A·N·N·U·A·L E·D·I·T·I·O·N·S

Human Development

05/06

Thirty-third Edition

EDITOR

Karen L. Freiberg

University of Maryland, Baltimore County

Dr. Karen Freiberg has an interdisciplinary educational and employment background in nursing, education, and developmental psychology. She received her B.S. from the State University of New York at Plattsburgh, her M.S. from Cornell University, and her Ph.D. from Syracuse University. Dr. Freiberg has worked as a school nurse, a pediatric nurse, a public health nurse for the Navajo Indians, an associate project director for a child development clinic, a researcher in several areas of child development, and a university professor. She is the author of an award-winning textbook, *Human Development: A Life-Span Approach*, which is now in its fourth edition. Dr. Freiberg is currently on the faculty at the University of Maryland, Baltimore County.

McGraw-Hill/Dushkin

2460 Kerper Blvd., Dubuque, IA 52001

Visit us on the Internet
http://www.dushkin.com

Credits

1. **Genetic and Prenatal Influences on Development**
   Unit photo—© by PhotoDisc, Inc.
2. **Development During Infancy and Early Childhood**
   Unit photo—© Getty Images/Punchstock
3. **Development During Childhood: Cognition and Schooling**
   Unit photo—© Getty Images/PhotoLink/ D.Berry
4. **Development During Childhood: Family and Culture**
   Unit photo—© Getty Images/Doug Menuez
5. **Development During Adolescence and Young Adulthood**
   Unit photo—© Getty Images/Ryan McVay
6. **Development During Middle and Late Adulthood**
   Unit photo—© Getty Images/Ryan McVay

Copyright

Cataloging in Publication Data
Main entry under title: Annual Editions: Human Development. 2005/2006.
1. Human Development—Periodicals. I. Freiberg, Karen L., *comp.* II. Title: Human Development.
ISBN 0–07–310222–9   658'.05   ISSN 0278–4661

© 2005 by McGraw-Hill/Dushkin, Dubuque, IA 52001 A Division of The McGraw-Hill Companies.

Thirty-third Edition

Cover image © Corbis Royalty Free and Punchstock/Getty Images
Printed in the United States of America   1234567890QPDQPD987654   Printed on Recycled Paper

Editors/Advisory Board

Members of the Advisory Board are instrumental in the final selection of articles for each edition of ANNUAL EDITIONS. Their review of articles for content, level, currentness, and appropriateness provides critical direction to the editor and staff. We think that you will find their careful consideration well reflected in this volume.

Preface

The process of human development is always changing. It is exciting and scary, joyful and disappointing.

This compendium of articles about human development covers the life span, considering physical, cognitive, and psychosocial components. Development should be viewed as a circle of life. Conception begins each new human being, but each unique individual carries genetic materials from biological relatives alive and dead.

Development through infancy and childhood proceeds from sensory and motor responses to verbal communication, thinking, conceptualizing, and learning from others. In adolescence the individual begins to test out sexual maturity. Values and identity are questioned.

Early adulthood usually establishes the individual as an independent person. Employment, further education, the beginning of one's own family are all aspects of setting up a distinct life, with both its own characteristics and the characteristics and customs of previous generations.

During middle adulthood persons have new situations to face, new transitions with which to cope. Children grow up and leave home. Signs of aging become apparent. Relationships change, roles shift. New abilities may be found and opportunities sought.

Finally, during late adulthood, people assess what they've accomplished. Some are pleased. Some feel they could have done more or lived differently. In the best of instances, individuals accept who they are and are comfortable with themselves.

As you explore this anthology, you will discover that many articles ask questions that have no answers. As a student, I felt frustrated by such writing. I wanted answers, right answers, right away. However, over time I learned that lessons that are necessary to acquire maturity include accepting relativity and acknowledging extenuating circumstances. Life frequently has no right or wrong answers, but rather various alternatives with multiple consequences. Instead of right versus wrong, a more helpful consideration is "What will bring about the greater good for the greater number?" Controversies, whether about terrorism or war, good or evil, stem cells or organ trans-plants, body-soul separate or unified, can promote healthy discussions. Different viewpoints should be weighed against societal standards. Different philosophies should be celebrated for what they offer in creativity of intellect and human beings' ability to adapt to changing circumstances.

The Greek sophists were philosophers who specialized in argumentation, rhetoric (using language persuasively), and dialectics (finding synthesis or common ground between contradictory ideas). From their skilled thinking came the derogatory term "sophism," suggesting that some argumentation was deceptive or fallacious rather than wise. The term sophomore, which now means second-year student, comes from this variation of sophism, combining "sophos" (wise) with "moros" (dull or foolish). "Sophomoric" translates to exhibiting immaturity and lack of judgment, while "sophisticated" translates to having acquired knowledge. Educators strive to have their students move from knowing all the answers (sophomoric) to asking intelligent questions (sophisticated).

This anthology is dedicated to seekers of knowledge and searchers for what is true, right, or lasting. To this end, articles have been selected to provide you with information which will stimulate discussion and which will give your thoughts direction, but not articles which tell you what to think. May you be "seeking" learners all through your own years of human development. May each suggestive answer you discover open your mind to more erudite (instructive) learning, questioning, and sophistication.

Karen Freiberg

Karen Freiberg, Ph.D.
Editor

Contents

UNIT 1
Genetic and Prenatal Influences on Development

Five selections discuss genetic influences on development and the role of lifestyle, including the effects of substance abuse on prenatal development.

UNIT 2
Development During Infancy and Early Childhood

Six selections profile the impressive abilities of infants and young children, examine the ways in which children learn, and discuss the development of ethics and morality in early childhood.

The concepts in bold italics are developed in the article. For further expansion, please refer to the Topic Guide.

UNIT 3
Development During Childhood: Cognition and Schooling

Eight selections examine human development during childhood, paying specific attention to social and emotional development, cognitive and language development, and development problems.

Unit Overview   **58**

The concepts in bold italics are developed in the article. For further expansion, please refer to the Topic Guide.

UNIT 4
Development During Childhood: Family and Culture

Five selections discuss the impact of home and culture on child rearing and child development. The topics include parenting styles, family structure, violence, and cultural influences.

Unit Overview

The concepts in bold italics are developed in the article. For further expansion, please refer to the Topic Guide.

UNIT 5
Development During Adolescence and Young Adulthood

Six selections explore a wide range of issues and topics concerning adolescence
and early adulthood.

Unit Overview   **140**

The concepts in bold italics are developed in the article. For further expansion, please refer to the Topic Guide.

UNIT 6
Development During Middle and Late Adulthood

Eight selections review a variety of biological and psychological aspects of aging, questioning the concepts of set life stages.

The concepts in bold italics are developed in the article. For further expansion, please refer to the Topic Guide.

The concepts in bold italics are developed in the article. For further expansion, please refer to the Topic Guide.

Topic Guide

This topic guide suggests how the selections in this book relate to the subjects covered in your course. You may want to use the topics listed on these pages to search the Web more easily.

On the following pages a number of Web sites have been gathered specifically for this book. They are arranged to reflect the units of this *Annual Edition*. You can link to these sites by going to the DUSHKIN ONLINE support site at *http://www.dushkin.com/online/*.

ALL THE ARTICLES THAT RELATE TO EACH TOPIC ARE LISTED BELOW THE BOLD-FACED TERM.

Adolescence
21. When Safety is the Name of the Game
24. Brown v. Board: A Dream Deferred
25. The 100 Best High Schools in America
26. Choosing Virginity
27. Hello to College Joys: Keep Stress Off Campus

Adulthood
2. Brave New Babies
26. Choosing Virginity
28. She Works, He Doesn't
29. We're Not in the Mood
32. Alcohol's Deadly Triple Threat
33. The Great Back Pain Debate
34. 12 Things You Must Know to Survive and Thrive in America

Aggression
11. Raising a Moral Child
20. Raising Happy Achieving Children in the New Millennium
21. When Safety is the Name of the Game

Aging
35. Aging's Changing Face
36. Secrets of the Centenarians
37. The Nun Study: Alzheimer's
38. Navigating Practical Dilemmas in Terminal Care

Anxiety
8. Vaccines and Autism, Beyond the Fear Factors
10. Guilt Free TV
24. Brown v. Board: A Dream Deferred
27. Hello to College Joys: Keep Stress Off Campus
28. She Works, He Doesn't
29. We're Not in the Mood
32. Alcohol's Deadly Triple Threat

Attachment
6. Four Things You Need to Know About Raising Baby
9. Four Perspectives on Child Care Quality

Birth and birth defects
3. Inside the Womb
32. Alcohol's Deadly Triple Threat

Brain development
3. Inside the Womb
8. Vaccines and Autism, Beyond the Fear Factors
17. The New Gender Gap
30. The Battle for Your Brain
31. Emotions and the Brain: Laughter
32. Alcohol's Deadly Triple Threat

Career
26. Choosing Virginity
28. She Works, He Doesn't
29. We're Not in the Mood
34. 12 Things You Must Know to Survive and Thrive in America

Children
6. Four Things You Need to Know About Raising Baby
9. Four Perspectives on Child Care Quality
13. The New Science of Dyslexia
15. Trick Question
22. The Blank Slate
23. Parents or Pop Culture? Children's Heroes and Role Models
24. Brown v. Board: A Dream Deferred
30. The Battle for Your Brain

Cognition
4. The Mystery of Fetal Life: Secrets of the Womb
6. Four Things You Need to Know About Raising Baby
10. Guilt Free TV
12. Implicit Learning
13. The New Science of Dyslexia
14. Metacognitive Development
16. The Future of Computer Technology in K–12 Education
20. Raising Happy Achieving Children in the New Millennium
30. The Battle for Your Brain
36. Secrets of the Centenarians

Creativity
15. Trick Question
16. The Future of Computer Technology in K–12 Education
19. "High Stakes Are for Tomatoes"
20. Raising Happy Achieving Children in the New Millennium
25. The 100 Best High Schools in America

Culture
11. Raising a Moral Child
16. The Future of Computer Technology in K–12 Education
17. The New Gender Gap
18. Girls, Boys and Autism
19. "High Stakes Are for Tomatoes"
20. Raising Happy Achieving Children in the New Millennium
22. The Blank Slate
23. Parents or Pop Culture? Children's Heroes and Role Models
24. Brown v. Board: A Dream Deferred
25. The 100 Best High Schools in America
28. She Works, He Doesn't
30. The Battle for Your Brain
34. 12 Things You Must Know to Survive and Thrive in America

Death
32. Alcohol's Deadly Triple Threat
38. Navigating Practical Dilemmas in Terminal Care

Depression
20. Raising Happy Achieving Children in the New Millennium
29. We're Not in the Mood
32. Alcohol's Deadly Triple Threat
34. 12 Things You Must Know to Survive and Thrive in America
35. Aging's Changing Face

Divorce
29. We're Not in the Mood
32. Alcohol's Deadly Triple Threat

World Wide Web Sites

The following World Wide Web sites have been carefully researched and selected to support the articles found in this reader. The easiest way to access these selected sites is to go to our DUSHKIN ONLINE support site at *http://www.dushkin.com/online/*.

AE: Human Development 05/06

The following sites were available at the time of publication. Visit our Web site—we update DUSHKIN ONLINE regularly to reflect any changes.

General Sources

Association for Moral Education
http://www.amenetwork.org/

This association is dedicated to fostering communication, cooperation, training, curriculum development, and research that links moral theory to educational practices.

Behavior Analysis Resources
http://www.coedu.usf.edu/behavior/bares.htm

Dedicated to promoting the experimental, theoretical, and applied analysis of behavior, this site encompasses contemporary scientific and social issues, theoretical advances, and the dissemination of professional and public information.

Healthfinder
http://www.healthfinder.gov

Healthfinder is a consumer health site that contains the latest health news, prevention and care choices, and information about every phase of human development.

UNIT 1: Genetic and Prenatal Influences on Development

American Academy of Pediatrics (AAP)
http://www.aap.org

AAP provides data on optimal physical, mental, and social health for all children. The site links to professional educational sources and current research.

Basic Neural Processes
http://psych.hanover.edu/Krantz/neurotut.html

An extensive tutorial on brain structures is provided here.

Evolutionary Psychology: A Primer
http://www.psych.ucsb.edu/research/cep/

A link to an evolutionary psychology primer is available on this site. Extensive background information is included.

Genetics Education Center
http://www.kumc.edu/gec/

The University of Kansas Medical Center provides information on human genetics and the human genome project at this site. Included are a number of links to research areas.

MedlinePlus Health Information/Prenatal Care
http://www.nlm.nih.gov/medlineplus/prenatalcare.html

On this site of the National Library of Medicine and the National Institutes of Health, you'll find prenatal-related sections such as General Information, Diagnosis/Symptoms, Nutrition, Organizations, and more.

UNIT 2: Development During Infancy and Early

Childhood

BabyCenter
http://www.babycenter.com

This well-organized site offers quick access to practical information on a variety of baby-related topics that span the period from preconception to toddlerhood.

Children's Nutrition Research Center (CNRC)
http://www.bcm.tmc.edu/cnrc/

CNRC is dedicated to defining the nutrient needs of healthy children, from conception through adolescence, and of pregnant and nursing mothers.

Early Childhood Care and Development
http://www.ecdgroup.com

Child development theory, programming and parenting data, and research can be found on this site of the Consultative Group. It is dedicated to the improvement of conditions of young children at risk.

Zero to Three: National Center for Infants, Toddlers, and Families
http://www.zerotothree.org

Zero to Three is dedicated solely to infants, toddlers, and their families. Organized by recognized experts in the field, it provides technical assistance to communities, states, and the federal government.

UNIT 3: Development During Childhood: Cognition and Schooling

Children Now
http://www.childrennow.org

Children Now focuses on improving conditions for children who are poor or at risk. Articles include information on education, the influence of media, health, and security.

Council for Exceptional Children
http://www.cec.sped.org

This is the home page of the Council for Exceptional Children, which is dedicated to improving education for exceptional children and the gifted child.

Educational Resources Information Center (ERIC)
http://www.eric.ed.gov/

Sponsored by the U.S. Department of Education, this site will lead to numerous documents related to elementary and early childhood education.

Federation of Behavioral, Psychological, and Cognitive Science
http://federation.apa.org

The federation's mission is fulfilled through legislative and regulatory advocacy, education, and information dissemination to the scientific community. Hotlink to the National Institutes of Health's Project on the Decade of the Brain.

www.dushkin.com/online/

The National Association for the Education of Young Children (NAEYC)
http://www.naeyc.org

NAEYC is the nation's largest organization of early childhood professionals. It is devoted to improving the quality of early childhood education programs for children from birth through the age of eight.

Project Zero
http://pzweb.harvard.edu

Following 30 years of research on the development of learning processes in children and adults, Project Zero is now helping to create communities of reflective, independent learners; to enhance deep understanding within disciplines; and to promote critical and creative thinking.

UNIT 4: Development During Childhood: Family and Culture

Childhood Injury Prevention Interventions
http://depts.washington.edu/hiprc/

Systematic reviews of childhood injury prevention and interventions on such diverse subjects as adolescent suicide, child abuse, accidental injuries, and youth violence are offered on this site.

Families and Work Institute
http://www.familiesandwork.org/index.html

The Families and Work Institute conducts policy research on issues related to the changing workforce, and it operates a national clearinghouse on work and family life.

Parentsplace.com: Single Parenting
http://www.parentsplace.com/

This resource focuses on issues concerning single parents and their children. The articles range from parenting children from infancy through adolescence.

UNIT 5: Development During Adolescence and Young Adulthood

ADOL: Adolescent Directory On-Line
http://education.indiana.edu/cas/adol/adol.html

The ADOL site contains a wide array of Web documents that address adolescent development. Specific content ranges from mental health issues to counselor resources.

Adolescence: Change and Continuity
http://www.personal.psu.edu/nxd10/adolesce.htm

This site offers a discussion of puberty, sexuality, biological changes, cross-cultural differences, and nutrition for adolescents, including a look at obesity.

AMA—Adolescent Health On-Line
http://www.ama-assn.org/ama/pub/category/1947.html

This AMA adolescent health initiative describes clinical preventive services that primary care physicians and other health professionals can provide to young people.

American Academy of Child and Adolescent Psychiatry
http://www.aacap.org/

Up-to-date data on a host of topics that include facts for families, public health, and clinical practice may be found here.

Ask NOAH About: Mental Health
http://www.noah-health.org/english/illness/mentalhealth/mental.html

NOAH's Web site contains information about child and adolescent family problems, mental conditions and disorders, suicide prevention, and much more.

UNIT 6: Development During Middle and Late Adulthood

Alzheimer's Disease Research Center
http://alzheimer.wustl.edu/adrc2//

ADRC facilitates advanced research on clinical, genetic, neuropathological, neuroanatomical, biomedical, neuropsychological, and psychosocial aspects of Alzheimer's disease and related brain disorders.

American Psychological Association's Division 20, Adult Development and Aging
http://www.aging.ufl.edu/apadiv20/apadiv20.htm

Dedicated to studying the psychology of adult development and aging, this division provides links to research guides, laboratories, instructional resources, and other related areas.

Grief Net
http://rivendell.org

Produced by a nonprofit group, Rivendell Resources, this site provides many links to the Web on the bereavement process, resources for grievers, and support groups.

Lifestyle Factors Affecting Late Adulthood
http://www.school-for-champions.com/health/lifestyle_elderly.htm

The way a person lives his or her life in the later years can affect the quality of life. Find here information to improve a senior's lifestyle plus a few relevant links.

National Aging Information Center (NAIC)
http://www.aoa.dhhs.gov/naic/

This service by the Administration on Aging is a central source of data on demographic, health, economic, and social status of older Americans.

We highly recommend that you review our Web site for expanded information and our other product lines. We are continually updating and adding links to our Web site in order to offer you the most usable and useful information that will support and expand the value of your Annual Editions. You can reach us at: *http://www.dushkin.com/annualeditions/*.

UNIT 1

Genetic and Prenatal Influences on Development

Unit Selections

1. **The Age of Genetic Technology Arrives**, Leon R. Kass
2. **Brave New Babies**, Claudia Kalb
3. **Inside the Womb**, J. Madeleine Nash
4. **The Mystery of Fetal Life: Secrets of the Womb**, John Pekkanen
5. **The War Over Fetal Rights**, Debra Rosenberg

Key Points to Consider

• Will genetic technology fulfill our existence or dehumanize us in the twenty-first millennium?

• Will sex selection of babies at conception become widespread? Will this result in a world overpopulated by males?

• Why should embryonic development become a political priority in the twenty-first century?

• Describe the long-term effects of health status during pregnancy on the development of mental abilities in infants and children.

• Why are lawyers, religious leaders, and ethicists going to war over fetal rights?

 **Links: www.dushkin.com/online/**
These sites are annotated in the World Wide Web pages.

American Academy of Pediatrics (AAP)
http://www.aap.org
Basic Neural Processes
http://psych.hanover.edu/Krantz/neurotut.html
Evolutionary Psychology: A Primer
http://www.psych.ucsb.edu/research/cep/
Genetics Education Center
http://www.kumc.edu/gec/
MedlinePlus Health Information/Prenatal Care
http://www.nlm.nih.gov/medlineplus/prenatalcare.html

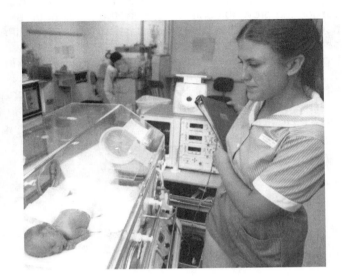

The total human genome was fully mapped in 2003. This knowledge of the human complement of twenty-three pairs of chromosomes with their associated genes in the nucleus of every cell has the potential for allowing genetic manipulation. The use of stem cells (undifferentiated embryonic cells) in animal research has documented the possibility of morphing stem cells into any kind of human cells. Stem cells will turn into desired tissue cells when the gene sequences of cytosine, adenine, thymine, and guanine (CATG) of the desired tissues are expressed. Scientists can eventually use their knowledge of the human genome, plus embryonic stem cells, to treat or cure diseases. Should they be allowed to? Are stem cells human life or property to be used for research purposes? Will cloning (complete reproduction) of a human become a reality? Within this unit you will find answers to some of the questions about how the decoding of the human genome may change your lives in the near future.

Genetic precursors of human development and the use of stem cells, morphing, and cloning will be hot topics of the next several years as genetic manipulation becomes feasible. As DNA sequences associated with particular human traits (genetic markers) are uncovered, pressure will appear to alter these traits, not just cure diseases. How far will scientists go in altering human behaviors?

Human embryology (the study of the first through seventh weeks after conception) and human fetology (the study of the eighth week of pregnancy through birth) have given verification to the idea that behavior precedes birth. The genetic hardwiring of CATG directs much of this behavior. However, the developing embryo/fetus reacts to the internal and external environments provided by the mother as well. Substances diffuse through the placental barrier from the mother's body. The embryo reacts to toxins (viruses, antigens) that pass through the umbilical cord. The fetus reacts to an enormous number of other stimuli, such as the sounds from the mother's body (digestive rumblings, heartbeat) and the mother's movements, moods, and medicines. How the embryo/fetus reacts (weakly to strongly, positively to negatively) depends, in large part, on his or her genetic preprogramming. Genes and environment are so inextricably intertwined that the effect of each cannot be studied separately. Prenatal development always has strong environmental influences and vice versa.

The two articles in the genetic influences section of this unit are state-of-the-science expositions on how decoding of the human genome will affect our future views about human development. The information in them is central to many ongoing discussions of human development. The potentialities for altering structures and behaviors, by altering the CATG messages of DNA on chromosomes within cells or by cloning humans, are massive. We all need to understand what is happening. We need to make knowledgeable and well-thought-out choices for our futures.

The first article, "The Age of Genetic Technology Arrives," addresses some of the moral and ethical implications of allowing science and genetic technicians to alter human DNA. While some people argue that no "playing God" or "tampering with human genes" is acceptable, others point out the potential benefits of curing cancer, enhancing immunity, and extending life. What will we, the human race, choose to do with the technology in our hands: human fulfillment or human debasement? The author poses several questions about human dignity which should stimulate lively debates.

The second article, "Brave New Babies," discusses the use of genetic technology to choose the sex of a child at the time of conception. The price tag approaches $20,000, but many parents are willing to pay this price for a boy or for a girl. The science behind this sex selection is illustrated and described. More parents choose boys than girls. If gender selection becomes widespread, will we have a world overpopulated with males?

The first article in the prenatal section of this unit discusses what scientists have learned about the nine months from conception through birth. Are these the first months of life, or does life begin at birth? New sophisticated ultrasound technology and computer-enhanced images now can reveal in exquisite detail what goes on

"Inside the Womb." Parents viewing their unborn child(ren) in this way find it difficult not to believe in life before birth. The human race may give more priority to embryonic and fetal development as this knowledge is disseminated. Concern for maternal and prenatal health care may move from a low-order need to one of our highest priorities.

The fourth article, "The Mystery of Fetal Life: Secrets of the Womb," answers questions on fetal psychological development. Human behaviors such as intelligence and personality may be profoundly influenced by the environment of the mother's uterus. Nurture occurs before and after birth. John Pekkanen addresses issues such as over-the-counter drugs, caffeine, infections, pets, and environmental pollutants. He reviews what is known about fetal memory, including the much misunderstood "Mozart effect."

The fifth article, "The War Over Fetal Rights," discusses the growing controversy over the rights of an unborn baby. Central to this is the question "When does life begin?" If life exists before birth, does this life form have legal claims for rights accorded to post-birth life forms in the country of origin? When is abuse, abuse? When is murder, murder? The politics of the womb are made more complicated now due to our ability to visualize and hear prenatal fetal life.

The Age of Genetic Technology Arrives

BY LEON R. KASS

As one contemplates the current and projected state of genetic knowledge and technology, one is astonished by how far we have come in the less than fifty years since Watson and Crick first announced the structure of DNA. True, soon after that discovery, scientists began seriously to discuss the futuristic prospects of gene therapy for genetic disease and of genetic engineering more generally. But no one then imagined how rapidly genetic technology would emerge. The Human Genome Project, disclosing the DNA sequences of all thirty thousand human genes, is all but completed. And even without comprehensive genomic knowledge, biotech business is booming. According to a recent report by the research director for GlaxoSmithKline, enough sequencing data are available to keep his researchers busy for the next twenty years, developing early-detection screening techniques, rationally designed vaccines, genetically engineered changes in malignant tumors leading to enhanced immune response, and, ultimately, precise gene therapy for specific genetic diseases. The age of genetic technology has arrived.

Genetic technology comes into existence as part of the large humanitarian project to cure disease, prolong life, and alleviate suffering. As such, it occupies the moral high ground of compassionate healing. Who would not welcome personal genetic profiling that would enable doctors to customize the most effective and safest drug treatments for individuals with hypertension or rheumatoid arthritis? Who would not welcome genetic therapy to correct the defects that lead to sickle cell anemia, Huntington's disease, and breast cancer, or to protect against the immune deficiency caused by the AIDS virus?

And yet genetic technology has also aroused considerable public concern, for it strikes most people as different from other biomedical technologies. Even people duly impressed by the astonishing genetic achievements of the last decades and eager for the medical benefits are nonetheless ambivalent about these new developments. For they sense that genetic technology, while in some respects continuous with the traditional medical project of compassionate healing, also represents something radically new and disquieting. Often hard-pressed to articulate the precise basis of their disquiet, they talk rather in general terms about the dangers of eugenics or the fear of "tampering with human genes" or, for that matter, "playing God."

Enthusiasts for genetic technology, made confident by their expertise and by their growing prestige and power, are often impatient with the public's disquiet. Much of it they attribute to ignorance of science: "If the public only knew what we know, it would see things our way and give up its irrational fears." For the rest, they blame outmoded moral and religious notions, ideas that scientists insist no longer hold water and only serve to obstruct scientific progress.

In my own view, the scientists' attempt to cast the debate as a battle of beneficial and knowledgeable cleverness versus ignorant and superstitious anxiety should be resisted. For the public is right to be ambivalent about genetic technology, and no amount of instruction in molecular biology and genetics should allay its—our—legitimate human concerns. Rightly understood, these worries are, in fact, in touch with the deepest matters of our humanity and dignity, and we ignore them at our peril.

I will not dispute here which of the prophesied technologies will in fact prove feasible or how soon.[1] To be sure, as a practical matter we must address the particular ethical issues raised by each new technical power as it comes into existence. But the moral meaning of the entire enterprise does not depend on the precise details regarding what and when. I shall proceed by raising a series of questions, the first of which is an attempt to say how genetic technology is different.

IS GENETIC TECHNOLOGY SPECIAL?

What is different about genetic technology? At first glance, not much. Isolating a disease-inducing aberrant gene looks fairly continuous with isolating a disease-inducing intracellular virus. Supplying diabetics with normal genes for producing insulin has the same medical goal as supplying them with insulin for injection.

Nevertheless, despite these obvious similarities, genetic technology is also decisively different. When fully developed, it will wield two powers not shared by ordinary medical practice. Medicine treats only existing individuals, and it treats them only remedially, seeking to correct deviations from a more or less stable norm of health. By contrast, genetic engineering will, first of all, deliberately make changes that are transmissible into succeeding generations and may even alter in advance specific *future* individuals through direct "germ-line" or embryo interventions. Secondly, genetic engineering may be able, through so-called genetic enhancement, to create new human capacities and, hence, new norms of health and fitness.[2]

For the present, it is true, genetic technology is hailed primarily for its ability better to diagnose and treat *disease* in *existing* individuals. Confined to such practices, it would raise few questions (beyond the usual ones of safety and efficacy). Even intrauterine gene therapy for existing fetuses with diagnosable genetic disease could be seen as an extension of the growing field of fetal medicine.

But there is no reason to believe that the use of gene-altering powers can be so confined, either in logic or in practice. For one thing, "germ-line" gene therapy and manipulation, affecting not merely the unborn but also the unconceived,[3] is surely in our future. The practice has numerous justifications, beginning with the desire to reverse the unintended dysgenic effects of modern medical success. Thanks to medicine, for example, individuals who would have died from diabetes now live long enough to transmit their disease-producing genes. Why, it has been argued, should we not reverse these unfortunate changes by deliberate intervention? More generally, why should we not effect precise genetic alteration in disease-carrying sperm or eggs or early embryos, in order to prevent in advance the emergence of disease that otherwise will later require expensive and burdensome treatment? In short, even before we have had more than trivial experience with gene therapy for existing individuals—none of it successful—sober people have called for overturning the current (self-imposed) taboo on germ-line modification. The line between somatic and germ-line modification cannot hold.

Despite the naive hopes of many, neither will we be able to defend the boundary between therapy and genetic enhancement. Will we reject novel additions to the human genome that enable us to produce, internally, vitamins or amino acids we now must get in our diet? Will we

decline to make alterations in the immune system that will increase its efficacy or make it impervious to HIV? When genetic profiling becomes able to disclose the genetic contributions to height or memory or intelligence, will we deny prospective parents the right to enhance the potential of their children?[4] Finally, should we discover—as no doubt we will—the genetic switches that control our biological clock and that very likely influence also the maximum human life expectancy, will we opt to keep our hands off the rate of aging or our natural human life span? Not a chance.

We thus face a paradox. On the one hand, genetic technology really *is* different. It can and will go to work directly and deliberately on our basic, heritable, life-shaping capacities at their biological roots. It can take us beyond existing norms of health and healing—perhaps even alter fundamental features of human nature. On the other hand, precisely because the goals it will serve, at least to begin with, will be continuous with those of modern high-interventionist medicine, we will find its promise familiar and irresistible.

This paradox itself contributes to public disquiet: rightly perceiving a powerful difference in genetic technology, we also sense that we are powerless to establish, on the basis of that difference, clear limits to its use. The genetic genie, first unbottled to treat disease, will go its own way, whether we like it or not.

HOW MUCH GENETIC SELF-KNOWLEDGE IS GOOD FOR US?

Quite apart from worries about genetic engineering, gaining genetic knowledge is itself a legitimate cause of anxiety, not least because of one of its most touted benefits—the genetic profiling of individuals. There has been much discussion about how knowledge of someone's genetic defects, if leaked to outsiders, could be damaging in terms of landing a job or gaining health or life insurance, and legislative measures have been enacted to guard against such hazards. Little attention has been paid, however, to the implications of genetic knowledge for the person himself. Yet the deepest problem connected with learning your own genetic sins and unhealthy predispositions is neither the threat to confidentiality nor the risk of "genetic discrimination" in employment or insurance, important though these practical problems may be.[5] It is, rather, the various hazards and deformations in living your life that will attach to knowing in advance your likely or possible medical future. To be sure, in some cases such foreknowledge will be welcome, if it can lead to easy measures to prevent or treat the impending disorder, and if the disorder in question does not powerfully affect self-image or self-command. But will and should we welcome knowledge that we carry a predisposition to Alzheimer's disease or schizophrenia, or genes that will definitely produce, at an unknown future time, a serious but untreatable disease?

Still harder will it be for most people to live easily and wisely with less certain information—say, where multigenic traits are involved. The recent case of a father who insisted that ovariectomy and mastectomy be performed on his ten-year-old daughter because she happened to carry the BRCA-1 gene for breast cancer dramatically shows the toxic effective of genetic knowledge.

Less dramatic but more profound is the threat to human freedom and spontaneity, a subject explored twenty-five years ago by the philosopher Hans Jonas, one of our wisest commentators on technology and the human prospect. As Jonas observed, "Knowledge of the future, especially one's own, has always been excepted [from the injunction to 'Know thyself'] and the attempt to gain it by whatever means (astrology is one) disparaged—as futile superstition by the enlightened, but as sin by theologians." Everyone remembers that Prometheus was the philanthropic god who gave fire and the arts to humans. But it is often forgotten that he gave them also the greater gift of "blind hopes"—"to cease seeing doom before their eyes"—precisely because he knew that ignorance of one's own future fate was indispensable to aspiration and achievement. I suspect that many people, taking their bearings from life lived open-endedly rather than from preventive medicine practiced rationally, would prefer ignorance of the future to the scientific astrology of knowing their genetic profile. In a free society, that would be their right.

Or would it? This leads us to the third question.

WHAT ABOUT FREEDOM?

Even people who might otherwise welcome the growth of genetic knowledge and technology are worried about the coming power of geneticists, genetic engineers and, in particular, governmental authorities armed with genetic technology.[6] Precisely because we have been taught by these very scientists that genes hold the secret of life, and that our genotype is our essence if not quite our destiny, we are made nervous by those whose expert knowledge and technique touch our very being. Even apart from any particular abuses and misuses of power, friends of human freedom have deep cause for concern.

C. S. Lewis, no friend of ignorance, put the matter sharply in *The Abolition of Man:*

> If any one age really attains, by eugenics and scientific education, the power to make its descendants what it pleases, all men who live after it are the patients of that power.... But even within this master generation (itself an infinitesimal minority of the species) the power will be exercised by a minority smaller still. Man's conquest of Nature, if the dreams of some scientific planners are

realized, means the rule of a few hundreds of men over billions upon billions of men.

Most genetic technologists will hardly recognize themselves in this portrait. Though they concede that abuses or misuses of power may occur, especially in tyrannical regimes, they see themselves not as predestinators but as facilitators, merely providing increased knowledge and technique that people can freely choose to use in making decisions about their health or reproductive choices. Genetic power, they tell us, serves not to limit freedom, but to increase it.

But as we can see from the already existing practices of genetic screening and prenatal diagnosis, this claim is at best self-deceptive, at worst disingenuous. The choice to develop and practice genetic screening and the choices of which genes to target for testing have been made not by the public but by scientists—and not on liberty-enhancing but on eugenic grounds. In many cases, practitioners of prenatal diagnosis refuse to do fetal genetic screening in the absence of a prior commitment from the pregnant woman to abort any afflicted fetus. In other situations, pregnant women who still wish *not* to know prenatal facts must withstand strong medical pressures for testing.

In addition, economic pressures to contain health-care costs will almost certainly constrain free choice. Refusal to provide insurance coverage for this or that genetic disease may eventually work to compel genetic abortion or intervention. State-mandated screening already occurs for PKU (phenylketonuria) and other diseases, and full-blown genetic screening programs loom large on the horizon. Once these arrive, there will likely be an upsurge of economic pressure to limit reproductive freedom. All this will be done, of course, in the name of the well-being of children.

Already in 1971, geneticist Bentley Glass, in his presidential address to the American Association for the Advancement of Science, enunciated "the right of every child to be born with a sound physical and mental constitution, based on a sound genotype." Looking ahead to the reproductive and genetic technologies that are today rapidly arriving, Glass proclaimed: "No parents will in that future time have a right to burden society with a malformed or a mentally incompetent child." It remains to be seen to what extent such prophecies will be realized. But they surely provide sufficient and reasonable grounds for being concerned about restrictions on human freedoms, even in the absence of overt coercion, and even in liberal polities like our own.

WHAT ABOUT HUMAN DIGNITY?

Here, rather than in the more-discussed fears about freedom, lie our deepest concerns, and rightly so. For threats to human dignity can—and probably will—arise even with the free, humane, and "enlightened" use of these technologies. Genetic technology, the practices it will engender, and above all the scientific teachings about human life on which it rests are not, as many would have it, morally and humanly neutral. Regardless of how they are practiced or taught, they are pregnant with their own moral meanings and will necessarily bring with them changes in our practices, our institutions, our norms, our beliefs, and our self-conception. It is, I submit, these challenges to our dignity and humanity that are at the bottom of our anxiety over genetic science and technology. Let me touch briefly on four aspects of this most serious matter.

"PLAYING GOD"

Paradoxically, worries about dehumanization are sometimes expressed in the fear of superhumanization, that is, that man will be "playing God." This complaint is too facilely dismissed by scientists and nonbelievers. The concern has meaning, God or no God.

Never mind the exaggeration that lurks in this conceit of man's playing God. (Even at his most powerful, after all, man is capable only of *playing* God.) Never mind the implicit innuendo that nobody has given to others this creative and judgmental authority, or the implicit retort that there is theological warrant for acting as God's co-creator in overcoming the ills and suffering of the world. Consider only that if scientists are seen in this godlike role of creator, judge, and savior, the rest of us must stand before them as supplicating, tainted creatures. Despite the hyperbolic speech, that is worry enough.

Practitioners of prenatal diagnosis, working today with but a fraction of the information soon to be available from the Human Genome Project, already screen for a long list of genetic diseases and abnormalities, from Down syndrome to dwarfism. Possession of any one of these defects, they believe, renders a prospective child unworthy of life. Persons who happen still to be born with these conditions, having somehow escaped the spreading net of detection and eugenic abortion, are increasingly regarded as "mistakes," as inferior human beings who should not have been born.[7] Not long ago, at my own university, a physician making rounds with medical students stood over the bed of an intelligent, otherwise normal ten-year-old boy with spina bifada. "Were he to have been conceived today," the physician casually informed his entourage, "he would have been aborted." Determining who shall live and who shall die—on the basis of genetic merit—is a godlike power already wielded by genetic medicine. This power will only grow.

MANUFACTURE & COMMODIFICATION

But, one might reply, genetic technology also holds out the premise of redemption, of a *cure* for these life-crippling and life-forfeiting disorders. Very well. But in order truly to practice their salvific power, genetic technologists will have to increase greatly their manipulations and interventions, well beyond merely screening and weeding out. True, in some cases genetic testing and risk management aimed at prevention may actually cut down on the need for high-tech interventions aimed at cure. But in many other cases, ever-greater genetic scrutiny will lead necessarily to ever more extensive manipulation. And, to produce Bentley Glass's healthy and well-endowed babies, let alone babies with the benefits of genetic enhancement, a new scientific obstetrics will be necessary, one that will come very close to turning human procreation into manufacture.

This process was already crudely begun with in vitro fertilization. It is now taking giant steps forward with the ability to screen in vitro embryos before implantation (so-called pre-implantation genetic diagnosis). And it will come to maturity with interventions such as cloning and, eventually, with precise genetic engineering. Just follow the logic and the aspirations of current practice: the road we are traveling leads all the way to the world of designer babies—reached not by dictatorial fiat, but by the march of benevolent humanitarianism, and cheered on by an ambivalent citizenry that also dreads becoming merely the last of man's manmade things.

Make no mistake: the price to be paid for producing optimum or even only genetically sound babies will be the transfer of procreation from the home to the laboratory. Such an arrangement will be profoundly dehumanizing, no matter how genetically good or healthy the resultant children. And let us not forget the powerful economic interests that will surely operate in this area; with their advent, the commodification of nascent human life will be unstoppable.

STANDARDS, NORMS, & GOALS

According to Genesis, God, in His creating, looked at His creatures and saw that there were *good*—intact, complete, well-working wholes, true to the spoken idea that guided their creation. What standards will guide the genetic engineers?

For the time being, one might answer, the norm of health. But even before the genetic enhancers join the party, the standard of health is being deconstructed. Are you healthy if, although you show no symptoms, you carry genes that will definitely produce Huntington's disease? What if you carry, say, 40 percent of the genetic markers thought to be linked to the appearance of Alzheimer's disease? And what will "healthy" and "normal" mean when we discover your genetic propensities for alcoholism, drug abuse, pederasty, or violence?[8] The idea of health progressively becomes at once both imperial and vague: medicalization of what have hitherto been mental or moral matters paradoxically brings with it the disappearance of any clear standard of health itself.

Once genetic *enhancement* comes on the scene, standards of health, wholeness, or fitness will be needed more than ever, but just then is when all pretense of standards will go out the window. "Enhancement" is, of course, a euphemism for "improvement," and the idea of improvement necessarily implies a good, a better, and perhaps even a best. If, however, we can no longer look to our previously unalterable human nature for a standard or norm of what is good or better, how will anyone know what constitutes an improvement? It will not do to assert that we can extrapolate from what we like about ourselves. Because memory is good, can we say how much more memory would be better? If sexual desire is good, how much more would be better? Life is good, but how much extension of the life span would be good for us? Only simplistic thinkers believe they can easily answer such questions.[9]

More modest enhancers, like more modest genetic therapists and technologists, eschew grandiose goals. They are valetudinarians, not eugenicists. They pursue not some faraway positive good, but the positive elimination of evils: diseases, pain, suffering, the likelihood of death. But let us not be deceived. Hidden in all this avoidance of evil is nothing less than the quasi-messianic goal of a painless, suffering-free and, finally, immortal existence. Only the presence of such a goal justifies the sweeping-aside of any opposition to the relentless march of medical science. Only such a goal gives trumping moral power to the principle "cure disease, relieve suffering."

"Cloning human beings is unethical and dehumanizing, you say? Never mind: it will help us treat infertility, avoid genetic disease, and provide perfect materials for organ replacement." Such, indeed, was the tenor of the June 1997 report of the National Bioethics Advisory Commission, *Cloning Human Beings*. Notwithstanding its call for a temporary ban on the practice, the only moral objection the commission could agree upon was that cloning "is not safe to use in humans at this time," because the technique has yet to be perfected.[10] Even this elite ethical body, in other words, was unable to muster any other moral argument sufficient to cause us to forgo the possible health benefits of cloning.[11]

The same argument will also justify creating and growing human embryos for experimentation, revising the definition of death to increase the supply of organs for transplantation, growing human body parts in the peritoneal cavities of animals, perfusing newly dead bodies as factories for useful biological substances, or reprogramming the human body and mind with genetic or neurobiological engineering. Who can sustain an objection if these practices will help us live longer and with less overt suffering?

It turns out that even the more modest biogenetic engineers, whether they know it or not, are in the immortality business, proceeding on the basis of a quasi-religious faith that all innovation is by definition progress, no matter what is sacrificed to attain it.

THE TRAGEDY OF SUCCESS

What the enthusiasts do not see is that their utopian project will not eliminate suffering but merely shift it around. Forgetting that contentment requires that our desires do not outpace our powers, they have not noticed that the enormous medical progress of the last half-century has not left the present generation satisfied. Indeed, we are already witnessing a certain measure of public discontent as a paradoxical result of rising expectations in the health care field: although their actual health has improved substantially in recent decades, people's *satisfaction* with their current health status has remained the same or declined. But that is hardly the highest cost of success in the medical/humanitarian project.

As Aldous Huxley made clear in his prophetic. *Brave New World*, the road chosen and driven by compassionate humaneness paved by biotechnology, if traveled to the end, leads not to human fulfillment but to human debasement. Perfected bodies are achieved at the price of flattened souls. What Tolstoy called "real life"—life in its immediacy, vividness, and rootedness—has been replaced by an utterly mediated, sterile, and disconnected existence. In one word: dehumanization, the inevitable result of making the essence of human nature the final object of the conquest of nature for the relief of man's estate. Like Midas, bioengineered man will be cursed to acquire precisely what he wished for, only to discover—painfully and too late—that what he wished for is not exactly what he wanted. Or, worse than Midas, he may be so dehumanized he will not even recognize that in aspiring to be perfect, he is no longer even truly human. To paraphrase Bertrand Russell, technological humanitarianism is like a warm bath that heats up so imperceptibly you don't know when to scream.

The main point here is not the rightness or wrongness of this or that imagined scenario; all this is, admittedly, highly speculative. I surely have no way of knowing whether my worst fears will be realized, but you surely have no way of knowing they will not. The point is rather the plausibility, even the wisdom, of thinking about genetic technology like the entire technological venture, under the ancient and profound idea of tragedy in which success and failure are inseparably grown together like the concave and the convex. What I am suggesting is that genetic technology's way of approaching human life, a way spurred on by the utopian promises and perfectionist aims of modern thought and its scientific crusaders, may well turn out to be inevitable, heroic, and doomed. If this suggestion holds water, then the question regarding genetic technology is not "triumph OR tragedy," because the answer is "both together."

In the nineteenth and early twentieth century, the challenge came in the form of Darwinism and its seeming opposition to biblical religion, a battle initiated not so much by the scientists as by the beleaguered defenders of orthodoxy. In our own time, the challenge comes from molecular biology, behavioral genetics, and evolutionary psychology, fueled by their practitioners' overconfident belief in the sufficiency of their reductionist explanations of all vital and human phenomena. Never mind "created in the image of God"; what elevated *humanistic* view of human life or human goodness is defensible against the belief, asserted by most public and prophetic voices of biology, that man is just a collection of molecules, an accident on the stage of evolution, a freakish speck of mind in a mindless universe, fundamentally no different from other living—or even nonliving—things? What chance have our treasured ideas of freedom and dignity against the reductive notion of "the selfish gene" (or, for that matter, of "genes for altruism"), the belief that DNA is the essence of life, or the teaching that all human behavior and our rich inner life are rendered intelligible only in terms of their contributions to species survival and reproductive success?

These transformations are, in fact, welcomed by many of our leading scientists and intellectuals. In 1997 the luminaries of the International Academy of Humanism—including biologists Crick, Dawkins, and Wilson, and humanists Isaiah Berlin, W. V. Quine, and Kurt Vonnegut—issued a statement in defense of cloning research in higher mammals and human beings. Their reasons were revealing:

> Views of human nature rooted in humanity's tribal past ought not to be our primary criterion for making moral decisions about cloning.… The potential benefits of cloning may be so immense that it would be a tragedy if ancient theological scruples should lead to a Luddite rejection of cloning.

In order to justify ongoing research, these intellectuals were willing to shed not only traditional religious views, but any view of human distinctiveness and special dignity, their own included. They failed to see that the scientific view of man they celebrated does more than insult our vanity. It undermines our self-conception as free, thoughtful, and responsible beings, worthy of respect because we alone among the animals have minds and hearts that aim far higher than the mere perpetuation of our genes.

The problem may lie not so much with scientific findings themselves, but with the shallow philosophy that recognizes no other truths but these and with the arrogant pronouncements of the bioprophets. For example, in a letter to the editor complaining about a review of his book *How the Mind Works,* the well-known evolutionary psychologist and popularizer Stephen Pinker rails against any appeal to the human soul:

> Unfortunately for that theory, brain science has shown that the mind is what the brain does. The supposedly immaterial soul can be bisected with

a knife, altered by chemicals, turned on or off by electricity, and extinguished by a sharp blow or a lack of oxygen. Centuries ago it was unwise to ground morality on the dogma that the earth sat at the center of the universe. It is just as unwise today to ground it on dogmas about souls endowed by God.

One hardly knows whether to be more impressed by the height of Pinker's arrogance or by the depth of his shallowness. But he speaks with the authority of science, and few are able and willing to dispute him on his own grounds.

There is, of course, nothing novel about reductionism, materialism, and determinism of the kind displayed here; these are doctrines with which Socrates contended long ago. What is new is that, as philosophies, they seem (to many people) to be vindicated by scientific advance. Here, in consequence, is perhaps the most pernicious result of our technological progress, more dehumanizing than any actual manipulation or technique, present or future: the erosion, perhaps the final erosion, of the idea of man as noble, dignified, precious, or godlike, and its replacement with a view of man, no less than of nature, as mere raw material for manipulation and homogenization.

Hence our peculiar moral crisis. We are in turbulent seas without a landmark precisely because we adhere more and more to a view of human life that both gives us enormous power and, *at the same time,* denies every possibility of nonarbitrary standards for guiding its use. Though well equipped, we know not who we are or where we are going. We triumph over nature's unpredictability only to subject ourselves, tragically, to the still greater unpredictability of our capricious wills and our fickle opinions. Engineering the engineer as well as the engine, we race our train we know not where. That we do not recognize our predicament is itself a tribute to the depth of our infatuation with scientific progress and our naive faith in the sufficiency of our humanitarian impulses.

Does this mean that I am therefore in favor of ignorance, suffering, and death? Of killing the goose of genetic technology even before she lays her golden eggs? Surely not. But unless we mobilize the courage to look foursquare at the full human meaning of our new enterprise in biogenetic technology and engineering, we are doomed to become its creatures if not its slaves. Important though it is to set a moral boundary here, devise a regulation there, hoping to decrease the damage caused by this or that little rivulet, it is even more important to be sober about the true nature and meaning of the flood itself.

That our exuberant new biologists and their technological minions might be persuaded of this is, to say the least, highly unlikely. For all their ingenuity, they do not even seek the wisdom that just might yield the kind of knowledge that keeps human life human. But it is not too late for the rest of us to become aware of the dangers—not just to privacy or insurability, but to our very humanity. So aware, we might be better able to defend the increasingly beleaguered vestiges and principles of our human dignity, even as we continue to reap the considerable benefits that genetic technology will inevitably provide.

Notes

1. I will also not dispute here the scientists' reductive understanding of life and their treatment of rich vital activities solely in terms of the interactions of genes. I do, however, touch on the moral significance of such reductionism toward the end of this essay.

2. Some commentators, in disagreement with these arguments, insist that genetic technology differs only in degree from previous human practices that have existed for millennia. For example, they see no difference between the "social engineering" of education, which works on the next generation through speech or symbolic deed, and biological engineering, which inscribes its effects, directly and irreversibly, into the human constitution. Or they claim to see no difference between the indirect genetic effects of human mate selection and deliberate, direct genetic engineering to produce offspring with precise biological capacities. Such critics, I fear, have already bought into a reductionist view of human life and the relation between the generations. And they ignore the fact that most people choose their mates for reasons different from stud farming.

3. Correction of a genetically abnormal egg or sperm (that is, of the "germ cells"), however, worthy an activity, stretches the meaning of "therapy" beyond all normal uses. Just who is the "patient" being "treated"? The potential child-to-be that might be formed out of such egg or sperm is, at the time of the treatment, at best no more than a hope and a hypothesis. There is no medical analogue for treatment of nonexistent patients.

4. To be sure, not all attempts at enhancement will require genetic alterations. We have already witnessed efforts to boost height with supplementary growth hormone or athletic performance with steroids or "blood doping." Nevertheless, the largest possible changes in what is "normally" human are likely to come about only with the help of genetic alterations or the joining of machines (for example, computers) to human beings.

5. I find it odd that it is these issues that have been put forward as the special ethical problems associated with genetic technology and the Human Genome Project. Issues of privacy and risks of discrimination related to medical conditions are entirely independent of whether the medical condition is genetic in origin. Only if a special stigma were attached to having an inherited disease—for example, only if having thalassemia or sickle cell anemia were more shameful than having gonorrhea or lung cancer—would the genetic character of a disease create special or additional reasons for protecting against breaches of confidentiality or discrimination in the workplace.

6. Until the events of September 11 and the anthrax scare that followed, they did not worry enough. It is remarkable that most bioethical discussions of genetic technology had naively neglected its potential usefulness in creating biological weapons, such as, to begin with, antibiotic-resistant plague bacteria, or later, aerosols containing cancer-inducing or mind-scrambling viral vectors. The most outstanding molecular geneticists were especially naive in this area. When American molecular biologists convened the 1975 Asilomar Conference on recombinant DNA research, which called for a voluntary moratorium on experiments until the biohazards could be evaluated, they invited Soviet biologists to the meeting who said virtually nothing but who photographed every slide that was shown.

7. One of the most worrisome but least appreciated aspects of the godlike power of the new genetics is its tendency to "redefine" a human being in terms of his genes. Once a person is decisively characterized by his genotype, it is but a short step to justifying death solely for genetic sins.

8. Many scientists suspect that we have different inherited propensities for these and other behavioral troubles, though it is almost certain that there is no single "gene for x" that is responsible.

9. This strikes me as the deepest problem with positive eugenics: less the threat of coercion, more the presumption of thinking we are wise enough to engineer "improvements" in the human species.

10. This is, of course, not an objection to cloning itself but only to hazards tied to the technique used to produce the replicated children.

11. I forbear mentioning what is rapidly becoming another trumping argument: increasing the profits of my biotech company and its shareholders, an argument often presented in more public-spirited dress: if we don't do it, other countries will, and we will lose our competitive edge in biotechnology.

Leon R. Kass, M.D. is professor in social thought at the University of Chicago, Hertog fellow at the American Enterprise Institute, and chairman of the President's Council on Bioethics. Excerpted from Life, Liberty and the Defense of Dignity. *Published by Encounter Books, San Francisco, October 2002. Reprinted with permission.*

Brave New Babies

Parents now have the power to choose the sex of their children. But as technology answers prayers, it also raises some troubling questions.

BY CLAUDIA KALB

SHARLA MILLER OF GILLETTE, WYO., ALWAYS wanted a baby girl, but the odds seemed stacked against her. Her husband, Shane, is one of three brothers, and Sharla and her five siblings (four girls, two boys) have produced twice as many males as females. After the Millers' first son, Anthony, was born in 1991, along came Ashton, now 8, and Alec, 4. Each one was a gift, says Sharla, but the desire for a girl never waned. "I'm best friends with my mother;' she says. "I couldn't get it out of my mind that I wanted a daughter." Two years ago Sharla, who had her fallopian tubes tied after Alec's birth, began looking into adopting a baby girl. In the course of her Internet research, she stumbled upon a Web site for the Fertility Institutes in Los Angeles, headed by Dr. Jeffrey Steinberg, where she learned about an in vitro fertilization technique called pre-implantation genetic diagnosis. By creating embryos outside the womb, then testing them for gender, PGD could guarantee with almost 100 percent certainty—the sex of her baby. Price tag: $18,480, plus travel. Last November Sharla's eggs and Shane's sperm were mixed in a lab dish, producing 14 healthy embryos, seven male and seven female. Steinberg transferred three of the females into Sharla's uterus, where two implanted successfully. If all goes well, the run of Miller boys will end in July with the arrival of twin baby girls. "I have three wonderful boys," says Sharla, "but since there was a chance I could have a daughter, why not?"

The brave new world is definitely here. After 25 years of staggering advances in reproductive medicine—first test-tube babies, then donor eggs and surrogate mothers—technology is changing babymaking in a whole new way. No longer can science simply help couples have babies, it can help them have the kind of babies they want. Choosing gender may obliterate one of the fundamental mysteries of procreation, but for people who have grown accustomed to taking 3-D ultrasounds of fetuses, learning a baby's sex within weeks of conception and scheduling convenient delivery dates, it's simply the next logical step. That gleeful exclamation, "It's a boy!" or "It's a girl!" may soon just be a quaint reminder of how random births used to be.

Throughout history, humans have wished for a child of one sex or the other and have been willing to do just about anything to get it. Now that gender selection is scientifically feasible, interest in the controversial practice (banned, except for medical reasons, in the United Kingdom) is exploding. Despite considerable moral murkiness, Americans are talking to their doctors and visiting catchy Web sites like www.choosethesexofyourbaby.com and myboyorgirl.com—many of them offering money-back guarantees. In just the last six months, Steinberg's site has had 85,000 hits. At the Genetics and IVF Institute (GIVF) in Fairfax, Va., an FDA clinical trial of a sophisticated sperm-sorting technology called MicroSort is more than halfway to completion. Through radio, newspaper and magazine ads ("Do you want to choose the gender of your next baby?"), the clinic has recruited hundreds of eager couples, and more than 400 babies out of 750 needed for the trial have been born. Other couples continue to flock to older, more low-tech and questionable sperm-sorting techniques like the Ericsson method, which is offered at about two dozen clinics nationwide. By far, the most provocative gender-selection technique is PGD. Some clinics offer the procedure as a bonus for couples already going through fertility treatments, but a small number are beginning to provide the option for otherwise healthy couples. Once Steinberg decided to offer PGD gender selection to all comers, he says, "word spread like wildfire."

The ability to create baby Jack or baby Jill opens a high-tech can of worms. While the advances have received kudos from grateful families, they also raise loaded ethical questions about whether science is finally crossing a line that shouldn't be crossed. Even fertility specialists are divided over whether choosing a male or female embryo is acceptable. If couples can request a baby boy or girl, what's next on the slippery slope of modern reproductive medicine? Eye color? Height? Intelligence? Could picking one gender over the other become the 21st century's form of sex discrimination? Or, as in China, upset the ratio of males to females? Many European countries already forbid sex selection; should there be similar regulations in the United States? These explosive issues are being debated in medical journals, on university ethics boards and at the highest levels in Washington. Just last week the President's Council on Bioethics discussed proposals for possible legislation that would ban the buying and selling of human embryos and far-out reproductive experimentation, like creating human-animal hybrids. While the recommendations—part of a report due out this spring—do not suggest limiting IVF or gender selection, the goals are clear: the government should clamp down before technology goes too far. "Even though people have strong differences of opinion on some issues," says council chair and leading bioethieist Leon Kass, "all of us have a stake in keeping human reproduction human."

After their first son, Jesse, was born in 1988, Mary and Sam Toedtman tried all sorts of folksy remedies to boost their chances of having a girl. When Jesse was followed by Jacob, now 10, and Lucas, 7, it seemed clear that boys would be boys in the Toedtman family. Sam has two brothers and comes from a line of boys 70 years long. So, after a lot of serious thinking, the Toedtmans decided to enroll in GIVF's clinical trial of MicroSort for "family balancing." That's the popular new term for gender selection by couples who already have at least one child and want to control their family mix. Since MicroSort's family balance trial began in 1995, more than 1,300 couples have signed on—almost 10 times more than joined a companion trial aimed at avoiding genetic illnesses that strike boys. GIVF is actively recruiting new candidates for both trials. In 2003 a second MicroSort clinic was opened near Los Angeles, and a third is planned for Florida this year. GIVF hopes MicroSort will become the first sperm-sorting device to receive the FDA's stamp of approval for safety and effectiveness. "This will completely change reproductive choices for women, and that's very exciting," says MicroSort's medical director, Dr. Keith Blauer. "We hope to make it available to as many couples as possible."

The MicroSort technology—created originally by the Department of Agriculture to sort livestock sperm—works by mixing sperm with a DNA-specific dye that helps separate X's from Y's (graphic).The majority of couples who use MicroSort for gender selection have no fertility problems and use standard artificial insemination to conceive. The technique is far from perfect: most participants have to make more than one attempt, each costing at least $2,500, to get pregnant. And not all end up with the gender of choice. At last count, 91 per-

cent of couples who requested an "X sort" gave birth to a baby girl and 76 percent who chose a "Y sort" produced a boy. It worked for the Stock family. Six-month-old Amberlyn was spared the debilitating neuromuscular disorder that plagues her brother, Chancellor, 7. The Toedtmans were lucky, too. Though it took three tries to get pregnant, Mary finally delivered a girl, Natalie, last April. "She's a total joy," she says.

Determined as she was, Toedtman says she would not have felt comfortable creating embryos to ensure that Natalie was Natalie and not Nathaniel. But a small number of others, knowing that their chance of success with PGD is exponentially better, are becoming pioneers in the newest form of family planning. Available at a limited number of clinics nationwide, PGD was designed and originally intended to diagnose serious genetic diseases in embryos, like Tay-Sachs and cystic fibrosis, before implantation. Over the last decade the technology has allowed hundreds of couples, many of whom have endured the death of sick children, to have healthy babies. Today, some doctors are using PGD to increase the odds of successful IVF pregnancies by screening out chromosomally abnormal embryos. Some of those patients are asking about gender—and it's their right to do so, many doctors say. After an embryo screening, "I tell them it's normal and I tell them it's male or female," says PGD expert Yury Verlinsky of the Reproductive Genetics Institute in Chicago. "It's their embryo. I can't tell them which one to transfer."

It's one thing to allow infertile couples to choose gender after PGD. Creating embryos solely to sort boys from girls sets off ethical and moral alarm bells. In the last year or so, several clinics have begun to offer the procedure for gender balance without restrictions. Steinberg, of Fertility Institutes, says his team methodically debated the pros and cons before doing so. The logic, he says, is simple: "We've been offering sperm sorting for 20 years without any stipulations. Now, in 2004, I can offer almost 100 percent success with PGD. Why would I make it less available?" Steinberg.'s clinic, which also has offices in Las Vegas and Mexico, will soon perform its 100th PGD sex-selection procedure. So far, about 40 babies have been born, every one of them the desired sex. It's unclear how many couples will actually want to endure the hefty cost, time commitment and physical burden of fertility drugs and IVF just to ensure gender. But the idea is intriguing for a lot of couples. "I've had friends and neighbors discreetly inquire," says Dr. David Hill, head of ART Reproductive Center in Beverly Hills, Calif., where about 5 to 10 percent of patients are requesting PGD solely for sex selection. Hill has no problem offering it, but he respects colleagues who say no. "This is a really new area," he says. "It's pretty divided right now as to those who think it's acceptable and those who don't."

Dr. Mark Hughes, a leading PGD authority at Wayne State University School of Medicine in Detroit, is one of the latter. "The last time I checked, your gender wasn't a disease," he says. "There is no illness, no suffering and no reason for a physician to be involved. Besides, we're too busy helping desperate couples with serious disease build healthy families." At Columbia University, Dr. Mark Sauer balks at the idea of family balance. "What are you balancing? It discredits the value of an individual life." For those few patients who ask for it, "I look them straight in the face and say, 'We're not going to do that'." And at Northwestern, Dr. Ralph Kazer says bluntly: " 'Gattaca' was a wonderful movie. That's not what I want to do for a living."

One of the most vexing concerns is what some consider gender selection's implicit sexism. When you choose one sex, the argument goes, you reject the other. In Asia girls have been aborted or killed, and populations skewed, because of favoritism toward boys. Could the same thing happen here? GIVF's Blauer says the vast majority of MicroSort couples want girls, not boys, though that could change if Y-sort statistics improve. At Hill's clinic, about 65 percent request boys; at Steinberg's, 55 percent. "It's not going to tip the balance one way or the other," he says. But what if a couple doesn't get the boy or girl they desire? PGD comes as close as it gets to guaranteeing outcome, but there remains the thorny question of what to do with "wrong sex" embryos. Opponents worry that they'll be destroyed simply because they're male or female, but the options are identical for everyone going through IVF: discard the extras, freeze them for later use, donate them or offer them up for scientific research. As for MicroSort, of the more than 500 pregnancies achieved so far, four have been terminated at other facilities (GIVF won't perform abortions) because of "non-desired gender," says Blauer. "It's important to realize that couples have reproductive choice in this country," he says, but "the vast majority of patients want another healthy child and are happy with either gender."

Just beyond these clinical worries lies a vast swamp of ethical quandaries and inherent contradictions. People who support a woman's right to choose find themselves cringing at the idea of terminating a fetus based on sex. Those who believe that embryos deserve the status of personhood decry their destruction, but gender selection could result in fewer abortions. Choosing sex can skew male-female ratios, but it might also reduce overpopulation. Requesting a girl could mean she will be more desired by her parents, but it's also possible she'll grow up and decide she'd rather have been a boy. "Children are going to hold their parents responsible for having made them this way," says bioethicist Kass, "and that may not be as innocent as it sounds."

And then there is the most fundamental conflict of all: science versus religion. One Korean-American couple, with two daughters has been on both sides. Feeling an intense cultural pressure to produce a son, the woman, 31, attended a MicroSort information session, where Blauer reviewed the technique. Intrigued, she went back for a second session and convinced her husband to come along. When it was time to

move forward, though, a greater power took over. "I don't think God intended us to do that," she says. "We decided we should just pray about it and leave it up to God."

There are no laws against performing gender selection in the United States. Many people believe that the safety and effectiveness of reproductive technologies like PGD should be regulated, says Kathy Hudson, of the Genetics and Public Policy Center at Johns Hopkins, which recently polled 1,200 Americans on the topic. But, she says, many Americans "are uncomfortable with the government being the arbiter of how to use these technologies." Meanwhile, fertility doctors look to the American Society for Reproductive Medicine for professional standards. John Robertson, head of ASRM's ethics committee, says preconception techniques like MicroSort "would be fine once safety is established." So far, MicroSort reports, 2.4 percent of its babies have been born with major malformations, like Down syndrome, compared with 3 to 4 percent in the general population. But until the trial is completed, there are no definitive data. As for PGD, the ASRM currently discourages its use for sex selection, but Robertson says he wouldn't rule out the possibility that it might become acceptable in the future.

So what, in the end, should we make of gender selection? Will programming of human DNA before birth become inevitable? "I learned a long time ago never to say never," says Rick Myers, chief of Stanford's genetics department. Still, he says, traits we're all worried about, like height, personality and intelligence, aren't the products of single genes. They're cooked in a complex stew of DNA and environment—a stew that boggles scientists, even those with IQs so high you'd swear they were bioengineered. And even if we could create designer Uma Thurmans, would we want to? Sharla Miller and Mary Toedtman say absolutely not. "That's taking it too far," says Miller.

We wouldn't be human if we didn't fantasize about the sci-fi universe around the corner. Steinberg, who has worked in IVF since its conception in the 1970s, remembers finding notes on his windshield in the early days that said, TEST-TUBE BABIES HAVE NO SOUL. The very idea of creating life outside the womb "was unthinkable," he says. And yet, some 1 million test-tube babies later, the practice has become routine. The same will likely be true of gender selection, says Robin Marantz Henig, author of the new book "Pandora's Baby," a history of IVF "The more it's done," she says, "the less you're going to see concerns."

Lizette Frielingsdorf doesn't have any. She and her husband have three boys—Jordan, 8, Justin, 6, and Jake, 5—and one MicroSort girl, Jessica, who just turned 2. "I call her my $15,000 baby. We felt like we won the lottery," says Frielingsdorf "Probably once a week someone will say, 'You got your girl. How did you do that?' and I'll say, 'Here's the number.' I want others to experience the same joy we have." No doubt, many will.

Inside The Womb

What scientists have learned about those amazing first nine months—
and what it means for mothers

By J. Madeleine Nash

As THE CRYSTAL PROBE SLIDES ACROSS HER BELLY, HILDA Manzo, 33, stares wide-eyed at the video monitor mounted on the wall. She can make out a head with a mouth and two eyes. She can see pairs of arms and legs that end in tiny hands and feet. She can see the curve of a backbone, the bridge of a nose. And best of all, she can see movement. The mouth of her child-to-be yawns. Its feet kick. Its hands wave.

Dr. Jacques Abramowicz, director of the University of Chicago's ultrasound unit, turns up the audio so Manzo can hear the gush of blood through the umbilical cord and the fast thump, thump, thump of a miniature heart. "Oh, my!" she exclaims as he adjusts the sonic scanner to peer under her fetus' skin. "The heart is on the left side, as it should be," he says, "and it has four chambers. Look—one, two, three, four!"

Such images of life stirring in the womb—in this case, of a 17-week-old fetus no bigger than a newborn kitten—are at the forefront of a biomedical revolution that is rapidly transforming the way we think about the prenatal world. For although it takes nine months to make a baby, we now know that the most important developmental steps—including laying the foundation for such major organs as the heart, lungs and brain—occur before the end of the first three. We also know that long before a child is born its genes engage the environment of the womb in an elaborate conversation, a two-way dialogue that involves not only the air its mother breathes and the water she drinks but also what drugs she takes, what diseases she contracts and what hardships she suffers.

One reason we know this is a series of remarkable advances in MRIs, sonograms and other imaging technologies that allow us to peer into the developmental process at virtually every stage—from the fusion of sperm and egg to the emergence, some 40 weeks later, of a miniature human being. The extraordinary pictures on these pages come from a new book that captures some of the color and excitement of this research: *From Conception to Birth: A Life Unfolds* (Doubleday), by photographer Alexander Tsiaras and writer Barry Werth. Their com-

puter-enhanced images are reminiscent of the remarkable fetal portraits taken by medical photographer Lennart Nilsson, which appeared in Life magazine in 1965. Like Nilsson's work, these images will probably spark controversy. Antiabortion activists may interpret them as evidence that a fetus is a viable human being earlier than generally believed, while pro-choice advocates may argue that the new technology allows doctors to detect serious fetal defects at a stage when abortion is a reasonable option.

The other reason we know so much about what goes on inside the womb is the remarkable progress researchers have made in teasing apart the sequence of chemical signals and switches that drive fetal development. Scientists can now describe at the level of individual genes and molecules many of the steps involved in building a human, from the establishment of a head-to-tail growth axis and the budding of limbs to the sculpting of a four-chambered heart and the weaving together of trillions of neural connections. Scientists are beginning to unroll the genetic blueprint of life and identify the precise molecular tools required for assembly. Human development no longer seems impossibly complex, says Stanford University biologist Matthew Scott. "It just seems marvelous."

How is it, we are invited to wonder, that a fertilized egg—a mere speck of protoplasm and DNA encased in a spherical shell—can generate such complexity? The answers, while elusive and incomplete, are beginning to come into focus.

Only 20 years ago, most developmental biologists thought that different organisms grew according to different sets of rules, so that understanding how a fly or a worm develops—or even a vertebrate like a chicken or a fish—would do little to illuminate the process in humans. Then, in the 1980s, researchers found remarkable similarities in the molecular tool kit used by organisms that span the breadth of the animal kingdom, and those similarities have proved serendipitous beyond imagining. No matter what the species, nature uses virtually the same nails

How They Did It

With just a few keystrokes, Alexander Tsiaras does the impossible. He takes the image of a 56-day-old human embryo and peers through its skin, revealing liver, lungs, a bulblike brain and the tiny, exquisite vertebrae of a developing spine.

These are no ordinary baby pictures. What Tsiaras and his colleagues are manipulating are layers of data gathered by CT scans, micro magnetic resonance imaging (MRI) and other visualization techniques. When Lennart Nilsson took his groundbreaking photographs in the 1960s, he was limited to what he could innovatively capture with a flash camera. Since then, says Tsiaras, "there's been a revolution in imaging."

What's changed is that development can now be viewed through a wide variety of prisms, using different forms of energy to illuminate different aspects of the fetus. CT scans, for example, are especially good at showing bone, and MRI is excellent for soft tissue. These two-dimensional layers of information are assembled, using sophisticated computer software, into a three-dimensional whole.

The results are painstakingly accurate and aesthetically stunning. Tsiaras, who trained as a painter and sculptor, used medical specimens from the Carnegie Human Embryology Collection at the National Museum of Health and Medicine in Washington as models for all but a few images. The specimens came from a variety of sources, according to museum director Adrianne Noe, including miscarriages and medically necessary procedures. None were acquired from elective abortions.

—By David Bjerklie

sory committee recommended that embryos be considered the same as human subjects in clinical trials.)

To be sure, the marvel of an embryo transcends the collection of genes and cells that compose it. For unlike strands of DNA floating in a test tube or stem cells dividing in a Petri dish, an embryo is capable of building not just a protein or a patch of tissue but a living entity in which every cell functions as an integrated part of the whole. "Imagine yourself as the world's tallest skyscraper, built in nine months and germinating from a single brick," suggest Tsiaras and Werth in the opening of their book. "As that brick divides, it gives rise to every other type of material needed to construct and operate the finished tower—a million tons of steel, concrete, mortar, insulation, tile, wood, granite, solvents, carpet, cable, pipe and glass as well as all furniture, phone systems, heating and cooling units, plumbing, electrical wiring, artwork and computer networks, including software."

Given the number of steps in the process, it will perhaps forever seem miraculous that life ever comes into being without a major hitch. "Whenever you look from one embryo to another," observes Columbia University developmental neurobiologist Thomas Jessell, "what strikes you is the fidelity of the process."

Sometimes, though, that fidelity is compromised, and the reasons why this happens are coming under intense scrutiny. In laboratory organisms, birth defects occur for purely genetic reasons when scientists purposely mutate or knock out specific sequences of DNA to establish their function. But when development goes off track in real life, the cause can often be traced to a lengthening list of external factors that disrupt some aspect of the genetic program. For an embryo does not develop in a vacuum but depends on the environment that surrounds it. When a human embryo is deprived of essential nutrients or exposed to a toxin, such as alcohol, tobacco or crack cocaine, the consequences can range from readily apparent abnormalities— spina bifida, fetal alcohol syndrome—to subtler metabolic defects that may not become apparent until much later.

and screws, the same hammers and power tools to put an embryo together.

Among the by-products of the torrent of information pouring out of the laboratory are new prospects for treating a broad range of late-in-life diseases. Just last month, for example, three biologists won the Nobel Prize for Medicine for their work on the nematode *Caenorhabditis elegans*, which has a few more than 1,000 cells, compared with a human's 50 trillion. The three winners helped establish that a fundamental mechanism that *C. elegans* embryos employ to get rid of redundant or abnormal cells also exists in humans and may play a role in AIDS, heart disease and cancer. Even more exciting, if considerably more controversial, is the understanding that embryonic cells harbor untapped therapeutic potential. These cells, of course, are stem cells, and they are the progenitors of more specialized cells that make up organs and tissues. By harnessing their generative powers, medical researchers believe, it may one day be possible to repair the damage wrought by injury and disease. (That prospect suffered a political setback last week when a federal advi-

IRONICALLY, EVEN AS SOCIETY AT LARGE CONTINUES TO WORRY almost obsessively about the genetic origins of disease, the biologists and medical researchers who study development are mounting an impressive case for the role played by the prenatal environment. A growing body of evidence suggests that a number of serious maladies—among them, atherosclerosis, hypertension and diabetes—trace their origins to detrimental prenatal conditions. As New York University Medical School's Dr. Peter Nathanielsz puts it, "What goes on in the womb before you are born is just as important to who you are as your genes."

Most adults, not to mention most teenagers, are by now thoroughly familiar with the mechanics of how the sperm in a man's semen and the egg in a woman's oviduct connect, and it is at this point that the story of development begins. For the sperm and the egg each contain only 23 chromosomes, half the amount of DNA needed to make a human. Only when the sperm and the egg fuse their chromosomes does the tiny zygote, as a fertilized egg is called, receive its instructions to grow. And grow it does, replicating its DNA each time it divides—into two cells, then four, then eight and so on.

If cell division continued in this fashion, then nine months later the hapless mother would give birth to a tumorous ball of literally astronomical proportions. But instead of endlessly dividing, the zygote's cells progressively take form. The first striking change is apparent four days after conception, when a 32-cell clump called the morula (which means "mulberry" in Latin) gives rise to two distinct layers wrapped around a fluid-filled core. Now known as a blastocyst, this spherical mass will proceed to burrow into the wall of the uterus. A short time later, the outer layer of cells will begin turning into the placenta and amniotic sac, while the inner layer will become the embryo.

The formation of the blastocyst signals the start of a sequence of changes that are as precisely choreographed as a ballet. At the end of Week One, the inner cell layer of the blastocyst balloons into two more layers. From the first layer, known as the endoderm, will come the cells that line the gastrointestinal tract. From the second, the ectoderm, will arise the neurons that make up the brain and spinal cord along with the epithelial cells that make up the skin. At the end of Week Two, the ectoderm spins off a thin line of cells known as the primitive streak, which forms a new cell layer called the mesoderm. From it will come the cells destined to make the heart, the lungs and all the other internal organs.

At this point, the embryo resembles a stack of Lilliputian pancakes—circular, flat and horizontal. But as the mesoderm forms, it interacts with cells in the ectoderm to trigger yet another transformation. Very soon these cells will roll up to become the neural tube, a rudimentary precursor of the spinal cord and brain. Already the embryo has a distinct cluster of cells at each end, one destined to become the mouth and the other the anus. The embryo, no larger at this point than a grain of rice, has determined the head-to-tail axis along which all its body parts will be arrayed.

How on earth does this little, barely animate cluster of cells "know" what to do? The answer is as simple as it is startling. A human embryo knows how to lay out its body axis in the same way that fruit-fly embryos know and *C. elegans* embryos and the embryos of myriad other creatures large and small know. In all cases, scientists have found, in charge of establishing this axis is a special set of genes, especially the so-called homeotic homeobox, or HOX, genes.

HOX genes were first discovered in fruit flies in the early 1980s when scientists noticed that their absence caused striking mutations. Heads, for example, grew feet instead of antennae, and thoraxes grew an extra pair of wings. HOX genes have been found in virtually every type of animal, and while their number varies—fruit flies have nine, humans have 39—they are invariably arrayed along chromosomes in the order along the body in which they are supposed to turn on.

Many other genes interact with the HOX system, including the aptly named Hedgehog and Tinman genes, without which fruit flies grow a dense covering of bristles or fail to make a heart. And scientists are learning in exquisite detail what each does at various stages of the developmental process. Thus one of the three Hedgehog genes—Sonic Hedgehog, named in honor of the cartoon and video-game character—has been shown to play a role in making at least half a dozen types of spinal-cord neurons. As it happens, cells in different places in the neural tube are exposed to different levels of the protein encoded by this gene; cells drenched in significant quantities of protein mature into one type of neuron, and those that receive the barest sprinkling mature into another. Indeed, it was by using a particular concentration of Sonic Hedgehog that neurobiologist Jessell and his research team at Columbia recently coaxed stem cells from a mouse embryo to mature into seemingly functional motor neurons.

At the University of California, San Francisco, a team led by biologist Didier Stainier is working on genes important in cardiovascular formation. Removing one of them, called Miles Apart, from zebra-fish embryos results in a mutant with two nonviable hearts. Why? In all vertebrate embryos, including humans, the heart forms as twin buds. In order to function, these buds must join. The way the Miles Apart gene appears to work, says Stainier, is by detecting a chemical attractant that, like the smell of dinner cooking in the kitchen, entices the pieces to move toward each other.

The crafting of a human from a single fertilized egg is a vastly complicated affair, and at any step, something can go wrong. When the heart fails to develop properly, a baby can be born with a hole in the heart or even missing valves and chambers. When the neural tube fails to develop properly, a baby can be born with a brain not fully developed (anencephaly) or with an incompletely formed spine (spina bifida). Neural-tube defects, it has been firmly established, are often due to insufficient levels of the water-soluble B vitamin folic acid. Reason: folic acid is essential to a dividing cell's ability to replicate its DNA.

Vitamin A, which a developing embryo turns into retinoids, is another nutrient that is critical to the nervous system. But watch out, because too much vitamin A can be toxic. In another newly released book, *Before Your Pregnancy* (Ballantine Books), nutritionist Amy Ogle and obstetrician Dr. Lisa Mazzullo caution would-be mothers to limit foods that are overly rich in vitamin A, especially liver and food products that contain lots of it, like foie gras and cod-liver oil. An excess of vitamin A, they note, can cause damage to the skull, eyes, brain and spinal cord of a developing fetus, probably because retinoids directly interact with DNA, affecting the activity of critical genes.

Folic acid, vitamin A and other nutrients reach developing embryos and fetuses by crossing the placenta, the remarkable temporary organ produced by the blastocyst that develops from the fertilized egg. The outer ring of cells that compose the placenta are extremely aggressive, behaving very much like tumor cells as they invade the uterine wall and tap into the pregnant woman's blood vessels. In fact, these cells actually go in and replace the maternal cells that form the lining of the uterine arteries, says Susan Fisher, a developmental biologist at the University of California, San Francisco. They trick the pregnant woman's immune system into tolerating the embryo's presence rather than rejecting it like the lump of foreign tissue it is.

In essence, says Fisher, "the placenta is a traffic cop," and its main job is to let good things in and keep bad things out. To this

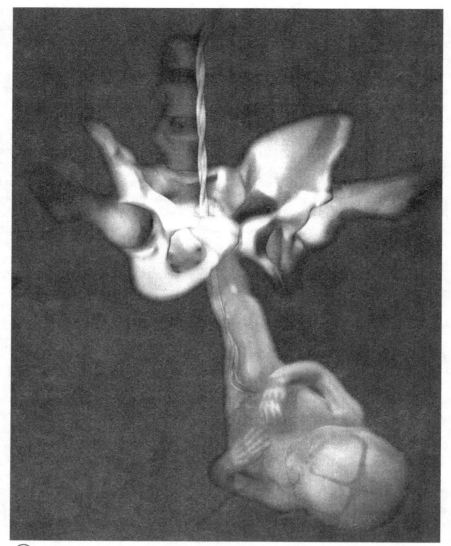

⑨ months—shows how a baby emerges from the birth canal began with an unusual delivery that required doctors to place the mother in a spiral CT scanner. The image was merged with CT and ultrasound data from other babies to create this re-enacted birth.

Photo © Alexander Tsiaras/SPL/Photo Researchers, Inc.

end, the placenta marshals platoons of natural killer cells to patrol its perimeters and engages millions of tiny molecular pumps that expel poisons before they can damage the vulnerable embryo.

ALAS, THE PLACENTA'S DEFENSES ARE SOMETIMES BREACHED— by microbes like rubella and cytomegalovirus, by drugs like thalidomide and alcohol, by heavy metals like lead and mercury, and by organic pollutants like dioxin and PCBs. Pathogens and poisons contained in certain foods are also able to cross the placenta, which may explain why placental tissues secrete a nausea-inducing hormone that has been tentatively linked to morning sickness. One provocative if unproved hypothesis says morning sickness may simply be nature's crude way of making sure that potentially harmful substances do not

reach the womb, particularly during the critical first trimester of development.

Timing is decisive where toxins are concerned. Air pollutants like carbon monoxide and ozone, for example, have been linked to heart defects when exposure coincided with the second month of pregnancy, the window of time during which the heart forms. Similarly, the nervous system is particularly vulnerable to damage while neurons are migrating from the part of the brain where they are made to the area where they will ultimately reside. "A tiny, tiny exposure at a key moment when a certain process is beginning to unfold can have an effect that is not only quantitatively larger but qualitatively different than it would be on an adult whose body has finished forming," observes Sandra Steingraber, an ecologist at Cornell University.

Among the substances Steingraber is most worried about are environmentally persistent neurotoxins like mercury and lead (which directly interfere with the migration of neurons formed during the first trimester) and PCBs (which, some evidence suggests, block the activity of thyroid hormone). "Thyroid hormone plays a noble role in the fetus," says Steingraber. "It actually goes into the fetal brain and serves as kind of a conductor of the orchestra."

PCBs are no longer manufactured in the U.S., but other chemicals potentially harmful to developing embryos and fetuses are. Theo Colborn, director of the World Wildlife Fund's contaminants program, says at least 150 chemicals pose possible risks for fetal development, and some of them can interfere with the naturally occurring sex hormones critical to the development of a fetus. Antiandrogens, for example, are widely found in fungicides and plastics. One in particular—DDE, a breakdown product of DDT—has been shown to cause hypospadias in laboratory mice, a birth defect in which the urethra fails to extend to the end of the penis. In humans, however, notes Dr. Allen Wilcox, editor of the journal *Epidemiology*, the link between hormone-like chemicals and birth defects remains elusive.

THE LIST OF POTENTIAL THREATS TO EMBRYONIC LIFE IS LONG. It includes not only what the mother eats, drinks or inhales, explains N.Y.U.'s Nathanielsz, but also the hormones that surge through her body. Pregnant rats with high blood-glucose levels (chemically induced by wiping out their insulin) give birth to female offspring that are unusually susceptible to developing gestational diabetes. These daughter rats are able to produce enough insulin to keep their blood glucose in check, says Nathanielsz, but only until they become pregnant. At that point, their glucose level soars, because their pancreases were damaged by prenatal exposure to their mother's sugar-spiked blood. The next generation of daughters is, in turn, more susceptible to gestational diabetes, and the transgenerational chain goes on.

In similar fashion, atherosclerosis may sometimes develop because of prenatal exposure to chronically high cholesterol levels. According to Dr. Wulf Palinski, an endocrinologist at the University of California at San Diego, there appears to be a kind of metabolic memory of prenatal life that is permanently retained. In genetically similar groups of rabbits and kittens, at least, those born to mothers on fatty diets were far more likely to develop arterial plaques than those whose mothers ate lean.

But of all the long-term health threats, maternal undernourishment—which stunts growth even when babies are born full term—may top the list. "People who are small at birth have, for life, fewer kidney cells, and so they are more likely to go into renal failure when they get sick," observes Dr. David Barker, director of the environmental epidemiology unit at England's University of Southampton. The same is true of insulin-producing cells in the pancreas, so that low-birth-weight babies stand a higher chance of developing diabetes later in life because their pancreases—where insulin is produced—have to work that much harder. Barker, whose research has linked low birth weight to heart disease, points out that undernourishment can trigger lifelong metabolic changes. In adulthood, for example, obesity may become a problem because food scarcity in prenatal life causes the body to shift the rate at which calories are turned into glucose for immediate use or stored as reservoirs of fat.

But just how does undernourishment reprogram metabolism? Does it perhaps prevent certain genes from turning on, or does it turn on those that should stay silent? Scientists are racing to answer those questions, along with a host of others. If they succeed, many more infants will find safe passage through the critical first months of prenatal development. Indeed, our expanding knowledge about the interplay between genes and the prenatal environment is cause for both concern and hope. Concern because maternal and prenatal health care often ranks last on the political agenda. Hope because by changing our priorities, we might be able to reduce the incidence of both birth defects and serious adult diseases.

—With reporting by David Bjerklie and Alice Park/New York and Dan Cray/Los Angeles

THE MYSTERY OF FETAL LIFE:
SECRETS OF THE WOMB

JOHN PEKKANEN

In the dim light of an ultrasound room, a wand slides over the abdomen of a young woman. As it emits sound waves, it allows us to see into her womb. The video screen brightens with a grainy image of a 20-week-old fetus. It floats in its amniotic sac, like an astronaut free of gravity.

The fetal face stares upward, then turns toward us, as if to mug for the camera. The sound waves strike different tissues with different densities, and their echoes form different images. These images are computer-enhanced, so although the fetus weights only 14 ounces and is no longer than my hand, we can see its elfin features.

Close up, we peek into the fetal brain. In the seconds we observe, a quarter million new brain cells are born. This happens constantly. By the end of the nine months, the baby's brain will hold 100 billion brain cells.

The sound waves focus on the chest, rendering images of a vibrating four-chambered heart no bigger than the tip of my little finger. The monitor tells us it is moving at 163 beats a minute. It sounds like a frightened bird fluttering in its cage.

We watch the rib cage move. Although the fetus lives in an airless environment, it "breathes" intermittently inside the womb by swallowing amniotic fluid. Some researchers speculate that the fetus is exercising its chest and diaphragm as its way of preparing for life outside the womb.

The clarity of ultrasound pictures is now so good that subtle abnormalities can be detected. The shape of the skull, brain, and spinal cord, along with the heart and other vital organs, can be seen in breathtaking detail.

In this ultrasound exam, there are no hints to suggest that anything is abnormal. The husband squeezes his wife's hand. They both smile.

The fetus we have just watched is at the midpoint of its 40-week gestation. At conception 20 weeks earlier, it began as a single cell that carried in its nucleus the genetic code for the human it will become.

After dividing and redividing for a week, it grew to 32 cells. Like the initial cell, these offspring cells carry 40,000 or so genes, located on 23 pairs of chromosomes inherited from the mother and father. Smaller than the head of a pin, this clump of cells began a slow journey down the fallopian tube and attached itself to the spongy wall of the uterus.

Once settled, some embryonic cells began to form a placenta to supply the embryo with food, water, and nutrients from the mother's bloodstream. The placenta also filtered out harmful substances in the mother's bloodstream. The embryo and mother exchange chemical information to ensure that they work together toward their common goal.

Instructed by their genes, the cells continued to divide but didn't always produce exact replicas. In a process still not well understood, the cells began to differentiate to seek out their own destinies. Some helped build internal organs, others bones, muscles, and brain.

At 19 days postconception, the earliest brain tissues began to form. They developed at the top end of the neural tube, a sheath of cells that ran nearly the entire length of the embryo.

The human brain requires virtually the entire pregnancy to emerge fully, longer than the other organ systems. Even in the earliest stage of development, the fetus knows to protect its brain. The brain gets the most highly oxygenated blood, and should there be any shortage, the fetus will send the available blood to the brain.

Extending downward from the brain, the neural tube began to form the spinal cord. At four weeks, a rudimentary heart started to beat, and four limbs began sprouting. By eight weeks, the two-inch-long embryo took human form and was more properly called a fetus. At 10 to 12 weeks, it began moving its arms and legs, opened its jaws, swallowed, and yawned, Mostly it slept.

"We are never more clever than we are as a fetus," says Dr. Peter Nathanielsz, a fetal researcher, obstetrician, and professor of reproductive medicine at Cornell University. "We pass far more biological milestones before we are born than we'll ever pass after we're born."

Not long ago, the process of fetal development was shrouded in mystery. But through the power of scanning techniques, biotechnology, and fetal and animal studies, much of the mystery of fetal life has been unveiled.

We now know that as the fetus matures it experiences a broad range of sensory stimulation. It hears, sees, tastes, smells, feels, and has rapid eye movement (REM) sleep, the sleep stage we associate with dreaming. From observation of its sleep and wake cycles, the fetus appears to know night from day. It learns and remembers, and it may cry. It seems to do everything in utero that it will do after it is born. In the words of one researcher, "Fetal life is us."

Studies now show that it's the fetus, not the mother, who sends the hormonal signals that determine when a baby will be born. And we've found out that its health in the womb depends in part on its mother's health when she was in the womb.

Finally, we've discovered that the prenatal environment is not as benign, or as neutral, as once thought. It is sensitive to the mother's health, emotions, and behavior.

The fetus is strongly affected by the mother's eating habits. If the mother exercises more than usual, the fetus may become temporarily short of oxygen. If she takes a hot bath, the fetus feels the heat. If she smokes, so does the fetus. One study has found that pregnant women exposed to more sunlight had more-outgoing children.

We now know that our genes do not encode a complete design for us, that our "genetic destiny" is not hard-wired at the time of conception. Instead, our development involves an interplay between genes and the environment, including that of the uterus. Because genes take "cues" from their environment, an expectant mother's physical and psychological health influences her unborn child's genetic well-being.

Factors such as low prenatal oxygen levels, stress, infections, and poor maternal nutrition may determine whether certain genes are switched on or off. Some researchers believe that our time in the womb is the single most important period of our life.

"Because of genetics, we once thought that we would unfold in the womb like a blueprint, but now we know it's not that simple," says Janet DiPietro, an associate professor of maternal and child health at the Johns Hopkins School of Public Health and one of a handful of fetal-behavior specialists. "The mother and the uterine environment she creates have a major impact on many aspects of fetal development, and a number of things laid down during that time remain with you throughout your life."

The impact of the womb on our intelligence, personality, and emotional and physical health is beginning to be understood. There's also an emerging understanding of something called fetal programming, which says that the effects of our life in the womb may be not felt until decades after we're born, and in ways that are more powerful than previously imagined.

Says Dr. Nathanielsz, whose book *Life in the Womb* details the emerging science of fetal development: "It's an area of great scientific importance that until recently remained largely unknown."

"I'm pregnant. Is it okay to have a glass of wine? Can I take my Prozac? What about a Diet Coke?"

Years ago, before she knew she was pregnant, a friend of mine had a glass of wine with dinner. When she discovered she was pregnant, she worried all through her pregnancy and beyond. She feels some guilt to this day, even though the son she bore turned out very well.

Many mothers have experienced the same tangled emotions. "There's no evidence that a glass of wine a day during pregnancy has a negative impact on the developing fetus," says Dr. John Larsen, professor and chair of obstetrics and gynecology at George Washington University. Larsen says that at one time doctors gave alcohol by IV to pregnant women who were experiencing preterm labor; it relaxed the muscles and quelled contractions.

Larsen now sometimes recommends a little wine to women who experience mild contractions after a puncture from an amniocentesis needle, and some studies suggest that moderate alcohol intake in pregnancy may prevent preterm delivery in some women.

Even though most experts agree with Larsen, the alcohol message that most women hear calls for total abstinence. Experts worry that declaring moderate alcohol intake to be safe in pregnancy may encourage some pregnant women to drink immoderately. They say that pregnant women who have an occasional drink should not think they've placed their baby at risk.

What is safe? Some studies show children born to mothers who consumed three drinks a day in pregnancy averaged seven points lower on IQ tests than unexposed children. There is evidence that six drinks a day during pregnancy puts babies at risk of fetal alcohol syndrome (FAS), a constellation of serious birth defects that includes mental retardation. The higher the alcohol intake, the higher the FAS risk.

Are there drugs and drug combinations that women should avoid or take with caution during pregnancy? Accutane (isotretinoin), a prescription drug for acne and psoriasis, is known to cause birth defects. So too are some anticonvulsant drugs, including Epitol, Tegretol, and Valproate. Tetracycline, a widely prescribed antibiotic, can cause bone-growth delays and permanent teeth problems for a baby if a mother takes it during pregnancy.

Most over-the-counter drugs are considered safe in pregnancy, but some of them carry risks. Heavy doses of aspirin and other nonsteroidal anti-inflammatory drugs such as ibuprofen can delay the start of labor. They are also linked to a life-threatening disorder of newborns called persistent pulmonary hypertension (PPHN), which diverts airflow away from the baby's lungs, causing oxygen depletion. The March issue of the journal

Pediatrics published a study linking these nonprescription pain-killers to PPHN, which results in the death of 15 percent of the infants who have it.

OTC DRUGS

In 1998, researchers at the University of Nebraska Medical Center reported dextromethorphan, a cough suppressant found in 40 or more OTC drugs including Nyquil, Tylenol Cold, Dayquil, Robitussin Maximum Strength, and Dimetapp DM, caused congenital malformations in chick embryos. The research was published in *Pediatric Research* and supported by the National Institutes of Health.

Although no connection between dextromethorphan and human birth defects has been shown, the Nebraska researchers noted that similar genes regulate early development in virtually all species. For this reason, the researchers predicted that dextromethorphan, which acts on the brain to suppress coughing, would have the same harmful effect on a human fetus.

Many women worry about antidepressants. Some need them during pregnancy or took them before they knew they were pregnant. A study published in the *New England Journal of Medicine* found no association between fetal exposure to antidepressants and brain damage. The study compared the IQ, temperament, activity level, and distractibility of more than 125 children whose mothers took antidepressants in pregnancy with 84 children whose mothers took no drugs known to harm the fetus.

The two groups of children, between 16 months and eight years old when tested, were comparable in every way. The antidepressants taken by the mothers included both tricyclates such as Elavil and Tofranil and selective serotonin reuptake inhibitors such as Prozac.

Not all mood-altering drugs may be safe. There is some evidence that minor tranquilizers taken for anxiety may cause developmental problems if taken in the first trimester, but there is no hard proof of this. Evidence of fetal damage caused by illegal drugs such as cocaine is widely accepted, as is the case against cigarette smoking. A 1998 survey found that 13 percent of all mothers who gave birth smoked. Evidence is striking that cigarette smoking in pregnancy lowers birth weight and increases the risks of premature birth, attention deficit hyperactive disorder, and diminished IQ.

A long-running study based on information from the National Collaborative Perinatal Project found that years after they were born, children were more apt to become addicted to certain drugs if their mother took them during delivery.

"We found drug-dependent individuals were five times more likely to have exposure to high doses of painkillers and anesthesia during their delivery than their nonaddicted siblings," says Stephen Buka of the Harvard School of Public Health. Buka suspects this is caused by a modification in the infant's brain receptors as the drugs pass from mother to child during an especially sensitive time.

CAFFEINE

Coffee consumption has worried mothers because there have been hints that caffeine may be harmful to the fetus. Like most things in life, moderation is the key. There's no evidence that 300 milligrams of caffeine a day (about three cups of coffee, or four or five cups of most regular teas, or five to six cola drinks) harms a developing baby. Higher caffeine consumption has been weakly linked to miscarriage and difficulty in conceiving.

Expectant mothers concerned about weight gain should be careful of how much of the artificial sweetener aspartame they consume. Marketed under brand names such as NutraSweet and Equal, it's found in diet soft drinks and foods.

The concern is this: In the body, aspartame converts into phenylalanine, a naturally occurring amino acid we ingest when we eat protein. At high levels, phenylalanine can be toxic to brain cells.

When we consume phenylalanine in protein, we also consume a number of other amino acids that neutralize any ill effects. When we consume it in aspartame, we get none of the neutralizing amino acids to dampen phenylalanine's impact. And as it crosses the placenta, phenylalanine's concentrations are magnified in the fetal brain.

If a fetal brain is exposed to high levels of phenylalanine because its mother consumes a lot of aspartame, will it be harmed? One study found average IQ declines of ten points in children born to mothers with a fivefold increase of phenylalanine blood levels in pregnancy. That's a lot of aspartame, and it doesn't mean an expectant mother who drinks moderate amounts of diet soda need worry.

Researchers say consuming up to three servings of aspartame a day—in either diet soda or low-calorie foods—appears to be safe for the fetus. However, a pregnant woman of average weight who eats ten or more servings a day may put her unborn baby at risk. In testimony before Congress, Dr. William Pardridge, a neuroscience researcher at UCLA, said it's likely that the effect of high phenylalanine levels in the fetal brain "will be very subtle" and many not manifest until years later.

One wild card concerns the 10 to 20 million Americans who unknowingly carry a gene linked to a genetic disease called phenylketonuria (PKU), which can lead to severe mental retardation. Most carriers don't know it, because PKU is a recessive genetic disorder, and both mother and father must carry the defective gene to pass PKU on to their child. A carrier feels no ill effects. According to researchers, a pregnant woman who unknowingly carries the PKU gene might place her unborn child at risk if she consumes even relatively moderate amounts of aspartame. There is no hard evidence that this will happen, but it remains a serious concern. PKU can be detected in the fetus by amniocentesis; a restrictive diet can prevent the worst effects of PKU on the child.

How does a mother's getting an infection affect her unborn baby? And should she be careful of cats?

Many experts think pregnant women should be more concerned about infections and household pets than a glass of wine or can of diet drink. There's overwhelming evidence of the potential harm of infections during pregnancy. We've known for a long time that rubella (German measles), a viral infection, can cause devastating birth defects.

More worrisome are recent studies showing that exposure to one of the most common of winter's ills—influenza—may put an unborn child at risk of cognitive and emotional problems. If flu strikes in the second trimester, it may increase the unborn baby's risk of developing schizophrenia later in life. While the flu may be a trigger, it's likely that a genetic susceptibility is also needed for schizophrenia to develop.

Some evidence exists that maternal flu may also lead to dyslexia, and suspicions persist that a first-trimester flu may cause fetal neural-tube defects resulting in spina bifida. The common cold, sometimes confused with the flu, has not been linked to any adverse outcomes for the baby.

"Infections are probably the most important thing for a pregnant woman to protect herself against," says Lise Eliot, a developmental neurobiologist at the Chicago Medical School. "She should always practice good hygiene, like washing her hands frequently, avoiding crowds, and never drinking from someone else's cup." She adds that the flu vaccine has been approved for use during pregnancy.

Some researchers recommend that pregnant women avoid close contact with cats. Toxoplasmosis, a parasitic infection, can travel from a cat to a woman to her unborn child.

Most humans become infected through cat litter boxes. An infected woman might experience only mild symptoms, if any, so the illness usually goes undetected. If she is diagnosed with the infection, antiparasitic drugs are helpful, but they don't completely eliminate the disease. The infection is relatively rare, and the odds of passing it from mother to child are only one in five during the first two trimesters, when the fetal harm is most serious. The bad news is that a fetus infected by toxoplasmosis can suffer severe brain damage, including mental retardation and epilepsy. Some researchers also suspect it may be a latent trigger for serious mental illness as the child grows older.

CEREBRAL PALSY

An expectant mother may not realize she has potentially harmful infections. The prime suspects are infections in the reproductive tract. Researchers suspect most cerebral-palsy cases are not caused by delivery problems, as has been widely assumed. There's strong evidence that some cases of cerebral-palsy may be linked to placental infections that occur during uterine life. Other cerebral-palsy cases may be triggered by oxygen deprivation in early development, but very few appear to be caused by oxygen deprivation during delivery. It's now estimated that only 10 percent of cerebral-palsy cases are related to delivery problems.

Maternal urinary-tract infections have been linked to lower IQs in children. Another infection, cytomegalovirus (CMV), has been linked to congenital deafness. Sexually transmitted diseases such as chlamydia are suspected to be a trigger for pre-term birth. Despite the serious threat posed to developing babies, infections during pregnancy remain poorly understood.

"We just don't know right now when or how the uterine infections that really make a difference to the fetus are transmitted

in pregnancy," says Dr. Karin Nelson, a child neurologist and acting chief of the neuro-epidemiology branch of the National Institute of Neurologic Disorders and Stroke at NIH. "Nor do we know all the potential problems they may cause."

Because of this, researchers offer little in the way of recommendations other than clean living and careful sex. They recommend that any woman contemplating pregnancy get in her best physical condition, because a number of studies have found that a woman's general health before she becomes pregnant is vital to fetal health. They also recommend a thorough gynecological exam because it may detect a treatable infection that could harm the fetus.

Rachel Carson was right about pesticides. So if you're pregnant, how careful should you be about what you eat?

In her book *Silent Spring,* author Rachel Carson noted that when pregnant mammals were exposed to synthetic pesticides, including DDT and methoxychlor, the pesticides caused developmental abnormalities in offspring. Carson, a scientist, noted that some pesticides mimicked the female hormone estrogen and caused the male offspring to be feminized.

About the time of Carson's 1962 book, another story was emerging about diethylstilbestrol (DES), a man-made female hormone administered in the 1940s and '50s to prevent miscarriages. In the 1960s it became clear that many young daughters of DES mothers were turning up reproductive malformations and vaginal cancers. Sons born to DES mothers suffered reproductive problems, including undescended testicles and abnormal sperm counts.

ENDOCRINE DISRUPTERS

Over the years, suspicion grew from both animal and human studies that something in the environment was disrupting fetal development. In the 1990s it was given a name—endocrine disruption. The theory was that DES and the pesticides cited by Carson caused defects in offspring because they disrupted the normal endocrine process. They did this by mimicking hormones inside the human body.

It's now clear that DDT and DES are the tip of the iceberg. Today more than 90,000 synthetic chemicals are used, most made after World War II. New chemicals are produced every week. They are used in everything from pesticides to plastics.

How many of these man-made chemicals might act as endocrine disrupters? More than 50 have been identified, and hundreds more are suspects.

To understand the threat from endocrine disrupters, it helps to understand what human hormones do. Secreted by endocrine glands, these tiny molecules circulate through the bloodstream to the organs. They include estrogen, adrenalin, thyroid, melatonin, and testosterone. Each is designed to fit only into a specific receptor on a cell, like a key that fits only one lock. When a hormone connects with the cell receptor, it enters the cell's nucleus. Once there, the hormone acts as a signaling agent to direct the cell's DNA to produce specific proteins.

During fetal life, the right type and concentration of hormones must be available at the right time for normal fetal development to occur. Produced by both mother and fetus, hormones are involved in cell division and differentiation, the development of the brain and reproductive organs, and virtually everything else needed to produce a baby.

"We know from animal experiments and wildlife observations that periods in development are very sensitive to alterations in the hormone levels," says Robert Kavlock, director of reproductive toxicology for the Environmental Protection Agency.

The damage is done when chemical mimickers get into cells at the wrong time, or at the wrong strength, or both. When this happens, something in the fetus will not develop as it should.

After years of witnessing the harmful impact on wildlife, we now know that humans are not immune to endocrine disrupters. More troubling, because of the pervasiveness of these chemicals, is that we can't escape them. We get them in the food we eat, the water we drink, the products we buy.

One of the most dramatic examples came to light in the 1970s when researchers wanted to find out why so many babies born in the Great Lakes region suffered serious neurological defects. They found the answer in polychlorinated biphenyls (PCBs), organic chemicals once used in electrical insulation and adhesives. Heavy PCB contamination of Great Lakes fish eaten by the mothers turned out to be the cause.

It is not clear how PCBs cause fetal brain damage, but it's believed to happen when they disrupt thyroid hormones. Severe thyroid deficiency in pregnancy is known to cause mental retardation. Another study found reduced penis size in boys born to mothers exposed to high levels of PCBs.

The U.S. manufacture of PCBs ended in 1977. PCB levels found in the mothers and the fish they ate suggested at the time that only very high exposure caused a problem for developing babies. Now we know this isn't true.

Because PCBs don't break down, they've remained a toxin that continues to enter our bodies through the food we eat. They have leached into soil and water and are found in shellfish and freshwater fish and to a smaller degree in ocean fish. Bottom-feeding freshwater fish, such as catfish and carp, have the highest PCB concentrations.

PCBs store in fat tissue and are found in dairy products and meats. Fatty meats, especially processed meats like cold cuts, sausages, and hot dogs, are usually heaviest in PCBs. They get into these products because farm animals graze on PCB-contaminated land. However, eating fish from PCB-contaminated water remains the primary way we get these chemicals into our systems. In pregnant women, PCBs easily cross the placenta and circulate in the fetus.

PCBs are ubiquitous. They've been detected in the Antarctic snow. If you had detection equipment sensitive enough, you'd find them in the milk at the supermarket.

What concerns experts are findings from studies in the Netherlands and upstate New York that found even low maternal PCB exposures pose risk to a fetus.

The Dutch study followed 418 children from birth into early childhood. In the final month of pregnancy, researchers mea-sured the maternal PCB blood levels, and at birth they measured PCB levels in the umbilical cord. None of the mothers was a heavy fish eater or had any history of high PCB exposure, and none of their PCB levels was considered high by safety standards.

At 3 1/2 years of age, the children's cognitive abilities were assessed with tests. After adjusting for other variables, the researchers found that maternal and cord blood PCB levels correlated with the children's cognitive abilities. As the PCB blood levels went up, the children suffered more attention problems and their cognitive abilities went down. It should be noted that the brain damage in these Dutch children was not devastating. They were not retarded or autistic. But on a relative scale, they had suffered measurable harm.

The Dutch researchers concluded that the in utero PCB exposure, and not any postnatal exposure, caused the children's brain damage. The study also revealed that these children had depressed immune function.

"All we can say now," says Deborah Rice, a toxicologist at the EPA's National Center for Environmental Assessment in Washington, "is we have strong evidence that PCB levels commonly found among women living in industrialized society can cause subtle neurological damage in their offspring." But one of the difficulties, according to Rice, is that we really don't yet know what an unsafe maternal PCB level might be.

"I think the bottom line is that women should be aware of PCBs and aware of what they're putting in their mouth," adds Rice.

The Dutch study is a warning not only about the potential impact of low levels of PCBs but about the potential harm from low levels of other endocrine disrupters.

More news arrived in March when the results from the federal government's on-going Fourth National Health and Nutrition Examination Survey (NHANES) became public. The survey of 38,000 people revealed that most of us have at least trace levels of pesticides, heavy metals, and plastics in our body tissues. In all, NHANES tested for 27 elements.

The survey found widespread exposure to phthalates, synthetic chemicals used as softeners in plastics and other products. Phthalates are one of the most heavily produced chemicals and have been linked in animal studies to endocrine disruption and birth defects. The likely sources of human exposure are foods and personal-care products such as shampoos, lotions, soaps, and perfumes; phthalates are absorbed through the skin.

Dr. Ted Schettler, a member of the Greater Boston Physicians for Social Responsibility, suspects endocrine disrupters may be linked to increases in the three hormone-driven cancers—breast, prostate, and testicular. The rate of testicular cancer among young men has nearly doubled in recent years, and the rates of learning disabilities and infertility also have increased.

"We can't blame all that is happening on toxic chemicals," says Schettler, who coauthored *In Harm's Way,* a report on how chemical contaminants affect human health. "But we need to ask ourselves if we're seeing patterns that suggest these chemicals are having a major impact on fetal development and human populations. We also need to ask what level of evidence we're going to need before we take public-health measures. That's a political question."

The EPA's Kavlock says, "We don't know the safe or unsafe levels for many of these chemicals." Nor do we know how many of the thousands of man-made chemicals in the environment will turn out to be endocrine disrupters or cause human harm. The EPA received a mandate from Congress in 1996 to find the answers, but it will be a long wait.

"If we devoted all the toxicology testing capacity in the entire world to look for endocrine-disrupting chemicals, we couldn't do all the chemicals. There's just not enough capacity," Kavlock says. "So we are focusing on 500 to 1,000 chemicals that are the major suspects. It will take many years and a lot of money just to understand how they interact with hormonal-system and fetal development."

What is all this bad stuff we can get from eating fish or from microwaving food in plastics? Do vitamins help?

Methylmercury is a heavy metal that can cause fetal brain damage. NHANES revealed that 10 percent of American women of child-bearing age—a representative sample of all American women—had methylmercury blood and hair levels close to "potentially hazardous levels." The EPA and some nongovernment experts consider these existing methylmercury levels already above what is safe.

Dr. Jill Stein, an adolescent-medicine specialist and instructor at Harvard Medical School, has studied methylmercury's toxicity. She says the acceptable levels of methylmercury in the NHANES report were too high and that many more women are in the danger zone. "The NHANES data tells me that more than 10 percent of American women today are carrying around enough mercury to put their future children at risk for learning and behavior problems," she says.

Like PCBs and other toxic chemicals, mercury is hard to avoid because it is abundant in our environment. It comes from natural and man-made sources, chiefly coal-fired power plants and municipal waste treatment. Each year an estimated 160 tons of mercury is released into the nation's environment. In water, mercury combines with natural bacteria to form methylmercury, a toxic form of the metal. It is easily absorbed by fish. When a pregnant woman consumes the contaminated fish, methylmercury crosses the placenta and the fetal blood-brain barrier.

The world became aware of methylmercury's potential for harm more than 40 years ago in the fishing village of Minamata in Japan. People there were exposed to high levels of the heavy metal from industrial dumping of mercury compounds into Minamata Bay. The villagers, who ate a diet heavy in fish caught in the bay, experienced devastating effects. The hardest hit were the unborn. Women gave birth to babies with cerebral-palsy-like symptoms. Many were retarded.

MERCURY

Fish are the major source of mercury for humans. The Food and Drug Administration recommends that pregnant women not eat swordfish, king mackerel, shark, and tilefish. These fish are singled out because large oceangoing fish contain more methylmercury. Smaller ocean fish, especially cod, haddock, and pollock, generally have low methylmercury levels. A whitefish found off the coast of Alaska, pollock is commonly found in fish sticks and fast-food fish. Salmon have low methylmercury levels, but they are a fatty fish and apt to carry higher levels of PCBs.

Like the Dutch PCB studies, recent studies of maternal methylmercury exposure have turned up trouble. They've shown that the so-called "safe" maternal levels of the metal can cause brain damage during fetal development.

One study was carried out in the 1990s by a Danish research team that studied 917 children in the Faroe Islands, where seafood is a big part of the diet. Children were grouped into categories depending on their level of maternal methylmercury exposure; they were assessed up to age seven by neurological tests. None of the children's methylmercury exposure levels was considered high, yet many of the children had evidence of brain damage, including memory, attention, and learning problems.

"Subtle effects on brain function therefore seem to be detectable at prenatal methylmercury exposure levels currently considered safe," the study concluded. In a follow-up report published in a 1999 issue of the *Journal of the American Medical Association,* the authors said the blood concentrations of methylmercury found in the umbilical cord corresponded with the severity of the neurological damage suffered by the children.

In a study of 237 children, New Zealand researchers found similar neurological harm, including IQ impairment and attention problems, in children whose mothers' exposure to methylmercury came from fish they ate during pregnancy.

"The children in these studies were not bathed in methylmercury," notes Rita Schoeny, a toxicologist in the EPA's Office of Water. "Can people in the U.S. be exposed to the same levels of mercury in the course of their dietary practice? We think so."

Jill Stein and other experts worry that the more scientific studies we do, the more we'll realize that in fetal development there may be no such thing as a "safe" maternal level for methylmercury, PCBs, and scores of other synthetic chemicals.

"We keep learning from studies that these chemicals are harmful to fetal development at lower and lower doses," Stein says. "It's what we call the declining threshold of harm."

What about canned tuna? It has been assumed to contain low methylmercury levels because most of it comes from smaller fish. The FDA offers no advisories about it. But according to EPA researchers, a recent State of Florida survey of more than 100 samples of canned tuna found high levels of methylmercury. The more-expensive canned tuna, such as albacore and solid white tuna, usually carried higher methylmercury levels, according to the survey. This apparently is because more expensive canned tuna comes from larger tuna. In some of the canned tuna, the methylmercury levels were high enough to prevent their export to several countries, including Canada.

Some of the methylmercury levels were "worrisomely high," according to Kathryn Mahaffey, a toxicologist and director of the division of exposure assessment at the EPA. They were high enough to cause concern for pregnant women.

"A big problem is the tremendous variability out there in the tuna supply," adds Stein. "You have no idea when you're eating a can of tuna how much methylmercury you're getting."

"Even if you ate just a small serving of some of these canned tunas each day," says Mahaffey, "you'd be substantially above a level we would consider safe."

Mahaffey and Stein agree that an expectant mother who ate even a few servings a week with methylmercury levels found in some of the canned tuna would put her developing baby at risk of brain and other neurological damage.

Now that we know a developing fetus is sensitive to even low levels of toxic chemicals, women can exercise some basic precautions to help protect their developing babies.

Don't microwave food that is wrapped in plastic or is still in plastic containers. "There are endocrine-disrupting chemicals in these plastics," Schettler says, "that leach right into the food when it's microwaved. This has been well documented and measured." Studies suggest that even at very low levels these chemicals can have an adverse effect on the fetus's hormonal system.

The EPA's Kavlock considers the fruits and vegetables you buy at the supermarket to be safe in pregnancy, but Schettler says you should try to eat organic foods to avoid even trace amounts of pesticides. Wash fruits and vegetables before eating them. Avoid pesticides or insecticide use around the house during pregnancy as well as the use of chemical solvents for painting or remodeling.

Herbicides and pesticides have leached into reservoirs that supply home drinking water, and filtration plants can't remove them all. Some are known to be endocrine disrupters. Home water filters can reduce contaminants; the best ones use active charcoal as a filtering agent.

Experts agree that a pregnant woman, or a woman who may get pregnant, can eat fish but should be careful about the kind she eats and how much of it. EPA's Rice cautions any woman who is pregnant or thinking of becoming pregnant to avoid eating any sport fish caught in a lake or river.

VEGETABLE FATS

Rice adds that the PCB risk with fish can be reduced. "Trim the fish of fat and skin, and broil or grill it," see says. "That way you cook off fat and minimize your PCB exposure." There is not much you can do to reduce the methylmercury levels in fish because it binds to protein.

"Fat is important for a baby's neurological development before and after birth, so pregnant women should consider vegetable fats like olive oil and flaxseed oil as a source," Rice adds. She says low fat dairy and meat products carry fewer PCBs than higher-fat ones.

The EPA has issued a PCB advisory for the Potomac River in the District, Virginia, and Maryland, citing in particular catfish and carp. You can go to *www.epa.gov/ost/fish/epafish.pdf* for EPA advisories on PCB and methylmercury environmental contamination. From there you can connect to state Web sites for advisories on local waters and specific fish.

Women can help prevent neurological and other birth defects by taking vitamin supplements before pregnancy. A daily dose of 400 micrograms of folic acid can reduce the risk of such problems as spina bifida by more than 70 percent as well as prevent brain defects and cleft lip and palate. Indirect evidence from a study published last year in the *New England Journal of Medicine* suggests that folic acid may also help prevent congenital heart defects.

To be effective, folic acid should be taken before pregnancy to prevent developmental defects. Folic acid comes in multivitamins and prenatal vitamins and is found naturally in legumes, whole-wheat bread, citrus fruits, fortified breakfast cereal, and leafy green vegetables. Despite the proven value of folic acid, a recent March of Dimes survey found that only 32 percent of American women of childbearing age—including pregnant women—took folic-acid supplements.

What can a fetus learn in the womb? And does playing Mozart make a baby lots smarter?

Developmental psychologist Anthony DeCasper wanted to answer two questions: What does a fetus know, and when does it know it?

DeCasper's aim was to find out if a fetus could learn in utero and remember what it learned after it was born. He enlisted the help of 33 healthy expectant mothers and asked each to tape-record herself reading passages from Dr. Seuss's *The Cat in the Hat* or from another children's book, *The King, the Mice, and the Cheese*. The mothers were randomly assigned to play one of these readings, each of which lasted two or three minutes, to their unborn children three times a day during the final three weeks of their pregnancies.

DeCasper, a professor of developmental psychology at the University of North Carolina at Greensboro, could do the experiment because it was known that fetuses could hear by the third trimester and probably earlier. DeCasper had shown earlier that at birth, babies preferred their mother's voice to all other voices. Studies in the early 1990s found that fetuses could be soothed by lullabies and sometimes moved in rhythm to their mother's voice. Fetuses hear their mother's voice from the outside, just as they can hear any other voice, but they hear the mother's voice clearer and stronger through bone conduction as it resonates inside her.

A little more than two days after birth, each of the newborns in DeCasper's study was given a specially devised nipple. The device worked by utilizing the baby's sucking reflex. When the baby sucked on the nipple, it would hear its mother's voice. But if it paused for too long a time between sucks, it would hear another woman's voice. This gave the baby control over whose voice it would hear by controlling the length of its pause between sucks.

DeCasper also placed small earphones over the infant's ears through which it could hear its mother's voice read from the books.

"Now two days or so after it was born, the baby gets to choose between two stories read by its own mother," DeCasper said. "One was the story she'd recited three times a day for the last three weeks of pregnancy, and the other is one the baby's never heard before, except for the one day his mother recorded it. So the big question was: Would the babies prefer the story they'd heard in the womb, or wouldn't they? The answer was a clear yes—the babies preferred to hear the familiar story."

DeCasper did a second experiment by having women who were not the baby's mothers recite the same two stories. The babies again showed a strong preference for the story they'd heard in the womb.

"These studies not only tell us something about the fidelity with which the fetal ear can hear," DeCasper says, "but they also show that during those two or three weeks in the womb, fetal learning and memory are occurring."

British researchers observed expectant mothers who watched a TV soap opera. The researchers placed monitors on the mother's abdomens to listen in on fetal movements when the program aired. By the 37th week of pregnancy, the babies responded to the show's theme music by increasing their movements, an indication they remembered it.

Soon after the babies were born, the researchers replayed the theme music to them. This time, instead of moving more, the babies appeared to calm down and pay attention to the music. The researchers considered this a response to familiar music.

FETAL MEMORY

"The fact that we find evidence of fetal memory doesn't mean fetuses carry conscious memories, like we remember what we ate for breakfast," explains Lise Eliot, author of *What's Going On in There?*, a book on early brain development. "But we now know there is a tremendous continuity from prenatal to postnatal life, and the prenatal experience begins to shape a child's interaction with the world it will confront after birth. Babies go through the same activity patterns and behavioral states before and after birth. Well before it is born, the baby is primed to gravitate to its mother and its mother's voice."

Some researchers speculate a baby's ability to remember in the womb may be a way of easing its transition from prenatal life to postnatal life. A baby already accustomed to and comforted by its mother's voice may be reassured as it enters a new world of bright lights, needle pricks, curious faces, and loud noises.

The question arises: Can the uterine environment affect a baby's intelligence? Twins studies have shown that genes exert an all-powerful influence on IQ. The role of environment in IQ has traditionally meant the nurturance and stimulation the baby receives after birth.

Bernie Devlin, a biostatistician and assistant professor of psychiatry at the University of Pittsburgh, did an analysis of 212 twins studies on intelligence. In a paper published in *Nature*, he concluded that the accepted figure of 60 to 80 percent for IQ heritability is too high. It should be closer to 50 percent, he says, which leaves more room for environmental factors. Devlin says the one environmental factor that's been missing in understanding human intelligence is time in the womb.

"I'm surprised that the impact of fetal life on a child's intelligence had not been accounted for in these IQ studies," Devlin says. "I know it's very complicated, but it's surprising that people who study the heritability of intelligence really haven't considered this factor."

What is the impact of life in the womb on intelligence? Devlin thinks it's equal to if not greater than the impact of a child's upbringing. In other words, it's possible a mother may have more influence over her child's intelligence before birth than after.

As the brain develops in utero, we know it undergoes changes that affect its ultimate capacity. Nutritional and hormonal influences from the mother have a big impact. And twins studies show that the heavier twin at birth most often has the higher IQ.

A number of studies from the United States and Latin America also found that a range of vitamins, as well as sufficient protein in the mother's prenatal diet, had an impact on the child's intelligence.

Links between specific vitamins and intelligence have been borne out in two studies. An animal study conducted at the University of North Carolina and published in the March issue of *Developmental Brain Research* found that rats with a choline deficiency during pregnancy gave birth to offspring with severe brain impairments. Choline, a B-complex vitamin involved in nerve transmission, is found in eggs, meat, peanuts, and dietary supplements.

The August 1999 issue of the *New England Journal of Medicine* reported that expectant mothers with low thyroid function gave birth to children with markedly diminished IQs as well as motor and attention deficits. The study said one cause of hypothyroidism—present in 2 to 3 percent of American women—is a lack of iodine in the American diet. Women whose hypothyroidism was detected and treated before pregnancy had children with normal test scores. Hypothyroidism can be detected with a blood test, but expectant mothers who receive little or late prenatal care often go undiagnosed or are diagnosed too late to help their child.

Although most American women get the nutrition they need through diet and prenatal vitamins, not all do. According to a National Center for Health Statistics survey, more than one in four expectant mothers in the U.S. received inadequate prenatal care.

Devlin's *Nature* article took a parting shot at the conclusions reached in the 1994 book *The Bell Curve*, in which Richard J. Herrnstein and Charles Murray argued that different social classes are a result of genetically determined, and therefore unalterable, IQ levels. The lower the IQ, the argument goes, the lower the social class.

Not only does the data show IQ to be far less heritable than that book alleges, Devlin says, but he suspects improvements in the health status of mostly poor expectant mothers would see measurable increases in the IQs of their offspring.

Devlin's argument is supported by Randy Thornhill, a biologist at the University of New Mexico. Thornhill's research suggests that IQ differences are due in part to what he calls "heritable vulnerabilities to environmental sources of developmental stress." In other words, vulnerable genes interact with environmental insults in utero resulting in gene mutations that affect fetal development. Thornhill says environmental insults may include viruses, maternal drug abuse, or poor nutrition.

"The developmental instability that results," Thornhill says, "is most readily seen in the body's asymmetry when one side of the body differs from the other. For example, on average an individual's index fingers will differ in length by about two millimeters. Some people have much more asymmetries than others."

But the asymmetries we see on the outside also occur in the nervous system. When this happens, neurons are harmed and memory and intelligence are impaired. Thornhill says the more physical asymmetries you have, the more neurological impairment you have. He calculates that these factors can account for as much as 50 percent of the differences we find in IQ.

Thornhill adds that a fetus that carries these genetic vulnerabilities, but develops in an ideal uterine environment, will not experience any serious problems because the worrisome mutations will not occur.

"The practical implications for this are tremendous," Thornhill says. "If we can understand what environmental factors most disrupt fetal development of the nervous system, then we'll be in a position to remove them and have many more intelligent people born."

Studies on fetal IQ development suggest that the current emphasis on nurturance and stimulation for young children be rethought. The philosophy behind initiatives such as Zero to Three and Early Head Start makes sense. The programs are based on evidence that the first three years are very important for brain development and that early stimulation can effect positive changes in a child's life. But Devlin and Thornhill's research suggests a stronger public-health emphasis on a baby's prenatal life if we are to equalize the opportunities for children.

Does that mean unborn babies need to hear more Mozart? Companies are offering kits so expectant mothers can play music or different sounds to their developing babies—the prenatal "Mozart effect." One kit promises this stimulation will lead to "longer new-born attention span, better sleep patterns, accelerated development, expanded cognitive powers, enhanced social awareness and extraordinary language abilities." Will acceptance to Harvard come next?

"The number of bogus and dangerous devices available to expectant parents to make their babies smarter constantly shocks me," says DiPietro. "All these claims are made without a shred of evidence to support them."

Adds DeCasper: "I think it is dangerous to stimulate the baby in the womb. If you play Mozart and it remembers Mozart, is it going to be a smarter baby? I haven't got a clue. Could it hurt the baby? Yes, I think it could. If you started this stimulation too early and played it too loud, there is evidence from animal studies that you can destroy the ear's ability to hear sounds in a particular range. That's an established fact. Would I take a risk with my fetus? No!"

DeCasper and other researches emphasize that no devices or tricks can enhance the brainpower of a developing baby. Their advice to the expectant mother: Take the best possible care of yourself.

"The womb is a quiet, protective place for a reason," DiPietro concludes. "Nature didn't design megaphones to be placed on the abdomen. The fetus gets all the stimulation it needs for its brain to develop."

Mr. Pekkanen is a contributing editor to The Washingtonian. *From "Secrets of the Womb," by John Pekkanen,* The Washingtonian, *August 2001, pages 44–51, 126–135.*

The War Over Fetal Rights

The politics of the womb are becoming ever more personal—and complex.
The Peterson murder case, changing state laws and startling new science
are causing many Americans to rethink long-held beliefs.

BY DEBRA ROSENBERG

IT WAS NEARLY VALENTINE'S DAY, 1992, WHEN TRACY Marciniak's estranged husband, Glenndale Black, showed up at her Wisconsin apartment. A 28-year-old mother of two, Marciniak was expecting another baby in just five days. But the night was hardly romantic. Within hours, the two argued and Black punched her in the stomach. "It felt like it had gone all the way through me," says Marciniak, now 39. The baby, whom she'd already named Zachariah, had seemed fine on a prenatal visit just the day before, she says. But when she arrived at the hospital that night, doctors couldn't find his heartbeat. Marciniak pulled through, but the baby did not.

Because Zachariah was not considered a "born person," prosecutors could not charge Black with homicide. They attempted to try him under an old state law banning illegal abortion, but Black's lawyer argued that the baby would have been stillborn anyway. In the end, a jury convicted Black of reckless injury and sentenced him to 12 years in prison. Though Marciniak has long supported abortion rights, she became furious when she discovered that the law didn't protect her unborn son—and that women's groups wouldn't back her quest for a state law punishing his killer. Now she is allied with the National Right to Life, appearing in an ad for the federal Unborn Victims of Violence Act. "There were two victims," Marciniak says. "He got away with murder."

Halfway across the country, in Connecticut, Pieter and Monica Coenraads want to defend their child, too. But as observant Roman Catholics, they've had to confront a question that strikes at the core of their religious and moral beliefs: Monica, 40, is so opposed to abortion she decided to skip amniocentesis in all three of her pregnancies, even though such testing is standard in older mothers. Whatever the test results, Monica knew she would never choose to terminate a pregnancy. Their first daughter, Chelsea, was born apparently healthy, but at the age of 2 she was diagnosed with Rett syndrome, a debilitating neurological disorder (which would not have been picked up by the amnio in any case). Now 6, Chelsea thinks clearly but cannot feed herself, walk without assistance or speak.

The Coenraadses believe that the only hope for their daughter and for the estimated 15,000 children like her is embryonic stem-cell research—which requires destroying human embryos. "My conscience tells me that for me personally having an abortion would not be the right thing to do. That same conscience tells me that stem-cell research is needed," says Monica, who now helps run the Rett Syndrome Research Foundation from her dining room.

The politics of the womb have never been more personal—or more complicated. When abortion foes are willing to destroy embryos for lifesaving medical research and abortion-rights supporters are willing to define a fetus as a murder victim, the black-and-white rhetoric of the 1970s abortion wars no longer applies. People on all sides of the debate are confronting long-held beliefs, often sending their most private emotions on a collision course with their political principles. With the Laci Peterson case making headlines and Congress poised to tackle both the Unborn Victims of Violence Act and the ban on partial-birth abortion this month, fetal rights have found new prominence on the public stage.

Recent dramatic breakthroughs in fetal and reproductive medicine only add to the confusion. Once just grainy blobs on a TV monitor, new high-tech fetal ultrasound images allow prospective parents to see tiny fingers and toes, arms, legs and a beating heart as early as 12 weeks. But while these images can make parents' hearts leap for joy, they also pack such an emotional punch that even the most hard-line abortion-rights supporters may find themselves questioning their beliefs. When 100,000 times a year, doctors are joining sperm and egg in a petri dish, and sometimes freezing the leftovers to be implanted in a woman at a later date, the question "When does life begin?" takes on new resonance. When specialists can do lifesaving surgery in utero, fetuses that once might have been terminated now have a shot at a normal life.

Along with forcing Americans into more-nuanced stances, the new science is also fanning longstanding, divisive political feuds—over the legality and morality of ending a pregnancy, about the rights of a woman versus the rights of an embryo or fetus, and, ultimately, over the meaning of human life. Abortion foes hope to take advantage of the new technology and sympathetic political environment to win fresh support. For their part, abortion-rights activists worry that the new focus on the fetus is part of a broad strategy to undermine the very bedrock of *Roe v. Wade*.

ACTIVISTS ON BOTH SIDES ARE STRUGGLING TO TREAD THIS new territory without losing their political footing. For decades, abortion opponents have offered moral and ethical arguments about protecting the fetus. Now they're building a legal case, defining the fetus—and even the embryo—as an individual entitled to basic human rights. With the recent murders of Laci Peterson and her unborn son, Conner, nearly 9 months old, abortion-rights supporters are finding it increasingly difficult to claim credibly that a fetus just a few weeks, or even days, from delivery is not entitled to at least some protections under the law—but they vigorously argue against such laws anyway, fearing that giving a fetus rights will lead to the collapse of abortion protections. "If they are able to make fetuses people in law with the same standing as women and men, then *Roe* will be moot," says Planned Parenthood president Gloria Feldt. On the other side of the debate, the anti-abortion camp strives to make laws protecting a woman's right to choose seem absurd. "It's not OK for the husband to kill his wife's child, but it's OK for the mother [to have an abortion]?" asks Ken Connor, president of the anti-abortion Family Research Council. But by equating any use of embryonic research with murder, and even objecting to the storage of undeveloped embryos for future use by potential parents, anti-abortion activists risk alienating many Americans. (According to the NEWSWEEK Poll, 49 percent of Americans think it's OK for an IVF clinic to destroy human embryos with the parents' approval.)

Without any nationwide consensus, individual states have begun settling on their own answers. Last month Gov. Jeb Bush asked a Florida court to appoint a guardian for the fetus of a 22-year-old developmentally disabled woman. A judge is scheduled to rule on the request this week. Within the past year, lawmakers in Georgia and Oklahoma introduced long-shot bills that would routinely require a woman seeking an abortion to obtain a "death warrant" for her fetus. Courts would then appoint a guardian for the fetus and hold a hearing to determine whether a woman could end her pregnancy. Neither bill is considered likely to pass, but they are visible signs of how abortion foes are using fetal rights as new ammunition in the abortion war.

In Wisconsin, Tracy Marciniak's case ultimately prompted the governor at the time, Tommy Thompson, to sign a law that counts fetuses as murder victims. Now 28 states have fetal-homicide laws on the books. In many states, the laws take effect only after a fetus is able to live outside the uterus, around 24 weeks. But 14 states cover a developing child from the moment an embryo is implanted in a woman's uterus—well within the legal time frame for an abortion. When Corinne Wilcott found out that 19-year-old Sheena Carson was having an affair with Wilcott's boyfriend and was 17 weeks pregnant, she attacked Carson, kicking her stomach repeatedly. "I hope the bastard dies," Wilcott said, according to prosecutors. Now Wilcott, one of the first convicted of murder in March under Pennsylvania's Crimes Against the Unborn Child Act, faces up to 40 years in prison.

As a state senator, Rep. Melissa Hart helped pass the Pennsylvania law. Now she's plugging the issue again in the U.S. House. The House passed the Unborn Victims of Violence Act in 1999 and again in 2001. The law would apply only to federal crimes—like bank robberies or domestic violence on military bases—when "a child in utero" is harmed or killed "at any stage of development." Penalties depend on the exact crime, but harming the fetus alone is counted as a separate crime that earns offenders as much jail time as harming the mother. The bill is expected to pass the Senate this time; it didn't hurt that Laci's family wrote and asked lawmakers to call it "Laci and Conner's Law" (even though it would not apply in their specific case). Seated behind a large desk, Hart insisted the law does not conflict with abortion because it applies only in cases where the mother wants the baby. "I don't think there's anybody who can argue the other side of this," she said, gesturing with a crucifix-shaped letter opener.

Across town, NARAL Pro-Choice America president Kate Michelman sighs deeply when she learns the bill has been renamed after Laci and Conner. She accuses lawmakers of exploiting the tragic case. "It's so crass, so offensive," she says. "It's part of a larger strategy to establish the embryo with separate distinct rights equal to if not greater than the woman." But Michelman does not want to seem callous. She calls back later to stress how terminating a wanted pregnancy is "an especially heinous crime that deserves enhanced penalties." Yet because Michelman and her group refuse to grant the fetus any rights at any stage of development, she awkwardly argues in favor of alternative laws that would add harsh penalties for attacking pregnant women—up to 20 years for harming a pregnancy and a life sentence for ending it. "That's not inconsistent," she argues. "It centers on the violence against the pregnant woman."

Michelman and her allies suspect that the conservatives' movement to protect fetuses is all part of a plan by the Bush administration to lay extensive legal groundwork to upend *Roe*. George W. Bush himself has spoken out in favor of the Unborn Victims Act and against destruction of embryos for medical research. In the past year, his administration has expanded the State Children's Health Insurance Program to cover children from "conception to birth to age 19," and added embryos to the list of vulnerable "human research subjects"—like children and prisoners—deserving extra oversight.

The courts are the other major weapon in the fetal-rights arsenal. If they can't overturn *Roe* directly, abortion opponents would like nothing more than to have sympathetic judges in as many courtrooms as possible. Many of Bush's candidates for the federal bench have strong anti-abortion records. One pending nominee to a federal district court, J. Leon Holmes, is even a former president of Arkansas Right to Life. Democrats in the Senate are already filibustering two of Bush's picks, in part because of their attitudes on abortion. The fight is certain to grow even uglier if, as expected, there's at least one vacancy on the high court before Bush leaves office.

THE PRO-LIFE VIEW
A conservative bioethicist argues on behalf of the embryo

'The Capacity Is There'

Hadley Arkes is the author of "Natural Rights and the Right to Choose" and is a fellow in Princeton University's politics department. He has testified before Congress on behalf of anti-abortion legislation. Excerpts from an interview by NEWSWEEK's Debra Rosenberg.

ROSENBERG: What rights does a fetus have?
ARKES: On what ground would one consider a child in the womb as anything less than a human being? Doesn't speak yet: neither do deaf-mutes. Doesn't have arms and legs: There are many people who are born without limbs or lose limbs in the course of their lives and they don't lose anything necessary to their standing as human beings. The fetus certainly wouldn't have a right to practice law, wouldn't have the right to use the squash courts, it wouldn't have the right to a driver's license. But certain kinds of rights that reside in human beings would not really be variable by height and weight. So the right not to be killed for a casual reason or an insubstantial reason would really not depend on the height or the weight of the baby—or its degrees of articulateness or even consciousness.

Does viability matter?
No, I don't think so.

Would it be inconsistent to say that a fetus could be a crime victim but abortion is legal?
Not particularly. If the abortion were done not with the intention of destroying the child but with the intention of saving the mother, if we could say that the abortion were justified, then we wouldn't say that the fetus was the victim of a wrong.

What should be done with frozen embryos in IVF clinics?
To the extent it's practicable, we ought to arrange for the adoption of these embryos by people who are willing to gestate them. If not, then they perish. The question is whether anyone should have a veto, or whether the law itself should contain a preference for life.

So you're saying the embryo could be implanted without the natural parents' consent?
Sure. The embryo doesn't encumber any longer the body of the woman. She's not being affected by it. It doesn't encumber her interests because she doesn't have to deal with an unwanted pregnancy. There's a tricky question here as to whether the natural parents can have property rights. The law doesn't ascribe property rights to bodies.

HUMAN ENTITIES
Once its life begins, the embryo's 'right not to be killed' is paramount, says Arkes

Can embryos be adopted?
The laws are mixed on this one. If these are human entities and they're adrift out there somewhere, they're abandoned, you can argue that we should be treating them with the same perspective we bring to other abandoned human beings.

So it's not OK to donate them to medical research?
Not any more than it would be OK for people to donate their own born children to medical research.

Is cloning OK for research or reproduction?
The matter of cloning for reproduction may actually be more arguably OK, though I have a strong aversion to it. But the case against so-called therapeutic cloning, cloning for research, could raise even greater moral questions. Would you allow parents to commit the bodies of their children [to research] without the consent of those children? Or sell the body parts of their children—not for any procedure involving the treatment of the child or the well-being of their own child, but for some speculative gain or benefit that could accrue to some other children or some other generation?

So when does life begin?
The leading textbooks on embryology say it's the union of two gametes, a male gamete or spermatozoon and a female gamete or mature ovum. You can phrase it in different ways, but on the medical side there is no dissent on this matter. What we find is that people are not arguing over the science, they're arguing over the social definition of a human being. People throw in all these other attributes—it has to be alert, and articulate. Well, many of those things aren't manifest in a newborn child. He's not snapping off witty sentences. He's not doing syllogisms. But we know that the capacity for it is there. If we know that about the child, we know that about the zygote or the embryo.

In the meantime, Bush has filled administration posts with officials who share his outlook. Under the careful direction of White House adviser Karl Rove, aides hold regular conference calls with evangelical Christians and Catholics to make sure they're happy. "The strategy is simply to create a principle that is at the heart of all this legislation that the unborn should be and are protected by law," says Deal Hudson, a Catholic adviser to the president. "There's a great deal of coordination within the administration on these issues."

Abortion opponents are setting their sights on ever-tinier targets, including the thousands of frozen embryos in storage at in vitro fertilization clinics across the country. During an IVF cycle, women take powerful drugs that stimulate their ovaries to produce many eggs at once. Because doctors haven't perfected

---

THE PRO-CHOICE VIEW
For this philosopher, 'viability' makes the moral difference

'When Can It Feel Pain'

Bonnie Steinbock has written several books on medical ethics, including "Life Before Birth: The Moral and Legal Status of Embryos and Fetuses." She is chair of philosophy at SUNY Albany. She spoke with NEWSWEEK's Debra Rosenberg. Here are excerpts:

ROSENBERG: What rights does a fetus have? Is it a crime victim?
STEINBOCK: I think the context matters tremendously. For example, when we're talking about the right to terminate a pregnancy, we're talking partly about the status of the fetus—whether it's a legal person, whether it's a moral person. When we're talking about an attack on a pregnant woman, then those issues are no longer relevant. And so it is consistent to say that a woman has a constitutional right to terminate a pregnancy up until viability and even afterwards if her life or health is in danger. But if somebody attacks a pregnant woman and beats her viciously and causes her to have a miscarriage, that could very easily be seen as a crime.
Does viability matter?
Viability matters, again, depending on context. The reason that viability seems morally important is that the more developed the fetus gets, the later in gestation it is, the more it's like a newborn baby—and the more it seems to deserve our protection. Which is why the Supreme Court said that states could prohibit abortion after viability [about 24 weeks].
How should the law treat someone who knowingly attacks a pregnant woman?
A number of states have done something I think is very sensible; they talk about whether the attacker should have known. So, if a reasonable person should have known that he [or she] was attacking a pregnant woman and was putting her pregnancy at risk, then he should be responsible. But if the attacker didn't know she was pregnant—or it's so early that no one could know—then it's probably not relevant.
What should be done with all the frozen embryos left over from IVF clinics?
My own view is that the pre-implantation embryo is so far from being a baby that it would be absurd to treat it as if it were a full human person like you or me, or even as if it were a newborn infant. If people want to donate their leftover

embryos to research, they should be able to do that. They shouldn't have to keep them frozen forever or discard them, especially if they can be used in such a way that will eventually save lives, prolong lives and alleviate pain.
Can embryos be adopted?
Sure they can. Usually it's called donating your embryos to an infertile couple. And in the beginning that's what people did. Now there are some people who don't want to donate their embryos because they think of the embryos as their potential children.

CONTEXT MATTERS
Steinbock says both women's wishes and the fetus's viability must be considered

How do medical advances change the debate?
Sonograms have definitely had an effect on the abortion debate. The minute people were able to actually see the fetus, it affected them emotionally, even if it didn't affect them theoretically.
Is cloning OK?
I think there are very good reasons to go slowly on reproductive cloning. So far there have been many indications that it is not safe. Cloned animals have had various kinds of birth defects; we need to be extremely careful. But I think it's entirely different when you're talking about using the same technology to create stem cells with the potential for treating Parkinson's, diabetes, Alzheimer's, burn victims, spinal-cord victims.
So when does life begin?
If we're talking about life in the biological sense, eggs are alive, sperm are alive. Cancer tumors are alive. For me, what matters is this: When does it have the moral status of a human being? When does it have some kind of awareness of its surroundings? When it can feel pain, for example, because that's one of the most brute kinds of awareness there could be. And that happens, interestingly enough, just around the time of viability. It certainly doesn't happen with an embryo.

techniques for freezing extra eggs alone, they fertilize them all, implant a few into a woman's uterus, then freeze the remaining embryos—a situation that troubles many abortion opponents. "As we see it, there's already a human being in a human embryo," says Douglas Johnson, legislative director of National Right to Life. Until recently no one knew exactly how many frozen embryos were in storage. But last month a new study calculated that there are nearly 400,000 embryos in clinic freezers, and nearly all of them—88 percent—are set aside for future family building by patients. Only about 3 percent have been earmarked for medical research and just 2 percent for donation to other couples.

Even families who've reserved their embryos for future use are often conflicted about what to do with them. Sue DiSilvestro and her husband, John, have 5-year-old triplets from IVF—and three embryos in cryostorage. Before their IVF cycle, the couple had planned to donate any extras to research. But now, the first photo in their baby book is a grainy cluster of six- or eight-celled embryos.

With triplets and a limited income—she's a nurse and he's a firefighter—the DiSilvestros don't think they want more kids, and they're agonizing, even disagreeing, over what to do next. Sue is still somewhat open to giving them to research, but John is strongly against it. He would prefer to donate them to another infertile couple, giving the cells a chance at life, and two more people the family they dreamed of. "Everything changes once you have kids," he says. "I now realize those embryos are my children. It's a different ball game."

The decision over what to do can be so wrenching that couples often pay hundreds of dollars a year in storage fees to avoid making it. "It's like a security blanket," says Dr. David Hoffman, who coauthored last month's embryo study. Patients who decide they want more children usually have several embryos implanted at once: live births occur only about 20 percent of the time when frozen embryos are transferred to the womb.

EVEN SEN. ARLEN SPECTER, A CHAMPION OF EMBRYONIC stem-cell research, has had second thoughts about what to do with the frozen embryos. He debated the issue during a train ride last year with Rep. Chris Smith, a strong abortion opponent. Smith, who disputed the notion that the embryos were "leftovers" that would be destroyed anyway, mentioned that they could be adopted instead. This conversation represented a turning point in Specter's thinking. "If these embryos could be adopted, I wouldn't use them for research," Specter told Smith. Last year he added $1 million to the federal budget for a pilot program to promote embryo-adoption efforts.

The whole question of embryo "adoption" is controversial. The American Society for Reproductive Medicine believes embryos can be donated like kidneys, but not adopted like living children. But one federal grant recipient, a project called Snowflakes, is part of a Christian adoption agency that goes so far as to conduct home studies of prospective parents. In the past five years, Snowflakes has had 27 babies born; an additional 18 are due by the end of the year.

The question is whether the law can protect fetuses without eroding the rights their mothers fought for

But dealing with embryos is always a delicate business. The federal government refuses to fund any research on human embryos—a situation that's already slowed fertility research to a trickle. And now researchers worry that the new scrutiny could lead to further crackdowns on the work they're already doing, perhaps setting limits on the number of embryos they can create or banning procedures that might inadvertently harm the growing cells. Dr. Jamie Grifo, a reproductive endocrinologist at New York University who has helped pioneer new infertility techniques such as pre-implantation genetic diagnosis, says the worry over working with embryos has already had a chilling effect. "There are no projects that we're doing right now because we're afraid of the politics," he says angrily. "We're making people parents who wouldn't be otherwise. What's the problem here?"

So far, the fight over fetal and embryonic rights is in a delicate stalemate. Each side risks overreaching. One government department that handles family-planning funds is already marshaling evidence about whether various birth-control methods—like the pill or IUDs—work by interfering with implantation of an embryo in the uterus. Trying to crack down on birth control may be a step too far. But arguing against "Laci and Conner's Law"—which Congress will likely pass—could also be a losing battle. For now, with the majority of Americans behind it, *Roe* remains the law of the land. The question is whether the law can protect fetuses without eroding the rights their mothers fought so hard to win.

With SUZANNE SMALLEY and RENA KIRSCH

UNIT 2

Development During Infancy and Early Childhood

Unit Selections

Key Points to Consider

- What are the four new ways of thinking about infant development that all parents and caregivers should know?

- What purposes are served by involving babies in hectic activity schedules and introducing them to academics as early as possible?

- Do infant and toddler immunizations cause autism? What risks ensue when a child is not immunized? Why have vaccines been linked to autism and its related disorders?

- Should child care quality be judged from a professional perspective? What do parents and children want?

- How much television should infants and preschoolers be allowed to watch? What shows are good for them? What aspects of television viewing are bad for them?

- When should children know right from wrong? How is it learned?

 **Links: www.dushkin.com/online/**
These sites are annotated in the World Wide Web pages.

BabyCenter
http://www.babycenter.com
Children's Nutrition Research Center (CNRC)
http://www.bcm.tmc.edu/cnrc/
Early Childhood Care and Development
http://www.ecdgroup.com
Zero to Three: National Center for Infants, Toddlers, and Families
http://www.zerotothree.org

Developmental researchers go back and forth between demonstrating environmental causes of behavior, genetic influences on behavior, and the interactions of both. The articles selected for inclusion in this unit reflect both the known influences of nurture (environment) and nature (biology) and the relationships and interactions of multiple variables and child outcomes about which we hope to know more in the new millennium.

Newborns are quite well developed in some areas, and incredibly deficient in others. Babies' cerebral hemispheres already have their full complement of neurons (worker cells). The neuroglia (supportive cells) are almost completely developed and will reach their final numbers by age one. In contrast, babies' legs and feet are tiny, weak, and barely functional. Look at newborns from another perspective, however, and their brains seem somewhat less superior. The neurons and neuroglia present at birth must be protected. We may discover ways to make more cerebral neurons in the future, but such knowledge now is in its infancy and does not go very far. By contrast, the cells of the baby's legs and feet (skin, fat, muscles, bones, blood vessels) are able to replace themselves by mitosis indefinitely. Their numbers will continue to grow through early adulthood; then their quantity and quality can be regenerated through advanced old age.

The developing brain in infancy is a truly fascinating organ. At birth it is poorly organized. The lower (primitive) brain parts (brain stem, pons, medulla, cerebellum) are well enough developed to allow the infant to live. The lower brain directs vital organ systems (heart, lungs, kidneys, etc.). The higher (advanced) brain parts (cerebral hemispheres) have all their neurons, but the nerve cells and cell processes (axons, dendrites) are small, underdeveloped, and unorganized. During infancy, these higher

(cerebral) nerve cells (that allow the baby to think, reason, and remember) grow at astronomical rates. They migrate to permanent locations in the hemispheres, develop myelin sheathing (insulation), and conduct messages. Many twentieth-century researchers, including Jean Piaget, the father of cognitive psychology, believed that all brain activity in the newborn was reflexive, based on instincts for survival. They were wrong. New research has documented that fetuses can learn and newborns can think as well as learn.

The role played by electrical and chemical activity of neurons in actively shaping the physical structure of the brain is particularly awe-inspiring. The neurons are produced prenatally. After birth, the flood of sensory inputs from the environment (sights, sounds, smells, tastes, touch, balance, and kinesthetic sensations) drives the neurons to form circuits and become wired to each other. Trillions of connections are established in a baby's brain. During childhood the connections that are seldom or never used are eliminated or pruned. The first 3 years are critical for establishing these connections. Environments that provide both good nutrition and lots of sensory stimulation really do produce richer, more connected brains.

The first article in this section on infancy explains what mothers, fathers, and all other infant caregivers need to know immediately upon birth of their precious baby. The Human Genome Project gives new life to attempts to integrate all the separate pieces of knowledge about infant development from biology and psychology. Joanna Lipari articulates the old thinking with its counterpoint new thinking.

The next selection on infancy asks and partially answers the question, "Who's Raising Baby?" Anne Pierce discusses the challenges to modern day parenting from a mother's-eye view.

Contemporary parents seem to be on a competitive merry-go-round to have their offspring involved in as many "enriching" activities as their neighbors, friends, co-workers, etc. What is the purpose of all this activity? The article cites the opinions of renowned child psychologists such as David Elkind and Stanley Greenspan that this race for supremacy is not healthy. In infancy, emotional learning and the ability to relate to others are more important than literacy. Home life is valuable. The author believes lessons learned at home supercede those obtained in daycare.

The third selection on infancy, "Vaccines and Autism," addresses a concern of many parents today: To immunize or not to immunize? The alarming increase in diagnoses of autism and its related syndromes is still unexplained. The preservative thimerosal, which contains mercury, is used in some vaccines (diphtheria, tetanus, flu, hepatitis) and in some eardrops and nasal sprays. There is not enough evidence today to link thimerosal and autism, although it is still being studied. Meanwhile, failure to immunize puts infants at risk of contacting many severe illnesses which can cause brain damage or death.

The selections about toddlers and preschoolers included in this anthology continue looking at development physically, cognitively, and socioemotionally. Each of the articles, while focusing on one topic more than others, views the whole child across all three domains, considering both hereditary and environmental factors.

The first early childhood article addresses "Child Care Quality." Nearly three-fourths of preschool-aged American children spend time in non-parental care. A key concern addressed by this article is "How do parents and children evaluate this care?" Most research focuses on the perspective of what professional persons judge to be high quality rather than what the consumers need and desire.

Daniel McGinn, in the next early childhood selection, praises what has happened to children's television programming in recent years. Nickelodeon, Fox, and the Disney Channel now compete with the public broadcasting station in the United States (PBS) for early childhood education excellence. Despite more and better programs, parents need to monitor what, and how much, is consumed by toddlers. Play is still the best brain-enhancer, and interaction with live humans vastly outweighs the possible benefits of television.

The last article in this unit discusses how parents can instill and nurture moral values and behaviors in young children. Although states vary in the ages that they hold children legally accountable for knowing right from wrong, child developmentalists believe that preschoolers can grasp, and should be taught, moral values.

FOUR THINGS YOU NEED TO KNOW ABOUT RAISING BABY

New thinking about the newborn's brain, feelings and behavior are changing the way we look at parenting

BY JOANNA LIPARI, M.A.

Bookstore shelves are crammed with titles purporting to help you make your baby smarter, happier, healthier, stronger, better-behaved and everything else you can imagine, in what I call a shopping-cart approach to infant development. But experts are now beginning to look more broadly, in an integrated fashion, at the first few months of a baby's life. And so should you.

Psychological theorists are moving away from focusing on single areas such as physical development, genetic inheritance, cognitive skills or emotional attachment, which give at best a limited view of how babies develop. Instead, they are attempting to synthesize and integrate all the separate pieces of the infant-development puzzle. The results so far have been enlightening, and are beginning to suggest new ways of parenting.

The most important of the emerging revelations is that the key to stimulating emotional and intellectual growth in your child is your own behavior—what you do, what you don't do, how you scold, how you reward and how you show affection. If the baby's brain is the hardware, then you, the parents, provide the software. When you understand the hardware (your baby's brain), you will be better able to design the software (your own behavior) to promote baby's well-being.

The first two years of life are critical in this regard because that's when your baby is building the mental foundation that will dictate his or her behavior through adulthood. In the first year alone, your baby's brain grows from about 400g to a stupendous 1000g. While this growth and development is in part predetermined by genetic force, exactly how the brain grows is dependent upon emotional interaction, and that in-

volves you. "The human cerebral cortex adds about 70% of its final DNA content after birth," reports Allan N. Schore, Ph.D., assistant clinical professor of psychiatry and biobehavioral sciences at UCLA Medical School, "and this expanding brain is directly influenced by early environmental enrichment and social experiences."

Failure to provide this enrichment during the first two years can lead to a lifetime of emotional disability, according to attachment theorists. We are talking about the need to create a relationship and environment that allows your child to grow up with an openness to learning and the ability to process, understand and experience emotion with compassion, intelligence and resilience. These are the basic building blocks of emotional success.

Following are comparisons of researchers' "old thinking" and "new thinking." They highlight the four new insights changing the way we view infant development. The sections on "What To Do" then explain how to apply that new information.

1 FEELINGS TRUMP THOUGHTS

It is the emotional quality of the relationship you have with your baby that will stimulate his or her brain for optimum emotional and intellectual growth.

OLD THINKING: In this country, far too much emphasis is placed on developing babies' cognitive abilities. Some of this push came out of the promising results of the Head Start program. Middle-class families reasoned that if a little stimulation in an under-endowed home environment is beneficial, wouldn't "more" be better? And the race to create the "superbaby" was on.

Gone are the days when parents just wished their child were "normal" and could "fit in" with other kids. Competition for selective schools and the social pressure it generates has made parents feel their child needs to be "gifted." Learning exercises, videos and educational toys are pushed on parents to use in play with their children. "Make it fun," the experts say. The emphasis is on developing baby's cognitive skills by using the emotional reward of parental attention as a behavior-training tool.

THE NEW THINKING: Flying in the face of all those "smarter" baby books are studies suggesting that pushing baby to learn words, numbers, colors and shapes too early forces the child to use lower-level thinking processes, rather than develop his or her learning ability. It's like a pony trick at the circus: When the pony paws the ground to "count" to three, it's really not counting; it's simply performing a stunt. Such "tricks" are not only not helpful to baby's learning process, they are potentially harmful. Tufts University child psychologist David Elkind, Ph.D., makes it clear that putting pressure on a child to learn information sends the message that he or she needs to "perform" to gain the parents' acceptance, and it can dampen natural curiosity.

Instead, focus on building baby's emotional skills. "Emotional development is not just the foundation for important capacities such as intimacy and trust," says Stanley Greenspan, M.D., clinical professor of psychiatry and pediatrics at George Washington University Medical School and author of the new comprehensive book *Building Healthy Minds*. "It is also the foundation of intelligence and a wide variety of cognitive skills. At each stage of development, emotions lead the way, and learning facts and skills follow. Even math skills, which appear [to be] strictly an impersonal cognition, are initially learned through the emotions: 'A lot' to a 2-year-old, for example, is more than he would expect, whereas 'a little' is less than he wants."

It makes sense: Consider how well you learn when you are passionate about a subject, compared to when you are simply required to learn it. That passion is the emotional fuel driving the cognitive process. So the question then becomes not "what toys and games should I use to make my baby smarter?" but "how should I interact with my baby to make him 'passionate' about the world around him?"

WHAT TO DO: When you read the baby "milestone" books or cognitive development guides, keep in mind that the central issue is your baby's *emotional* development. As Greenspan advises, "Synthesize this information about milestones and see them with emotional development as the central issue. This is like a basketball team, with the coach being our old friend, emotions. Because emotions tell the child what he wants to do—move his arm, make a sound, smile or frown. As you look at the various 'milestone components'—motor, social and cognitive skills—look to see how the whole mental team is working together."

Not only will this give you more concrete clues as to how to strengthen your emotional relationship, but it will also serve to alert you to any "players" on the team that are weak or injured, i.e., a muscle problem in the legs, or a sight and hearing difficulty.

2 NOT JUST A SCREAMING MEATLOAF: BIRTH TO TWO MONTHS It's still largely unknown how well infants understand their world at birth, but new theories are challenging the traditional perspectives.

OLD THINKING: Until now, development experts thought infants occupied some kind of presocial, precognitive, preorganized life phase that stretched from birth to two months. They viewed newborns' needs as mainly physiological—with sleep-wake, day-night and hunger-satiation cycles, even calling the first month of life "the normal autism" phase, or as a friend calls it, the "screaming meatloaf" phase. Certainly, the newborn has emotional needs, but researchers thought they were only in response to basic sensory drives like taste, touch, etc.

THE NEW THINKING: In his revolutionary book, *The Interpersonal World of the Infant*, psychiatrist Daniel Stern, Ph.D., challenged the conventional wisdom on infant development by proposing that babies come into this world as social beings. In research experiments, newborns consistently demonstrate that they actively seek sensory stimulation, have distinct preferences and, from birth, tend to form hypotheses about what is occurring in the world around them. Their preferences are emotional ones. In fact, parents would be unable to establish the physiological cycles like wake-sleep without the aid of such sensory, emotional activities as rocking, touching, soothing, talking and singing. In turn, these interactions stimulate the child's brain to make the neuronal connections she needs in order to process the sensory information provided.

WHAT TO DO: "Take note of your baby's own special biological makeup and interactive style," Greenspan advises. You need to see your baby for the special individual he is at birth. Then, "you can deliberately introduce the world to him in a way that maximizes his delight and minimizes his frustrations." This is also the time to learn how to help your baby regulate his emotions, for example, by offering an emotionally overloaded baby some soothing sounds or rocking to help him calm down.

3 THE LOVE LOOP: BEGINNING AT TWO MONTHS At approximately eight weeks, a miraculous thing occurs—your baby's vision improves and for the first time, she can fully see you and can make direct eye contact. These beginning visual experiences of your baby play an important role in social and emotional development. "In particular, the mother's emotionally expressive face is, by far, the most potent visual stimulus in the infant's environment," points out UCLA's Alan Schore, "and the child's intense interest in her face, especially in her eyes, leads him/her to track it in space to engage in periods of intense mutual gaze." The result: Endorphin levels rise in the baby's brain, causing pleasurable feelings of joy and excitement. But the key is for this joy to be interactive.

OLD THINKING: The mother pumps information and affection into the child, who participates only as an empty receptacle.

THE NEW THINKING: We now know that the baby's participation is crucial to creating a solid attachment bond. The loving gaze of parents to child is reciprocated by the baby with a loving gaze back to the

parents, causing their endorphin levels to rise, thus completing a closed emotional circuit, a sort of "love loop." Now, mother (or father) and baby are truly in a dynamic, interactive system. "In essence, we are talking less about what the mother is doing to the baby and more about how the mother is being with the baby and how the baby is learning to be with the mother," says Schore.

The final aspect of this developing interactive system between mother and child is the mother's development of an "emotional synchronization" with her child. Schore defines this as the mother's ability to tune into the baby's internal states and respond accordingly. For example: Your baby is quietly lying on the floor, happy to take in the sights and sounds of the environment. As you notice the baby looking for stimulation, you respond with a game of "peek-a-boo." As you play with your child and she responds with shrieks of glee, you escalate the emotion with bigger and bigger gestures and facial expressions. Shortly thereafter, you notice the baby turns away. The input has reached its maximum and you sense your child needs you to back off for awhile as she goes back to a state of calm and restful inactivity. "The synchronization between the two is more than between their behavior and thoughts; the synchronization is on a biological level—their brains and nervous systems are linked together," points out Schore. "In this process, the mother is teaching and learning at the same time. As a result of this moment-by-moment matching of emotion, both partners increase their emotional connection to one another. In addition, the more the mother fine-tunes her activity level to the infant during periods of play and interaction, the more she allows the baby to disengage and recover quietly during periods of nonplay, before initiating actively arousing play again."

Neuropsychological research now indicates that this attuned interaction—engaged play, disengagement and restful nonplay, followed by a return to play behavior—is especially helpful for brain growth and the development of cerebral circuits. This makes sense in light of the revelation that future cognitive development depends not on the cognitive stimulation of flashcards and videos, but on the attuned, dynamic and emotional interactions between parent and child. The play periods stimulate baby's central nervous system to excitation, followed by a restful period of alert inactivity in which the developing brain is able to process the stimulation and the interaction.

In this way, you, the parents, are the safety net under your baby's emotional highwire; the act of calming her down, or giving her the opportunity to calm down, will help her learn to handle ever-increasing intensity of stimulation and thus build emotional tolerance and resilience.

WHAT TO DO: There are two steps to maximizing your attunement ability: spontaneity and reflection. When in sync, you and baby will both experience positive emotion; when out of sync, you will see negative emotions. If much of your interactions seem to result in negative emotion, then it is time to reflect on your contribution to the equation.

In these instances, parents need to help one another discover what may be impeding the attunement process. Sometimes, on an unconscious level, it may be memories of our own childhood. For example, my friend sings nursery rhymes with a Boston accent, even though she grew up in New York, because her native Bostonian father sang them to her that way. While the "Fah-mah in the Dell" will probably not throw baby into a temper tantrum, it's a good example of how our actions or parenting style may be problematic without our realizing it.

But all parents have days when they are out of sync with baby, and the new perspective is that it's not such a bad thing. In fact, it's quite valuable. "Misattunement" is not a bioneurological disaster if you can become attuned again. The process of falling out of sync and then repairing the bond actually teaches children resilience, and a sense of confidence that the world will respond to them and repair any potential hurt.

Finally, let your baby take the lead. Schore suggests we "follow baby's own spontaneous expression of himself," which lets the child know that another person, i.e., mom or dad, can understand what he is feeling, doing, and even thinking. Such experiences, says Schore, assist in the development of the prefrontal area, which controls "empathy, and therefore that which makes us most 'human.'"

4 THE SHAME TRANSACTION Toward the end of the first year, as crawling turns to walking, a shift occurs in the communication between child and parents. "Observational studies show that 12-month-olds receive more positive responses from mothers, while 18-month-olds receive more instructions and directions," says Schore. In one study, mothers of toddlers expressed a prohibition—basically telling the child "no"—approximately every nine minutes! That's likely because a mobile toddler has an uncanny knack for finding the most dangerous things to explore!

Yesterday, for example, I walked into the living room to find my daughter scribbling on the wall with a purple marker. "NO!" shot out of my mouth. She looked up at me with stunned shock, then realized what she had done. Immediately, she hung her head, about to cry. I babbled on a bit about how markers are only for paper, yada-yada and then thought, "Heck, it's washable." As I put my arm around my daughter, I segued into a suggestion for another activity: washing the wall! She brightened and raced to get the sponge. We had just concluded a "shame transaction."

OLD THINKING: Researchers considered all these "no's" a necessary byproduct of child safety or the socialization process. After all, we must teach children to use the potty rather than wet the bed, not to hit another child when mad, to behave properly in public. Researchers did not consider the function of shame vis-à-vis brain development. Instead, they advised trying to limit situations in which the child would feel shame.

NEW THINKING: It's true that you want to limit the shame situations, but they are not simply a necessary evil in order to civilize your baby. Neurobiological studies indicate that episodes of shame like the one I described can actually stimulate the development of the right hemisphere, the brain's source of creativity, emotion and sensitivity, as long as the shame period is short and followed by a recovery. In essence, it's not the experience of shame that can be damaging, but rather the inability of the parent to help the child recover from that shame.

WHAT TO DO: It's important to understand "the growth-facilitating importance of small doses of shame in the socialization process of the infant," says Schore. Embarrassment (a component of shame) first emerges around 14 months, when mom's "no" results in the child lowering his head and looking down in obvious sadness. The child goes from excited (my daughter scribbling on the wall) to sudden deflation (my "NO!") back to excitement ("It's okay, let's wash the wall together"). During this rapid process, various parts of the brain get quite a workout and experience heightened connectivity, which strengthens these systems. The result is development of the orbitofrontal cortex (cognitive area) and limbic system (emotional area) and the ability for the two systems to interrelate emotional resiliency in the child and the ability to self-regulate emotions and impulse control.

What is important to remember about productive shame reactions is that there must be a quick recovery. Extended periods of shame result in a child learning to shut down, or worse, become hyperirritable, perhaps even violent. It's common sense: Just think how you feel when someone embarrasses you. If that embarrassment goes on without relief, don't you tend to either flee the situation or rail against it?

From these new research findings, it's clear that successful parenting isn't just about intuition, instinct and doing what your mother did. It's also not about pushing the alphabet, multiplication tables or violin lessons. We now believe that by seeing the newborn as a whole person—as a thinking, feeling creature who can and should participate in his own emotional and cognitive development—we can maximize the nurturing and stimulating potential of our relationship with a newborn baby.

Joanna Lipari is pursuing a Psy.D. at Pepperdine University in Los Angeles.

READ MORE ABOUT IT

The Irreducible Needs of Children: What Every Child Must Have to Grow, Learn and Flourish, T. Berry Brazelton, M.D., and Stanley Greenspan, M.D. (Perseus Books, 2000).

Building Healthy Minds, Stanley Greenspan, M.D. (Perseus Books, 1999).

WHO'S RAISING BABY?

Challenges To Modern-Day Parenting

Anne R. Pierce

Drive through the empty streets of our neighborhoods and ask yourself not merely where the children have gone but where childhood has gone. It is most unlikely you will see such once-familiar scenes as these: a child sitting under a tree with a book, toddlers engaged in collecting leaves and sticks, friends riding bikes or playing tag, parents and their offspring working together in the yard, families (in no hurry to get anywhere) strolling casually along. Today's children are too busy with other things to enjoy the simple pleasures children used to take for granted. Preoccupied with endless "activities" and diversions, they have little time for simply going outside.

Where are the children and what are they doing? They are in day-care centers, now dubbed "learning centers." They are in "early childhood programs" and all-day kindergarten. They are acquiring new skills, attending extracurricular classes, and participating in organized sports. They are sitting in front of the computer, the TV, and the Play Station. They are not experiencing the comfortable ease of unconditional love, nor the pleasant feeling of familiarity. They are not enjoying a casual conversation, nor are they playing. They are working—at improving their talents, at competing with their peers, at "beating the enemy" in a video game, at just getting by, at adapting to the new baby-sitter or coach, at not missing Mom or Dad. They, like their computers, are "on." Being, for them, is doing, adjusting, coping. Parenting, for us, is providing them with things to do.

Young children expend their energy on long days in group situations, in preschool and after-school programs, in music and athletic lessons. For much-needed relaxation, they collapse in front of the TV or computer, the now-defining features of "homelife." Relaxation no longer signifies quiet or repose. The hyperactive pace of children's television shows and video games, always accompanied by driving music, exacerbates and surpasses the fast pace of modern life. Children stare at the screen, though the inanity, violence, and doomsday sociopolitical messages of the programming are anything but reassuring.

From doing to staring, from staring to doing. There is little room in this scenario for idle contentment, playful creativity, and the passionate pursuit of interests. Alternatives to this framework for living are provided neither in thought nor in deed by busy parents who, themselves, end their rushed days with television and escapism.

Before nursery school starts, most children who can afford it have attended "classes," from gymnastics to ballet, piano, or swimming. Infant "swim lessons," in which an instructor in diving gear repeatedly forces screaming babies underwater so that they are forced to swim, are now commonplace. Day-care centers claim to give toddlers a head start in academic advancement and socialization. Increasing numbers of bright young children spend time with tutors or at the learning center to attain that ever-elusive "edge."

Children in elementary school now "train" and lift weights in preparation for their sports. Football and track are new options for first-graders. A recent trend in elementary athletic programs is to recruit professional coaches, due to the supposed competitive disadvantage of amateur coaching done by parents. It is more common for young children to "double up," participating in two team sports at a time. A constantly increasing selection of stimulating activities lures modern families, making downtime more elusive.

What used to be "time for dinner" (together) is, more often than not, time for family members to rush and scatter in different directions. A typical first-grade soccer team practices two evenings a week, from 6:00 to 7:30. The stress involved in getting six-year-olds fed and in gear by practice time and, after practice, bathed and in bed at an appropriate hour is obvious. And yet, if you attend a first-grade soccer game, you'll likely find parents eager to discover the activities of other people's children and anxious to sign their children up for—whatever it might be. Some parents appear to be jealous of the activities others have discovered.

THE NEW CONFORMISM—AFRAID OF MISSING OUT

In asking scores of parents about the purpose of all this activity, I have never received a clear or, to my mind, satisfactory answer. The end, apparently, is unclear apart from the idea, often expressed, that if one's child starts activities later than other children, he (or she) will be "left behind." Some of the more cohesive explanations I have received are these: A mother described herself as being "swept along by the inevitable"; she didn't want her young daughter to be "the only one missing out." A couple explained their determination to expose their toddler to a wide variety of opportunities so that he would know which sports he excelled in "by the time things get competitive." A father said, simply, that he saw his role in terms of making sure his children were "the best at something," and with all the other kids starting activities at such an early age, this meant that his kids "had to start even earlier."

In effect, this is the "do what everyone else does, only sooner and more intensely" theory of child rearing. This theory creates a constant downward pressure upon children of a younger and younger age. This was evident to me when my youngest son entered kindergarten and I discovered he was within a small minority of boys who had not *already* participated in team sports. Only five years earlier, my oldest son was within the sizable majority of kindergartners whose parents had decided kindergarten was a little too early for such endeavors. (First grade was then the preferred starting point.)

The more families subscribe to this "lifestyle," the more there is another reason for pushing kids off to the races: If no children are around to play with, then, especially for only children, organized activities become their only opportunity to "play" with other kids. Playing is thus thoroughly redefined.

The philosophy of child rearing as a race and of homelife as oppressive for women compels families toward incessant action. Love, nurture, and, concomitantly, innocence have been demoted as compared to experience and exposure. The family is viewed as a closedness to experience, the nurturing role within the family as the most confining of all. Indeed, busyness supplants togetherness in many modern families.

One legacy of Freud, Piaget, Pavlov, and the behaviorists, neodevelopmentalists, and social scientists who followed them has been the decreasing respect for the child's being and the increasing emphasis upon his "becoming." The child is seen as "socializable" and is studied as a clinical object whose observable response to this or that "environmental stimulus" becomes more important than his deeper, more complicated features. With the clinical interpretation of childhood, social engineering projects and "activities" that make the child's world more stimulating gain momentum.

In addition to the advantage that all this activity supposedly gives children, there is also the element of convenience. If parents are too busy to supervise their children, it behooves them to keep the kids so busy and under the auspices of so many (other) adults that they are likely to "stay out of trouble." Such is the basis of many modern

choices. Children spend much of their time exhausted by activities, the purposes of which are ill construed.

Conformism, convenience, and new interpretations of childhood are, then, contributing factors in the hectic existence and the premature introduction to academics that parents prescribe for their children.

Conformism, convenience, and new interpretations of childhood are, then, contributing factors in the hectic existence and the premature introduction to academics that parents prescribe for their children. For example, before the 1960s, it was generally believed that placing young children in out-of-home learning programs was harmful. The concern for the harmfulness of such experiences was abandoned when these learning programs became convenient and popular.

EDUCATION AS 'SOCIALIZATION'

In *Miseducation: Preschoolers at Risk*, David Elkind expressed dismay at the fact that age-inappropriate approaches to early education have gained such momentum despite the undeniable evidence that pushing children into formal academics and organized activities before they are ready does more harm than good. He lamented, "In a society that prides itself on its preference for facts over hearsay, on its openness to research, and on its respect for 'expert' opinion, parents, educators, administrators, and legislators are ignoring the facts, the research and the expert opinion about how young children learn and how best to teach them.... When we instruct children in academic subjects, or in swimming, gymnastics, or ballet, at too early an age, we miseducate them; we put them at risk for short-term stress and long-term personality damage for no useful purpose."

Elkind pointed to the consistent result of reputable studies (such as that conducted by Benjamin Bloom) that a love of learning, not the inculcation of skills, is the key to the kind of early childhood development that can lead to great things. These findings, warned Elkind, point to the fallacy of early instruction as a way of producing children who will attain eminence. He noted that with gifted and talented individuals, as with children in general, the most important thing is an excitement about learning: "Miseducation, by focusing on skills to the detriment of motivation, pays an enormous price for teaching infants and young children what amounts to a few tricks."

He further observed that those advocating early instruction in skills and early out-of-home education rely upon youngsters who are very disadvantaged to tout early education's advantages. "Accordingly, the image of the competent child introduced to remedy the understimulation of low-income children now serves as the rationale for the overstimulation of middle-class children."

Dr. Jack Westman of the Rockford Institute, renowned child psychiatrist Dr. Stanley Greenspan, and brain researcher Jane Healy are among the many unheeded others who warn of the implications of forcing the "childhood as a race" approach upon young children. Laments Westman, "The result is what is now referred to as the 'hothousing movement' for infants and toddlers devoted to expediting their development. This is occurring in spite of the evidence that the long-term outcomes of early didactic, authoritarian approaches with younger children relate negatively to intellectual development."

In an interview for Parent and Child *magazine, Dr. Greenspan insisted that young children suffer greatly if there is inadequate "emotional learning" in their daily lives.*

In an interview for *Parent and Child* magazine, Dr. Greenspan insisted that young children suffer greatly if there is inadequate "emotional learning" in their daily lives. Such learning, he explained, is both a requisite for their ability to relate well with others and the foundation of cognitive learning. "Emotional development and interactions form the foundation for all children's learning—especially in the first five years of life. During these years, children abstract from their emotional experiences constantly to learn even the most basic concepts. Take, for example, something like saying hello or learning when you can be aggressive and when you have to be nice—and all of these are cues by emotions."

In *Endangered Minds: Why Children Don't Think and What We Can Do About It*, Healy states the case for allowing young children to play with those who love them before requiring them to learn academic skills. She intones, "Driving the cold spikes of inappropriate pressure into the malleable heart of a child's learning may seriously distort the unfolding of both intellect and motivation. This self-serving intellectual assault, increasingly condemned by teachers who see its warped products, reflects a more general ignorance of the growing brain.... Explaining things to children won't do the job; they must have the chance to experience, wonder, experiment, and act it out for themselves. It is this process, throughout life, that enables the growth of intelligence."

Healy goes so far as to describe the damaging effect on the "functional organization of the plastic brain" in pushing too hard too soon: "Before brain regions are myelinated, they do not operate efficiently. For this reason, trying to 'make' children master academic skills for which they do not have the requisite maturation may re-

sult in mixed-up patterns of learning.... It is possible to force skills by intensive instruction, but this may cause a child to use immature, inappropriate neural networks and distort the natural growth process."

Play is a way for children to relish childhood, prepare for adulthood, and discover their inner passions.

Play is important for intellectual growth, the exploration of individuality, and the growth of a conscience. Play is a way for children to relish childhood, prepare for adulthood, and discover their inner passions. Legendary psychoanalyst D.W. Winnicott warned us not to underestimate the importance of play. In *The Work and Play of Winnicott*, Simon A. Grolnick elucidates Winnicott's concept of play.

> Play in childhood and throughout the life cycle helps to relieve the tension of living, helps to prepare for the serious, and sometimes for the deadly (e.g., war games), helps define and redefine the boundaries between ourselves and others, helps give us a fuller sense of our own personal and bodily being. Playing provides a trying-out ground for proceeding onward, and it enhances drive satisfaction.... Winnicott repeatedly stressed that when playing becomes too drive-infested and excited, it loses its creative growth-building capability and begins to move toward loss of control or a fetishistic rigidity.... Civilization's demands for controlled, socialized behavior gradually, and sometimes insidiously, supersedes the psychosomatic and aesthetic pleasures of open system play.

When we discard playtime, we jeopardize the child's fresh, creative approach to the world. The minuscule amount of peace that children are permitted means that thinking and introspection are demoted as well. Thought requires being, not always doing. Children who are not allowed to retreat once in a while into themselves are not allowed to find out what is there. Our busy lives become ways of hiding from the recesses of the mind. Teaching children to be tough and prepared for the world, making them into achieving doers instead of capable thinkers, has its consequences. Children's innate curiosity is intense. When that natural curiosity has no room to fulfill itself, it burns out like a smothered flame.

In an age when "socialization" into society's ideals and mores is accepted even for babies and toddlers, we should remember that institutionalized schooling even for older children is a relatively new phenomenon. Mass education was a post-Industrial Revolution invention, one that served the dual purposes of preparing children for work and freeing parents to contribute fully to the industrial structure. No longer was work something that families did together, as a unit.

The separation of children from the family's work paved the way for schools and social reformers to assume the task of preparing children for life. This is a lofty role. As parents, we need to inform ourselves as to what our children are being prepared *for* and *how* they are being prepared.

Although our children's days are filled with instruction, allowing them little time of their own, we seem frequently inattentive as to just what they are learning. As William Bennett, Allan Bloom, and others have pointed out, recent years have been characterized by the reformulation of our schools, universities, and information sources according to a relativist, left-leaning ideology saturated with cynicism. This ideology leaves students with little moral-intellectual ground to stand on, as they are taught disrespect not only for past ideas and literary works but for the American political system and Judeo-Christian ethics. Such works as *The Five Little Peppers and How They Grew* and *Little Women* are windows into the soul of a much less cynical (and much less hectic) time.

Teaching children about the great thinkers, writers, and statesmen of the past is neglected as the very idea of greatness and heroism is disputed. Thus, the respect for greatness that might have caused children to glance upward from their TV show or activity and the stories about their country's early history that might have given them respect for a time when computer games didn't exist are not a factor in their lives. The word *preoccupied* acquires new significance, for children's minds are stuffed with the here and now.

THE DEVALUATION OF HOMELIFE

The busyness of modern child rearing and the myopia of the modern outlook reinforce each other. The very ideas that education is a race and that preschool-age children's participation in beneficial experience is more important than playing or being with the family are modern ones that continually reinforce themselves for lack of alternatives. Our busy lives leave insufficient time to question whether all this busyness is necessary and whether the content of our childrens' education is good.

The possibility that children might regard their activities less than fondly when they are older because these activities were forced upon them is not addressed. The possibility that they may never find their own passionate interests is not considered. (I came across an interesting television show that discussed the problem middle-school coaches are having with burned-out and unenthusiastic participants in a wide range of sports. The coaches attributed this to the fact that children had already been doing these sports for years and were tired of the pressure.)

One needs time to be a thinker, freedom to be creative, and some level of choice to be enthusiastic. Families can bestow upon children opportunities for autonomy while at the same time giving them a stable base to fall back upon and moral and behavioral guidelines. Having a competitive edge is neither as important nor as lasting as the ability to lead a genuine, intelligently thought-out, and considerate life.

Some of the best learning experiences happen not in an institution, not with a teacher, but in a child's independent "research" of the world at hand.

Some of the best learning experiences happen not in an institution, not with a teacher, but in a child's independent "research" of the world at hand. As the child interprets the world around her, creates new things with the materials available to her, and extracts new ideas from the recesses of her mind, she is learning to be an active, contributing participant in the world. She occupies her physical, temporal, and intellectual space in a positive, resourceful way. Conversely, if she is constantly stuffed with edifying "opportunities," resentment and lack of autonomy are the likely results.

In *The Erosion of Childhood*, Valerie Polakow insists upon the child's ability to "make history" as opposed to simply receiving it. Lamenting the overinstitutionalization of children in day care and school, she warns, "Children as young as a year old now enter childhood institutions to be formally schooled in the ways of the social system and emerge eighteen years later to enter the world of adulthood having been deprived of their own history-making power, their ability to act upon the world in significant and meaningful ways." She adds, "The world in which children live—the institutional world that babies, toddlers and the very young have increasingly come to inhabit and confront—is a world in which they become the objects, not the subjects of history, a world in which history is being made of them."

Day care provides both too much stimulation of the chaotic, disorganized kind, which comes inevitably from the cohabitation of large numbers of babies and toddlers, and too much of the organized kind that comes, of necessity, from group-centered living. It provides too little calm, quiet, space, or comfort and too little opportunity to converse and relate to a loving other.

Imagine, for example, a parent sitting down with her child for a "tea party." As she pours real tea into her own cup and milk into her child's, the "how to do things" is taken seriously. The child is encouraged to say "thank you" and to offer cookies to his mother, and their chat begins. Although they are pretending to be two adults, the ritual is real; it occurs in a real home setting; it provides the child with real food and a real opportunity for "mature" conversation. The mother says, "I'm so glad to be here for tea. How have you been?" The child, enjoying the chance to play the part of his mother's host, answers, "Fine! Would you like another cookie?" "Oh yes, thank you," answers his mother. "These cookies are delicious!" The child is learning about civilized behavior.

Children living in the new millennium need a refuge from the impersonal, the mechanical, and the programmed. We must provide them with more than opportunities for skill learning, socialization, and competition.

Then, picture the toy tea set at the learning center. Two children decide "to have tea." They fight over who has asked whom over. When one child asks, "How have you been?" the other loses interest and walks away. Too much of this peer-centered learning and not enough of adult-based learning clearly has negative implications for social development. The child simply cannot learn right from wrong, proper from improper, from other children who themselves have trouble making these distinctions.

Homelife that provides a break from group action has innumerable advantages for older children as well. Think of the different learning experiences a child receives from sitting down at the dinner table with his family and from gulping down a hamburger on the way to a nighttime game. In one case, the child has the opportunity to learn about manners and conversation. In the other, he is given another opportunity to compete with peers. (This is not to deny the benefits of being part of a team but simply to state that homelife itself is beneficial.) I hear many parents of high-school students complain about the compet-

itive, selfish manner of today's students. And, yet, most of these students have not a moment in their day that is not competitive.

How can we expect children to value kindness and cooperation when their free time has been totally usurped by activities wherein winning is everything? At home, winning is not everything (unless the child expends all his time trying to "beat the enemy" in a video game). At home, a child is much more likely to be reprimanded for not compromising with his siblings than for not "defeating" them. If homelife provides children with time to define their individuality and interact with family members (and all the give-and-take implied), then it is certainly an invaluable aspect of a child's advancement.

Children living in the new millennium need a refuge from the impersonal, the mechanical, and the programmed. We must provide them with more than opportunities for skill learning, socialization, and competition. Otherwise, something will be missing in their humanness. For to be human is to have the capacity for intimate attachments based upon love (which can grow more intimate because of the closeness that family life provides); it is to reason and to have a moral sense of things; it is to be capable of a spontaneity that stems from original thought or from some passion within.

We must set our children free from our frenetic, goal-oriented pace. We must create for them a private realm wherein no child-rearing "professional" can tread. Within this secure space, the possibilities are endless. With this stable base to fall back upon, children will dare to dream, think, and explore. They will compete, learn, and socialize as the blossoming individuals that they are, not as automatons engineered for results.

Anne R. Pierce is an author and political philosopher who lives in Cincinnati with her husband and three children. As a writer, she finds that bringing up children in the modern world gives her much food for thought.

Vaccines and Autism:
Beyond the Fear Factors

By JANE E. BRODY

Over the years, any number of coincidental findings have suggested that exposure to a particular substance may cause a certain illness. But under the critical eye of careful research, most of these apparent associations turn out to have no cause-and-effect relationship.

The suspicion that vaccines given to infants and children can cause autism is one such association, with attention directed at the vaccines that use the preservative thimerosal, which contains mercury.

Experts have poked many holes in this theory, which arose because of two facts: that mercury is a known neurotoxin and that symptoms of autism typically appeared soon after children were given vaccines containing thimerosal.

While the final "i" has yet to be dotted on this question, overwhelming evidence so far suggests that thimerosal poses no significant threat to the developing brain.

Erring on the side of caution three years ago, vaccine makers stopped using thimerosal to prevent microbial contamination of certain vaccines given to infants and small children, although none of the existing batches were recalled and remained in use until supplies ran out. Also, thimerosal is still used in flu vaccine, which is now recommended for otherwise healthy children ages 6 months to 2 years.

Keeping Open Minds

It is easy for parents to become convinced that thimerosal is the culprit in the current rise in autism rates if they consider only the arguments presented by those who believe in this association.

So it is important to review the evidence that experts have marshaled against it, which is described in the current issue of the journal Pediatrics by two neuropathologists, Dr. Karin B. Nelson of the National Institute of Neurological Disorders and Stroke and Dr. Margaret L. Bauman of Harvard Medical School.

In October 2001, a 15-member expert panel of the Institute of Medicine, an arm of the National Academy of Sciences, concluded that there was not enough evidence to prove or disprove a link between thimerosal and autism.

Meanwhile, Dr. Marie C. McCormick, the Harvard professor of maternal and child health who led the panel, suggested that parents ask their doctors to use mercury-free vaccines. But, she said, even if they are not available, parents should still have their children vaccinated.

The diseases that vaccines prevent can cause severe illness, brain damage and even death, and these real risks are far greater than anything that may be imagined to result from the vaccines themselves.

To be sure, the numbers of reported cases of autism and its milder forms are alarming: an increase from about 1 child in 2,000 before 1970 to a prevalence today of 1 in 500, 1 in 250 and possibly even 1 in 150, according to various estimates.

What accounts for the change remains a mystery: some environmental agent may be acting on the brains of susceptible children, or the change may simply reflect better recognition and diagnosis.

Thimerosal has been used to protect vaccines since the 1930's. But the change in diagnosis rates of autism has coincided with an increased exposure of American infants to vaccines preserved with thimerosal, which have included Haemophilus influenzae (HiB), hepatitis B, diphtheria and tetanus. This preservative is also used in some immunoglobulins given to pregnant Rh-negative women and some over-the-counter eardrops and nasal sprays.

Claims vs. Facts

Typically, children who are found to be autistic appear normal for their first months or year, then they seem to lose natural developmental landmarks. Many parents of affected children have noted that this reversal occurs suddenly or gradually soon after the vaccinations received in the child's first 15 months. But Dr. Nelson and Dr. Bauman point out that "age of onset of symptoms can be highly misleading as an indicator that some environmental event has caused or precipitated a disorder."

For example, in two disorders known to be caused solely by a defect in a single gene, a period of normal development occurs before symptoms appear—about 18 months in Rett syndrome and 45 years in Huntington's chorea, the disease that killed the songwriter Woody Guthrie.

Those who have focused on mercury as a cause of autism list nearly 100 clinical signs that they say are shared by autism and mercury poisoning. But Dr. Nelson and Dr. Bauman say this list does not distinguish between "typical and characteristic manifestations" and those that are "rare, unusual and highly atypical."

For example, the scientists said, in mercury poisoning, including the few cases of poisoning caused by ethyl mercury, the form in thimerosal, characteristic motor symptoms are lack of coordination, unsteadiness and difficulty speaking because of poor muscle control, along with tremors, muscle pains and weakness and, in severe cases, spasticity. But in autism, they said, the only common motor symptoms are "repetitive behaviors such as flapping, circling or rocking."

As for sensory symptoms, mercury poisoning is associated with extreme sensitivity to touch, a function of peripheral nerve damage. But in autism a reduced sensitivity to pain accompanies a hypersensitivity to sound, suggesting involvement of the central nervous system, not peripheral nerves.

There is even debate over ethyl mercury and whether it gets into the brain. Methyl mercury has an "active transport system" to carry it across the blood-brain barrier, but there is no such transport for ethyl mercury, which is further hindered from entering the brain by being a larger molecule that is rapidly decomposed once in the body.

Also striking, the scientists report, are differences in the brains, including size and the kinds of cells and areas that are damaged in autism and mercury poisoning. Children with mercury poisoning experience a shrinkage of the brain; those with autism tend to have abnormally large brains, with an enlarged cortex and white matter and more nerve processes than normal.

In an interview, Dr. Nelson suggested that the normal "pruning process"—the loss of extraneous neurons and connections that occur as children mature and gain experience—fails to happen in autism, leading to an enlarged brain. More studies should be done, she said, to reveal why autistic children seem unable to focus and are overwhelmed by environmental stimuli.

A further brain difference, she noted, lies in the brain cells: those that are relatively spared in mercury poisoning are damaged in autism, and vice versa.

Autism is known to have hereditary influences, and Dr. Nelson, among others, says that it "probably begins in the womb," the result of abnormal brain development. Although the symptoms usually do not become apparent until months or longer after birth, some mothers of autistic children have reported noticing abnormalities in their newborns before any mercury-containing vaccine was administered.

Through the years, several cases of serious mercury poisoning have occurred, including one involving a mercury-containing teething powder and another related to the contamination of fish consumed by millions of people in Japan. But still, no increase was seen in the incidence of autism or in behavior changes suggestive of autism.

Millions of children get vaccines every year, but fewer than 1 percent end up with autism. If vaccines are a factor, why would so many be spared? The hypothesis put forth by Sallie Bernard and colleagues at the parent organization Safe Minds in Cranford, N.J., is that some children are either born sensitive to mercury or fail to eliminate mercury normally and thus accumulate large amounts that can damage the brain.

Clearly, this matter deserves thorough scientific attention. Autism is a devastating condition that is very costly for child and family and, if cases can be prevented, they should be. If thimerosal is an important cause, the phasing out of its use in vaccines that is now occurring should result in a significant decline in cases in the next few years.

Four Perspectives on Child Care Quality

Deborah Ceglowski[1,2] and Chiara Bacigalupa[1]

National and state child care policies are shaped in part by studies of child care quality. The majority of these studies focus on variables that influence child outcomes. Katz suggests that this is but one of four perspectives on child care quality, and that parents, children, and child care staff have perspectives on child care quality that have not been adequately addressed. This article reviews the variables, measures, and studies associated with each of these four perspectives. The authors argue that given the preponderance of studies conducted from the professional/researcher perspective, more effort should be directed to studying child care quality from parents' children's, and child care staff members' viewpoints.

INTRODUCTION

As more and more mothers have entered the paid labor force, children increasingly spend part of their time in nonparental care, often in paid child care settings (Cohen, 1996). Parents often choose child care for educational or developmental reasons as well, for example, using preschool even when not employed. Nearly 75% of children under 5 years and between 5 and 12 years of age are in child care (Capizzano and Adams, 2000).

At the same time, welfare reform and a strong economy have increased the number of low-income mothers who are working. Children from low-income families in which the parents are entering the work force will attend formal and informal early care and education programs (Howes, 1992). Formal early care and education is defined as licensed family child care and an array of nonprofit and for-profit licensed child care programs. Informal arrangements include care arrangements consisting of (a) relative care and care provided by friends and neighbors, and (b) illegal, nonlicensed care out of compliance with legally licensed or legally unlicensed care regulations.

Research on child care issues and policy has been expanding rapidly in the past few years. Our knowledge of the factors affecting quality of care, the effects on children's development and education, and the outcomes for family income and self-sufficiency are growing. The rapidly changing policy environment and increasing involvement of government in child care

(Edwards, 2002) mean that policymakers at state and local levels of government are increasingly involved in program changes.

WHY STUDY CHILD CARE QUALITY?

Child care policies support enhanced practices for child care and the outcomes for families and children in a number of ways. One key concern is the level of quality of care. Substantial evidence has demonstrated that variation in the quality of early care and education—within the range available in typical community and family child care programs—affects a wide range of child outcomes including cognitive, social, and health outcomes. For example, the Cost, Quality, and Outcomes Study (Peisner-Feinberg et al., 2000) found high quality child care had positive effects on children's language ability and sociability through kindergarten, and on math ability, thinking/attention skills, and problem behaviors through second grade. Several other major studies have shown similar gains in cognitive and social skills (Burchinal, Roberts, Nabors, and Bryant, 1996; NICHD Early Childhood Research Network, 200 I; Phillips, McCartney, and Scarr, 1987; Whitebook, Howes, and Phillips, 1990).

Another compelling reason to study the quality of care is to understand the impact of welfare reform upon the child care system. The quality of care that is available to low-income families is highly uneven (Phillips, 1995). A sizable minority of care falls into a range of quality that some conclude may compromise development, and there is a very limited supply of arrangements at the high end of the quality spectrum (major studies summarized by Phillips, 1995). When selecting child care, many working-poor and low-income families must choose from a seriously constrained set of options. These families face obstacles that derive primarily from the structure of low-wage

[1]University of Minnesota, Minneapolis.
[2]Correspondence should be directed to Deborah Ceglowski, Department of Curriculum and Instruction, Center for Early Education and Development, University of Minnesota, 360 Peik Hall, 159 Pillsbury Drive SE. Minneapolis, MN 55455. E-mail: deber@umn.edu

jobs, the low incomes these jobs provide, and the availability of various child care arrangements (Hofferth, 1995; Hofferth, Brayfield, Oeich, and Holcomb, 1991). They rely on free care by relatives and friends or very inexpensive care (National Center for Education Statistics, 1995). Their nonstandard and often rotating work hours restrict them to arrangements with flexible and weekend or evening hours of operation (Meyers, 1993). These factors typically lead to greater reliance on multiple providers and expose young children to shifting child care arrangements (Phillips, 1995).

Another reason to study the quality of care is to expand the current understanding of child care quality to include all child care settings, both formal and informal. To date, child care quality has focused on family child care homes or child care centers. Only recently have studies involved the observation and assessment of children in the vast, informal child care market consisting of care by relatives, friends, or neighbors. While we do have evidence that high quality center-based programs such as the Perry Preschool Project (Schweinhart, Barnes, Weikart, Barnett, and Epstein, 1993) provide substantial benefits to children considered to be at risk, we do not know whether the informal settings often used by low-income children provide similar benefits.

FOUR PERSPECTIVES ON CHILD CARE QUALITY

Katz (1993) suggests there are four perspectives on the quality of child care: (a) the perspective of researchers and professionals in the field, (b) the perspective of parents using child care, (c) the perspective of child care staff, and (d) the perspective of the children in child care. Although Katz argues that all four perspectives must inform child care policy, the researcher/professional perspective is considered far more often than are the other three.

The researcher/professional perspective focuses on program attributes and consists of structural, global, and process components. Structural quality includes group size, staff qualifications and levels of experience, and child/teacher ratio. Global quality entails classroom practices and environments that promote children's growth and learning. Process quality entails adult responsiveness to and behavior with children. The researcher/professional perspective has been used in every major study of

child care quality and dominates current views of child care quality. The major aim of these studies is to identify and measure the key program variables associated with child outcomes.

Of the remaining three perspectives, the parent perspective has been studied modestly, and the staff and child perspectives have been studied minimally. Studies of parent perspectives focus on parent's perceptions of quality, including program flexibility and staff responsiveness to family needs. Staff perceptions of quality might include administrative, collegial, parental, and sponsor relationships. Child perceptions of quality would investigate quality from a child's perspective and might include information about children's comfort, level of acceptance, and engagement in activities. Figure 1 presents Katz's model.

Katz's view of "quality" in early childhood services and care remind us that it is a "relative concept....subjective in nature and based on values, beliefs, and interest, rather than an objective and universal reality" (Pence and Moss, 1994, p. 172). Definitions of quality may be narrower or broader, depending on the groups identified. Children, parents, families, employers, providers, and society all have different needs and values and will define quality differently. This outlook on quality presents "quality" as a more loosely defined construct, whose meaning can change depending on specific circumstances.

In the next two sections, we review the major variables, measures, and studies associated with these four views of child care quality. The first section focuses on the researcher/professional perspective and is substantially longer than the second section because the vast majority of child care research has been done from this perspective. The second section groups the remaining three perspectives together. The article concludes with a discussion of the current state of child care research and recommendations for future studies.

CHILD CARE QUALITY FROM RESEARCHERS' AND PROFESSIONALS' PERSPECTIVES

Child care quality has been studied extensively since the 1970s. To date, the vast majority of this research has used a top-down perspective aiming to determine the variables that influence child outcomes. Early research focused on the effects of child care on children, especially on infant-maternal attachment (Cornelius and Denney, 1975). Beginning in the late-1970s, many researchers turned their attention to the question of how variations in child care affected children's development. New questions were asked about what constituted quality in child care and how quality influenced children's development, especially in the areas of cognitive and social development (Anderson, Nagle, Roberts, and Smith, 1981; McCartney, Scarr, Phillips, Grajek, and Schwarz, 1982). Since then, discussions of child care quality have focused on the following variables: classroom composition, curriculum and program philosophy, physical environment, staff characteristics, adult–child interactions, and parent–staff communication.

Discussions of child care quality usually involve an analysis of adult/child ratio, group size, and the age mix of children in the room. Low adult/child ratios (Field, 1980; NICHD Early Child Care Research Network, 1996; Kontos, Howes,

Researcher/Professional Perceptions of Child Care Quality

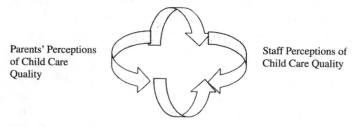

Parents' Perceptions of Child Care Quality

Staff Perceptions of Child Care Quality

Children's Perceptions of Child Care Quality

Fig. 1. Katz's model of four perspectives of child care quality.

Shinn, and Galinsky, 1995) and small group size (Clarke-

Table 1. Measures Used in Major Studies of Child Care Quality

Instrument	Description	Examples of Studies Using This Measure
The Early Childhood Environmental Rating Scale—Revised (Harms, Clifford, and Cryer, 1998)	7-point rating scale used to measure the appropriateness of classroom environment and practices. Additional versions rate family child care, infant/toddler, and school-age settings.	Cost, Quality, and Child Outcomes; National Child Care Staffing Study; Florida Child Care Quality Improvement Study; Quality in Family Child Care and Relative Care
Assessment Profile for Early Childhood Programs (Abbott-Shinn and Sibley, 1992)	Checklist of global quality indicators. Different versions available for infant/toddler, preschool, school-age, and family child care.	NICHD Study of Early Child Care
Assessment of School-Age Child Care Quality (Wellesley College School-Age Child Care Project, 1991)	Rating scale used to measure 14 aspects of classroom environment and caregiver practices.	National Study of Before- and After-School Programs
Caregiver Interaction Scale (Arnett, 1989)	26-item scale measuring process quality. Subscales measure provider sensitivity and harshness toward a group of children.	National Child Care Staffing Study; Cost, Quality, and Outcomes Study; Florida Child Care Quality Improvement Study; Quality in Family Child Care and Relative Care
Observational Record of the Caregiving Environment (N1CHD Early Child Care Research Network, 1996)	Measures process quality: caregiver attachment, sensitivity, and responsiveness to individual children.	NICHD Study of Early Child Care
UCLA Early Childhood Observation Form (Stipek, Daniels, Galuzzo, and Milburn, 1992)	Measures whether teaching style in a particular classroom is didactic or child-centered.	Cost, Quality, and Child Outcomes; Florida Child Care Quality Improvement Study; Quality in Family Child Care and Relative Care
Parent and Teacher Questionnaires, Interviews, and Surveys	Used to measure parent and teacher perceptions of quality and child outcomes. Usually developed by the authors of the study.	NICHD Study of Early Child Care; National Child Care Staffing Study; Cost, Quality, and Outcomes Study; Florida Child Care Quality Improvement Study; Quality in Family Child Care and Relative Care: National Study of Before- and After-School Programs

Stewart, Gruber, and Fitzgerald, 1994) are associated with higher quality settings. The age mix of children has not been addressed extensively.

The physical environment is another widely recognized indicator of quality from the researcher/professional perspective. Researchers and state licensing boards agree that health and safety criteria must be met first. Additional factors such as the amount of space per child, the presence of age-appropriate toys and materials, accessibility of materials to children, and even aesthetic considerations such as the amount of "soft" materials in the environment also play a role in the quality of the physical environment (Howes, 1983; Kontos and Keyes, 1999; NICHD Early Child Care Research Network, 1996).

A third set of factors that researchers and professionals have included in their quality definition center on characteristics of child care staff. The most important factors in this area are (1) the amount and content of staff training/education (Arnett, 1989; Howes, Smith, and Galinsky 1995; Love, Ryer, and Faddis,

1992; Peisner-Feinberg et al., 2000; Whitebook et al., 1990), and (2) stability of staff (Howes and Hamilton, 1993). Provider education is linked with higher quality care in all settings—home, center, and relative care. Staff with formal training in early childhood education are more likely to recognize children's interests, ask and answer questions, speak at the child's eye-level, be sensitive to children's needs, and generally be warm and attentive to children (Bredekamp and Copple, 1997; Holloway and Reichhart-Erickson, 1988). Finally, Ghazvini and Readdick (1994) found that frequency of parent-caregiver communication was positively correlated with quality.

Studies of child care have tended to collect data in the following ways: direct observation of child care quality, indirect measures of child care quality, assessment measures of individual children, caregiver or parent ratings of individual children, and records of child care and parent information. The main instruments used to assess child care quality are presented in Table 1.

CHILD CARE QUALITY FROM PARENTS', CHILDREN'S, AND STAFF MEMBERS' PERSPECTIVES

Researchers have only begun to ask parents, teachers, and children—the people who participate most directly in child care—how they define quality child care. Parents in the National Child Care Survey (Hofferth, Brayfield, Deich, and Holcomb, 1991) said that the most important factors in how they chose child care were health and safety criteria and personal characteristics of the caregiver, such as warmth and sensitivity. A third factor valued by parents is a high level of parent–caregiver communication (Cryer and Burchinal, 1997; Kontos et al., 1995).

Emlen (1999) suggests that a fourth variable, flexibility, is the major factor in parental selection and definition of quality child care. Families that have limited flexibility in work choose child care arrangements that are very flexible. For example, a single parent who does not have nearby relatives and who works evening hours seeks a child care arrangement that can accommodate her working schedule. Often such parents choose from a limited number of family child care arrangements that offer evening care or informal care (a neighbor or friend). Families that have job flexibility and/or relative support can choose child care arrangements that are less flexible. In a two-parent household where one parent works during the day and one during the evening, the children could attend a child care center or a half-day early childhood program followed by parental care.

When teachers have been asked about quality of care, they chose the same factors that parents chose, including caregiver traits such as warmth and sensitivity (Galinsky, Howes, Kontos, and Shinn, 1994). Despite the fact that children are the people most affected by variations in quality of child care, almost no one has studied their perspective. The little research that has been done indicates they would like their child care program to be similar to home, that the staff be "nice," and that there be appealing children with whom to play (Langsted, 1994).

Surveys and interview protocols have been developed to assess parents', children's, and staffs' perspectives about quality of care. These measures are usually developed by authors to assess areas of interest in each particular study. For example, the Oregon Child Care Research Partnership developed a questionnaire to measure how parents define and assess quality (Emlen, 1999). Cryer and Burchinal (1997) adapted versions of the Early Childhood Environmental Rating Scale for parent use. Deborah Yandell (personal communication) wrote and used scripts of common child care occurrences to elicit responses from preschool children. The Cost, Quality, and Outcomes overview refers to interviews conducted with children, but the technical report (Helburn, 1995) does not contain findings from these interviews nor is the interview protocol easily accessible.

DISCUSSION

The prevailing definition of child care quality—that which researchers and early childhood professionals have defined as good for the child—has dominated child care research. Although this is an important perspective to investigate when studying child care quality, it is only one of several perspectives to consider. For example, studies comparing parental ratings of program quality to that of educators indicate that parents give programs higher ratings than do educators (Helbum, 1995). Explanations for this difference center on the lack of information parents have about the indicators of quality, or the different perspectives that parents have of quality. Another explanation is that the description and evaluation of quality care has been dominated by experts from government, certain professions, and academic research—to the exclusion of others (Pence and Moss, 1994). Some conclude that we need to understand what parental visions are for their children, both at home and in child care, because parents' perspectives may broaden the prevailing parameters of program quality (Cryer and Burchinal, 1997; Zinzeleta and Little, 1997).

The near exclusionary focus on this one perspective has limited our understanding of child care quality. We do not know how various stakeholder groups might define this concept differently, nor do we know how these various perspectives interact with each other. For instance, if parents are provided with a "high quality child outcome" program and make other choices, one might assume that the parents have made "bad" choices. However, from a parent's perspective, such a program may not meet the family's criteria for care. This may be due to differences in cultural values and expectations, work schedule, or family finances.

While Emlen's analysis of parents' perceptions of child care quality (based on family flexibility) seems to be in opposition to the "child care outcomes" definitions of child care quality, it might be viewed instead as another perspective on child care quality, namely families' perception of child care quality. This would not eliminate or lessen the importance of the top-down "child outcomes" definition of child care quality but expand it to include parents', children's, and staff members' perspectives.

Certainly disregarding children's perspectives on child care is not unique. Children are rarely asked, for example, about their lives in school and school culture (Graue and Walsh, 1998). However, children's perspectives on child care quality would broaden the current understanding of best practices and may influence and improve the current system of formal and informal care. Similarly, child care staff member's perspectives of child care quality have not been studied systematically.

With the majority of children being cared for in out-of-home programs, it is critical that we broaden our understanding of quality child care programs. This broader understanding could augment how we currently allocate funding for and deliver child care services and how local services are designed to meet specific community needs. For instance, if parents who have recently immigrated from Somalia define quality child care in terms of providers who speak Somali and observe Muslim eating customs, then programs could be developed to fit the families' definitions of quality while also conforming to traditional definitions of quality. In the same manner, staff definitions and children's definitions of quality could influence current child care service delivery.

REFERENCES

Abbott-Shinn, M., and Sibley, A. (1992). *Assessment Profile for Early Childhood Programs.* Quality Assist, Inc., 368 Moreland Ave. NE Suite 210, Atlanta, GA.

Anderson, C., Nagle, R., Roberts, W., and Smith, J. (1981). Attachment to substitute caregivers as a function of center quality and caregiver involvement. *Child Dev.* 52: 53-61.

Arnett, J. (1989). Caregivers in day-care centers: Does training matter? J. *Appl. Dev. Psychol.* 10: 541-552.

Bredekamp, S., and Copple, C. (eds.) (1997). *Developmentally Appropriate Practices in Early Childhood Programs, Revised Edition,* National Association for the Education of Young Children, Washington, DC.

Burchinal, M. R., Roberts, J. E., Nabors, L. A., and Bryant, D. M. (1996). Quality of center child care and infant cognitive and language development. *Child Dev.* 67: 606-615.

Capizzano, J., and Adams, G. (2000). The number of child care arrangements used by children under five: Variations across states, Urban Institute, Washington, DC.

Clarke-Stewart, K. A., Gruber, C. P., and Fitzgerald, L. M. (1994). *Children at Home and in Day Care,* Lawrence Erlbaum Associates, Hillsdale, NJ.

Cohen, A. J. (1996). A brief history of federal financing for child care in the United States. *Future Child.* 6: 26-40.

Cornelius, S., and Denney, N. (1975). Dependency in daycare and home care children. *Dev. Psychol.* 11: 575-582.

Cryer, D., and Burchinal, M. (1997). Parents as child care consumers. *Early Child Res. Q.* 12: 35-58.

Edwards, V. B. (ed.) (2002). Quality Counts 2002. *Education Week, 21(17).*

Emlen, A. (1999). *From a Parent's Point of View: Measuring the Quality of Child Care,* Portland State University, Portland OR.

Field, T. (1980). Preschool play: Effects of teacher: Child ratios and organization of classroom space. *Child Study J.* 10: 191-205.

Galinsky, E., Howes, C., Kontos, S., and Shinn, M. (1994). *The study of children in family child care and relative care: Highlights of findings,* Families and Work Institute, New York.

Ghazvini, A., and Readdick, C. (1994). Parent-caregiver communication and quality of care in diverse child care settings. *Early Child Res. Q.* 9: 207-222.

Graue, M. E., and Walsh, D. J. (1998). *Studying Children in Context: Theories, Methods, and Ethics,* Sage, Thousand Oaks, CA.

Harms, T., Clifford, R., and Cryer, D. (1998). *Early Childhood Environmental Rating Scale, Revised Edition,* Teachers College Press, New York.

Helburn, S. (ed.) (1995). Cost, Quality, and Child Outcomes in Child Care Centers: Technical Report, Department of Economics, Center for Research in Economic and Social Policy, University of Colorado, Denver.

Hofferth, S. (1995). Caring for children at the poverty line. *Child Youth Serv. Rev.* 17: 61-90.

Hofferth, S., Brayfield, A., Deich, S., and Holcomb, P. (1991). *National Child Care Survey, 1990,* The Urban Institute Press, Washington, DC.

Holloway, S. D., and Reichhart-Ericksoil, M. (1988). The relationship of day care quality to children's free-play behavior and social problem-solving skills. *Early Child Res. Q.* 3: 39-53.

Howes, C. (1983). Caregiver behavior in center and family day-care. *J. Appl. Dev. Psychol.* 4: 99-107.

Howes, C. (1992). *Preschool Experiences,* National Center for Educational Statistics, Los Angeles.

Howes, C., and Hamilton, C. (1993). The changing experience of child care: Changes in teachers and in teacher-child relationships and children's social competence with peers. *Early Child Res. Q.* 8: 15-32.

Howes, C., Smith, E., and Galinsky, E. (1995). *Florida Child Care Quality Improvement Study: Interim Report,* Families & Work Institute, New York.

Katz, L. (1993). Multiple perspectives on the quality of early childhood programs. ERIC # ED355 041.

Kontos, S., Howes, C., Shinn, M., and Galinsky, E. (1995). *Quality in Family Child Care and Relative Care,* Teachers College Press, New York.

Kontos, S., and Keyes, L. (1999). An ecobehavioral analysis of early childhood classrooms. *Early Child Res. Q.* 14: 35-50.

Langsted, O. (1994). Looking at quality from the child's perspective. In: Moss, P. and Pence, A. (eds.), *Valuing Quality in Early Childhood Services: New Approaches to Defining Quality,* Teachers College Press, New York, pp. 28-42.

Love, J., Ryer, P., and Faddis, B. (1992). *Caring Environments: Program Quality in California's Publicly Funded Child Development Programs: Report on the Legislatively Mandated 1990-91 Staff / Child Ratio Study,* RMC Research Corporation, Portsmouth, NH.

McCartney, K., Scarr, S., Phillips, D., Grajek, D., and Schwarz, C. (1982). Environmental differences among day care centers and their effects on children's level of intellectual, language and social development. In: Zigler, E., and Gordon, E. (eds.), *Daycare: Scientific and Social Policy Issues,* Auburn House. Boston, pp. 126-151.

Meyers, M. K. (1993). Child care in JOBS employment and training program: What difference does quality make? *J. Marriage Fam.* 55: 767-783.

National Center for Education Statistics (October 1995). *Approaching Kindergarten: A Look at Preschoolers in the United States,* U.S. Department of Education, Office of Educational Research and Improvement, Washington, DC.

NICHD Early Child Care Research Network (1996). Characteristics of infant childcare: factors contributing to positive caregiving. *Early Child Res. Q.* 11: 269-306.

NICHD Early Childhood Research Network (2001). Before Head Start: Income and ethnicity, family characteristics, child care experiences, and child development. *Early Educ. Dev.* 12: 545-576.

Peisner-Feinberg, E. S., Burchinal, M. R., Clifford, R. M., Culkin, M. L., Howes, C., Kagan, S.L., Yazejian, N., Byler, P., Rustici, J., and Zelazo, J. (2000). The Children of the Cost, Quality, and Outcomes Study Go to School: Technical Report, University of North Carolina at Chapel Hill, Frank Porter Graham Development Center, Chapel Hill.

Pence, A., and Moss, P. (1994). Towards an inclusionary approach in defining quality. In: Moss, P., and Pence, A. (eds.). *Valuing Quality in Early Childhood Services: New Approaches to Defining Quality,* Teachers' College Press, New York, pp. 172-179.

Phillips, D., McCartney, K., and Scarr, S. (1987). Child-care quality and children's social development. *Dev. Psychol.* 23: 537-543.

Phillips, D. A. (ed) (1995). *Child Care for Low-Income Families,* National Academy Press, Washington, DC.

Schweinhart, L. J., Barnes, H. V., and Weikart, D. P., with Barnett, W.S., and Epstein, A. (1993). *Significant Benefits: The High/ Scope Perry Preschool Study Through Age 27,* High/Scope Press, Ypsilanti, MI.

Stipek, D., Daniels, D., Galluzzo, D., and Milburn, S. (1992). Characterizing early childhood education programs for poor and middle-class children. *Early Child Res. Q.* **7:** 1-19.

Wellesley College School-Age Child Care Project (1991). *AS: Assessing School-Age Child Care Quality*, Wellesley, MA, Author.

Whitebook, M., Howes, C., and Phillips, D. (1990), *Who Cares: Child Care Teachers and the Quality of Care in America: Final Report of the National Child Care Staffing Study,* Child Care Employee Project, Oakland, CA.

Zinzeleta, E., and Little, N. (1997). How do parents really choose early childhood programs? *Young Child.* **52:** 8-11.

Guilt Free TV

In the beginning, there was Big Bird. Now, thanks to intense competition from Disney and Nick, there are more quality shows for preschoolers than ever.

BY DANIEL McGINN

WHEN ALICIA LARGE WAS GROWING up, her parents rarely let her watch television. Even the Muppets were off-limits, she says, because her parents disliked the sexual tension between Kermit and Miss Piggy. Now 31 and raising her own sons—ages 2 and 3—Large views TV more benevolently. Her boys love "Dora the Explorer," so when she takes them on errands, she draws a map—the bank, the grocery store—so they can track their progress as Dora does. Among Large's friends, kids' TV—what and how much are yours watching?—is a constant conversation. Yes, many parents still use TV as a babysitter. But increasingly, she says, parents are looking to TV to help them do a better job of raising kids. "Our generation is using it completely differently," she says.

Parents have felt conflicted about television since its earliest days. Even Philo T. vision since its earliest days. Even Philo T. Farnsworth, TV's inventor, fretted over letting his son watch cowboy shows, according to biographer Evan I. Schwartz. That anxiety continues. In a survey released last week by Public Agenda, 22 percent of parents said they'd "seriously considered getting rid of [their TV] altogether" because it airs too much sex and bad language. But at the same time, for parents of the youngest viewers—ages 2 to 5—there are new reasons for optimism. Now that PBS, which invented the good-for-kids genre, has new competition from Nickelodeon and Disney, there are more quality choices for preschoolers than ever.

Inside those networks, a growing number of Ph.D.s are injecting the latest in child-development theory into new programs. In Disney's "Stanley," meet a freckle-faced kid who's fascinated with animals; in one episode, he and his pals explore the life and habitat of a platypus.

Nickelodeon now airs 4.5 hours of quality preschool shows daily (in addition to learning-free fare like "SpongeBob" for older kids). Shows like "Dora" and "Blue's Clues" goad kids into interacting with the television set; studies show this improves problem-solving skills. Even the grand-daddy of this genre, "Sesame Street," has undergone a makeover to better serve today's precocious viewers. The newcomers provide stiff competition to Mister Rogers, whose show stopped production in 2000 (it still airs on PBS). But he welcomes his new TV neighbors. "I'm just glad that more producers —and purveyors of television have signed the pledge to protect childhood," says Fred Rogers, who now writes parenting books.

That's the good news. The bad news is that working these shows into kids' lives in a healthy way remains a challenge. Much of what kids watch remains banal or harm-

Puppets to Muppets: A Hit Parade

Children's television has been evolving for more than half a century. A time line of highs and lows.

1947
Howdy Doody and pal Buffalo Bob were the first superstars of kids' TV. Puppet power!

1949
The first-made-for-TV animated show was **Crusader Rabbit**, created by Jay Ward, who later gave us "Rocky and His Friends."

1949
Bozo the Clown debuts. The red-haired funny man also made hit records and generated millions in merchandise sales.

1953
The first interactive kids' show was **Winky Dink and You**. Viewers put a sheet of acetate over the screen and used crayons to help Winky Dink solve problems.

1955
For 30 years, **Captain Kangaroo** and his cast of gentle characters offered simple lessons in morality.

1955
The Mickey Mouse Club. Who needs friends when the Mouseketeers are in your living room every afternoon?

1961
Say what? The FCC's **Newton Minow** dubs TV "a vast wasteland."

1961
Brilliant writing and sharp satire make **The Bullwinkle Show** a draw for kids and parents alike.

1963
Mister Rogers moves in. Three years later, the mayhem of **The Road Runner Show** arrives.

1969
The big one. Designed by experts to help children learn, **Sesame Street** set new standards for the medium and established PBS as the home of good kids' TV.

1971
Children raised on "Sesame Street" moved on to **The Electric Company**'s more mature lessons.

1979
The launch of **Nickelodeon**. The network, initially, was commercial-free.

1981
The Smurfs, a marketing juggernaut, was seen as sexist at first. It evolved into a message-heavy show by 1987.

1984
One of many shows based on boys' toys, **The Transformers** was inherently violent.

1987
It had plenty of action, but **Teenage Mutant Ninja Turtles** felt less dangerous because of an emphasis on character. Teen turtles named for Italian artists can't be *that* violent.

1990
Thanks to the **Children's Television Act**, networks must broadcast three hours of educational programming per week. Saturday's superheroes become an endangered species.

1992
Kids love **Barney**, but the purple dinosaur annoys anyone over the age of 5.

1993
Mighty Morphin Power Rangers. Finally, a girl superhero, the Pink Ranger.

1996
Blue's Clues. Detective work with an adorable pup. A fresh idea.

2002
Meet **Rolie Polie Olie**, the 6-year-old robot boy.

---

ful. Many kids watch too much. There are also troubling socioeconomic factors at work. In lower-income homes, for instance, kids watch more and are more likely to have TV in their bedrooms, a practice pediatricians discourage. But even as some families choose to go TV-free, more parents are recognizing that television can be beneficial. In the Public Agenda survey, 93 percent of parents agree that "TV is fine for kids as long as he or she

is watching the right shows and watching in moderation."

When it comes to the right shows, "Sesame Street" remains the gold standard. Last week, as the crew taped an episode for its 34th season, the set looked comfortingly familiar: while Telly and Baby Bear worked on a skit near Hooper's Store, Snuffleupagus hung from the rafters, sleeping under a sheet. The show's longevity is a testament to the research-driven

process founder Joan Ganz Cooney invented in the late 1960s. Then, as now, each season begins with Ph.D.s working alongside writers to set goals and review scripts. Any time there's a question—will kids understand Slimey the Worm's mission to the moon?—they head to day-care centers to test the material.

When "Sesame" began reinventing kids' TV in the early '70s, Daniel Anderson was a newly minted professor of psychology at the University of Massachusetts, Amherst. Like most child-development pros at that time, he assumed TV was bad for kids. Then one day Anderson taught his class that young children have very short attention spans. One student challenged him: "So why do kids sit still for an hour to watch 'Sesame Street'?" "I genuinely didn't know the answer," Anderson recalls. So he went to a lab and placed kids in front of TVs to find it.

What he found surprised him. Like most researchers, he assumed that fast-moving images and sounds mesmerized young viewers. But videotapes of kids' viewing showed that their attention wandered most during transitions between segments and when dialogue or plotlines became too complex. He hypothesized that even young children watch TV for the same reason adults do: to enjoy good stories. To test that theory, he sliced up "Sesame Street" skits so the plot no longer made sense. Even 2-year-olds quickly realized the story was amiss and stopped watching. Some knocked on the TV screen. Others called out: "Mommy, can you fix this?" Over years of research, Anderson reached a startling conclusion: "Television viewing is a much more intellectual activity for kids than anybody had previously supposed."

THIS RESEARCH MIGHT HAVE STAYED hidden in psych journals if it hadn't been for the work of two equally powerful forces: the U.S. Congress and a purple dinosaur named Barney. In 1990 Congress passed the Children's Television Act, increasing demand for quality kids' shows. Then "Barney & Friends" was launched as a PBS series in 1992. Kids went wild, and merchandise flew off shelves. Until then, Nickelodeon and Disney had been content to leave preschool shows to the do-gooders at PBS. Now they saw gold. "The success of 'Barney' just changed everybody's feeling—it became 'OK, we should be able to do that, too'," says Marjorie Kalins, a former "Sesame" executive.

It was a profitable move. By 2001 Nick and Disney's TV businesses had generated a combined $1.68 billion in revenue, according to Paul Kagan Associates. Everyone admits that licensing money influences programming decisions. (Ironically, merchandisers at Nickelodeon lobbied *against* "Dora" because they believed that another show would generate more sales.) Ads and toys can detract from many parents' enthusiasm for the shows; no matter how much your kid may learn from "Sagwa" or "Rolie Polie Olie," the characters are hard to love when you can't get through Wal-Mart without a giant case of "I-WANT-itis."

Until there's a way to make shows free, that overcommercialization will continue. But for parents, there's some comfort from knowing that more TV producers are applying the latest research to make their shows better. This happened partly because researchers of Anderson's generation helped grow a new crop of Ph.D.s, who began graduating into jobs at "Sesame" and Nickelodeon. And like seeds from a dandelion blown at by a child, folks who'd trained at "Sesame" began taking root inside other networks. Anne Sweeney, who'd studied at Harvard with "Sesame" cofounder Gerald Lesser, interned with television activist Peggy Charren and spent 12 years at Nickelodeon, took over the Disney Channel in 1996. She hired a team (led by ex-Nick programmer Rich Ross) to design pre-school shows. By 1999 Disney had a full block of little-kid programming it branded Playhouse Disney. Today it uses a 28-page "Whole Child Curriculum" detailing what shows should teach.

To see how research can drive these new-generation shows, come along, neighbor, as we visit a day-care center on Manhattan's Upper West Side. Dr. Christine Ricci sits in a child-size chair, holding a script and tapping a red pen against her lip.

Ricci, who holds a psychology Ph.D. from UMass, is research director for "Dora the Explorer," which airs on Nick Jr., Nickelodeon's preschool block. In each episode Dora, an animated Latina girl, goes on a journey with a monkey named Boots. Using a map to guide them (which helps kids' spatial skills), they visit three locations ("Waterfall, mountain, forest!" kids yell) and solve problems. As in "Blue's Clues," Nick Jr.'s groundbreaking hit in which a dog named Blue and the host Joe help kids solve puzzles, "Dora" encourages kids to yell back at the screen (often in Spanish) or do physical movements (like rowing a boat).

Today Ricci shows 4-year-olds a crudely animated "Dora" episode slated for next season. As they watch, Ricci's team charts, moment by moment, whether the kids are paying attention and interacting with the screen. At first the kids sit transfixed, but during a pivotal scene (in which Swiper the fox, Dora's nemesis, throws a boot down a hole) their attention wanders. One child picks up a Magic Marker, and suddenly every child is seeking out toys. All the while the researchers scribble furiously. When the episode ends, an adult asks the children questions: "What color button on the fix-it machine matched the tire?" Their recall is astonishing. "Sesame Street" has done this kind of testing off and on since the '70s. Ricci's team, however, is relentless, testing and revising every "Dora" episode repeatedly.

The following afternoon, Ricci, "Dora" creator Chris Gifford and their team study a bar graph showing how kids interacted with the episode minute by minute. To boost the numbers, sometimes they suggest better animation. Sometimes they call for a better "money shot": a big close-up of Dora. Fixing one segment—"Only 15 out of 26 kids were still watching," Ricci informs them gravely—requires more drastic measures. Gifford stands up, motioning like a cheerleader, to suggest livelier movements to get kids moving along with Dora during a song. "So often when you work on a TV show for kids, you forget about your audience," Gifford says. "We've set up a system where we can't ignore them." Similar work goes on at "Blue's Clues." Says Nick Jr. chief Brown Johnson: "It's science meets story."

For a parent, it's natural to get excited when kids shout back at the TV during "Dora" or dance to "The Wiggles," a music-and-dance show that airs on Disney. That leads some parents to look at their TVs the way a previous generation looked to Dr. Spock. Colleen Breitbord of

Framingham, Mass., sees these programs as so vital to the development of her children, 7 and 2, that she installed a TV in the kitchen so they can watch "Arthur" and "Clifford" while they eat. "They learn so much," Breitbord says. "I think children who don't have the opportunity to watch some of this excellent programming miss out." In Ansonia, Conn., Patti Sarandrea uses Playhouse Disney, Nick Jr. and PBS "to reinforce what I teach the kids: colors, shapes, counting." At 3 1/2, her daughter can count to 25. Thanks to "Dora," her 18-month-old says "Hola."

As kids that young start tuning in, even "Sesame" is rethinking its approach. The show was originally designed for kids 3 to 5, but by the mid-1990s, many viewers were 2 or younger. The tykes seemed to tire of 60 minutes of fast-paced Muppet skits (the pacing was originally modeled after "Laugh-In" and TV commercials). So in 1999 "Sesame" introduced "Elmo's World," a 15-minute segment that ended every show. Even after that change, "Sesame" VP Lewis Bernstein noticed how today's little kids would sit still to watch 90-minute videotaped movies. So last February "Sesame" unveiled more longer segments. In "Journey to Ernie," Big Bird and Ernie play hide-and-seek against an animated background. Today ratings are up. The cast likes the new format, too. Before, stories were constantly cut short. "It was a little discombobulating," says Kevin Clash, the muscular, deep-voiced Muppet captain who brings Elmo to life. Now Elmo l-o-o-o-ves the longer stories.

So just how much good do these shows do? On a recent afternoon five undergrads sit around a table in the Yale University psychology department, playing a bizarre variation of bingo to try to find out. Together they watch three episodes of "Barney & Friends," each filling in hash marks on six sheets of paper. After each screening, they tally how many "teaching elements" they've counted. "I've got 9 vocabulary, 6 numbers... 11 sharing," says one student. Afterward Yale researcher Dorothy Singer will crunch the data and compare them with past seasons'. Her work has shown that the higher an episode's score, the more accurately children will be able to recount the plot and use the vocabulary words.

PBS does more of this postproduction "summative" research than other networks. Study after study shows "Sesame" viewers are better prepared for school. "Dragon Tales," a "Sesame"-produced animated show, helps kids become more

What's Right for My Kid?

We asked a panel of experts what kinds of shows are good for kids of various ages. In general, they said, trust your gut, avoid violent programs and stay tuned in to what they're watching.

Ages 2–5
The best shows for this age group—like **Dora the Explorer** and **Clifford the Big Red Dog**—are slow-moving and repetitive.

Ages 5–8
Kids begin to understand the vocabulary of TV: good and bad guys, for example. Try **Sagwa, the Chinese Siamese Cat**, based on a book by novelist Amy Tan.

Ages 9–11
At this age, kids, like adults, want TV that entertains. Shows like **Doug**, **Lizzie McGuire** and **The Wild Thornberrys** are appropriate. Characters have inner lives and complex motives.

Adolescents
Each family—and teenager—is different; TV-watching guidelines vary. Experts recommend **Gilmore Girls** and **Nick News** for "tweens" and younger teens. It's difficult to monitor older teens.

goal-oriented, and "Between the Lions," a puppet show produced by Boston's WGBH, helps kids' reading. Nick research offers proof of the effectiveness of "Dora" and "Blue's Clues." Disney doesn't do summative research; Disney execs say for now they'd rather devote resources to creating more shows for new viewers. Competitors suggest another reason: Disney's shows may not measure up. "It's scary to test," says "Sesame" research chief Rosemarie Truglio. "Maybe that's a piece of it—they're afraid."

Network-funded research won't change the minds of folks who say kids are better off with no television at all. That view gained strength in 1999, when the American

Academy of Pediatrics began discouraging any television for kids under 2. But when you parse the pro- and anti-TV rhetoric, the two sides don't sound as far apart as you'd suspect. The pro-TV crowd, for instance, quickly concedes that violent TV is damaging to kids, and that too many kids watch too many lousy shows. The anti-TV crowd objects mostly to TV's widespread overuse. Like Häagen-Dazs, TV seems to defy attempts at moderation, they suggest, so it's safer to abstain entirely. They believe overviewing especially affects children because of what Marie Winn, author of "The Plug-In Drug," calls the "displacement factor." That's when kids watch so much TV that they don't engage in enough brain-enhancing free play as toddlers or read enough during elementary school. Although pro-TV researchers say there are no data to support those fears, they agree it could be true. In fact, Anderson is currently conducting an experiment to measure whether having adult shows (like "Jeopardy!") playing in the background interferes with children's play. Bad news, soap-opera fans: the early data suggest it might.

Even shows the academics applaud could be better. In his UMass office, Anderson pops in a videotape of "Dora." It's one of the handful of shows that he advised during their conception. In this episode, Dora and Boots paddle a canoe down a river, around some rocks, toward a waterfall. *Toward* a waterfall? "If I'd read this script I'd have completely blocked this," he says, because it models unsafe behavior. Anderson has his arms crossed, his eyebrows scrunched; occasionally he talks to the screen, like an NFL fan disputing a bad call. "Oh, God, another dangerous thing," he says as Dora and Boots canoe under downed tree limbs. He still likes "Dora," but not this episode. "The education is a little thinner than I would wish, and it's a little dubious sending them on such a dumb journey." Then he watches "Bear" and "Blue's Clues," still nitpicking but happier.

EVEN AS THE KIDS' TV ENVIRONMENT improves, shortcomings remain. Only PBS airs educational shows for older elementary kids (examples: "Zoom" and "Cyberchase"). In focus groups, says Nickelodeon president Herb Scannell, older kids say they get enough learning in school; what commercial broadcaster is going to argue with the audience? Producers have other worries. Mitchell Kriegman, creator of "Bear in the Big Blue House," says parents could grow too enamored of obviously educational, A-

B-C/1-2-3-type shows. One of the most successful episodes of "Bear" involves potty training. "The [network's] reaction was 'Oh, my God, you can't say poop and pee on TV,'" Kriegman says. "Bear" did, and families loved it. Tighter curricula could dampen that creativity.

But those are worries for the future. For now, it's worth celebrating the improvements—however incremental—in shows for TV's youngest audience. Not everyone will want to raise a glass: like alcohol or guns, TV will be used sensibly in some homes and wreak havoc in others. Debating its net societal value will remain a never-ending pursuit. In the meantime parents live through these trade-offs daily. A recent issue of Parenting magazine offered the following question to help assess parenting skills: "I let my child watch TV only when... A) There's an educational show on public television, B) I have time to narrate the action for him... or C) I want to take a shower." The scoring code rates the answers: "A) Liar, B) Big fat liar, and C) You may not be perfect, but at least you're honest." As kids' TV raises the bar, parents who choose a different answer—D) All of the above—have a little less reason to feel guilty.

Raising a Moral Child

For many parents, nothing is more important than
teaching kids to know right from wrong. But when does
a sense of morality begin?

By Karen Springen

NANCY ROTERING BEAMS AS she recalls how her 3-year-old son Jack recently whacked his head against a drawer hard enough to draw blood. It's not that she found the injury amusing. But it did have a silver lining: Jack's wails prompted his 2-year-old brother, Andy, to offer him spontaneous consolation in the form of a cup of water and a favorite book, "Jamberry." "Want 'Berry' book, Jack?" he asked. Nancy loved Andy's "quick-thinking act of sympathy." "I was thrilled that such a tiny person could come up with such a big thought," she says. "He stepped up and offered Jack refreshment—and entertainment—to take his mind off the pain."

All parents have goals for their children, whether they center on graduating from high school or winning the Nobel Prize. But for a great many, nothing is more important than raising a "good" child—one who knows right from wrong, who is empathetic and who, like Andy, tries to live by the Golden Rule, even if he doesn't know yet what it is. Still, morality is an elusive—and highly subjective—character trait. Most parents know it when they see it. But how can they instill and nurture it in their children? Parents must lead by example. "The way to raise a moral child is to be a moral person," says Tufts University psychologist David Elkind. "If you're honest and straightforward and decent and caring, that's what children learn." Humans seem innately inclined to behave empathetically; doctors talk about "contagious crying" among newborns in the hospital nursery. And not all children of murderers or even tax cheats follow in their parents' footsteps. "What's surprising is how many kids raised in immoral

homes grow up moral," says New York psychiatrist Alvin Rosenfeld.

81% of mothers and 78% of fathers say they plan eventually to send their young child to Sunday school or some other kind of religious training

Parents have always been preoccupied with instilling moral values in their children. But in today's fast-paced world, where reliable role models are few and acts of violence by children are increasingly common, the quest to raise a moral child has taken on new urgency. Child criminals grow ever younger; in August, a 6-year-old California girl (with help from a 5-year-old friend) smothered her 3-year-old brother with a pillow. Such horrific crimes awaken a dark, unspoken fear in many parents: Is my child capable of committing such an act? And can I do anything to make sure that she won't?

There are no guarantees. But parents are increasingly aware that even very young children can grasp and exhibit moral behaviors—even if the age at which they become "morally accountable" remains under debate. According to the Roman Catholic Church, a child reaches "the age of reason"

by 7. Legally, each state determines how old a child must be to be held responsible for his acts, ranging from 7 to 15. Child experts are reluctant to offer a definitive age for accountability. But they agree that in order to be held morally responsible, children must have both an emotional and a cognitive awareness of right and wrong—in other words, to know in their heads as well as feel in their hearts that what they did was wrong. Such morality doesn't appear overnight but emerges slowly, over time. And according to the latest research, the roots of morality first appear in the earliest months of an infant's life. "It begins the day they're born, and it's not complete until the day they die," says child psychiatrist Elizabeth Berger, author of "Raising Children with Character."

It's never too early to start. Parents who respond instantly to a newborn's cries lay an important moral groundwork. "You work to understand what the baby's feeling," says Barbara Howard, a specialist in developmental behavioral pediatrics at the Johns Hopkins University School of Medicine. "Then the baby will work to understand what other people are feeling." Indeed, empathy is among the first moral emotions to develop. Even before the age of 2, children will try to comfort an upset child—though usually in an "egocentric" way, says Marvin Berkowitz, professor of character education at the University of Missouri-St. Louis: "I might give them *my* teddy even though your teddy is right there." To wit: Andy Rotering brought his brother his own favorite book.

Morality consists of not only caring for others but also following basic rules of conduct. Hurting another child, for instance, is never OK. But how you handle it depends on your child's age. If a 1-year-old is hitting or biting, "you simply say 'no' firmly, and you remove the child from the situation," says Craig Ramey, author of "Right From Birth." But once a child acquires language skills, parents can provide more detail. "You can say, 'We don't hit in this family'," says David Fassler, chairman of the American Psychiatric Association's council on children, adolescents and their families. "You can say, 'Everyone feels like hitting and biting from time to time. My job is to help you figure out what to do with those kinds of feelings'." Suggest alternatives—punching a pillow, drawing a sad picture or lying quietly on a bed.

Children grow more moral with time. As Lawrence Kohlberg of Harvard University has said, kids go through progressive stages of moral development. Between 1 and 2, children understand that there are rules—but usually follow them only if an adult is watching, says Barbara Howard. After 2, they start obeying rules—inconsistently—even if an adult isn't there. And as any adult who has ever driven faster than 65mph knows, people continue "circumstantial" morality throughout life, says Howard. "People aren't perfect, even when they know what the right thing to do is."

Though all children are born with the capacity to act morally, that ability can be lost. Children who are abused or neglected often fail to acquire a basic sense of trust and belonging that influences how people behave when they're older. "They may be callous because no one has ever shown them enough of the caring to put that into their system," says Howard. Ramey argues that "we come to expect the world to be the way we've experienced it"—whether that means cold and forbidding or warm and loving. According to Stanford developmental psychologist William Damon, morality can also be hampered by the practice of "bounding"—limiting children's contact with the world only to people who are like them—as opposed to "bridging," or exposing them to people of different backgrounds. "You can empathize with everyone who looks just like you and learn to exclude everyone who doesn't," says Damon. A juvenile delinquent may treat his sister gently—but beat up an old woman of another race. "The bridging approach ends up with a more moral child," says Damon.

No matter how hard you try, you can't force your child to be moral. But there are things you can do to send him in the right direction:

If you're honest, straightforward, decent and caring, that's what children learn'

• Decide what values—such as honesty and hard work—are most important to you. Then do what you want your children to do. "If you volunteer in your community, and you take your child, they will do that themselves," says Joseph Hagan, chairman of the American Academy of Pediatrics' committee on the psychosocial aspects of child and family health. "If you stub your toe, and all you can say is the F word, guess what your child is going to say when they stub their toe?"

Always help your child see things from the other person's point of view

---

• Praise children liberally. "You have to ignore the behaviors you don't want and highlight the behaviors you do want," says Kori Skidmore, a staff psychologist at Children's Memorial Hospital in Chicago. Rather than criticizing a toddler for his messy room, compliment him on the neat corner, recommends Darien, Ill., pediatrician Garry Gardner. Use "no" judiciously, otherwise "a child starts to feel like 'I'm always doing something wrong'," says the APA's Fassler. "If you're trying to teach a child to share, then praise them when they share. Don't just scold them when they're reluctant to."

• Take advantage of teachable moments. When Gardner's kids were 3 and 4, they found a $10 bill in front of a store. Gardner talked to them about the value of the money—and they agreed to give it to the shopkeeper in case someone returned for it. They mutually decided "finders keepers" shouldn't apply to anything worth more than a quarter. "Certainly you wouldn't go back and say, 'I found a penny'," says Gardner. Parents can also use famous parables, like "The Boy Who Cried Wolf," or Bible stories to illustrate their point.

• Watch what your child watches. TV and computer games can glorify immoral behavior. "If children are unsupervised, watching violence or promiscuity on TV, they're going to have misguided views about how to treat other people," says Karen Bohlin, director of Boston University's Center for the Advancement of Ethics and Character. "Children by nature are impulsive and desperately need guidance to form good habits. That can come only from a loving caregiver who's by their side, teaching them how to play nicely, safely, fairly, how to take turns, how to put things back where they belong, how to speak respectfully."

• Discuss consequences. Say, " 'Look how sad Mary is because you broke her favorite doll'," explains Berkowitz. Parents can also ask their children to help them pick fair punishments—for example, no TV. "They're learning that their voice is valued," says Berkowitz. Allowing kids to make choices—even about something as trivial as what to have for lunch—will enable them to make moral ones later. "If they don't learn peanut butter and jelly at 2, how are they going to decide about drinking when they're 14?" asks family physician Nancy Dickey, editor in chief of Medem, an online patient-information center.

• Always help them see things from the other person's point of view. If a child bops his new sibling, try to reflect the newborn's outlook. Say, " 'Oh, my, that must hurt. How would you feel if someone did that to you?'" says Howard. Gardner encourages parents whose kids find stray teddy bears to ask their children how sad they would feel if they lost their favorite stuffed animal—and how happy they would be if someone returned it. "It's one thing to hear about it at Sunday school," he says. And another to live the "do unto others" rule in real life.

In the end, the truest test of whether a parent has raised a moral child is how that young person acts when Mom or Dad is not around. With a lot of love and luck, your child will grow up to feel happy and blessed—and to want to help others who aren't as fortunate. Now, *that's* something to be proud of.

UNIT 3

Development During Childhood: Cognition and Schooling

Unit Selections

Key Points to Consider

- What is implicit learning? Why is it of interest to cognitive scientists?

- If dyslexia is a biologically based brain glitch, can instruction repair the short circuitry?

- Should metacognitive strategies be taught to children? Why?

- Is attention deficit hyperactivity disorder (ADHD) real? Should children with ADHD be given Ritalin, a stimulant drug?

- Will computer technology change the way students are educated? How?

- Are there gender differences in brain development? Should boys and girls be educated differently to optimize their learning based on brain development?

- Are the autistic spectrum disorders an exaggerated version of the male-type brain?

 **Links: www.dushkin.com/online/**
These sites are annotated in the World Wide Web pages.

Children Now
http://www.childrennow.org

Council for Exceptional Children
http://www.cec.sped.org

Educational Resources Information Center (ERIC)
http://www.eric.ed.gov/

Federation of Behavioral, Psychological, and Cognitive Science
http://federation.apa.org

The National Association for the Education of Young Children (NAEYC)
http://www.naeyc.org

Project Zero
http://pzweb.harvard.edu

The mental process of knowing—cognition—includes aspects such as sensing, understanding, associating, and discriminating. Cognitive research has been hampered by the limitations of trying to understand what is happening inside the minds of living persons without doing harm. It has also been challenged by problems with defining concepts such as intuition, unconsciousness, unawareness, implicit learning, incomprehension, and all the aspects of knowing situated behind our mental perceptions (metacognition). Many kinds of achievement that require cognitive processes (awareness, perception, reasoning, judgment) cannot be measured with intelligence tests or with achievement tests. Intelligence is the capacity to acquire and apply knowledge. It is usually assumed that intelligence can be measured. The ratio of tested mental age to chronological age is expressed as an intelligence quotient (IQ). For years, school children have been classified by IQ scores. The links between IQ scores and school achievement are positive, but no significant correlations exist between IQ scores and life success. Consider, for example, the motor coordination and kinesthetic abilities of former baseball player Cal Ripken, Jr. He had an intelligence about the use of his body that surpassed the capacity of most other athletes and nonathletes. A Harvard psychologist, Howard Gardner, has suggested that there are at least eight different kinds of intelligences.

Some psychologists have suggested that uncovering more about how the brain processes various types of intelligences will soon be translated into new educational practices. Today's tests of intelligence only measure abilities in the logical/mathematical, spatial, and linguistic areas of intelligence, which is what schools now teach. Jean Piaget, the Swiss founder of cognitive psychology, was involved in the creation of the world's first intelligence test, the Binet-Simon Scale. He became disillusioned with trying to quantify how much children knew at different chronological ages. He was much more intrigued with what they did not know, what they knew incorrectly, and how they came to know the world in the ways in which they knew it. He started the Centre for Genetic Epistemology in Geneva, Switzerland, where he began to study the nature, extent, and validity of children's knowledge. He discovered qualitative, rather than quantitative, differences in cognitive processes over the life span. Infants know the world through their senses and their motor responses. After language develops, toddlers and preschoolers know the world through their language/symbolic perspectives. Piaget likened early childhood cognitive processes to bad thought, or thought akin to daydreams. By school age, children know things in concrete terms, which allows them to number, classify, conserve, think backwards and forwards, and think about their own thinking (metacognition). However, Piaget believed that children do not acquire the cognitive processes necessary to think abstractly and to use clear, consistent, logical patterns of thought until early adolescence. Their moral sense and personal philosophies of behavior are not completed until adulthood.

The first article in this unit, "Implicit Learning," considers the difficulties in defining and operationalizing what is meant by "implicit" (implied, but not directly apparent) knowledge. Learning which occurs without awareness is an active area of cognitive re-

search. The authors believe that it exists and also believe that it will be understood better in the near future thanks to improved methodology, brain-imaging, and computational modeling. Researchers must still resolve the issue of what is meant by implicit learning.

The second selection gives the reader a glimpse of the world of children with dyslexia (reading difficulties). One in five children, both girls and boys, struggles to learn to read. Neuroscientific research, using functional magnetic resonance imaging (FMRI), has new evidence that the causes of dyslexia are biological. The brain experiences glitches getting information from the sound producer to areas which analyze and detect words. Each child with dyslexia is different. Early appropriate instruction can give amazing results.

The third cognition selection deals with metacognitive knowledge, the mental process of reflecting on, monitoring, and regulating what one knows. Deanna Kuhn explains why metacognition is an important developmental and educational

goal. She traces its origins in childhood to its performance in adulthood, suggesting how it could be optimized. This article stimulates great discussions about the major concepts of critical thinking.

The first schooling selection addresses the issue of defining and assessing attention-deficit hyperactivity disorders (ADHD) for purposes of school placement and educational programming. Rush Limbaugh, other conservative commentators, and some politicians, have stated their beliefs that ADHD may be a hoax. They argue that giving the diagnosis to certain students (usually male, often problem children) may be an excuse to coddle them rather than teach them. Many people, even those who believe ADHD is real, feel that it is wrong to medicate children with ADHD with Ritalin. The author explains why he has accepted both the disorder and the need for treatment.

The second school-related article, "The Future of Computer Technology in K-12 Education," discusses the power of computers in the new millennium. How will this emerging technological force change education? Frederick Bennett believes that exceptionally good teachers are in the minority, and many teachers are not talented in teaching. So far computers in schools have not improved the quality of academics very much either. Dr. Ben-

nett's alternate solution is to allow computers to tutor students directly and individually. He cites the successes of some school systems that have tried this approach. Teachers would assume new roles as group leaders, guides, and leader-teachers.

The third school-related article, "The New Gender Gap," opens the door for discussing gender equality in contemporary schooling. Are boys being short-changed educationally in order to promote girls?

"Girls, Boys, and Autism" presents new information about the spectrum of brain differences given the umbrella coverage of autistic disorders. Neuroscientists are beginning to view these disabilities (including Asperger's syndrome) as an exaggerated version of the male-type brain. Autistic people are extreme systemizers with an inability to intuit feelings and empathize (abilities of the female-type brain). They may find fractal geometry easier than communicating.

In the last article of this section, Peter Schrag discusses the backlash against proficiency testing in "High Stakes Are for Tomatoes," questioning whether accountability in math, science, and English discriminates against other children who have high motivation and potential but different types of intelligences.

Implicit Learning

Peter A. Frensch[1] and Dennis Rünger
Department of Psychology, Humboldt University, Berlin, Germany

Abstract
Implicit learning appears to be a fundamental and ubiquitous process in cognition. Although defining and operationalizing implicit learning remains a central theoretical challenge, scientists' understanding of implicit learning has progressed significantly. Beyond establishing the existence of "learning without awareness," current research seeks to identify the cognitive processes that support implicit learning and addresses the relationship between learning and awareness of what was learned. The emerging view of implicit learning emphasizes the role of associative learning mechanisms that exploit statistical dependencies in the environment in order to generate highly specific knowledge representations.

Keywords
cognitive psychology; learning; consciousness; awareness

Have you ever wondered why it is that you can speak your native language so well without making any grammatical errors although you do not know many of the grammatical rules you follow? Have you ever wondered how it is that you can walk properly although you cannot describe the rules of mechanics your body must certainly follow? These two examples point to an important human property, namely, the ability to adapt to environmental constraints—to learn—in the absence of any knowledge about how the adaptation is achieved. *Implicit learning*—laxly defined as learning without awareness—is seemingly ubiquitous in everyday life.

In this article, we try to provide an overview of the difficulties research on implicit learning has been facing and of the advances that have been made in scientists' understanding of the concept. More specifically, we discuss three separate issues. First, we address what is meant by implicit learning and how the concept has been empirically approached in the recent past. Second, we summarize what is currently known with some certainty about the cognitive processes underlying implicit learning and the mental representations that are acquired through it. Third, we discuss some of the most important current topics of investigation.

DEFINITION AND OPERATIONALIZATION

The one basic theoretical issue that reigns supreme among the difficulties facing researchers concerns the definition and operationalization of implicit learning. Although it seems clear that implicit learning needs to be viewed in opposition to learning that is not implicit (often called explicit, hypothesis-driven learning), it has so far proven extremely difficult to provide a satisfactory definition of implicit learning. At least a dozen different definitions have been offered in the field.

One important consequence of the heterogeneity of definitions is that different researchers have operationalized implicit learning in different ways. For example, Arthur Reber, whose early work in the 1960s rekindled interest in implicit learning, has done most of his empirical work with artificial-grammar-learning tasks. In these tasks, participants are asked to memorize a set of letter strings, such as "XXRTRXV" and "QQWMWQP," that are, unbeknownst to the participants, generated by some rules. After the memorization phase, participants are told that the strings they memorized followed certain rules, and are asked to classify new strings as grammatical (i.e., following the rules) or not. Typically, participants can perform this classification task with accuracy better than would be expected by chance, despite remaining unable to verbally describe the rules.

Thus, in a grammar-learning task, participants learn about permissible and nonpermissible combinations of letters that are presented simultaneously. By comparison, in another task often used to investigate implicit learning, the serial reaction time task (SRTT), participants learn about permissible and nonpermissible combinations of spatial locations that occur over time. In the SRTT, participants are asked to select and depress a key that matches each of the locations at which a stimulus appears on a screen. The sequence of locations at which the stimulus appears is fixed. In general, participants seem to be able to learn the sequence of spatial locations even when they are not able to verbally describe it.

Divergent definitions of implicit learning entail divergent operationalizations of the concept, but even researchers who agree in their definitions might use experimental tasks that differ in what exactly participants might learn. Therefore, it remains an open empirical issue to what extent results from a given task that has been used to probe implicit learning can be generalized to other tasks. This point leads to our first conclusion:

- *Conclusion 1.* Implicit learning of Task A is not necessarily comparable to implicit learning of Task B. Neither the properties of the learning mechanisms involved nor the acquired mental representations need be the same. It is even conceivable that implicit learning of Task A might be possible, but implicit learning of Task B might not.

THE KEY ISSUE

Regardless of how implicit learning is defined and operationalized, the key empirical issue that research needs to address is whether or not learning that is "implicit" is possible, and if it is, whether implicit learning is different from learning that is "not implicit." Many researchers have for practical reasons adopted as their definition of implicit learning "the capacity to learn without awareness of the products of learning." Thus, learning is assumed to be "implicit" when participants are unaware of what they learned. Alternatively, learning is assumed not to be implicit when participants are aware of what they learned. In other words, implicit learning is defined in terms of its product rather than the properties of the learning process.

Various measures have been proposed to assess awareness of the products of learning. The most notable measures are verbal reports and forced-choice tests (such as recognition tests).

Participants in implicit-learning experiments have consistently been shown to be able to acquire knowledge that they cannot verbally describe. This appears to be true for a wide variety of tasks, including the grammar-learning and sequence-learning tasks we described earlier. Thus, if verbal report is used to assess awareness of acquired knowledge, many experimental findings appear to support the conclusion that implicit learning is possible.

However, many authors have argued that verbal reports may have poor validity. First, it has been argued that the verbal-report

data do not pass the information criterion; that is, the information assessed by verbal recall tests is not always the same information that has led to the demonstrated learning. Second, verbal recall tests might not pass the sensitivity criterion; that is, they may not provide a level of sensitivity that is comparable to that of tests demonstrating learning in the first place. Many researchers have therefore suggested that awareness should be assessed by forced-choice tests, such as recognition tests, rather than verbal recall.

In the grammar-learning paradigm, participants are sometimes asked to complete recognition tests after they have categorized letter strings as grammatical or nongrammatical. For example, in some studies participants were asked to indicate for each letter string which particular letters they thought made the string grammatical or not. It was found that participants' markings correlated with their classification performance, suggesting at least partial awareness of the knowledge learned.

Similar findings have been obtained in studies that have used other implicit-learning paradigms. For example, after participants had completed the SRTT, they were presented sequence patterns of varying lengths in numerical form. Each sequence (e.g., 123432) denoted a series of locations on the computer screen. Participants were asked to mark patterns that they had encountered during the experiment as true and patterns that they had not seen as false. It was found that participants' recognition scores correlated with their learning scores for the SRTT. In general, many different studies using different experimental paradigms have used forced-choice tests to assess awareness of the acquired knowledge, and these studies appear not to support the existence of implicit learning.

However, it has been argued that this particular interpretation rests on the assumption that the forced-choice tests are pure assessments of awareness (i.e., are process pure). This is almost certainly not the case. Indeed, participants might choose a correct answer on a forced-choice test not because they are aware of the fact that it is the correct answer but because they rely on some intuition that they are not able to express. The growing understanding that tests are rarely process pure has fostered the use of new methodologies that are not based on this assumption. For example, Jacoby's process dissociation procedure offers a measure of awareness that is derived from experimental conditions that are believed to trigger both implicit and nonimplicit processes simultaneously. This consideration of how awareness should be assessed leads to our second conclusion:

- *Conclusion 2.* Many researchers have tried to avoid the difficult issue of how to define implicit learning and have, often without stating so explicitly, adopted the stance that implicit learning is the capacity to learn without awareness of the products of learning. However, it has become clear that the amount of support for implicit learning varies considerably with the specific measure that is selected to assess awareness of what was learned. Thus, by avoiding the issue of how to define implicit learning, researchers have introduced the problem of how to define awareness. In the end, the definitional question has not been resolved, but has merely been transferred from one concept to another.

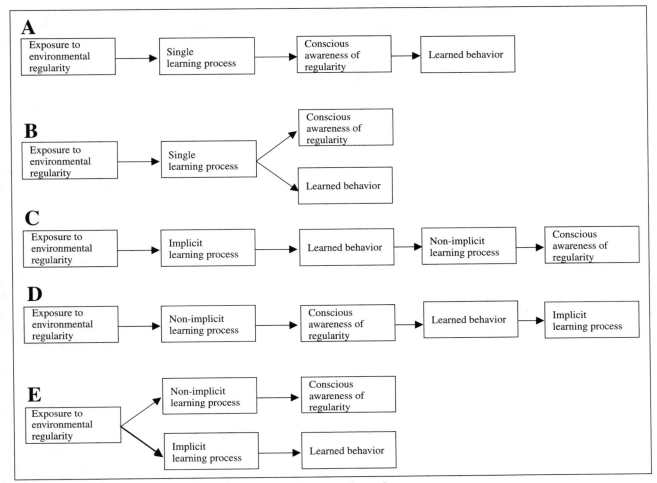

Fig. 1 Possible relations between learning and awareness of what was learned.

MECHANISMS OF LEARNING AND AWARENESS

Even when implicit learning (in the sense of learning that yields knowledge the learner is not aware of) is demonstrated conclusively, one learns little about the mechanisms underlying implicit learning. It is helpful to consider the different ways in which, in principle, learning and awareness of the products of learning might be related. Figure 1 depicts five of the many distinct possibilities that have been proposed.

First, it is, of course, conceivable that learning and awareness of what has been learned are perfectly correlated. According to this proposal, implicit learning does not exist. As is shown in Figure 1a, learning might be achieved by a single mechanism that generates memory representations a learner is always aware of.

According to the four remaining possibilities, learning and awareness need not be—but might be—perfectly correlated. According to the second possibility, depicted in Figure 1b, a single learning mechanism is assumed to create memory representations that control behavior. Some of the learned memory representations might be open to awareness; some might not be.

The last three possibilities (Figs. 1c–1e) allow for truly implicit learning. According to the third possibility, an implicit-learning mechanism might generate memory representations that control behavior. The perception of one's own behavior, in turn, might lead to nonimplicit (i.e., hypothesis-testing) learning that might generate awareness of what was learned (Fig. 1c). Under this view, the effects of implicit learning are an important trigger for nonimplicit learning. For example, a tennis player might perceive an increased accuracy of her serve. She might then conclude that the reason for this improvement is to be found in a slightly higher toss of the ball.

The fourth possibility is that nonimplicit learning might lead to awareness of what was learned, and might control behavior. The expression of behavior, in turn, might provide the input for the operation of an implicit-learning mechanism (Fig. 1d). For example, most tennis players know that solid ground strokes require a player to move toward the approaching ball instead of away from it. The conscious effort to engage in a forward movement may lead to learning within the motor systems that lies largely outside of conscious awareness.

The fifth possibility, shown in Figure 1e, is that there exist two distinct learning mechanisms, with one of the mechanisms generating memory representations that a learner is aware of, and the other mechanism generating representations that a learner is not aware of but that nevertheless control behavior.

Most of the research that has been concerned with the difference between implicit and nonimplicit learning has not addressed which possibility in Figure 1 describes the nature of implicit learning, but rather has tried to demonstrate that learning is possible in the absence of learners' awareness of the acquired knowledge. However, several attempts have been made to distinguish the two-systems hypothesis (i.e., that there are separate systems for implicit and nonimplicit learning), represented by the possibilities depicted in 1c through 1e, from the single-system hypothesis, represented by the possibilities depicted in 1a and 1b. The relative adequacy of these two hypotheses can be assessed by exploring the potentially differing influence of variables such as intention to learn, attention, age of participants, individual differences in intelligence, stimulus complexity, and task demands on learning with awareness and on learning without awareness.

For example, researchers have explored the possibility that implicit and nonimplicit learning might be differentially affected by age. With the SRTT, it has been found that implicit learning is less affected by age than is learning that is based on hypothesis testing. Indeed, implicit learning in the SRTT does not appear to begin to decline until relatively old age, and even then, the elderly display performance levels that are much closer to those of younger adults for implicit-learning tasks than for nonimplicit-learning tasks involving, for example, problem solving, reasoning, and long-term memory. On the whole, this research therefore lends some credibility to the multiple-systems view.

Also, both neuropsychological studies and neuroimaging studies have addressed the adequacy of the multiple-systems and single-system hypotheses. For example, early studies suggested that even densely amnesic patients can show near-normal implicit learning in both the grammar-learning and the sequence-learning paradigms, although they are specifically impaired on recognition and prediction tasks. More recent critical reexaminations have, however, demonstrated that amnesic patients do seem to show a deficit in implicit learning compared with normal control participants; it is therefore unclear whether or not the findings, on the whole, support the multiple-systems view.

Brain-imaging techniques have increasingly been used to study implicit learning in the SRTT. Although some results suggest that partially distinctive brain areas are involved in implicit and nonimplicit forms of learning, it is, at present, not clear whether these findings should be interpreted as evidence supporting the multiple-systems view or as evidence supporting a "single-system plus awareness" view (depicted in Fig. 1b).

Consideration of the cognitive mechanisms that might be involved in implicit learning leads to our third conclusion:

• *Conclusion 3.* Defining implicit learning with respect to awareness of the products of learning has drawn attention away from the mechanisms that are responsible for the generation of different forms of knowledge. Despite a continuously increasing amount of empirical data, the debate between multiple-systems proponents and single-system

proponents has not been settled yet. Furthermore, the question of how exactly awareness and learning might be interrelated has only recently begun to be addressed empirically.

IMPORTANT ADVANCES MADE

If one agrees with the use of verbal-report measures to assess awareness, then recent research on implicit learning has modified earlier theoretical beliefs in important ways. Earlier work had characterized implicit learning as a mechanism by which abstract knowledge of regularities that are present in the environment is acquired automatically and unintentionally by mere exposure to relevant instances. The proposal of a smart unconscious was based, to a large extent, on empirical findings with the grammar-learning task that appeared to show that participants possessed abstract knowledge about the rules of the grammar that went beyond the surface characteristics of the information encountered. This claim seemed further supported by findings indicating that implicitly acquired knowledge may transfer across modalities; for example, learning from a task involving written letters (visual stimuli) can transfer to performance in a task involving letter sounds (auditory stimuli).

This view has been challenged, however, by many recent findings. For example, it has been repeatedly shown that implicitly acquired knowledge might consist of little more than short fragments or chunks of the materials encountered in an implicit-learning situation. In the wake of these findings, neural-network models and fragment-based models that are capable of simulating a great deal of the available experimental findings have been developed. These models utilize representations of elementary stimuli in the learning situation (e.g., representations of letters in a grammar-learning task) and associations between the representations. Learning consists of a continuous, incremental change in the associative pattern that is sensitive to the statistical features of the set of items or events encountered. Thus, a representation of the implicit-learning situation that is shaped by statistical constraints gradually evolves. Although the characterization of implicitly acquired knowledge is still a matter of debate, the current trend is to assume that abstract knowledge might not be implicitly generated.

Many recent studies have explored whether implicit learning, unlike nonimplicit learning (i.e., explicit hypothesis testing), proceeds automatically, without the use of attentional resources. By far, most of these studies have used the SRTT, often manipulating the amount of attentional resources available to participants by asking them to perform the SRTT either by itself or together with a secondary task (typically a tone-counting task).

In general, it has been found that implicit learning takes place both in the presence and in the absence of a secondary task. What remains unclear, at present, is the extent to which implicit learning is affected by the attention manipulation. Some researchers argue that the secondary task interferes with task performance rather than with implicit learning proper (i.e., that the secondary task impedes the expression of what has been learned). Under this view, implicit learning does not depend on the availability of attentional resources. Others take the stance that the learning process itself is adversely affected by the presence of a secondary task and thus requires attentional resources.

On the whole, the experiments that have been conducted all suffer from the problem that attention itself is an ill-defined concept that might refer to both mental capacity and selection. In the latter sense, "attention" points to the problem of allocating cognitive resources to a specific item or event. When "attention" is used synonymously with "mental capacity," it instead refers to a limitation of cognitive resources that becomes apparent when resources have to be shared by concurrent cognitive processes. When these two factors are separately and experimentally manipulated, it appears that implicit learning occurs only when stimuli are relevant to the task and are attended to, but that implicit learning may require no or very little mental capacity.

Recent advances in researchers' understanding of implicit learning lead to our fourth conclusion:

- *Conclusion 4.* The early proposal of a smart unconscious capable of acquiring abstract knowledge in an effortless, automatic manner has been replaced recently by the assumption of one or more implicit learning mechanisms that operate mostly associatively. These mechanisms pick up statistical dependencies encountered in the environment and generate highly specific knowledge representations. It is likely that the mechanisms operate only on information that is attended to and that is relevant to the response to be made.

CONCLUSIONS

Researchers' understanding of implicit learning has come a long way. Today, many believe that implicit learning exists, and furthermore that it is based on relatively simple learning mechanisms. These mechanisms associate environmental stimuli that are attended to and that are relevant for behavior. Despite the re-

cent advances, however, the field still suffers from a number of unresolved empirical and theoretical issues. First, there exist conflicting results regarding the role of attention in implicit learning. Second, the exact relation between learning and awareness (see Fig. 1) is very much unknown. Third, the key theoretical issue of how to define implicit learning has still not been resolved.

We strongly believe that progress on the former two (empirical) issues will be made soon and will be based on improved methodology and the joint use of computational modeling and functional brain-imaging techniques. Progress on the key theoretical issue can come, however, only from theoretical advances in understanding of the concepts of "consciousness," "awareness," and "intention." To achieve this progress might require the joint efforts of philosophers, neuroscientists, and cognitive psychologists.

Recommended reading

Berry, D.C., & Dienes, Z. (1993). *Implicit learning: Theoretical and empirical issues.* Hove, England: Erlbaum.

Cleeremans, A. (1993). *Mechanisms of implicit learning: Connectionist models of sequence processing.* Cambridge, MA: MIT Press.

Reber, A.S. (1993). *Implicit learning and tacit knowledge: An essay on the cognitive unconscious.* New York: Oxford University Press.

Stadler, M.A., & Frensch, P.A. (Eds.). (1998). *Handbook of implicit learning.* Thousand Oaks, CA: Sage.

Note

1. Address correspondence to Peter A. Frensch, Department of Psychology, Humboldt University, Hausvogteiplatz 5-7, D-10177 Berlin, Germany; e-mail: peter.frensch@psychologie.hu-berlin.de.

The New Science of
DYSLEXIA

Why some children struggle so much with reading used to be a mystery. Now researchers know what's wrong—and what to do about it

By Christine Gorman

WHEN SEAN SLATTERY, 17, LOOKS AT A PAGE OF text, he can see the letters. He can tell you the letters' names. He can even tell you what sounds those letters make. But it often takes a while for the articulate high school student from Simi Valley, Calif., to tell you what words those letters form. "I see a wall," he says. "I see a hurdle I have to get over." Some words are easier for Sean to figure out than others. "I can get longer words, like *electricity*," he says. "But I have trouble with shorter words, like *four* or *year*."

Slattery has dyslexia, a reading disorder that persists despite good schooling and normal or even above-average intelligence. It's a handicap that affects up to 1 in 5 schoolchildren. Yet the exact nature of the problem has eluded doctors, teachers, parents and dyslexics themselves since it was first described more than a century ago. Indeed, it is so hard for skilled readers to imagine what it's like not to be able to effortlessly absorb the printed word that they often suspect the real problem is laziness or obstinacy or a

proud parent's inability to recognize that his or her child isn't that smart after all.

The mystery—and perhaps some of the stigma—may finally be starting to lift. The more researchers learn about dyslexia, the more they realize it's a flaw not of character but of biology—specifically, the biology of the brain. No, people with dyslexia are not brain damaged. Brain scans show their cerebrums are perfectly normal, if not extraordinary. Dyslexics, in fact, seem to have a distinct advantage when it comes to thinking outside the box.

But a growing body of scientific evidence suggests there is a glitch in the neurological wiring of dyslexics that makes reading extremely difficult for them. Fortunately, the science also points to new strategies for overcoming the glitch. The most successful programs focus on strengthening the brain's aptitude for linking letters to the sounds they represent. (More later on why that matters.) Some studies suggest that the right kinds of instruction provided early enough may rewire the brain so

thoroughly that the neurological glitch disappears entirely.

The new science may even be starting to change public policy. When the U.S. government launched an education initiative in 2001 called No Child Left Behind, its administrators made clear that their funding would go only to reading programs that are based on solid evidence of the sort that has been uncovered in dyslexia research. "In education, the whole idea that there is evidence that some programs are more effective than others is new," says Dr. Sally Shaywitz, a Yale neuroscientist who has written a fascinating new book, *Overcoming Dyslexia* (Alfred A. Knopf; April 2003), that details the latest brain-scan research—much of it done in her lab. "The good news is we really understand the steps of how you become a reader and how you become a skilled reader," she says.

Along the way, a number of myths about dyslexia have been exploded. You may have heard, for example, that it's all about flipping letters, writing them backward, Toys "R" Us style. Wrong. Practically all children make mirror copies of letters as they learn to write, although dyslexics do it more. You may believe that more boys than girls are dyslexic. Wrong again. Boys are just more likely to get noticed because they often vent their frustration by acting out. You may think that dyslexia can be outgrown. This is perhaps the most damaging myth, because it leads parents to delay seeking the extra instruction needed to keep their children from falling further behind. "The majority of students who get identified with learning disorders get identified between the ages of 11 and 17," says Robert Pasternack, U.S. assistant secretary for Special Education and Rehabilitative Services. "And that's too late." They can still learn to read, but it will always be a struggle.

This is not to say that dyslexics can't succeed despite their disability. In fact, dyslexics are overrepresented in the top ranks of artists, scientists and business executives. Perhaps because their brains are wired differently, dyslexics are often skilled problem solvers, coming at solutions from novel or surprising angles and making conceptual leaps that leave tunnel-visioned, step-by-step sequential thinkers in the dust. They talk about being able to see things in 3-D Technicolor or as a multidimensional chess game. It may also be that their early struggle with reading better prepares them for dealing with adversity in a volatile, fast-changing world.

But that struggle can cut both ways. Dyslexics are also overrepresented in the prison population. According to Frank Wood, a professor of neurology at Wake Forest University in Winston-Salem, N.C., new research shows that children with dyslexia are more likely than nondyslexics to drop out of school, withdraw from friends and family or attempt suicide.

T HE STAKES HAVE NEVER BEEN HIGHER. Right now in the U.S. there are almost 3 million students in spe-

cial-education classes specifically because they can't read. Most of them are probably dyslexic. But there are other slow readers who are simply overlooked—ignored in crowded classrooms or dismissed as discipline problems. Unless corrective action is taken, their self-confidence often crumbles as they see other students progressing. Even worse, their peers may taunt or ostracize them—a situation that Sean Slattery's mother Judy remembers all too well. "Sean cried for four hours every day after kindergarten," she says. "He was so unhappy."

To be sure, researchers still don't understand everything there is to know about learning disabilities. Dyslexia, for one, may consist of several subtypes. "It would be very dangerous to assume that every child with reading problems is uniform and has the same kinds of breakdowns preventing him from learning to read," says Dr. Mel Levine, a pediatrician and author of several influential books about learning disabilities and dyslexia, including *A Mind at a Time*. But whatever the exact nature of the deficit, the search for answers begins with the written word.

When you think about it, that anyone can read at all is something of a miracle. Reading requires your brain to rejigger its visual and speech processors in such a way that artificial markings, such as the letters on a piece of paper, become linked to the sounds they represent. It's not enough simply to hear and understand different words. Your brain has to pull them apart into their constituent sounds, or phonemes. When you *see* the written word cat, your brain must *hear* the sounds /k/ ... /a/... /t/ and associate the result with an animal that purrs.

Unlike speech, which any developmentally intact child will eventually pick up by imitating others who speak, reading must be actively taught. That makes sense from an evolutionary point of view. Linguists believe that the spoken word is 50,000 to 100,000 years old. But

the written word—and therefore the possibility of reading—has probably been around for no more than 5,000 years. "That's not long enough for our brains to evolve certain regions for just that purpose," says Guinevere Eden, a professor of pediatrics at Georgetown University in Washington, who also uses brain scans to study reading. "We're probably using a whole network of areas in the brain that were originally designed to do something slightly different." As Eden puts it, the brain is moonlighting—and some of the resulting glitches have yet to be ironed out.

To understand what sorts of glitches we're talking about, it helps to know a little about how the brain works. Researchers have long been aware that the two halves, or hemispheres, of the brain tend to specialize in different tasks. Although the division of labor is not absolute, the left side is particularly adept at processing language while the right is more attuned to analyzing spatial cues. The specialization doesn't stop there. Within each hemisphere, different regions of the brain break down various tasks even further. So reading a sonnet, catching a ball or recognizing a face requires the complex interaction of a number of different regions of the brain.

Most of what neuroscientists know about the brain has come from studying people who were undergoing brain surgery or had suffered brain damage. Clearly, this is not the most convenient way to learn about the brain, especially if you want to know more about what passes for normal. Even highly detailed pictures from the most advanced computer-enhanced X-ray imaging machines could reveal only the organ's basic anatomy, not how the various parts worked together. What researchers needed was a scanner that didn't subject patients to radiation and that showed which parts of the brain are most active in healthy subjects as they perform various intellectual tasks. What was needed was a breakthrough in technology.

That breakthrough came in the 1990s with the development of a technique called functional magnetic resonance imaging (fMRI). Basically, fMRI allows researchers to see which parts of the brain are getting the most blood—and hence are the most active—at any given point in time.

Neuroscientists have used fMRI to identify three areas of the left side of the brain that play key roles in reading. Scientifically, these are known as the left inferior frontal gyrus, the left parieto-temporal area and the left occipito-temporal area. But for our purposes, it's more helpful to think of them as the "phoneme producer," the "word analyzer" and the "automatic detector." We'll describe these regions in the order in which they are activated, but you'll get closer to the truth if you think of them as working simultaneously, like the sections of an orchestra playing a symphony.

Using fMRI, scientists have determined that beginning readers rely most heavily on the phoneme producer and the word analyzer. The first of these helps a person say things—silently or out loud—and does some analysis of the phonemes found in words. The second analyzes words more thoroughly, pulling them apart into their constituent syllables and phonemes and linking the letters to their sounds.

As readers become skilled, something interesting happens: the third section—the automatic detector—becomes more active. Its function is to build a permanent repertoire that enables readers to recognize familiar words on sight. As readers progress, the balance of the symphony shifts and the automatic detector begins to dominate. If all goes well, reading eventually becomes effortless.

In addition to the proper neurological wiring, reading requires good instruction. In a study published in the current issue of *Biological Psychiatry*, Shaywitz and colleagues identified a group of poor readers who were not classically dyslexic, as their phoneme producers, word analyzers and automatic

detectors were all active. But the three regions were linked more strongly to the brain's memory processors than to its language centers, as if the children had spent more time memorizing words than understanding them.

The situation is different for children with dyslexia. Brain scans suggest that a glitch in their brain prevents them from easily gaining access to the word analyzer and the automatic detector. In the past year, several fMRI studies have shown that dyslexics tend to compensate for the problem by overactivating the phoneme producer.

Here at last is physical evidence that the central weakness in dyslexia is twofold. First, as many dyslexia experts have long suspected, there is an inherent difficulty in deriving sense from phonemes. Second, because recognizing words doesn't become automatic, reading is slow and labored. This second aspect, the lack of fluency, has for the most part not been widely appreciated outside the research community.

Imagine having to deal with each word you see as if you had never come across it before, and you will start to get the idea. That's exactly what Abbe Winn of Atlanta realized her daughter Kate, now 9, was doing in kindergarten. "I noticed that when her teacher sent home a list of spelling words, she had a real hard time," Abbe says. "We'd get to the word the and come back five minutes later, and she had no idea what it was."

So much for what dyslexia is. What many parents would like to know is what can be done about it. Fortunately, the human brain is particularly receptive to instruction. Otherwise practice would never make perfect. Different people respond to different approaches, depending on their personality and the nature of their disability. "The data we have don't show any one program that is head and shoulders above the rest," says Shaywitz. But

the most successful programs emphasize the same core elements: practice manipulating phonemes, building vocabulary, increasing comprehension and improving the fluency of reading.

This kind of instruction leaves nothing to chance. "In most schools the emphasis is on children's learning to read sentences," says Gina Callaway, director of the Schenck School in Atlanta, which specializes in teaching dyslexic students using the Orton-Gillingham approach. "Here we have to teach them to recognize sounds, then syllables, then words and sentences. There's lots of practice and repetition." And a fair number of what the kids call tricks, or rules, for reading. (Among the most important and familiar: the magic *e* at the end of a word that makes a vowel say its name, as in *make* or *cute*.) A particularly good route to fluency is to practice reading aloud with a skilled reader who can gently correct mistakes. That way the brain builds up the right associations between words and sounds from the start.

BOYS AND GIRLS ARE EQUALLY LIKELY TO SUFFER FROM DYSLEXIA

There is no reason to assume that the public school system, despite its myriad problems, isn't up to the task. But it's a sad fact of life, particularly in larger or cash-starved institutions, that many kids fall through the cracks. A parent may have to keep up the pressure on the child's school district. Unfortunately, some have had to sue to get results. In extreme cases, parents can be reimbursed for private schooling, as two unanimous decisions by the Supreme Court, in 1985 and 1993, have made clear.

It helps to tap into a student's interests. For Monique Beltran, 13, of Los Angeles, the turning point came with the computer game Pokémon.

"I had to read to get to more levels," she says matter-of-factly. The computer game also showed Monique the value of reading outside of schoolwork, and she is eagerly devouring the latest *Harry Potter* book.

As you might expect, early intervention gives the best results. Yet for decades most schools wouldn't consider special education for a child until he or she had fallen at least a year behind. That may be changing. In the U.S., Congress is considering legislation that would eliminate the need to show a discrepancy between a child's IQ and his or her achievements before receiving a diagnosis of dyslexia.

Ideally, all children should be screened in kindergarten—to minimize educational delay and preserve self-confidence. How do you know someone has dyslexia before he or she has learned to read? Certain behaviors—like trouble rhyming words—are good clues that something is amiss. Later you may notice that your child is memorizing books rather than reading them. A kindergarten teacher's observation that reading isn't clicking with your son or daughter should be a call to action.

If caught soon enough, can a child's dyslexia be reversed? The evidence looks promising. In her book, Shaywitz reports that brain scans of dyslexic kindergartners and first-graders who have benefited from a year's worth of targeted instruction start to resemble those of children who have never had any difficulty reading.

That doesn't mean older folks need despair. Shaywitz's brain scans of adult dyslexics suggest that they can compensate by tapping into the processing power on their brain's right side. Just don't expect what works for young children to work for adults. "If you're 18 and you're about to graduate and you don't have phonemic awareness, that may not be your top priority," says Chris Schnieders, director of teacher training at the Frostig Center in Pasadena, Calif. "It's a little bit late to start 'Buh is for baby' at that point."

Technology can play a supporting role. Some dyslexics supplement their reading with books on tape. (Indeed, in 1995, the Recording for the Blind organization changed its name to Recording for the Blind and Dyslexic in recognition of that fact.) Because their condition affects the ability to write as well as read, a growing number of dyslexics are turning to voice-recognition software for help in preparing term papers, memos and reports. A couple of small studies have shown that the software can also bolster the ability to read. "We found improvement in word recognition, in reading com-prehension and spelling," says Marshall Raskind, director of research at the Frostig Center. He suspects that the ability to say, hear and see words almost simultaneously provides good training for the brain.

UP TO 1 IN 5 U.S. SCHOOLCHILDREN ARE LIVING WITH DYSLEXIA

There are, alas, no quick fixes. Dyslexic students often have to put many more hours into their course work than naturally skilled readers do. But the results are worth it. In the seventh grade, Sean Slattery was barely reading on a first-grade level. Now, after four years at the Frostig Center, he has nearly caught up to where he should be. In May, on his third try, Slattery passed California's high school exit exam.

That's another thing about dyslexics: they learn to persevere. Now Slattery has his eye on a career as an underwater welder. "There's a lot of reading involved" between the course work and the instruction manuals, he says. "But I'm looking forward to it, actually." The written word is not going to hold him back anymore.

Metacognitive Development

Abstract

Traditional developmental research in memory and reasoning, as well as current investigations in such disparate areas as theory of mind, epistemological understanding, knowledge acquisition, and problem solving, share the need to invoke a meta-level of cognition in explaining their respective phenomena. The increasingly influential construct of metacognition can be conceptualized in a developmental framework. Young children's dawning awareness of mental functions lies at one end of a developmental progression that eventuates in complex metaknowing capabilities that many adults do not master. During its extended developmental course, metacognition becomes more explicit, powerful, and effective, as it comes to operate increasingly under the individual's conscious control. Enhancing (a) metacognitive awareness of what one believes and how one knows and (b) metastrategic control in application of the strategies that process new information is an important developmental and educational goal.

Keywords

metacognition; development; knowledge acquisition

Deanna Kuhn[1]

Teachers College, Columbia University, New York, New York

Metacognition—that is, cognition that reflects on, monitors, or regulates first-order cognition—was characterized by Flavell in 1979 as a "promising new area of investigation" (p. 906). He appears to have been on the right track. The claim that metacognition is "where the action is" in understanding intellectual performance would meet with approval in many (though not all) circles today. If so, what do we need to know about this construct? The answer is, a great many things, but here I focus on two fundamental questions that have lacked clear answers: Where does metacognition come from and what kinds of it are there? In addition, I examine the relation between metacognition and cognition. Do they work together closely, or is the relation a more distant and formal one, akin to that between metaphysics and physics?

The answer I propose to the first question is that metacognition develops. It does not appear abruptly from nowhere as an epiphenomenon in relation to first-order cognition. Instead, metacognition emerges early in life, in forms that are no more than suggestive of what is to come, and follows an extended developmental course during which it becomes more explicit, more powerful, and hence more effective, as it comes to operate increasingly under the individual's conscious control. Placing metacognition in this developmental framework helps to clarify its nature and significance.

DEVELOPMENTAL ORIGINS OF METACOGNITION IN THEORY OF MIND

Over the past decade, the wave of research on children's understanding of the mind has been valuable in highlighting the earliest forms of metacognition. By age 3, children have acquired some awareness of themselves and others as knowers. They distinguish thinking about an object from actually perceiving it, and begin to refer to their own knowledge states, using verbs such as *think* and *know* (Flavell, 1999). By age 4, they understand that others' behavior is guided by beliefs and desires and that such beliefs may not match their own and could be incorrect. This so-called false belief understanding is a developmental milestone because it connects assertions to their generative source in human knowers. These early years are also a period of rapidly developing awareness of how one has come to know that what one claims is so—that is, awareness of the sources of one's knowledge.

These early metacognitive achievements serve as foundations for much of the higher-order thinking that appears later. Understanding knowledge as the product of human knowing is a critical first step in the development of epistemological thinking, which is metacognitive in the sense of constituting an implicit theory of how things are known and increasingly is becoming recognized as influential in higher-order thinking (Hofer & Pintrich, 1997). Scientific thinking is another form of higher-order thinking whose roots lie in early metacognitive achievements (Kuhn & Pearsall, 2000). Awareness of the sources of one's knowledge is critical to understanding evidence as distinct from and bearing on theories—an understanding that lies at the heart of scientific thinking. In skilled scientific thinking, existing understandings are coordinated with new evidence, and new knowledge is thereby acquired, in a highly deliberate, rule-governed, and therefore metacognitively controlled process.

DEVELOPMENTAL ORIGINS OF METASTRATEGIC AWARENESS AND CONTROL

Are there different kinds of metacognition? A long-standing distinction in cognitive psychology is that between declarative (knowing that) and procedural (knowing how) knowing. If these two kinds of knowing are fundamentally different, perhaps meta-level operations on them also differ. Specifically, I propose, we would expect meta-level operations to have their greatest influence on procedural knowing. Meta-level awareness of strategies for comprehending a chapter in a textbook, for example, may influence comprehension efforts, whereas explicit meta-level awareness of the declarative knowledge gained from the chapter ("knowing that I know") has less obvious effects on the knowledge itself.

I have proposed *metastrategic knowing* as a separate term to refer to metaknowing about procedural knowing, reserving *metacognitive knowing* (addressed in the preceding section) to refer to metaknowing about declarative knowing. Metastrategic knowledge can be further divided into *metatask* knowing about task goals and *metastrategic* knowledge about the strategies one has available to address these goals (Kuhn & Pearsall, 1998).

How and when does metastrategic cognition originate? Central to Vygotsky's (1962) view of cognitive development is the child's acquisition of voluntary control in initiating or inhibiting actions, with Vygotsky attributing a major role to meta-level awareness in this achievement. More recently, Zelazo and his associates have investigated early origins of what they call executive control in the execution of a simple object-sorting task. To perform the task, an executive function is called on to select which of two previously learned rules (sort by shape or by color) to apply. Three-year-olds, these researchers have found, have difficulty selecting the called-for rule, even though they can easily execute either rule. The requisite executive control of cognitive functions, it is proposed, is acquired gradually and undergoes multiple developmental transitions (Zelazo & Frye, 1998).

META-LEVEL CONSTRUCTS IN THE STUDY OF DEVELOPMENTAL PROCESS

Why do metastrategic and metacognitive functions warrant our attention? One reason is that they help to explain how and why cognitive development both occurs and fails to occur (Kuhn, in press). Developmentalists have long been criticized for failing to address the core question of how change occurs. The picture has changed with the advent of microgenetic methods, in which the process of change is observed directly as individuals engage in the same task repeatedly. The consistent finding of microgenetic studies is that people possess a repertory of multiple strategies of varying adequacy that they apply variably to the same problem. Development, then, rather than constituting a single transition from one way of being to another, entails a shifting distribution in the frequencies with which more or less adequate strategies are applied, with the inhibition of inferior strategies as important an achievement as the acquisition of superior ones (Kuhn, 1995; Siegler, 1996).

This revised conception of the developmental process has important implications in the present context because it suggests a critical role for meta-level processes. If shifts in strategy usage cannot be satisfactorily explained at the level of performance (e.g., frequency of prior use dictates the probability of a strategy's appearance), the explanatory burden shifts from the performance level to a meta-level that dictates which strategies are selected for use on a given occasion. The meta-level directs the application of strategies, but feedback from this application is directed back to the meta-level. This feedback leads to enhanced meta-level awareness of the goal and the extent to which it is being met by different strategies, as well as enhanced awareness and understanding of the strategies themselves, including their power and limitations. These enhancements at the meta-level lead to revised strategy selection. These changes in strategy usage in turn feed back to further enhance understanding at the meta-level, in a continuous cycle in which the meta-level both directs and is modified by the performance level.

Such a model privileges the meta-level as the locus of developmental change. Developmentally, then, increasing meta-level awareness and control may be the most important dimension in terms of which we see change (Kuhn, in press). In addition, the model makes it clear why efforts to induce change directly at the performance level have only limited success, indicated by failures of a newly acquired strategy to transfer to new materials or contexts. Strategy training may appear successful, but if nothing has been done to influence the meta-level, the new behavior will quickly disappear once the instructional context is withdrawn and individuals resume meta-level management of their own behavior.

EXTENDING THE SCOPE OF METACOGNITION RESEARCH

A second reason that metacognition warrants our attention has to do with the phenomena to which it is applied. In the era in which Flavell wrote his 1979 article, almost all the research on metacognitive development was confined to metamemory—the study of what children and adults know about how to remember and about their own memory functions and how such knowledge relates to memory performance. Today, metacognition is conceptualized and studied in a much broader context. Metacognitive and metastrategic functions are being investigated within domains of text comprehension, problem solving, and reasoning, as well as memory. Metacognition in the year 2000, then, is "about" more than it was in 1979.

It thus becomes more feasible to construct and evaluate alternative theories of the role that meta-level processes play in regulating and advancing cognitive development (Crowley, Shrager, & Siegler, 1997; Kuhn, in press). It is a reasonable hypothesis that the nature of strategy-metastrategy relations shows some generality across different kinds of cognition, specifically in the ways in which meta-level processes operate to select and regulate performance strategies. Studies of these phenomena across different kinds of cognitive strategies stand to inform one another.

ENDPOINTS OF METACOGNITIVE DEVELOPMENT

A third reason that metacognition warrants attention has to do with the later rather than early portions of its developmental course. Despite the centrality of knowledge acquisition as a topic of theoretical and practical significance, we lack sufficient research observing individuals engaged in the process of acquiring new knowledge. Microgenetic methods allow us to study this process of "knowledge building" (Chan, Burtis, & Bereiter, 1997) during which existing understandings are modified in the course of their interaction with new information. In addition, we can examine how knowledge-acquisition strategies are themselves transformed in the course of their continuing application. Such studies point to the critical role of metacognitive and metastrategic processes in regulating knowledge-acquisition processes.

Adults show more skill in these respects than do children (Kuhn, Garcia-Mila, Zohar, & Andersen, 1995), but the performance of adults is far from optimum. Their beliefs are frequently modified by the new information they encounter, to be sure, and they may become more certain of these beliefs over

time, but they often lack awareness of why they are certain (i.e., of the process of theory-evidence coordination that has transpired), and they apply knowledge-acquisition and inference strategies in a selective way to protect their own, often erroneous, beliefs. Enhancing (a) metacognitive awareness of what one believes and how one knows and (b) metastrategic consistency in application of the strategies that select and interpret evidence is thus both a developmental and an educational (Olson & Astington, 1993) goal.

SUPPORTING METACOGNITIVE DEVELOPMENT

In sum, competence in metaknowing warrants attention as a critical endpoint and goal of childhood and adolescent cognitive development. Young children's dawning awareness of their own and others' mental functions lies at one end of a developmental progression that eventuates in complex metaknowing capabilities not realized before adulthood, if they are realized at all. Linking these diverse attainments within a developmental framework makes it possible to investigate ways in which earlier attainments prepare the way for later ones.

As I suggested in the introduction, much remains to be learned about metacognition. We need to know more about how it develops and how it comes to regulate first-order cognition, or, very often, fails to do so. The fact that such failure is a common occurrence raises what is perhaps the most consequential question in need of more investigation: How can metacognitive development be facilitated?

Flavell (1979) expressed a broad vision in this respect:

It is at least conceivable that the ideas currently brewing in this area could someday be parlayed into a method teaching children (and adults) to make wise and thoughtful life decisions as well as to comprehend and learn better in formal educational settings. (p. 910)

Although it has yet to be realized, this vision conveys the potential significance of achieving meta-level control of one's knowing processes. A promising ap-

proach to fostering metacognitive development focuses on the idea of exercising, at an external, social level, the cognitive forms we would hope to become operative as well at the individual level. One of a number of researchers who have pursued this approach is Brown (1997), whose "community of learners" curriculum relies on

the development of a discourse genre in which constructive discussion, questioning, querying, and criticism are the mode rather than the exception. In time, these reflective activities become internalized as self-reflective practices. (p. 406)

There would seem few more important accomplishments than people becoming aware of and reflective about their own thinking and able to monitor and manage the ways in which it is influenced by external sources, in both academic, work, and personal life settings. Metacognitive development is a construct that helps to frame this goal.

Recommended Reading

Crowley, K., Shrager, J., & Siegler, R. (1997). (See References)

Hofer, B., & Pintrich, P. (1997). (See References)

Kuhn, D. (1999). A developmental model of critical thinking. *Educational Researcher, 28*, 16–25.

Kuhn, D. (1999). Metacognitive development. In L. Balter & C. Tamis-LeMonda (Eds.), *Child psychology: A handbook of contemporary issues* (pp. 259–286). Philadelphia: Psychology Press.

Kuhn, D. (in press). How do people know? *Psychological Science.*

Olson, D., & Astington, J. (1993). (See References)

Note

1. Address correspondence to Deanna Kuhn, Box 119, Teachers College, Columbia University, New York, NY 10027.

References

Brown, A. (1997). Transforming schools into communities of thinking and learning about serious matters. *American Psychologist, 52,* 399–413.

Chan, C., Burtis, J., & Bereiter, C. (1997). Knowledge-building as a mediator of conflict in conceptual change. *Cognition and Instruction, 15,* 1–40.

Crowley, K., Shrager, J., & Siegler, R. (1997). Strategy discovery as a competitive negotiation between metacognitive and associative mechanisms. *Developmental Review, 17*, 462–489.

Flavell, J. (1979). Metacognition and cognitive monitoring: A new area of cognitive-developmental inquiry. *American Psychologist, 34*, 906–911.

Flavell, J. (1999). Cognitive development: Children's knowledge about the mind. *Annual Review of Psychology, 50*, 21–45.

Hofer, B., & Pintrich, P. (1997). The development of epistemological theories: Beliefs about knowledge and knowing and their relation to learning. *Review of Educational Research, 67*, 88–140.

Kuhn, D. (1995). Microgenetic study of change: What has it told us? *Psychological Science, 6*, 133–139.

Kuhn, D. (in press). Why development does (and doesn't) occur: Evidence from the domain of inductive reasoning. In R. Siegler & J. McClelland (Eds.), *Mechanisms of cognitive development: Neural and behavioral perspectives.* Mahwah, NJ: Erlbaum.

Kuhn, D., Garcia-Mila, M., Zohar, A., & Andersen, C. (1995). Strategies of knowledge acquisition. *Society for Research in Child Development Monographs, 60* (4, Serial No. 245).

Kuhn, D., & Pearsall, S. (1998). Relations between metastrategic knowledge and strategic performance. *Cognitive Development, 13*, 227–247.

Kuhn, D., & Pearsall, S. (2000). Developmental origins of scientific thinking. *Journal of Cognition and Development, 1*, 113–129.

Olson, D., & Astington, J. (1993). Thinking about thinking: Learning how to take statements and hold beliefs. *Educational Psychologist, 28*, 7–23.

Siegler, R. (1996). *Emerging minds: The process of change in children's thinking.* New York: Oxford University Press.

Vygotsky, L.S. (1962). *Thought and language.* Cambridge, MA: MIT Press.

Zelazo, P., & Frye, D. (1998). Cognitive complexity and control: II. The development of executive function in childhood. *Current Directions in Psychological Science, 7*, 121–125.

Trick Question

A liberal 'hoax' turns out to be true.

By MICHAEL FUMENTO

IT'S BOTH RIGHT-WING and vast, but it's not a conspiracy. Actually, it's more of an anti-conspiracy. The subject is Attention Deficit Disorder (ADD) and Attention Deficit Hyperactivity Disorder (ADHD), closely related ailments (henceforth referred to in this article simply as ADHD). Rush Limbaugh declares it "may all be a hoax." Francis Fukuyama devotes much of one chapter in his latest book, *Our Posthuman Future*, to attacking Ritalin, the top-selling drug used to treat ADHD. Columnist Thomas Sowell writes, "The motto used to be: 'Boys will be boys.' Today, the motto seems to be: 'Boys will be medicated.'" And Phyllis Schlafly explains, "The old excuse of 'my dog ate my homework' has been replaced by 'I got an ADHD diagnosis.'" A March 2002 article in *The Weekly Standard* summed up the conservative line on ADHD with this rhetorical question: "Are we really prepared to redefine childhood as an ailment, and medicate it until it goes away?"

Many conservative writers, myself included, have criticized the growing tendency to pathologize every undesirable behavior—especially where children are concerned. But, when it comes to ADHD, this skepticism is misplaced. As even a cursory examination of the existing literature or, for that matter, simply talking to the parents and teachers of children with ADHD reveals, the condition is real, and it is treatable. And, if you don't believe me, you can ask conservatives who've come face to face with it themselves.

MYTH: ADHD ISN'T A REAL DISORDER.

The most common argument against ADHD on the right is also the simplest: It doesn't exist. Conservative columnist Jonah Goldberg thus reduces ADHD to "ants in the pants." Sowell equates it with "being bored and restless." Fukuyama protests,

"No one has been able to identify a cause of ADD/ADHD. It is a pathology recognized only by its symptoms." And a conservative columnist approvingly quotes Thomas Armstrong, Ritalin opponent and author, when he declares, "ADD is a disorder that cannot be authoritatively identified in the same way as polio, heart disease or other legitimate illnesses."

The Armstrong and Fukuyama observations are as correct as they are worthless. "Half of all medical disorders are diagnosed without benefit of a lab procedure," notes Dr. Russell Barkley, professor of psychology at the College of Health Professionals at the Medical University of South Carolina. "Where are the lab tests for headaches and multiple sclerosis and Alzheimer's?" he asks. "Such a standard would virtually eliminate all mental disorders."

Often the best diagnostic test for an ailment is how it responds to treatment. And, by that standard, it doesn't get much more real than ADHD. The beneficial effects of administering stimulants to treat the disorder were first reported in 1937. And today medication for the disorder is reported to be 75 to 90 percent successful. "In our trials it was close to ninety percent," says Dr. Judith Rapoport, director of the National Institute of Mental Health's Child Psychiatry Branch, who has published about 100 papers on ADHD. "This means there was a significant difference in the children's ability to function in the classroom or at home."

Additionally, epidemiological evidence indicates that ADHD has a powerful genetic component. University of Colorado researchers have found that a child whose identical twin has the disorder is between eleven and 18 times more likely to also have it than is a non-twin sibling. For these reasons, the American Psychiatric Association (APA), American Medical Association, American Academy of Pediatrics, American Academy of Child

Adolescent Psychiatry, the surgeon general's office, and other major medical bodies all acknowledge ADHD as both real and treatable.

MYTH: ADHD IS PART OF A FEMINIST CONSPIRACY TO MAKE LITTLE BOYS MORE LIKE LITTLE GIRLS.

Many conservatives observe that boys receive ADHD diagnoses in much higher numbers than girls and find in this evidence of a feminist conspiracy. (This, despite the fact that genetic diseases are often heavily weighted more toward one gender or the other.) Sowell refers to "a growing tendency to treat boyhood as a pathological condition that requires a new three R's—repression, re-education and Ritalin." Fukuyama claims Prozac is being used to give women "more of the alpha-male feeling," while Ritalin is making boys act more like girls. "Together, the two sexes are gently nudged toward that androgynous median personality… that is the current politically correct outcome in American society." George Will, while acknowledging that Ritalin can be helpful, nonetheless writes of the "androgyny agenda" of "drugging children because they are behaving like children, especially boy children." Anti-Ritalin conservatives frequently invoke Christina Hoff Sommers's best-selling 2000 book, *The War Against Boys.* You'd never know that the drug isn't mentioned in her book—or why.

"Originally I was going to have a chapter on it," Sommers tells me. "It seemed to fit the thesis." What stopped her was both her survey of the medical literature and her own empirical findings. Of one child she personally came to know she says, "He was utterly miserable, as was everybody around him. The drugs saved his life."

MYTH: ADHD IS PART OF THE PUBLIC SCHOOL SYSTEM'S EFFORTS TO WAREHOUSE KIDS RATHER THAN TO DISCIPLINE AND TEACH THEM.

"No doubt life is easier for teachers when everyone sits around quietly," writes Sowell. Use of ADHD drugs is "in the school's interest to deal with behavioral and discipline problems [because] it's so easy to use Ritalin to make kids compliant: to get them to sit down, shut up, and do what they're told," declares Schlafly. The word "zombies" to describe children under the effects of Ritalin is tossed around more than in a B-grade voodoo movie.

Kerri Houston, national field director for the American Conservative Union and the mother of two ADHD children on medication, agrees with much of the criticism of public schools. "But don't blame ADHD on crummy curricula and lazy teachers," she says. "If you've worked with these children, you know they have a serious neurological problem." In any case, Ritalin, when taken as prescribed, hardly stupefies children. To the extent the medicine works, it simply turns ADHD children into normal children. "ADHD is like having thirty televisions on at one time, and the medicine turns off twenty-nine so you can

concentrate on the one," Houston describes. "This zombie stuff drives me nuts! My kids are both as lively and as fun as can be."

MYTH: PARENTS WHO GIVE THEIR KIDS ANTI-ADHD DRUGS ARE MERELY DOPING UP PROBLEM CHILDREN.

Limbaugh calls ADHD "the perfect way to explain the inattention, incompetence, and inability of adults to control their kids." Addressing parents directly, he lectures, "It helped you mask your own failings by doping up your children to calm them down."

Such charges blast the parents of ADHD kids into high orbit. That includes my Hudson Institute colleague (and fellow conservative) Mona Charen, the mother of an eleven-year-old with the disorder. "I have two non-ADHD children, so it's not a matter of parenting technique," says Charen. "People without such children have no idea what it's like. I can tell the difference between boyish high spirits and pathological hyperactivity.… These kids bounce off the walls. Their lives are chaos; their rooms are chaos. And nothing replaces the drugs."

Barkley and Rapoport say research backs her up. Randomized, controlled studies in both the United States and Sweden have tried combining medication with behavioral interventions and then dropped either one or the other. For those trying to go on without medicine, "the behavioral interventions maintained nothing," Barkley says. Rapoport concurs: "Unfortunately, behavior modification doesn't seem to help with ADHD." (Both doctors are quick to add that ADHD is often accompanied by other disorders that are treatable through behavior modification in tandem with medicine.)

MYTH: RITALIN IS "KIDDIE COCAINE."

One of the paradoxes of conservative attacks on Ritalin is that the drug is alternately accused of turning children into brain-dead zombies and of making them Mach-speed cocaine junkies. Indeed, Ritalin is widely disparaged as "kiddie cocaine." Writers who have sought to lump the two drugs together include Schlafly, talk-show host and columnist Armstrong Williams, and others whom I hesitate to name because of my long-standing personal relationships with them.

Mary Eberstadt wrote the "authoritative" Ritalin-cocaine piece for the April 1999 issue of *Policy Review*, then owned by the Heritage Foundation. The article, "Why Ritalin Rules," employs the word "cocaine" no fewer than twelve times. Eberstadt quotes from a 1995 Drug Enforcement Agency (DEA) background paper declaring methylphenidate, the active ingredient in Ritalin, "a central nervous system (CNS) stimulant [that] shares many of the pharmacological effects of amphetamine, methamphetamine, and cocaine." Further, it "produces behavioral, psychological, subjective, and reinforcing effects similar to those of d-amphetamine including increases in rating of euphoria, drug liking and activity, and decreases in sedation." Add to this the fact that the Controlled Substances Act lists it as a

Schedule II drug, imposing on it the same tight prescription controls as morphine, and Ritalin starts to sound spooky indeed.

What Eberstadt fails to tell readers is that the DEA description concerns methylphenidate *abuse*. It's tautological to say abuse is harmful. According to the DEA, the drugs in question are comparable when "administered the same way at comparable doses." But ADHD stimulants, when taken as prescribed, are neither administered in the same way as cocaine nor at comparable doses. "What really counts," says Barkley, "is the speed with which the drugs enter and clear the brain. With cocaine, because it's snorted, this happens tremendously quickly, giving users the characteristic addictive high." (Ever seen anyone pop a cocaine tablet?) Further, he says, "There's no evidence anywhere in literature of [Ritalin's] addictiveness when taken as prescribed." As to the Schedule II listing, again this is because of the potential for it to fall into the hands of abusers, not because of its effects on persons for whom it is prescribed. Ritalin and the other anti-ADHD drugs, says Barkley, "are the safest drugs in all of psychiatry." (And they may be getting even safer: A new medicine just released called Strattera represents the first true non-stimulant ADHD treatment.)

Indeed, a study just released in the journal *Pediatrics* found that children who take Ritalin or other stimulants to control ADHD cut their risk of future substance abuse by 50 percent compared with untreated ADHD children. The lead author speculated that "by treating ADHD you're reducing the demoralization that accompanies this disorder, and you're improving the academic functioning and well-being of adolescents and young adults during the critical times when substance abuse starts."

MYTH: RITALIN IS OVERPRESCRIBED ACROSS THE COUNTRY.

Some call it "the Ritalin craze." In *The Weekly Standard*, Melana Zyla Vickers informs us that "Ritalin use has exploded," while Eberstadt writes that "Ritalin use more than doubled in the first half of the decade alone, [and] the number of schoolchildren taking the drug may now, by some estimates, be approaching the *4 million mark*."

A report in the January 2003 issue of *Archives of Pediatrics and Adolescent Medicine* did find a large increase in the use of ADHD medicines from 1987 to 1996, an increase that doesn't appear to be slowing. Yet nobody thinks it's a problem that routine screening for high blood pressure has produced a big increase in the use of hypertension medicine. "Today, children suffering from ADHD are simply less likely to slip through the cracks," says Dr. Sally Satel, a psychiatrist, AEI fellow, and author of *PC, M.D.: How Political Correctness Is Corrupting Medicine*.

Satel agrees that some community studies, by the standards laid down in the APA's *Diagnostic and Statistical Manual of Mental Disorders (DSM)*, indicate that ADHD may often be over-diagnosed. On the other hand, she says, additional evidence shows that in some communities ADHD is *under*-diagnosed and *under*-treated. "I'm quite concerned with children who need the medication and aren't getting it," she says.

There *are* tremendous disparities in the percentage of children taking ADHD drugs when comparing small geographical areas. Psychologist Gretchen LeFever, for example, has compared the number of prescriptions in mostly white Virginia Beach, Virginia, with other, more heavily African American areas in the southeastern part of the state. Conservatives have latched onto her higher numbers—20 percent of white fifth-grade boys in Virginia Beach are being treated for ADHD—as evidence that something is horribly wrong. But others, such as Barkley, worry about the lower numbers. According to LeFever's study, black children are only half as likely to get medication as white children. "Black people don't get the care of white people; children of well-off parents get far better care than those of poorer parents," says Barkley.

MYTH: STATES SHOULD PASS LAWS THAT RESTRICT SCHOOLS FROM RECOMMENDING RITALIN.

Conservative writers have expressed delight that several states, led by Connecticut, have passed or are considering laws ostensibly protecting students from schools that allegedly pass out Ritalin like candy. Representative Lenny Winkler, lead sponsor of the Connecticut measure, told *Reuters Health*, "If the diagnosis is made, and it's an appropriate diagnosis that Ritalin be used, that's fine. But I have also heard of many families approached by the school system [who are told] that their child cannot attend school if they're not put on Ritalin."

Two attorneys I interviewed who specialize in child-disability issues, including one from the liberal Bazelon Center for Mental Health Law in Washington, D.C., acknowledge that school personnel have in some cases stepped over the line. But legislation can go too far in the other direction by declaring, as Connecticut's law does, that "any school personnel [shall be prohibited] from recommending the use of psychotropic drugs for any child." The law appears to offer an exemption by declaring, "The provisions of this section shall not prohibit *school medical staff* from recommending that a child be evaluated by an appropriate medical practitioner, or prohibit school personnel from consulting with such practitioner, with the consent of the parent or guardian of such child." [Emphasis added.] But of course many, if not most, schools have perhaps one nurse on regular "staff." That nurse will have limited contact with children in the classroom situations where ADHD is likely to be most evident. And, given the wording of the statute, a teacher who believed a student was suffering from ADHD would arguably be prohibited from referring that student to the nurse. Such ambiguity is sure to have a chilling effect on any form of intervention or recommendation by school personnel. Moreover, 20- year special-education veteran Sandra Rief said in an interview with the National Education Association that "recommending medical intervention for a student's behavior could lead to personal liability issues." Teachers, in other words, could be forced to choose between what they think is best for the health of their students and the possible risk of losing not only their jobs but their personal assets as well.

"Certainly it's not within the purview of a school to say kids can't attend if they don't take drugs," says Houston. "On the other hand, certainly teachers should be able to advise parents as to problems and potential solutions.... [T]hey may see things parents don't. My own son is an angel at home but was a demon at school."

If the real worry is "take the medicine or take a hike" ultimatums, legislation can be narrowly tailored to prevent them; broad-based gag orders, such as Connecticut's, are a solution that's worse than the problem.

THE CONSERVATIVE CASE FOR ADHD DRUGS.

There are kernels of truth to every conservative suspicion about ADHD. Who among us has not had lapses of attention? And isn't hyperactivity a normal condition of childhood when compared with deskbound adults? Certainly there are lazy teachers, warehousing schools, androgyny-pushing feminists, and far too many parents unwilling or unable to expend the time and effort to raise their children properly, even by their own standards. Where conservatives go wrong is in making ADHD a scapegoat for frustration over what we perceive as a breakdown in the order of society and family. In a column in *The Boston Herald*, Boston University Chancellor John Silber rails that Ritalin is "a classic example of a cheap fix: low-cost, simple and purely superficial."

Exactly. Like most headaches, ADHD is a neurological problem that can usually be successfully treated with a chemical. Those who recommend or prescribe ADHD medicines do not, as *The Weekly Standard* put it, see them as "discipline in pill-form." They see them as pills.

In fact, it can be argued that the use of those pills, far from being liable for or symptomatic of the Decline of the West, reflects and reinforces conservative values. For one thing, they increase personal responsibility by removing an excuse that children (and their parents) can fall back on to explain misbehavior and poor performance. "Too many psychologists and psychiatrists focus on allowing patients to justify to themselves their troubling behavior," says Satel. "But something like Ritalin actually encourages greater autonomy because you're treating a compulsion to behave in a certain way. Also, by treating ADHD, you remove an opportunity to explain away bad behavior."

Moreover, unlike liberals, who tend to downplay differences between the sexes, conservatives are inclined to believe that there are substantial physiological differences— differences such as boys' greater tendency to suffer ADHD. "Conservatives celebrate the physiological differences between boys and girls and eschew the radical-feminist notion that gender differences are created by societal pressures," says Houston regarding the fuss over the boy-girl disparity among ADHD diagnoses. "ADHD is no exception."

But, however compatible conservatism may be with taking ADHD seriously, the truth is that most conservatives remain skeptics. "I'm sure I would have been one of those smug conservatives saying it's a made-up disease," admits Charen, "if I hadn't found out the hard way." Here's hoping other conservatives find an easier route to accepting the truth.

MICHAEL FUMENTO is a senior fellow at the Hudson Institute in Washington, D.C., where he is completing his latest book, tentatively titled *Bioevolution: How Biotechnology Is Changing our World*, due this spring from Encounter Books.

The Future of Computer Technology in K–12 Education

American business was not able to take advantage of the power of computer technology until many of its basic practices changed, Mr. Bennett points out, and this is equally true in education. Until schools can permit a major alteration in the way teaching is carried on, they must necessarily continue to miss out on the improvement that computer technology can bring.

BY FREDERICK BENNETT

IN A PIECE published in February 2001, syndicated columnist George Will used Hippocrates and Socrates to illustrate the difficulties in contemporary American schooling. "If you were ill and could miraculously be treated by Hippocrates or by a young graduate of Johns Hopkins medical school, with his modern technologies and techniques, you would choose the latter. But if you could choose to have your child taught either by Socrates or by a freshly minted holder of a degree in education, full of the latest pedagogical theories and techniques? Socrates, please."

Teaching has always been more art than science and depends heavily on the talents of the practitioner. Some teachers are outstanding; some are not. In medicine, Hippocrates probably had more innate abilities than many of the new physicians, but his successors have the advantage of modern technology. Teachers, however, rely on basically the same approach that instructors have used throughout history, and, consequently, they must count on their own native skills. This situation presents a difficulty for education because exceptional instructors are in the minority. We see this easily if we think back over the teachers that we ourselves had in our school career. The number we remember as superb is not large.

THE PRESENT

Education today, as always, depends on the luck of the draw—who gets the good teachers and who gets the others? Meanwhile, technology has become a powerful force in the world. Theoretically, it might change education, just as it has made the new physician better equipped than

Hippocrates and has brought dazzling benefits to innumerable other areas of society. Education authorities apparently hoped for comparable results because they have placed millions of computers in schools. By 1999, there

was one computer for every six children.[1] Yet despite this massive infusion of technology, overall improvements in education have been minimal.

Scores on the National Assessment of Educational Progress point up this lack of advancement. Results for 1999 showed no significant change in reading, mathematics, or science for the three age groups tested—9-year-olds, 13-year-olds, and 17-year-olds—from 1994 through 1999.[2] During this five-year period, schools acquired huge numbers of computers and hoped earnestly that this influx of technology would improve education.

Since few people want to despair and conclude that K–12 education seems to be about the only major field that technology cannot benefit, authorities have sought reasons for the current failure. The most frequently suggested explanation is that teachers have not learned how to employ technology in their classrooms. Therefore, if schools could train teachers, the argument goes, technology would finally deliver major benefits to education. President Clinton joined those who wanted additional teacher training when in June 2000 he announced $128 million in grants to instruct teachers in the use of technology.

Lack of teacher training, however, is a myth. In 2000 the U.S. Department of Education issued a study in which half of all teachers reported that college and graduate work had prepared them to use technology. In addition, training continues after formal schooling. The same government document pointed out that, from 1996 to 1999, 77% of teachers participated in "professional development activities in the use of computers or the Internet."[3] Thirty-three percent to 39% of teachers responding to two surveys in 1999 said that they felt well prepared to use computers.[4] Although not the full universe of teachers, this percentage of well-prepared instructors ought to have brought some improvement if technology were going to lift education to a higher plateau.

The failure of test scores to change after schools have added millions of computers, after teachers have received considerable training, and after many years of computer usage leads to a troubling question: Is it possible that technology as currently used can never fundamentally improve today's K–12 education? I believe that such hopelessness is indeed warranted, for one obvious reason: the power of electronic interaction is necessarily diminished because of the way computers must be used in schools today.

Interaction takes place when the instructor and the student react directly to each other's contributions. Interaction between child and teacher has always been found in good instruction. It can make learning enjoyable, can adjust to the varied abilities of different students, and is effective with children of all ages. Very possibly, one of the attributes of the teachers that we remember as being superb was their ability to develop a high degree of interaction with us.

Computer games show the power of electronic interaction. The secret to a large portion of this technology's success in maintaining its iron grip on the attention of game players is the unparalleled ability of the machine to interact

continually with the participant. Theoretically, this same interactive power ought to make computers a potent force in education. When computers are used in classrooms today, however, interaction between the computer and the student cannot be strong and ongoing. This is because the teacher, not the computer, must control and direct instruction. Individual teachers must decide how they will use computer instruction in the dissemination of classroom material—how much the machine will teach the student and how much instruction the teacher will provide. These conditions are unalterable in the present system of education, and they drastically curtail interaction between the computer and the student.

BUSINESS AND COMPUTERS

American education, however, is not unique in its poor initial results with computers. Corporate America had a similar experience. For several years, businesses added large numbers of computers, but overall productivity did not improve. Many workers acquired the machines for their desks. They used them for important jobs such as word processing and spreadsheets, but the basic manner in which companies carried on their activities did not change. This kind of computer usage was bound to fail. In time, corporations made the necessary structural changes and thus altered the basic way they carried on their business. When that happened, productivity increased dramatically. In an extensive article about the increase in productivity that technology has brought to business, Erik Brynjolfsson and Lorin Hitt point out, "Investments in computers may make little direct contribution to overall performance of a firm or the economy until they are combined with complementary investments in work practices, human capital, and firm restructuring."[5]

Education is in a position today akin to that of American business in those early days. Despite the millions of computers in schools, teaching has not changed. In the encompassing evaluation of technology in schools mentioned above, the Department of Education notes, "According to the literature, the advent of computers and the Internet has not dramatically changed how teachers teach and how students learn."[6]

AN ALTERNATIVE

There is an alternative to the way we use computers in schools, an alternative that would take advantage of the power of interaction. We could allow computers to tutor children individually and directly, without a teacher in the usual role. This approach seems radical when first considered. Nonetheless, a few schools have tried it for some students or subjects. The usual students in these computerized classes are those who are at risk of dropping out of school. In many cases, these students have been so difficult to teach that authorities have allowed this new approach. The results have been uniformly good.

Several companies have developed fitting teaching software. Among these are Plato Learning, Inc., Scientific Learning, and NovaNet Learning, Inc. All three have Web pages on which the results of their programs are posted.[7]

Lakeland High School in Florida, Lawrence High School in Indianapolis, and Turner High School in Carrollton, Texas, provide three interesting examples of Plato programs. In retests in Lakeland, student FHSCT (Florida High School Competency Test) scores increased dramatically, and the school identified a significant positive relationship between some Plato student performance data and the FHSCT scores. Authorities at Lawrence implemented an extensive remediation program in 1998–99 to increase the passing rate of their students taking the state-mandated competency exam, ISTEP (Indiana Statewide Testing for Educational Progress). At the beginning of the year, 406 students failed either the math or the English component. At the end of the year, only 74 of those pupils continued to fail the exam. At Turner, the pass rate on TAAS (Texas Assessment of Academic Skills) reversed a trend and improved from 69% in 1998 to 83% in 2000.

Scientific Learning has concentrated on reading and comprehension, especially with students who are behind in these vital areas. Pretest and posttest results with standardized, nationally normed tests showed significant gains with various levels of students from kindergarten through grade 12.

Dillard High School in Fort Lauderdale, Florida, provides an example of the results of using NovaNet software. In this program there were 123 students, all of whom were below the 20th percentile on state standards. After three months of using the program, all pupils had made gains. Moreover, half of the students had advanced at least one full grade, and 27 of those pupils had improved by either two or three grade levels.

Although schools have used this form of computerized education primarily with at-risk children, there are other programs that teach average and bright students, and they have recorded equally exciting gains. For example, researchers at Carnegie Mellon University created software to teach algebra through computers. They installed the program in a number of high schools, including some in their hometown of Pittsburgh. The authors made a study of freshmen at three schools, none of whom had taken the subject in middle school. Approximately 470 students enrolled in 21 computer classes. At the end of the year the schools assessed results and compared math achievement for these students with that of a comparable group of 170 ninth-grade students in standard math courses. The results showed the power of the computerized learning. The computer students scored 15% better on standardized tests. Moreover, they scored 100% better on the more difficult questions that "focused on mathematical analysis of real-world situations and the use of computational tools."[8]

In all these successful programs the electronic instruction takes advantage of many of the strengths of computers: children are taught individually and at their own pace, and the software develops interaction between the computer and the student. Moreover, the electronic instructor never retires or gets sick, and programmers can continually improve the software. Teachers continue to be essential, but with a role that differs from our accustomed conception of what teachers do.

Careful consideration of results from these and other studies makes it seem possible that, if this type of computerized education were adopted universally, technology could begin to make real and beneficial changes for students, teachers, and schools. Under this scenario, not only would there be interaction between the computer and the student, but also each pupil would have, in effect, a private tutor throughout his or her educational career. Like a human tutor, the electronic instructor would teach the child at his or her learning level. For example, superior students would constantly have new vistas and challenges opened to them, with continual opportunities for advancement. With sub-par students, the computer would provide appropriate material but would also move at a speed that would fit each pupil's capacity for progress.

Through constant testing and continual interaction, the electronic instructor would be aware of the child's needs and would immediately provide proper material to correct any problems and to encourage and help the student to advance. Students who had more difficulty learning would never be overwhelmed because the class had proceeded beyond their level of scholarship. Moreover, there would be no embarrassment if the computer had to take longer to cover a given lesson for a particular student. The child's classmates would not know. Only the computer and the authorities receiving the computer reports would have this information. At the other end of the learning spectrum, students who were capable of advancing more rapidly would find new excitement and challenges, and much of the boredom that has always engulfed these students would be removed.

Moreover, the electronic instructor could be programmed to emulate the approaches that good teachers have always used with their students. It would point out errors and praise and reinforce all gains. Positive feedback helps the student and makes learning enjoyable, as all teachers recognize. In a classroom of 15 or 20 students, teachers are often unable to give each student individual encouragement. The computer, however, with only one child to attend to, would always be quick to praise his or her accomplishments. Since the computer would interact directly with the child, it could concentrate its power exclusively on the needs of the individual student without affecting the requirements of other children in the class. They would all have their own private tutors.

TEACHERS

Computerized education would change the role of teachers but would neither eliminate nor downgrade them. On the contrary, human instructors would remain extremely important but with a radically different focus. This possibility often frightens teachers, but computerization would actually enhance their position. Many of the tedious, boring duties that they must endure today, such as preparing daily lesson plans and correcting tests, would vanish. That would leave them more time to function in their true and essential position as educators. There are two basic roles that I foresee for teachers in computerized education: continuing to conduct group activities and acting as "leader teachers."

Many teachers today conduct a variety of group sessions, such as workshops, seminars, and discussions. In computerized education, these duties would not only continue but would take on more importance than in today's schools. In addition, some aspects of today's group meetings would change. The computer would handle the basic necessities of the assigned curriculum, giving teachers greater freedom to choose topics for a group setting and the prospect of dealing more deeply with those topics than is possible today. Group projects might continue for several class periods or for several days. Despite the length of time used in these activities, the students would not miss any of their computer classes because the computer would begin again exactly where the last lesson ended. Today, teachers usually have all the students from their own classes in their groups and no one else. In computerized education, preset conditions would not determine attendance. Students could choose the workshops that most interested them, and teachers could establish prerequisites for attendance. For a teacher, this type of group would form the ideal teaching environment.

One of the fears sometimes voiced about children learning extensively from computers is that they would lose the valuable human give-and-take that currently happens in classes. In actuality, because of the need for discipline, less interplay among students goes on in today's classrooms than is often imagined. But group sessions in computerized education would provide many legitimate opportunities for student interaction.

Another vitally important activity for humans in the education of children would be to function as leader teachers.[9] Every student at every age level would have a leader teacher whom the pupil and his or her parents would choose and who would be responsible for leading the child as he or she pursued an education. This relationship between student and teacher would last for at least a year at a time and might continue for several years. The student would meet this mentor privately and on a regular basis. These meetings would vary, depending on the age and needs of the child. For example, the leader teacher of a student in the first grade might see and talk with the child several times every day. The leader teacher of a student in high school might meet with the youth only once every couple of weeks if that seemed appropriate.

All children, however, at all age levels would sit down regularly with their teachers, who would have access to their computer records. Time would be available for the instructors to get to know the children well. This system would make directing the education of the children easier and more productive for the teachers and make the children comfortable with this kind of direction. In today's education system, many students go months or even years without meeting privately with a teacher. That could never happen if computers were teaching and leader teachers had both the responsibility of directing children's education and the time to carry out that responsibility.

Parents would have another advantage because a leader teacher directed their child. They would find it easier to arrange parent/teacher conferences. They would need to meet with only one instructor, who would have a thorough knowledge of the student and of all the subjects he or she was studying.

THE FUTURE

Can schools ever take advantage of true computerized education? When corporate America learned how it could use computers to improve productivity, the central role of the computer in business was assured. The need for improvement in education is present, as even such staunch defenders of today's schools as the Sandia National Laboratories and Gerald Bracey point out. Moreover, everybody would be delighted if there could be additional gains even among today's best schools.

Emulating the successful employment of computers by business, however, is not simple. There are unique difficulties in education. For example, school boards must alleviate the fears of teachers that they will lose their jobs. In addition, since education is much more involved in the political world, proportionately more people must take part in the process of making changes. The numbers of citizens who must become aware of the potential of computerization in education will be larger than in business, where the decision makers are fewer. In corporate America, when software companies developed programs to enhance productivity, individual businesses bought that software because they wanted to improve and did not fear changes. Education, with some exceptions, has a history of resisting serious change. This tendency lessens the incentive for software companies to develop the necessary programming.

The solution, therefore, must be twofold. First, educators, politicians, parents, and concerned citizens must understand how schools can use computers more effectively to improve education and to benefit students and teachers. Second, commercial companies must create suitable software.

These seem to be monstrous tasks, but both are possible. Many teachers, parents, and administrators want improvements and are engaged in an ongoing search for answers. They will need to examine and debate the value of true computerization as they carry out their quest. If these many searchers for improved education decide that computerization can supply an important portion of the answer, then it will be up to the private corporations to do their part. Some of these are already developing programming, as noted above, and they and other companies could turn more of their resources and ingenuity toward developing outstanding and effective educational software. The potential market is huge, and software corporations will produce the programming as soon as they see that education will accept these changes.

Although there are differences in the paths of education and business in developing the use of computerization, there is one major similarity. American business was not able to take advantage of the power of computer technology until many of its basic practices changed. This is equally true in education. Until schools can permit a major alteration in the way teaching is carried on, they must necessarily continue to miss out on the improvement that computer technology can bring.

NOTES

1. Becky Smerdon et al., *Teachers' Tools for the 21st Century: A Report on Teachers' Use of Technology* (Washington, D.C.: National Center for Education Statistics, 2000), p. 5.
2. Jay R. Campbell, Catherine M. Hombo, and John Mazzeo, *NAEP 1999 Trends in Academic Progress: Three Decades of Student Performance* (Washington, D.C.: National Center for Education Statistics, 2000), Figure 1.
3. Smerdon et al., p. iii.
4. Ibid.; and Market Data Retrieval, "New Teachers and Technology: Examining Perceptions, Habits, and Professional Development Experiences," survey conducted in 1999.
5. Erik Brynjolfsson and Lorin M. Hitt, "Computing Productivity: Firm-Level Evidence," p. 2, available at http://grace.wharton.upenn.edu/~lhitt/ cpg.pdf.
6. Smerdon et al., chap. 7.
7. Plato Learning, Inc.: http://www.plato.com; Scientific Learning: http://www.scilearn.com; and NovaNet Learning, Inc.:http://www.nn.com.
8. Kenneth R. Koedinger et al., "Intelligent Tutoring Goes to School in the Big City," *Journal of Artificial Intelligence in Education*, vol. 8, no. 1, 1997, p. 31.
9. Frederick Bennett, *Computers as Tutors: Solving the Crisis in Education* (Sarasota, Fla.: Faben, 1999), chap. 19.

FREDERICK BENNETT is a retired psychologist and the author of Computers as Tutors: Solving the Crisis in Education *(Faben, 1999). He lives in Sarasota, Fla. E-mail address: bennett@fabenbooks.com*

THE NEW GENDER GAP

From kindergarten to grad school, boys are becoming the second sex.

BY MICHELLE CONLIN

Lawrence High is the usual fortress of manila-brick blandness and boxy 1960s architecture. At lunch, the metalheads saunter out to the smokers' park, while the AP types get pizzas at Marinara's, where they talk about—what else?—other people. The hallways are filled with lip-glossed divas in designer clothes and packs of girls in midriff-baring track tops. The guys run the gamut, too: skate punks, rich boys in Armani, and saggy-panted crews with their Eminem swaggers. In other words, they look pretty much as you'd expect.

But when the leaders of the Class of 2003 assemble in the Long Island high school's fluorescent-lit meeting rooms, most of these boys are nowhere to be seen. The senior class president? A girl. The vice-president? Girl. Head of student government? Girl. Captain of the math team, chief of the yearbook, and editor of the newspaper? Girls.

It's not that the girls of the Class of 2003 aren't willing to give the guys a chance. Last year, the juniors elected a boy as class president. But after taking office, he swiftly instructed his all-female slate that they were his cabinet and that he was going to be calling all the shots. The girls looked around and realized they had the votes, says Tufts University-bound Casey Vaughn, an Intel finalist and one of the alpha femmes of the graduating class. "So they impeached him and took over."

The female lock on power at Lawrence is emblematic of a stunning gender reversal in American education. From kindergarten to graduate school, boys are fast becoming the second sex. "Girls are on a tear through the educational system," says Thomas G. Mortenson, a senior scholar at the Pell Institute for the Study of Opportunity in Higher Education in Washington. "In the past 30 years, nearly every inch of educational progress has gone to them."

Just a century ago, the president of Harvard University, Charles W. Eliot, refused to admit women because he feared they would waste the precious resources of his school. Today, across the country, it seems as if girls have built a kind of scholastic Roman Empire alongside boys' languishing Greece. Although Lawrence High has its share of boy superstars—like this year's valedictorian—the gender takeover at some schools is nearly complete. "Every time I turn around, if something good is happening, there's a female in charge," says Terrill O. Stammler, principal of Rising Sun High School in Rising Sun, Md. Boys are missing from nearly every leadership position, academic honors slot, and student-activity post at the school. Even Rising Sun's girls' sports teams do better than the boys'.

At one exclusive private day school in the Midwest, administrators have even gone so far as to mandate that all awards and student-government positions be divvied equally between the sexes. "It's not just that boys are falling behind girls," says William S. Pollock, author of *Real Boys: Rescuing Our Sons from the Myths of Boyhood* and a professor of psychiatry at Harvard Medical School. "It's that boys themselves are falling behind their own functioning and doing worse than they did before."

It may still be a man's world. But it is no longer, in any way, a boy's. From his first days in school, an average boy is already developmentally two years behind the girls in reading and writing. Yet he's often expected to learn the same things in the same way in the same amount of time.

While every nerve in his body tells him to run, he has to sit still and listen for almost eight hours a day. Biologically, he needs about four recesses a day, but he's lucky if he gets one, since some lawsuit-leery schools have banned them altogether. Hug a girl, and he could be labeled a "toucher" and swiftly suspended—a result of what some say is an increasingly anti-boy culture that pathologizes their behavior.

If he falls behind, he's apt to be shipped off to special ed, where he'll find that more than 70% of his classmates are also boys. Squirm, clown, or interrupt, and he is four times as likely to be diagnosed with attention deficit hyperactivity disorder. That often leads to being forced to take Ritalin or risk being expelled, sent to special ed, or having parents accused of negligence. One study of public schools in Fairfax County, Va., found that more than 20% of upper-middle-class white boys were taking Ritalin-like drugs by fifth grade.

Once a boy makes it to freshman year of high school, he's at greater risk of falling even further behind in grades, extracurricular activities, and advanced placement. Not even science and math remain his bastions. And while the girls are busy working on sweeping the honor roll at graduation, a boy is more likely to be bulking up in the weight room to enhance his steroid-fed Adonis complex, playing Grand Theft Auto: Vice City on his PlayStation2, or downloading rapper 50 Cent on his iPod. All the while, he's 30% more likely to drop out, 85% more likely to commit murder, and four to six times more likely to kill himself, with boy suicides tripling since 1970. "We get a bad rap," says Steven Covington, a sophomore at Ottumwa High School in Ottumwa, Iowa. "Society says we can't be trusted."

As for college—well, let's just say this: At least it's easier for the guys who get there to find a date. For 350 years, men outnumbered women on college campuses. Now, in every state, every income bracket, every racial and ethnic group, and most industrialized Western nations, women reign, earning an average 57% of all BAs and 58% of all master's degrees in the U.S. alone. There are 133 girls getting BAs for every 100 guys—a number that's projected to grow to 142 women per 100 men by 2010, according to the U.S. Education Dept. If current trends continue, demographers say, there will be 156 women per 100 men earning degrees by 2020.

Overall, more boys and girls are in college than a generation ago. But when adjusted for population growth, the percentage of boys entering college, master's programs, and most doctoral programs—except for PhDs in fields like engineering and computer science—has mostly stalled out, whereas for women it has continued to rise across the board. The trend is most pronounced among Hispanics, African Americans, and those from low-income families.

The female-to-male ratio is already 60–40 at the University of North Carolina, Boston University, and New York University. To keep their gender ratios 50–50, many Ivy League and other elite schools are secretly employing a kind of stealth affirmative action for boys. "Girls present better qualifications in the application process—better grades, tougher classes, and more thought in their essays," says Michael S. McPherson, president of Macalester College in St. Paul, Minn., where 57% of enrollees are women. "Boys get off to a slower start."

The trouble isn't limited to school. Once a young man is out of the house, he's more likely than his sister to boomerang back home and sponge off his mom and dad. It all adds up to the fact that before he reaches adulthood, a young man is more likely than he was 30 years ago to end up in the new and growing class of underachiever—what the British call the "sink group."

For a decade, British educators have waged successful classroom programs to ameliorate "laddism" (boys turning off to school) by focusing on teaching techniques that re-engage them. But in the U.S., boys' fall from alpha to omega status doesn't even have a name, let alone the public's attention. "No one wants to speak out on behalf of boys," says Andrew Sum, director of the Northeastern University Center for Labor Market Studies. As a social-policy or educational issue, "it's near nonexistent."

Women are rapidly closing the M.D. and PhD gap and make up almost half of law students.

On the one hand, the education grab by girls is amazing news, which could make the 21st the first female century. Already, women are rapidly closing the M.D. and PhD gap and are on the verge of making up the majority of law students, according to the American Bar Assn. MBA programs, with just 29% females, remain among the few old-boy domains.

Still, it's hardly as if the world has been equalized: Ninety percent of the world's billionaires are men. Among the super rich, only one woman, Gap Inc. co-founder Doris F. Fisher, made, rather than inherited, her wealth. Men continue to dominate in the highest-paying jobs in such leading-edge industries as engineering, investment banking, and high tech—the sectors that still power the economy and build the biggest fortunes. And women still face sizable obstacles in the pay gap, the glass ceiling, and the still-Sisyphean struggle to juggle work and child-rearing.

But attaining a decisive educational edge may finally enable females to narrow the earnings gap, punch through more of the glass ceiling, and gain an equal hand in rewriting the rules of corporations, government, and society. "Girls are better able to deliver in terms of what modern society requires of people—paying attention, abiding by rules, being verbally competent, and dealing with interpersonal relationships in offices," says James Garbarino, a professor of human development at Cornell

University and author of *Lost Boys: Why Our Sons Turn Violent and How We Can Save Them.*

Righting boys' problems needn't end up leading to reversals for girls. But some feminists say the danger in exploring what's happening to boys would be to mistakenly see any expansion of opportunities for women as inherently disadvantageous to boys. "It isn't a zero-sum game," says Susan M. Bailey, executive director of the Wellesley Centers for Women. Adds Macalester's McPherson: "It would be dangerous to even out the gender ratio by treating women worse. I don't think we've reached a point in this country where we are fully providing equal opportunities to women."

Men could become losers in a global economy that values mental powers over might.

Still, if the creeping pattern of male disengagement and economic dependency continues, more men could end up becoming losers in a global economy that values mental powers over might—not to mention the loss of their talent and potential. The growing educational and economic imbalances could also create societal upheavals, altering family finances, social policies, and work-family practices. Men are already dropping out of the labor force, walking out on fatherhood, and disconnecting from civic life in greater numbers. Since 1964, for example, the voting rate in Presidential elections among men has fallen from 72% to 53%—twice the rate of decline among women, according to Pell's Mortenson. In a turn-around from the 1960s, more women now vote than men.

Boys' slide also threatens to erode male earnings, spark labor shortages for skilled workers, and create the same kind of marriage squeeze among white women that already exists for blacks. Among African Americans, 30% of 40- to 44-year-old women have never married, owing in part to the lack of men with the same academic credentials and earning potential. Currently, the never-married rate is 9% for white women of the same age. "Women are going to pull further and further ahead of men, and at some point, when they want to form families, they are going to look around and say, 'Where are the guys?'" says Mortenson.

Corporations should worry, too. During the boom, the most acute labor shortages occurred among educated workers—a problem companies often solved by hiring immigrants. When the economy reenergizes, a skills shortage in the U.S. could undermine employers' productivity and growth.

Better-educated men are also, on average, a much happier lot. They are more likely to marry, stick by their children, and pay more in taxes. From the ages of 18 to 65, the average male college grad earns $2.5 million over his lifetime, 90% more than his high school counterpart. That's

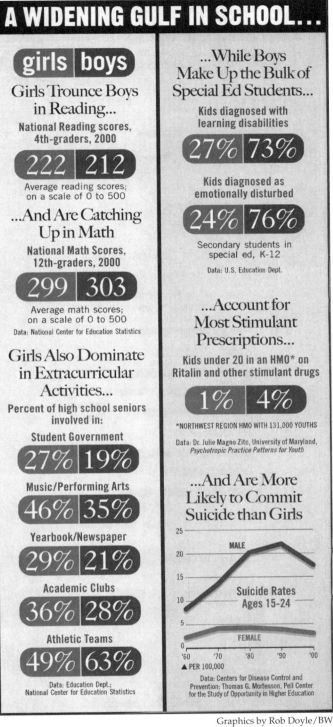

Graphics by Rob Doyle/BW

up from 40% more in 1979, the peak year for U.S. manufacturing. The average college diploma holder also contributes four times more in net taxes over his career than a high school grad, according to Northeastern's Sum. Meanwhile, the typical high school dropout will usually get $40,000 more from the government than he pays in, a net drain on society.

Certainly, many boys continue to conquer scholastic summits, especially boys from high-income families with

...LEADS MORE AND MORE TO A GIRLS' CLUB IN COLLEGE

The Gender Gap Spans Every Racial and Ethnic Group...

Bachelor's degrees awarded to students by race/ethnicity, as a percent of total

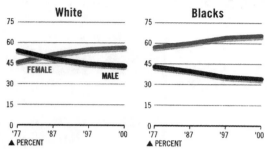

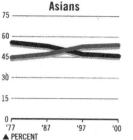

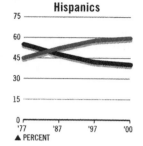

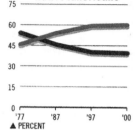

...And Most of the Industrialized World...

Ages 25 to 34, with at least a college education, plus advanced degrees

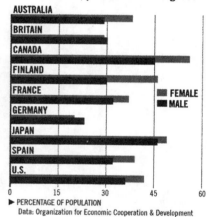

▶ PERCENTAGE OF POPULATION

Data: Organization for Economic Cooperation & Development

...And Is Projected to Get Worse...

Number of U.S. women awarded degrees per 100 men

Bachelor's Degrees

1999-2000	Est. 2009-10
133	142

Master's Degrees

1999-2000	Est. 2009-10
138	151

Data: Andrew Sum, Northeastern University Center for Labor Market Studies

...Threatening the Marriage Squeeze Among Whites That Blacks Already Face

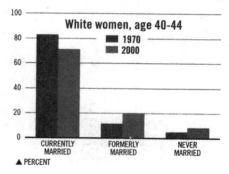

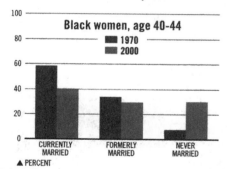

Data: *Mismatch*, by Andrew Hacker; National Center for Education Statistics; Bureau of Labor Statistics; Census Bureau

Graphics by Rob Doyle/BW

educated parents. Overall, boys continue to do better on standardized tests such as the scholastic aptitude test, though more low-income girls than low-income boys take it, thus depressing girls' scores. Many educators also believe that standardized testing's multiple-choice format favors boys because girls tend to think in broader, more complex terms. But that advantage is eroding as many colleges now weigh grades—where girls excel— more heavily than test scores.

Still, it's not as if girls don't face a slew of vexing issues, which are often harder to detect because girls are likelier to internalize low self-esteem through depression or the

THE NEW SHAPE OF THE WORKFORCE

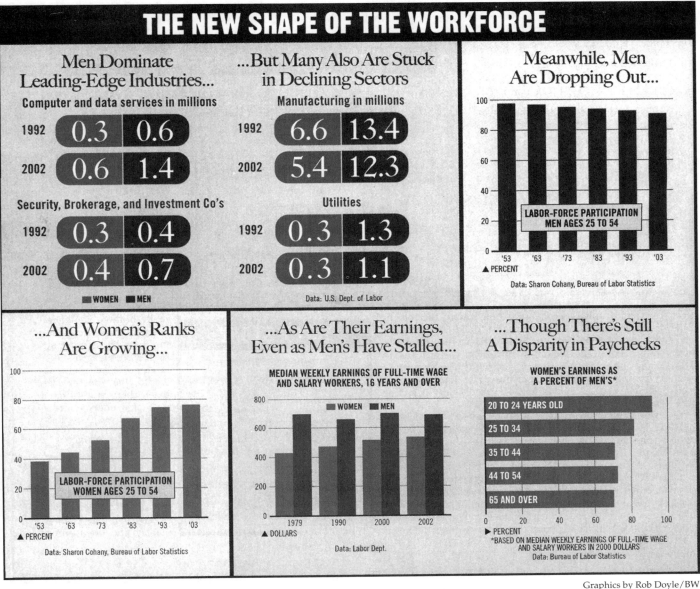

Men Dominate Leading-Edge Industries...

Computer and data services in millions

	WOMEN	MEN
1992	0.3	0.6
2002	0.6	1.4

Security, Brokerage, and Investment Co's

	WOMEN	MEN
1992	0.3	0.4
2002	0.4	0.7

■ WOMEN ■ MEN

...But Many Also Are Stuck in Declining Sectors

Manufacturing in millions

	WOMEN	MEN
1992	6.6	13.4
2002	5.4	12.3

Utilities

	WOMEN	MEN
1992	0.3	1.3
2002	0.3	1.1

Data: U.S. Dept. of Labor

Meanwhile, Men Are Dropping Out...

LABOR-FORCE PARTICIPATION MEN AGES 25 TO 54

▲ PERCENT

Data: Sharon Cohany, Bureau of Labor Statistics

...And Women's Ranks Are Growing...

LABOR-FORCE PARTICIPATION WOMEN AGES 25 TO 54

▲ PERCENT

Data: Sharon Cohany, Bureau of Labor Statistics

...As Are Their Earnings, Even as Men's Have Stalled...

MEDIAN WEEKLY EARNINGS OF FULL-TIME WAGE AND SALARY WORKERS, 16 YEARS AND OVER

■ WOMEN ■ MEN

▲ DOLLARS

Data: Labor Dept.

...Though There's Still A Disparity in Paychecks

WOMEN'S EARNINGS AS A PERCENT OF MEN'S*

20 TO 24 YEARS OLD
25 TO 34
35 TO 44
44 TO 54
65 AND OVER

► PERCENT
*BASED ON MEDIAN WEEKLY EARNINGS OF FULL-TIME WAGE AND SALARY WORKERS IN 2000 DOLLARS
Data: Bureau of Labor Statistics

Graphics by Rob Doyle/BW

desire to starve themselves into perfection. And while boys may act out with their fists, girls, given their superior verbal skills, often do so with their mouths in the form of vicious gossip and female bullying. "They yell and cuss," says 15-year-old Keith Gates, an Ottumwa student. "But we always get in trouble. They never do."

Before educators, corporations, and policymakers can narrow the new gender gap, they will have to understand its myriad causes. Everything from absentee parenting to the lack of male teachers to corporate takeovers of lunch rooms with sugar-and-fat-filled food, which can make kids hyperactive and distractable, plays a role. So can TV violence, which hundreds of studies—including recent ones by Stanford University and the University of Michigan—have linked to aggressive behavior in kids. Some believe boys are responding to cultural signals—downsized dads cast adrift in the New Economy, a dumb-and-

dumber dude culture that demeans academic achievement, and the glamorization of all things gangster that makes school seem so uncool. What can compare with the allure of a gun-wielding, model-dating hip hopper? Boys, who mature more slowly than girls, are also often less able to delay gratification or take a long-range view.

Schools have inadvertently played a big role, too, losing sight of boys—taking for granted that they were doing well, even though data began to show the opposite. Some educators believed it was a blip that would change or feared takebacks on girls' gains. Others were just in denial. Indeed, many administrators saw boys, rather than the way schools were treating them, as the problem.

Thirty years ago, educational experts launched what's known as the "Girl Project." The movement's noble objective was to help girls wipe out their weaknesses in math and science, build self-esteem, and give them the undisputed message: The opportunities are yours; take them. Schools focused on making the classroom more girl-friendly by including teaching styles that catered to them. Girls were also powerfully influenced by the women's movement, as well as by Title IX and the Gender & Equity Act, all of which created a legal environment in which discrimination against girls—from classrooms to the sports field—carried heavy penalties. Once the chains were off, girls soared.

For 30 years, the focus at schools has been to empower girls, in and out of the classroom.

Yet even as boys' educational development was flat-lining in the 1990s—with boys dropping out in greater numbers and failing to bridge the gap in reading and writing—the spotlight remained firmly fixed on girls. Part of the reason was that the issue had become politically charged and girls had powerful advocates. The American Association of University Women, for example, published research cementing into pedagogy the idea that girls had deep problems with self-esteem in school as a result of teachers' patterns, which included calling on girls less and lavishing attention on boys. Newspapers and TV newsmagazines lapped up the news, decrying a new confidence crisis among American girls. Universities and research centers sponsored scores of teacher symposiums centered on girls. "All the focus was on girls, all the grant monies, all the university programs—to get girls interested in science and math," says Steve Hanson, principal of Ottumwa High School in Iowa. "There wasn't a similar thing for reading and writing for boys."

Some boy champions go so far as to contend that schools have become boy-bashing laboratories. Christina Hoff Sommers, author of *The War Against Boys*, says the AAUW report, coupled with zero-tolerance sexual harassment laws, have hijacked schools by overly feminizing classrooms and attempting to engineer androgyny.

The "earliness" push, in which schools are pressured to show kids achieving the same standards by the same age or risk losing funding, is also far more damaging to boys, according to Lilian G. Katz, co-director of ERIC Clearinghouse on Elementary and Early Childhood Education. Even the nerves on boys' fingers develop later than girls', making it difficult to hold a pencil and push out perfect cursive. These developmental differences often unfairly sideline boys as slow or dumb, planting a distaste for school as early as the first grade.

Instead of catering to boys' learning styles, Pollock and others argue, many schools are force-fitting them into an unnatural mold. The reigning sit-still-and-listen paradigm isn't ideal for either sex. But it's one girls often tolerate better than boys. Girls have more intricate sensory capacities and biosocial aptitudes to decipher exactly what the teacher wants, whereas boys tend to be more anti-authoritarian, competitive, and risk-taking. They often don't bother with such details as writing their names in the exact place instructed by the teacher.

Experts say educators also haven't done nearly enough to keep up with the recent findings in brain research about developmental differences. "Ninety-nine-point-nine percent of teachers are not trained in this," says Michael Gurian, author of *Boys and Girls Learn Differently*. "They were taught 20 years ago that gender is just a social function."

In fact, brain research over the past decade has revealed how differently boys' and girls' brains can function. Early on, boys are usually superior spatial thinkers and possess the ability to see things in three dimensions. They are often drawn to play that involves intense movement and an element of make-believe violence. Instead of straitjacketing boys by attempting to restructure this behavior out of them, it would be better to teach them how to harness this energy effectively and healthily, Pollock says.

As it stands, the result is that too many boys are diagnosed with attention-deficit disorder or its companion, attention-deficit hyperactivity disorder. The U.S.—mostly its boys—now consumes 80% of the world's supply of methylphenidate (the generic name for Ritalin). That use has increased 500% over the past decade, leading some to call it the new K–12 management tool. There are school districts where 20% to 25% of the boys are on the drug, says Paul R. Wolpe, a psychiatry professor at the University of Pennsylvania and the senior fellow at the school's Center for Bioethics: "Ritalin is a response to an artificial social context that we've created for children."

Instead of recommending medication—something four states have recently banned school administrators from doing—experts say educators should focus on helping boys feel less like misfits. Experts are designing new developmentally appropriate, child-initiated learning that concentrates on problem-solving, not just test-taking. This approach benefits both sexes but especially boys, given that they tend to learn best through action, not just talk. Activities are geared toward the child's interest level and temperament. Boys, for example, can learn math through counting pinecones, biology through mucking around in a pond. They can read *Harry Potter* instead of *Little House on the Prairie*, and write about aliens attacking a hospital rather than about how to care for people in the hospital. If they get antsy, they can leave a teacher's lecture and go to an activity center replete with computers and manipulable objects that support the lesson plan.

Paying attention to boys' emotional lives also delivers dividends. Over the course of her longitudinal research project in Washington (D.C.) schools, University of Northern Florida researcher Rebecca Marcon found that boys who attend kindergartens that focus on social and emotional skills—as opposed to only academic learning—perform better, across the board, by the time they reach junior high.

Indeed, brain research shows that boys are actually more empathic, expressive, and emotive at birth than girls. But Pollock says the boy code, which bathes them in a culture of stoicism and reticence, often socializes those aptitudes out of them by the second grade. "We now have executives paying $10,000 a week to learn emotional intelligence," says Pollock. "These are actually the skills boys are born with."

The gender gap also has roots in the expectation gap. In the 1970s, boys were far more likely to anticipate getting a college degree—with girls firmly entrenched in the cheerleader role. Today, girls' expectations are ballooning, while boys' are plummeting. There's even a sense, including among the most privileged families, that today's boys are a sort of payback generation—the one that has to compensate for the advantages given to males in the past. In fact, the new equality is often perceived as a loss by many boys who expected to be on top. "My friends in high school, they just didn't see the value of college, they just didn't care enough," says New York University sophomore Joe Clabby. Only half his friends from his high school group in New Jersey went on to college.

They will face a far different world than their dads did. Without college diplomas, it will be harder for them to find good-paying jobs. And more and more, the positions available to them will be in industries long thought of as female. The services sector, where women make up 60% of employees, has ballooned by 260% since the 1970s. During the same period, manufacturing, where men hold 70% of jobs, has shrunk by 14%.

These men will also be more likely to marry women who outearn them. Even in this jobless recovery, women's wages have continued to grow, with the pay gap the smallest on record, while men's earnings haven't managed to keep up with the low rate of inflation. Given that the recession hit male-centric industries such as technology and manufacturing the hardest, native-born men experienced more than twice as much job loss as native-born women between 2000 and 2002.

Some feminists who fought hard for girl equality in schools in the early 1980s and '90s say this: So what if girls have gotten 10, 20 years of attention—does that make up for centuries of subjugation? Moreover, what's wrong with women gliding into first place, especially if they deserve it? "Just because girls aren't shooting 7-Eleven clerks doesn't mean they should be ignored," says Cornell's Garbarino. "Once you stop oppressing girls, it stands to reason they will thrive up to their potential."

Moreover, girls say much of their drive stems from parents and teachers pushing them to get a college degree because they have to be better to be equal—to make the same money and get the same respect as a guy. "Girls are more willing to take the initiative... they're not afraid to do the work," says Tara Prout, the Georgetown-bound senior class president at Lawrence High. "A lot of boys in my school are looking for credit to get into college to look good, but they don't really want to do the grunt work."

A new world has opened up for girls, but unless a symmetrical effort is made to help boys find their footing, it may turn out that it's a lonely place to be. After all, it takes more than one gender to have a gender revolution.

BOYS' STORY

For further reading:

- *Lost Boys* by James Garbarino
- *Boys and Girls Learn Differently* by Michael Gurian
- *Mismatch* by Andrew Hacker
- *Raising Cain* by Dan Kindlon and Michael Thompson
- *Real Boys* by William Pollack
- *The War Against Boys* by Christina Hoff Sommers

Girls, Boys and Autism

Is this mysterious and sometimes devastating condition just an extreme version of normal male intelligence? That's one provocative new theory. Behind autism's gender gap.

By Geoffrey Cowley

ANDREW BACALAO has a good, sharp mind. At 13, he's a decent pianist, a devotee of Frank Lloyd Wright, a master at video-games and jigsaw puzzles. He remembers phone numbers like a Pocket PC, and he can dismantle a radio or a flashlight in the time it takes some people to find the power switch. But drop in on Andrew at home in Oak Park, Ill., and you quickly sense that something is amiss. "Can you look at her?" his mom, Dr. Cindy Mears, prompts, as a NEWSWEEK correspondent greets him in the living room. He stays on the couch, feet up, mesmerized by a handheld game called Bop It Extreme. Soon he's making soap bubbles and running outside to bang on the windows. Andrew does eventually talk, but conversation doesn't come easily. When his mom asks him not to burp, he tells the guest, "I'm going to unbutton your outfit." He's merely offering to take her jacket—and he seems to think his choice of words is just fine.

What do you make of such a kid? A generation ago, he might have been written off as a discipline problem or a psychopath—someone who insists on misbehaving even though he's smart enough to know better.

But we now know there are different kinds of intelligence, which can crop up in unusual combinations. The world, as it turns out, is full of people who find fractal geometry easier than small talk, people who can spot a tiny lesion on a chest X-ray but can't tell a smile from a smirk. Most of these folks qualify as "autistic," but not in the traditional sense. Classic autism is a devastating neurological disorder. Though its causes are unclear, it has a strong genetic component and is marked by rapid brain growth during early childhood. Many sufferers are mentally retarded and require lifelong institutional care. But autism has many other faces. The condition, as experts now conceive it, is like high blood pressure—a "spectrum disorder" in which affected people differ from the rest of us only by degrees. The question is, degrees of what? Can autistic tendencies be measured on some scale? If so, is there a clear boundary between normal and abnormal? And is abnormality always a bad thing? What promise does life hold for people like Andrew?

Cambridge University psychologist Simon Baron-Cohen has a thesis that bears on all these questions. In a bold new book called "The Essential

A SPECTRUM

In general, females relate more to feelings, and males to facts. Autistic kids fit an extreme male patern

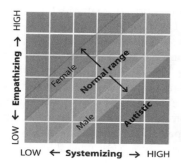

Difference," he defines autism as an imbalance between two kinds of intelligence: the kind used to understand people (he calls it "empathizing") and the kind used to understand things ("systemizing"). Though most of us have both abilities, studies suggest that females are better than males at empathizing, while males have a stronger knack for systemizing. By Baron-Cohen's account, autism is just an exaggerated version of the male profile—an extreme fondness for rule-based systems, coupled with an inability to intuit people's feelings and intentions. The truth may not be quite that simple, but the concepts of "E" and "S" offer a powerful new framework for thinking about boys, girls and autism. If Baron-Cohen is right, autism is not just a disease in need of a cure. It's a mental style that people can learn to accommodate. Sometimes it's even a gift.

It's no secret that autism affects boys more than girls. Males account for more than 80 percent of the million-plus Americans with autistic disorders. Are these conditions partly an expression of male thought patterns? Do boys live closer to the autistic spectrum than girls? Not in every case. But when researchers study groups of people—infants, toddlers, teens or adults—an interesting pattern emerges. Newborn girls gaze longer at faces than at mechanical mobiles, while boys show the opposite preference. By the age of 3, girls are more adept than boys at imagining fictional characters' feelings, and by 7 they're better at identifying a faux pas in a story. The disparity is just as striking when adults are asked to interpret facial expressions and tones of voice. Women rule.

Males aren't hopeless, though. They show a lifelong advantage on tests of spatial and mechanical reasoning. In fact they're nearly twice as likely as women to score more than 700 on the SAT math test, and four times as likely to become engineers. Social conditioning may account for

some of that gap. It may also help explain the thrill that 2-year-old boys get from trucks, blocks and other mechanical toys. But there has to be more to the story. Consider what happened when psychologists Gerianne Alexander and Melissa Hines tried out six toys on vervet monkeys at UCLA's Non-Human Primate Laboratory. Male monkeys favored the boy toys (a ball and a car). Females spent more time with a doll and a pot. And the gender-neutral toys (a picture book and a stuffed dog) got equal attention from both groups. The findings suggest that sex hormones may sculpt our brains as well as our bodies, priming males and females for different styles of thought—what Baron-Cohen calls a "Type E" style and a "Type S" style.

It's not hard to see how autism fits into this scheme. In its classic form, the condition leaves people virtually devoid of social impulses. Autistic kids have trouble communicating, and games like peekaboo leave them cold. They seem to perceive people as unpredictable objects. Yet they often excel at systemizing. "Even young autistic children love to classify and order things," says Dr. Bryna Siegel of the University of California, San Francisco. "They're interested in categorical information." Siegel recalls a mother's story about taking her autistic son and nonautistic daughters to see "Finding Nemo," a movie about a clown fish who loses his mom and gets separated from his dad. "The little girls wanted to know if Nemo was scared," she says. "The autistic boy wanted to know exactly what clown fish eat."

Autistic people are famous for collecting such facts, and many can recall them with breathtaking precision. Patricia Juhrs, director of a Rockville, Md., group called Community Services for Autistic Adults and Children, has an adult client who has memorized every top-10 song list Billboard magazine has published since 1947. Tell him which day you were born, and he'll tell you what was playing on the radio. Even when

they lack such savant skills, autistic people often excel at mundane, detail-oriented tasks. "I maintain that we should have autistic people running the scanners at airports," says Catherine Johnson, an author and activist whose two autistic sons amuse themselves by putting together jigsaw puzzles with the picture-side down. "No normal human being can process that much detail."

S HE'S HALF JOKING, but studies support her contention. As you'd expect, autistic people score even lower than typical males on tests that involve predicting people's feelings and interpreting their facial expressions. But when challenged to find the triangle embedded in a complex design, or predict the behavior of a rod attached to a lever, they fare as well as normal males, if not better. The same pattern holds when autistic people are polled directly about empathizing ("I can pick up quickly if someone says one thing and means another") and systemizing ("I am fascinated by how machines work"). In a recently published study, Baron-Cohen's team found that mildly autistic adults trailed normal women and men on a 40-item empathy test, but trumped both groups on a systemizing survey. In short, they were more male than the men.

The findings square nicely with Baron-Cohen's model, but the model takes us only so far. As it turns out, autistic people are not just extreme systemizers. They systemize in a distinct and unusual way. When normally developing kids draw a picture of a train, they start with a gestalt, or general idea: a series of long, flat rectangles with wheels underneath. Autistic kids often start with peripheral details and expand them into dazzling 3-D renderings. "They don't do it in a logical order," says Siegel of UCSF. "They do it as you would if you were tracing." Stephen Wiltshire, 29, had never spoken when he started sketching at the age of 5. He still lives with his mother in West London, but he has since achieved world renown

THE DETAIL-ORIENTED JOBS MOST OF US CAN'T STAND ARE OFTEN TASKS THAT AUTISTIC PEOPLE THRIVE ON

for his visionary portraits of buildings and vehicles. "Cadillac, Chevy, Lincoln," he says when asked about his passions. "Sears Tower, the Frick, the Chrysler building." His speech, like his work, is virtually free of generalizations. As a friend once observed, he is "rooted in the literal, the concrete."

Wiltshire may have Type S tastes, but his avoidance of abstractions can't be passed off as a typical Type S tendency. It gets at something more specific, says neuroscientist Laurent Mottron of Montreal's Hôpital Rivière-des-Prairies. It reveals a preference for parts over wholes, a tendency to process information one piece at a time instead of filtering it through general categories. Most of us simplify the world to make it more manageable. Whether we're taking in sights, sounds or sentences, our brains ignore countless details to create useful gestalts. Autistic people make generalizations, too ("it's a train," "it's a blender"), but studies suggest they work from the bottom up, attending doggedly to everything their senses take in. That has nothing to do with maleness, but it helps explain various aspects of autism—the encyclopedic memory, the lightning-fast calculation and the extreme sensitivity to sounds, lights and textures. It also ties in neatly with recent studies linking autism to superfast brain growth during the first years of life. Researchers believe that process may generate more sensory neurons than the brain can integrate into coherent networks.

Baron-Cohen doesn't dispute any of this. The E-S model may not capture all the nuances of autism, he says, but it sheds new light on the narrow interests and repetitive behaviors that people across the autistic spectrum display. "Consider the child who can spend hours watching

how a glass bottle rotates in the sunlight but who cannot talk or make eye contact," he says. "The old theories said that this was purposeless repetitive behavior. The new theory says that the child, given his or her IQ, may be doing something intelligent: looking for predictable rules or patterns in the data." In other words, the E-S model may be incomplete but it's still valuable—for it reveals the sanity and dignity of autistic behavior. "People with Asperger's syndrome [a mild form of autism] are like saltwater fish forced to live in fresh water," a patient once explained to Baron-Cohen. "We're fine if you put us into the right environment. But when the person and the environment don't match, we seem disabled."

Some advocates insist that conditions like Asperger's syndrome are not disorders at all, just personality variants that have been misconstrued as defects. They believe that people at the high-functioning end of the autistic spectrum should be spared psychiatric labels. But when the labels are applied without stigma, they can be liberating.

Dave Spicer had never thought of himself as autistic until 1994, when his 8-year-old son, Andrew, got a formal diagnosis and he was diagnosed too. Spicer, then 46, was a computer programmer and system designer, but his social ineptitude had cost him two marriages and blighted his career. He recalls leaving business meetings thinking all had gone well, only to discover that he had annoyed or offended people. "A social situation is like a square dance where the caller is speaking Swahili," he says. "There will be a cue and I won't get it, and I'll stumble into people." Spicer's son is now thriving in a mainstream high school after several years of special education, and Spicer himself has learned

to play to his strengths. He has gone back to college. He socializes on his own terms, and doesn't berate himself for being different. "My favorite story about autism is 'The Emperor's New Clothes'," he says. "The boy didn't understand social norms, but he spoke the truth. I think society needs us."

Gifted geeks aren't the only ones saying that. Juhrs, the social-service organizer, has found that even profoundly autistic adults are often highly employable. "If they're matched properly with work they enjoy," she says, "they can do as well or better than people who aren't disabled." In seeking out jobs for her clients, Juhrs never appeals to employers for charity. She asks if there are jobs they've had trouble filling. As it turns out, the Type S tasks that her people thrive on—inspecting garments, coding inventory, assembling components for the fuses on nuclear submarines—are often the same ones that ordinary people can't stand. "Once our folks get into going to work, they don't want to miss a day," she says. "We have to talk them into holidays."

Tapping these strengths makes obvious sense, but the deficits associated with autism are just as real. Are people like Spicer destined to fail in love and the workplace, or can their social handicaps be conquered? Unlike systemizing, empathy involves snap, intuitive judgments that you can't always make by following a recipe. "Most people learn to interact socially just by observation," says Stephen Shore, a mildly autistic Boston University doctoral student who heads the Asperger's Association of New England. "People on the autistic spectrum regard things as a set of rules. We have to figure them out or be taught." Like Tom Hanks in "Big," Shore thought *sleepover* the first time a woman invited him to spend the night. But through painstaking study and practice, he has developed a good enough social repertoire to sustain a career and a 13-year marriage.

Was Shore just lucky, or is there a lesson to be drawn from his experience? Can people on the autistic spectrum learn to compensate for their lack of natural empathizing ability? The answer depends on the person and the condition. Siegel estimates that 25 percent of classically autistic children respond to intensive interventions and that 7 percent do well enough to attend mainstream schools and lead normal lives. The response rates are much higher among mildly affected kids, and experts agree that early intervention is the key to success. "The earlier you can get into a treatment program," says Andy Shih of the National Alliance for Autism Research, "the better the prognosis."

The programs go by different names—applied behavioral analysis, discreet trial training, pivotal response treatment—but most of them use simple conditioning exercises to open lines of communication. "With an average child, you can point to something red and ask what color it is," says psychologist Robert Koegel of the University of California, Santa Barbara. "Autistic kids are screaming, trying to get out of it. But what if they love M&Ms? When we ask which one is red, they take a red one. They're highly motivated." Naming colors is simpler than decoding social signals, but they, too, can be mastered by unconventional means. Baron-Cohen's team has developed an interactive computer program that pairs 418 emotions with distinct facial expressions. Preliminary studies suggest that anyone, autistic or not, can develop a better eye for flattery, boredom or scorn simply by practicing for 10 weeks with these electronic flashcards.

As fate would have it, some of the best natural readers of feelings and faces are themselves profoundly disabled. People with a rare genetic disorder called Williams syndrome are often severely retarded. Yet they're hypersocial, highly verbal and often deeply empathetic. "In some ways," says research psychologist Teresa Doyle of the Salk Institute, "Williams syndrome is almost an opposite of autism." Ten-year-old A. J. Arciniega will never play Bop It Extreme the way Andrew Bacalao does, let alone dismantle a radio. But he shakes hands eagerly when greeted by a NEWSWEEK correspondent, and gladly engages in conversation, asking about the visitor's children and their interests. Settling in with a wordless picture book, he pages through the story of a boy and a dog who lose their frog and set out to find him. There is no plot in A.J.'s telling, but his feeling for the characters is irrepressible. "Ron! Ron! Where are you?" he exclaims when the boy is shown calling for his frog. " 'Woof! Woof!' the dog moans." Neither Andrew nor A.J. is in for an easy life—as Baron-Cohen might say, things are simpler in the middle of the E-S spectrum. But the world will be richer for both of them.

With ANNE UNDERWOOD, ANDREW MURR, KAREN SPRINGEN and SARAH SENNOTT

"High Stakes Are for Tomatoes"

Statewide testing of students, with penalties for failure, has run into opposition from parents across the political spectrum

by Peter Schrag

By now it's hardly news that as education has risen to the top of the national agenda, a great wave—some would say a frenzy—of school reform has focused on two related objectives: more-stringent academic standards and increasingly rigorous accountability for both students and schools.

In state after state, legislatures, governors, and state boards, supported by business leaders, have imposed tougher requirements in math, English, science, and other fields, together with new tests by which the performance of both students and schools is to be judged. In some places students have already been denied diplomas or held back in grade if they failed these tests. In some states funding for individual schools and for teachers' and principals' salaries—and in some, such as Virginia, the accreditation of schools—will depend on how well students do on the tests. More than half the states now require tests for student promotion or graduation.

But a backlash has begun.

- In Massachusetts this spring some 300 students, with the support of parents, teachers, and community activists, boycotted the Massachusetts Comprehensive Assessment System MCAS tests ("Be a hero, take a zero") and demanded that if students had good enough records or showed other evidence of achievement, they be allowed to graduate even if they hadn't passed the test. Last November, after a strong majority of students failed the test, the state board of education lowered the score for passing to the level that the state designates as "needs improvement."

- In Wisconsin last year the legislature, pressed by middle-class parents, refused to fund the exit examination that the state had approved just two years earlier. After an extended battle with Governor Tommy Thompson, who has been a national leader in the push for higher standards and greater ac-

countability, a compromise was reached under which student achievement will be assessed on a variety of criteria. Failing the exam will not result in the automatic denial of a diploma.

- In Virginia this spring parents, teachers, and school administrators opposed to the state's Standards of Learning assessments, established in 1998, inspired a flurry of bills in the legislature that called for revising the tests or their status as unavoidable hurdles for promotion and graduation. One bill would also have required that each new member of the state board of education "take the eighth grade Standards of Learning assessments in English, mathematics, science, and social sciences" and that "the results of such assessments… be publicly reported." None of the bills passed, but there's little doubt that if the system isn't revised and the state's high failure rates don't decrease by

2004, when the first Virginia seniors may be denied diplomas, the political pressure will intensify. Meanwhile, some parents are talking about Massachusetts-style boycotts.

- In Ohio, where beginning next year fourth-graders who fail the Ohio Proficiency Tests will be held back, a growing coalition of parents and teachers—members of the Freedom in Education Alliance, Parents Against Unfair Proficiency Testing, and other groups—are circulating petitions to place a referendum on the ballot to amend or repeal the state's testing laws.

- In New York a policy requiring that all students pass Regents examinations in a variety of subjects in order to graduate is increasingly the subject of controversy. Three former members of the State Board of Regents who helped to develop the policy issued a position paper earlier this year saying that they had never expected that all students would be held to a single standard, and calling for a re-examination of the policy. "The thinking [when I voted for the test requirement] was that everyone would take the exams," one of them told *The New York Times*, "but you could get a diploma through other channels."

THE backlash, touching virtually every state that has instituted high-stakes testing, arises from a spectrum of complaints: that the focus on testing and obsessive test preparation, sometimes beginning in kindergarten, is killing innovative teaching and curricula and driving out good teachers; that (conversely) the standards on which the tests are based are too vague, or that students have not been taught the material on which the tests are based; that the tests are unfair to poor and minority students, or to others who lack test-taking skills; that the tests overstress young children, or that they are too long (in Massachusetts they can take thirteen to seventeen hours) or too tough or simply not good enough. In Massachusetts, according to students protesting MCAS, some students designated as needing improvement out-

scored half their peers on national standardized tests. "Testing season is upon us," says Mickey VanDerwerker, a leader of Parents Across Virginia United to Reform SOL, "and a lot of kids are so nervous they're throwing up." In Oakland, California, a protest organizer named Susan Harman is selling T-shirts proclaiming HIGH STAKES ARE FOR TOMATOES.

Some of the backlash comes from conservatives who a decade ago battled state-imposed programs that they regarded as anti-family exercises in political correctness. Although she has always thought of herself as a "bleeding-heart liberal," Mary O'Brien, a parent in Ohio who calls herself "an accidental activist" and is the leader of the statewide petition drive against the Ohio Proficiency Tests, complains that the state has no business trying to control local school curricula. In suburban Maryland this spring some parents kept their children out of school on test days, because they regard the Maryland School Performance and Assessment Program as a waste of time. They complain that it is used only to evaluate schools, not students—thereby objecting to almost precisely what parents in some other states are demanding. "It's more beneficial to have my child in his seat in the fifth grade practicing long division," one Maryland parent told a *Washington Post* reporter.

But many more of the protesters—parents, teachers, and school administrators—are education liberals: progressive followers of John Dewey, who believe that children should be allowed to discover things for themselves and not be constrained by "drill-and-kill" rote learning. They worry that the tests are stifling students and teachers. Most come from suburbs with good, even excellent, schools. Instead of the tests they want open-ended exercises—portfolios of essays, art and science projects, and other "authentic assessments"—that in their view more genuinely measure what a student really knows and can do. They have gotten strong reinforcement from, among others, FairTest, of Cambridge, Massachusetts, which opposes standardized testing; Senator Paul Wellstone, of Minnesota, who is sponsoring an anti-testing bill in Congress; Alfie Kohn, a prolific writer and polemicist who ar-

gues that the standards movement is a travesty that has "turned teachers into drill sergeants" in the traditionalist belief that "making people suffer always produces the best results"; and Gerald Bracey, an education researcher and a critic of the widespread belief that U.S. students are far behind their peers overseas, which has given impetus to the standards movement.

In most cases tests and standards were imposed with little input from teachers or parents.

The anti-testing backlash is beginning to cohere as an integrated national effort. Earlier this year some 600 test critics attended a national conference on high-stakes testing, at Columbia University's Teachers College, to discuss effects, alternatives, and strategies: how to get the attention of legislators, what kinds of cases would be suited to civil-rights litigation, what assessments ensure accountability, how to achieve higher standards without high-stakes tests. Some on the left believe that the whole standards movement is a plot by conservatives to show up the public schools and thus set the stage for vouchers. All believe that poor and minority kids, who don't test well, are the principal victims of the tests and the standards movement. They contend (correctly) that almost no testing experts and none of the major testing companies endorse the notion of using just one test to determine promotion or graduation or, for that matter, the salaries of teachers and principals. But so far legislators and governors haven't paid much attention.

Among the most articulate critics of the tests are the boycotting students, who complain about narrowing opportunities and shrinking curricula. The most exciting ninth-grade course in his school, says Will Greene, a high school sophomore in Great Barrington, Massachusetts, is a science-and-technology class with a lot of hands-on experimentation. In the 1998–1999 school year, when students could take the class without worrying about MCAS, eighty students enrolled; this past year enrollment fell to thirty. Greene says that students feel the course will not help them pass the test, and failing the test next year could mean they don't get a diploma. "At least create a test," wrote Alison Maurer, an eighth-grader in Cambridge, Massachusetts, "that doesn't limit what students learn, something that shows what we have learned, not what we haven't."

THE movement is a long way from achieving critical mass. The two most prominent lawsuits brought to date—one in Texas, challenging the test as racially biased; the other in Louisiana, arguing that students hadn't had a chance to learn the material—have failed. The boycotts are still small, and polls, by Public Agenda and other organizations, continue to show that 72 percent of Americans—and 79 percent of parents—support tougher academic standards and oppose social promotion "even if [the outcome is] that significantly more students would be held back." Those numbers seem to reinforce the argument of Diane Ravitch, an education historian, an education official in the Bush Administration, and a strong supporter of standards, who has described the protesters as "crickets"— few in number, but making a disproportionate amount of noise. "There's tremendous support" for tests, Ravitch says, "among elected officials and in the business community." She may also be correct when she says that a great many of those who profess to oppose the high-stakes tests oppose all testing and all but the fuzziest standards. They are the same people, Ravitch argues, who in the end cheat kids by demanding too little and forever blaming children's inability to read or to do elementary math on the shortcomings of parents, neighborhoods, and the culture. Scrap the tests and we're back to the same neglect and indifference, particularly toward poor, marginal students, that we had before. Letting students who can't read, write, or do basic math graduate is doing no one a favor.

Yet even Ravitch is concerned about what she calls the "test obsession" and the backlash it could create if large numbers of students fail and the whole system unravels. The accountability structure in Virginia has been set up in such a way that even if the vast majority of students pass the tests, a large percentage of schools could fail the accompanying Standards of Accreditation. Under the SOA, any school in which more than 30 percent of students fail in 2007 will be subject to loss of accreditation. That, according to a study by the conservative Thomas Jefferson Institute for Public Policy, in Springfield, Virginia, is a formula that fosters public distrust of both the schools and the system. The study points out that because high-scoring students are concentrated in just a handful of districts, only 6.5 percent of Virginia schools met the SOA in 1999, when 35 percent of all Virginia students passed all the required SOL tests.

The Jefferson Institute study illustrates a wider set of problems underlying the new standards and tests. In an effort to look like the toughest guy on the block, some states have imposed standards that will be difficult if not impossible for many students and schools to meet. Members of the Virginia Board of Education are negotiating over allowing students to graduate without necessarily passing a standardized test. As noted, Massachusetts has already lowered the passing score on MCAS. A policy in Los Angeles to hold back all failing students has been modified. And merit-scholarship systems have been created in Michigan and California to keep top students from blowing off the test. The states that have had the least trouble with backlash are those, like Texas, that set standards low enough (and the Texas standards are far too low, in the view of some critics) that a large percentage of students can pass the tests.

Some protesters complain that students are being constrained by "drill-and-kill" rote learning.

It is, of course, in the public ambivalence about where the bar should be set that the larger uncertainty about the standards movement lies. Robert B. Schwartz, the president of Achieve, an organization created in 1996 by governors and business executives to defend the standards movement (at that time mostly against conservative attacks), recognizes that despite the polls, "not enough has been done to bring the public along." In most cases the tests and standards were imposed from the top down, with little input either from teachers—often regarded as the problem rather than the solution—or from parents (who in Arizona and California are not even allowed to see old test questions). What's needed now, Schwartz says, is to bolster public understanding and "capacity building," including professional development for teachers, to make the whole system work. "The good news," he told a reporter from *Education Week* in April, is that "states are not simply stopping with raising the bar, and shouting at kids and teachers to jump higher, but are moving to address the support question."

The question, as Schwartz knows, is whether resources—and particularly the quality of teaching in inner cities—will catch up with the demands on students. Since April, Schwartz has also acknowledged that as the day of reckoning approaches for millions of American students, the backlash will spread and intensify. "It's easy to assent in the abstract," he told me recently. "When it's my kid, it's something different." In the mid-1990s Delaware threw out a testing program because, in the words of Achieve, the legislature "had been unprepared for high rates of student failure."

In his state of education speech in February the U.S. Secretary of Education, Richard Riley, a strong advocate of accountability and standards, seemed to recognize the danger. "Setting high expectations," he said, "does not mean setting them so high that they are unreachable except for only a few.... If all of our efforts to raise standards get reduced to one test, we've gotten it wrong. If we force our teachers to teach only to the test, we will lose their creativity.... If we are so consumed with making sure students pass a multiple-choice test that we throw out the arts and civics then we will be going backwards instead of forward."

And yet the line between the political drive to be tough and indifference to standards in the name of creativity and diversity sometimes seems hard to draw. Diane Ravitch says that a person much missed in this debate is the late Albert Shanker, a longtime president of the American Federation of Teachers, who was relentless in his push for high standards for both students and teachers. But Shanker also pointed out that if only one standard for graduation exists, it will necessarily be low, because the political system can't support a high rate of failure. Shanker suggested two criteria: a basic competency level required of everyone, combined with honors diplomas, by whatever name, for students who do better and achieve more. The issue of the tradeoff between minimum competency and what is sometimes called "world-class standards" is rarely raised in any explicit manner, but it has bedeviled this debate since the beginning. As the standards requirements begin to take effect, and as more parents face the possibility that their children will not graduate, pressure to lower the bar or eliminate it entirely will almost certainly increase. Conversely, as more people come to understand that the "Texas miracle" and other celebrated successes are based on embarrassingly low benchmarks, those, too, will come under attack. The most logical outcome would be the Shanker solution. But in education politics, where ideology often reigns, logic is not always easy to come by.

From *The Atlantic Monthly*, August 2000, pp. 19-21. © 2000 by Peter Schrag. Reprinted by permission of the author.

UNIT 4

Development During Childhood: Family and Culture

Unit Selections

Key Points to Consider

- What contributes to raising emotionally happy, cognitively achieving children in the new millennium?

- Do sports programs encourage violence? How can sports injuries be curbed?

- Is it more efficient to reinforce good human traits and teach control of bad ones rather than trying to assign credit and blame for the behaviors of children?

- Who do children name as heroes and role models: parents or pop culture figures? What impact does hero worship have on child development?

- Are American schools equal? If not, why not? What is the future for school desegregation?

 **Links: www.dushkin.com/online/**
These sites are annotated in the World Wide Web pages.

Childhood Injury Prevention Interventions
   http://depts.washington.edu/hiprc/
Families and Work Institute
   http://www.familiesandwork.org/index.html
Parentsplace.com: Single Parenting
   http://www.parentsplace.com/

Most people accept the proposition that families and cultures have substantial effects on child outcomes. Do they? Are the anti-American, anti-Israeli terrorists in the Middle East socialized to hate? New interpretations of behavioral genetic research suggest that genetically predetermined child behaviors may also be having substantial effects on how families parent, how children react, and how cultures evolve. Nature and nurture are very interactive. Is it possible that there is a genetic predisposition towards more war-like, aggressive, and violent behaviors in some children and/or in some ethnic groups? Do genes, environment, or both cause the impulsive, aggressive behaviors of terrorists?

If parents and societies have a significant impact on child outcomes, is there a set of cardinal family values? Does one culture have more correct answers than another culture? Some Middle Eastern spokesmen have called the Western culture corrupt and decadent. Laypersons often assume that children's behaviors and personalities have a direct correlation with the behaviors and personality of the person or persons who provided their socialization during infancy and childhood. Have Americans become paranoid about weapons of mass destruction and the extent of terrorist intentions? Do we try to justify our culture's flaws by claims that other cultures are worse? Do we teach our children this fear?

Are you a mirror image of the person or persons who raised you? How many of their beliefs, preferences, and virtuous behaviors do you reflect? Did you learn their hatreds and vices as well? Do you model your family, your peers, your culture, all of them, or none of them? If you have a sibling, are you alike because the same person or persons raised you? What accounts for all the differences between people with similar genes, similar parenting, and the same cultural background?

During childhood, a person's family values get compared to and tested against the values of schools, community, and culture. Peers, schoolmates, teachers, neighbors, extracurricular activity leaders, religious leaders, and even shopkeepers play increasingly important roles. Culture influences and is influenced by children through holidays, styles of dress, music, television, world events, movies, slang, games played, parents' jobs, transportation, exposure to sex, drugs, and violence, and many other variables. The ecological theorist Urie Bronfenbrenner calls these cultural variables exosystem and macrosystem influences. The developing personality of a child has multiple interwoven influences: from genetic potentialities through family values and socialization practices to community and cultural pressures for behaviors.

The first article discusses "Raising Happy Achieving Children in the New Millennium." Alice Honig gives advice on how parents and teachers can build child self-esteem, how parents and teachers can cooperate in education, how to discipline positively, how to apply insights from the new brain research, and how parents can partner with professionals to increase children's happiness and achievement.

The second article addresses the issue of the learned aspects of violence and aggression. "When Safety is the Name of the Game" suggests that safety is not always an objective in sports contests in North America. Parents, coaches, and our culture encourage winning … at almost any cost. This results in millions of sports injuries every year in children and teens. Their rate of sports injuries are triple the rates of adults. David Noonan reports that injury prevention programs and safety education can go a long way to reduce this major public health concern. Parents, coaches, and referees should be more adamant about fair-play and come down harder on athletes who commit flagrant fouls. The presence of a sports trainer in school athletic programs is an effective way to prevent many of these life-threatening injuries.

The third article, "The Blank Slate," argues that family variables and cultural factors (such as fast foods loaded with sugars and fats as mentioned in the previous article) always interact with genetics. Parents and society cannot be blamed for every choice made by their children. While advice on how to raise happy, achieving children, and how to keep children healthy, physically fit, and well-nourished may be followed by parents and teachers, some children simply will not turn out as hoped. They cannot be molded like lumps of clay. The author suggests that social progress can proceed with acceptance of the inherent natures (both good and bad) of all humans. Blaming is a waste of time. Working with what we have makes more sense.

The first article in the culture subsection of this unit asks who are the heroes and role models of America's children in the twenty-first century: "Parents or Pop Culture?" The authors give an overview of many pop culture icons; from television, film, comic books, video games, computer games, and music. They report findings from a mixed age, sex, and ethnic sample of children in California. Boys picked heroes from pop culture more often than did girls. Asian-American and Latino children were more apt to pick pop culture role models than their parents or other known adults. Asian and Latino children had more white media heroes than heroes of their own ethnicity. Most children chose same-gender role models, although girls, lacking the number of same-gender media models as boys, often also chose opposite-gender heroes as well. Implications of these findings are raw materials for heated discussions of the heroes put forth by the American pop culture.

The last article in this subsection deals with the question of school desegregation in America. The Supreme Court decision that ended segregated schools happened 50 years ago. Other court decisions in the 1970's, 80's, and 90's weakened compliance with Brown v. Board of Education of 1954. Many inner city schools are not only segregated, they also have fewer resources, more crowded conditions, and less teachers than schools in the affluent suburbs. Ellis Cose describes the historical changes in education since the Brown decision. He discusses current issues such as high-states testing, charter schools, privatization, and vouchers. Are we serious about realizing the promise of Brown?

Raising Happy Achieving Children in the New Millennium*

ALICE STERLING HONIG—*Syracuse University (Received 12 April 2000)*

Key words: Children, happy, achieving

Raising happy achieving children is a tall order. The recipe is complicated. The ingredients are awesomely many! Some of the ingredients involve educators and the training of high quality caregivers and teachers. Some of the recipe requirements involve political advocacy for the poor. Some ingredients are challenging—such as how to provide sexual information and information about unwanted pregnancies and AIDS and how to provide internship opportunities for practicing excellent caregiving within a high school model childcare—for teens who need clear and helpful knowledge and skills. These recipe requirements mean changes in offering school courses in junior high and senior high school. Required courses in positive communication techniques and required courses in family life education are as urgent as studying the invasions of Ghenghis Khan or the history of the Norman invasion in England and its effect on enriching the vocabulary of the English language.

Changes in the way education is offered for medical, nursing, and legal professionals to include more knowledge about children's interests and needs must also be part of the complex societal recipe to support children's flourishing. Thus, part of the recipe lies in enhancing the training of obstetricians and nurses caring for pregnant first time parents. Sensitivity training and knowledge, in dealing with birthing situations for single parents and high-risk teens, are important for professionals involved with childbirth. They will be more likely then to provide nurturance to promote early bonding with the newborn and to support breast feeding for those who may be physically able to nurse but have no clue as to how or why.

Another political ingredient in this recipe will mean much wider monetary support for home visitation personnel who work with at-risk pregnant women PRIOR to the birth of the baby. Honig and Morin's (2000) research has shown that IF high-risk teens who dropped out of an intensive home visitation program had about 7 home visits, then they still had much lower rates of confirmed neglect/abuse several years later. These rates were actually comparable to rates for high risk teen moms who stayed in program for 18 to 24 months regardless of whether program teens' entry was prebirth or postbirth. High risk teens who started program after the birth of the baby and then dropped out had markedly higher confirmed abuse/neglect rates.

LOVING, KNOWLEDGEABLE, SKILLED CAREGIVERS: THE PRICELESS INGREDIENT

The priceless ingredient in the recipe for a happy achieving child is a strong and loving family foundation and highly competent caregivers in group care. Parents are young children's most precious resource. No other caregiver and no material resources can take the place of parents who genuinely treasure their children and are deeply committed to nourish their children's growth and optimal development. The dream of every family is a child who is able to grow up independent yet lovingly related to family and achieving work success and satisfaction in life. We still cannot improve on this formula of the old master, Sigmund Freud!

After their needs for food and comforting, for protection from distress and from danger are taken care of, young children most need a special person whom they know in their deepest self is their loving protector, teacher, and friend. This fundamental security base, this unpaid worker who puts in countless overtime hours without pay and often without much recognition from society, is a PARENT. Thus, this presentation will focus particularly on positive parental ingredients for raising happy achieving children.

Many excellent enrichment programs such as Head Start, Even Start, HIPPY, and Parent Child Development Centers actively work to enlist parental help in young children's learning. Yet sometimes programs that attempt to work with low-income, low education parents, or very young parents or upper class dual career busy parents, report frustrations they were not prepared to cope with. Often the program staff goal is to assist new parents in positive ways to deepen the love relationship with a child, become primary educators of their preschoolers and to encourage parents to work actively in partnership with child care providers. Yet staff report low turnout for meetings, missed appointments for home visits, and lack of parent attunement to program messages.

...quality parenting is the secret indispensible ingredient to provide the inner core of self-love and self-esteem that sustains each growing child.

What are the sources of difficulties? Part of the problem lies in the stressful lives of parents with limited time and often with aggravating lack of means of transportation to program sites. Some families may not have learned in their own families of origin the ability to empathize with child neediness. Struggling to cope with their own adult problems, some parents are not even aware of how important early consistent tender nurturing is in order to promote early child emotional attachment to parents. Chaos, drug abuse, spousal or partner abuse, depression and current lack of family supports account for some of the frustrations for families and for program staff. The deep reverberations of what Fraiberg (1980) calls "ghosts in the nursery"—angers, jealousies, resentments over being rejected or unloved or terrorized in own's own childhood—

intrude in dangerous ways into the parent's current relationship with a young child. Some staff frustrations stem from lack of access to technical skills, such a specific therapeutic techniques, book reading techniques, anger management skills, etc. on the part of staff. Sometimes staff is strong on wishing to do good but not trained thoroughly enough in sensitivity to client needs nor community mores. This can lead, for example, to family outreach workers becoming discouraged with parents and gradually working more and more directly with the child even though the program goals were to empower parents to become their children's most special enrichment person.

Part of the problem also results when service providers lack materials for parents with low literacy skills or for immigrant parents from different culture groups. Programs need to be proactive and create lending libraries that contain both videos (on infant massage and well-baby care, for example) and materials written in easy to read words or in a family's native language. Many publications available for encouraging optimal parenting are geared toward families with more resources, higher literacy, and fewer stresses.

Family support and information programs for parents need to brainstorm creatively to find ways to engage parents with their children. For example, a home visiting program can provide a weekly xeroxed "How to play the game" sheet with suggestions for **varying** an interactive learning game if a child needs more help OR, if a child needs more challenge (Honig, 1982b). And of course, staff needs to affirm steadily for parents how priceless is their role in supporting their children's emotional and intellectual learning.

PARENTS AND TEACHERS BUILD CHILD SELF ESTEEM

A caring adult committed to children's secure well-being is a person every society should honor or cherish. There could not be enough "awards" or medals for such special persons! Responsive caregivers permit hope that the fabric of society will not be rent with violence, alienation, school dropouts, suicides, drug abuse, and other tragic attempts by youngsters attempting to deaden their personal pain or to carve out a feeling of power. Watch the new films about kids in high school, for example. So many "in" youngsters in school cliques behave in ruthlessly ridiculing ways. Girls who aren't considered "sexy" or "beautiful" are called unkind names and treated with contempt socially. Boys who are shy or intellectual are labelled "nerds". Teachers need specialized training in working on cutting out bullying in classrooms, corridors, rest rooms and playing fields! In Norway, thanks to the work of Olweus on the noxious effects of school bullying, teachers are trained to address this issue and are responsible for proactive handling of bullying. Teaching as a profession needs more respect from society, and more in-depth training on how to enhance emotional intelligence as well as intellectual intelligence and knowledge! Teaching staff in childcare has very high turnover each year. Many caregivers earning minimum wage also have minimum training. We need to enhance the respect for quality caregiving. We need to support campaigns for worth wages! An even more intriguing question is how to help parents to see how important a quality child care provider in each child's life—not as paid servant but as a concerned, talented, hardworking extra "parenting" person in that young child's life.

Children need parents who provide for them as the parents in the fairy tale of the Three Bears, where the porridge was not too hot and not too cold, but just right!

Because of the hazards of changing providers and inconsistent care, we must still emphasize that quality parenting is the secret indispensable ingredient to provide the inner core of self-love and self-esteem that sustains each growing child. As Erik Erikson taught us long ago, this consistent core of cherishing permits that child in turn to grow up to care for others in ways that sustain family and community. As a young one is given unto, so does that little one grow up learning how to become a giver. Such caring gives inner courage to cope with problems so that the child can both lead a productive personal life as well as contribute to society (Honig, 1982a). Parents are the **mirror** wherein young children find their inner true selves reflected as either essentially lovable or sadly unworthy (Briggs, 1975).

In a women's dress store, a toddler wandered among the clothes. As she walked around, babbling "Da" and touching clothing, the mother called out over and over either "No! No! Don't touch!". Mostly she kept saying "I don't want you. I don't want you!" The toddler looked bewildered and started to cry. "It must feel frustrating to be among all these clothes racks while the grown ups are busy shopping" I remarked sympathetically to the mother. "Yeah, I've been frustrated with her every minute since she's born!" replied the mother as she reluctantly picked up the tiny tot and continued down the store aisle.

Just giving birth to a child is not the same as parenting! Bettelheim (1987) and Winnicott (1987), wise psychia-

trists, remind us, however, the young children do not need perfect parents to thrive. They will do very well with a "good enough parent". There is no "How-to" book that works for every child in every life situation.

Parents with profound good will for their children remember that cherishing does not mean smothering or intrusiveness.

A teen mother was waiting in the well-baby clinic for the pediatrician to see her child. The toddler, playing with a ring stack set (provided with other toys by a caring nursing staff in a play corner in the waiting room) put the rings on haphazardly. "That's not how you do it", the mom remarked with contempt. She snatched the ring stack from her child and put the rings on in graduated sizes. "There, that's the right way", she announced triumphantly as she handed back the toy to her child. The toddler took the ring stack, and turned it upside down as she let all the rings tumble in disarray to the floor. She gave her mother an angry look and walked silently away from her.

Insightful adults understand developmental stages. They understand that wanting a child to do well cannot be forced but must be supported. They let children have the leisure to try toys on their own. They don't constantly intrude with trying to force the child's attention. They LURE kids to new experiences. But they do not dominate the play situation. Rather they are responsive to children's cues, to children's curiosity, to children's explorations when the child seems calm and engrossed in play. If a toy seems too frustrating, they may move in quietly to provide a bit of unobtrusive support (such as steadying the elbow of a child trying to stack boxes), a quiet suggestion, a turning of a puzzle piece so that the child can better notice where it goes. TEMPO is an important skill in childrearing and in lovemaking! We need to talk more about tempo just as we need to address power issues more in society, with respect to marriages and childrearing as well as in business and politics!

Keeping the see-saw of daily life from bumping down too hard for some children is a major challenge!

Havighurst, a half-century ago, wrote about the developmental tasks of childhood. As a theorist he may be out of fashion nowadays. But he observed wisely that many adults need to become more aware emotionally that a young child first needs to be **allowed to be dependent** and kept safe in order to grow up brave enough to become **independent** and separate from the parents. Youth who feel they must belong to a gang, must cut classes and smoke and drink to be "cool" and grownup, who must act violent with a sex partner are NOT independent persons. They are acting out ancient wounds and scenarios. Their immature and scary actions show how much they lack skills for being independent, contributing helpful adults in society. As one adult remarked quietly to me about her teen years:

> I cut out emotionally. My parents were both quarreling a lot. They were so busy with their careers. They did not seem to have time really to talk with me or to see that their intellectual interest were not the same as my interests in music and sports. So I gave up caring about their world. I turned to peers and to drugs so my friends became my "family" support. It took me years to become my own person.

Parents and teachers together need to notice how special and *individual* each child is in a family. Children do not have the same temperament or wishes or abilities as a parent or as another youngster. A child who is very shy may be quite unlike a gregarious younger sibling. Children need parents who provide for them as the parents in the fairy tale of the Three Bears, where the porridge was not too hot and not too cold, but just right!

Too Much Enmeshment or Too Much Isolation Emotionally Withers The Souls of Young Children

What a strange job parenting is! We cherish and protect, worry over sniffles, blow noses, tie shoelaces, read stories, help with homework, patiently teach moral values and courtesies toward others (Lickona, 1983). Yet we do the job of parenting so that children can grow up to make their own choices and be able to live calmly and effectively on their own without parental help. If the job of parenting is done well, it is done so that parents work themselves OUT of a job!

Flexibility and Adaptability Help Caregivers and Parents Survive

Caregiving requirements change with children's ages and stages. Caregivers who are perceptive will note when to drop the baby talk that so delighted the 10-month-old and truly encouraged her to try words. Now they will use clearly pronounced adult words like "water" rather than "wa-wa" with their toddler whose vocabulary is growing by leaps and bounds. Adults will note that a toddler expresses fierce independence about what he wants, how much he wants and how he wants it right away. They

cannot let that child run in the street or go out without clothes on a winter morning! But, they will also note that a No-saying defiant toddler who tries adult patience in the household still needs his thumb or pacifier and definitely needs the reassurance of his parent's lap when tired, crabby, or coming down with a cold. Parents who are perceptive will note that the five-year-old can feed and dress herself rather well now and can even be allowed to choose clothes to lay out the night before going to kindergarten.

The mystery of growth and development is not steady or predictable. Perceptive caregivers balance firmness with sensible tuning in to a child's stages and needs. They work hard to figure out where each child is at in each domain in his or her learning career. Some children love tinkering with tools and are good at helping Mom or granddad with a repair job. But they may have many frustrations with reading and math in school work. Ridicule and nagging only increase a child's smoldering resentment or stubborn refusal to cooperate at home or school. Finding a warm caring tutor and also exploring the community for an excellent vocational high school may open the path to real job satisfaction later in life for this youngster. Adults need to be good noticers and good balancers in order to promote each child's well being. Keeping the see-saw of daily life from bumping down too hard for some children is a major challenge!

PARENTS AS TEACHERS: TEACHERS AS PARENT SUPPORTERS

Parents and caregivers must both be the emotional teachers of young children. They can teach empathy (sensitivity to feelings—of one's own and of other persons) and trustfulness; or they can teach mistrust and anger, insensitivity and uncaring.

> On the toddler playground, Donny pushed at another boy and snatched his shiny toy auto. Mama came over, kneeled down, held his hands and firmly reminded him of the social rules: "Donny, no pushing or hitting." The toddler nodded and added tearfully "And no biting and kicking!" Self-control is so hard to learn. But with the help of his mother's clear and patient teachings, Donny was learning.

Authoritative parents (as opposed to permissive parents or to authoritarian "Do as I say because I say so!" parents) bring up children who are easiest to live with at home and teachers report that they are a pleasure to have in the classroom (Baumrind, 1977). Such parents show genuine interest in their children. They provide firm clear rules and reasons for rules. And they need, of course, to be flexible about rules. A feverish school child may be excused from family chores. A child just starting a new day-care placement needs more lap time and more tolerance for his crankiness until he feels more secure in the new environment. A teenager who comes home with a really difficult and long set of homework problems feels grateful when a concerned parent offers to take on the teenager's chore of loading the dishwasher to free up some extra study time that evening. Teach generosity by being generous. Teach kindness by showing kindness.

Thus, every child needs caring adults who will promote emotional intelligence (Goleman, 1995). How to be assertive as differentiated from angry and hostile is a challenging emotional task. Children and parents need to focus on how to reframe daily hassles as opportunities to strengthen positive emotional skills, such as: giving a peer a chance to explain, being able to articulate well your point of view and trying to see another's point of view as well; searching for win-win reasonable solutions to social hassles; asking for help in ways that affirm the role of the helper, whether teacher or parents. Some folks believe that the job of teacher and the job of parent are totally different. Those of you who have cared for infants and toddlers know so well that diaper changing, holding a frightened tiny person, feeding, and soothing are intimate ministrations. The roles are indeed blurred when we care for the youngest little persons. Maybe a high school teacher can be sarcastic and put down a student in front of the class. Maybe that student will not feel resentment and anger. Maybe. Sometimes an adolescent with strong family supports achieves ego serenity and resilience and can handle such classroom stresses fairly well. The provider of care for your children is working with a small person whose ego is gradually building. Be sure that all the builders are cooperating, caring and knowledgeable or the structure being built will have troublesome flaws!

Learning Values

Parents are also on the frontiers of a child's learning values in the family. If parents deal their own problems by screaming and lashing out, or being sharply jeering and critical of weaknesses or mistakes made by a family member, then children will **model** their folks and learn those ways to cope with frustrations. If parents struggle to keep a family organized and functioning, then even though financial resources are limited, if they cherish children through hard times and good, their children will learn courage and caring (Honig, 1982a).

Children's empathy flows from experiencing their own parent's empathic response to their early fears and emotional upsets. Research by Yarrow and Zahn-Waxler reveals that during the first two years of life, the parent who shows empathy by soothing a child's hurt after a scare or a kneebruising fall, and who, in addition, clearly does not allow a child to hurt others as a way of solving social disagreements, will have a socially empathic child who is more likely to tune into and try to help other children who are hurt or scared (Pines, 1979).

If families provide models for punitive and vengeful actions, they need to realize that their children may gloat over the misfortune of others or else be indifferent to others' pain. Parents need to become aware of the emotional response that the old master, Sigmund Freud, called "Identification with the aggressor".

> In a rigidly organized household with innumerable rules posted on the refrigerator, the ten-year-old was being punished. She had tried to add her cuddly teddy bear, her comfort object for years, to her school backpack. The parents were angry. The toy animal could have been lost at school or taken by another child. They "punished" the child by having her sit for several hours at an empty dining room table without moving. The five-year-old in the family declared that her older sister "deserved" her punishment and announced that she "did not care" if her sister felt sad.

Parents Prime the Pump of Learning

How does a parent become the first, best teacher who ensures the child's early learning success? Varied are the programs that have been developed to teach parents how best to help their children learn. Some involve parents in groups together. Some programs invite parents as aides into classrooms. Some programs provide Home Visitation in order to promote parenting skills (see Honig, 1979 for an in-depth description of types of parent involvement programs).

Respect for the child is the foundation of good teaching. As parents notice early skills just emerging, they **scaffold, support, and lure** the child to a slightly more difficult accomplishment, to a slightly more subtle level of understanding, to a somewhat higher and more mature level of skill. I have called this technique "Dancing developmental ladders of learning" (Honig, 1982b). In each area of learning, the parent takes CUES from the child: Is the baby making new babbling sounds? Talk delightedly with a cooing baby. Express genuine interest in what baby seems to be trying to communicate. Turn-taking-talk primes language learning (Honig, 1985a). Does the baby smile when he sees animals? Snuggle together and point to pictures of animals during picture book story time with your little one and be sure to label objects baby points to.

Is your year-old child trying to feed herself? Provide Cheerios on the high chair tray to facilitate thumb and forefinger precise pincer prehension. Is your five-year old asking questions about where babies come from? Be an askable parent and provide simple, short calm explanations easy for that young child to understand (Gordon,

1983). Is your six-year-old determined to learn to ride a two-wheeler? Be sure that she is skillful with her tricycle; then advance to training wheels.

Facilitate learning by creating easy "steps" upward toward skill mastery. Figure out the **prerequisites** for success in any area of learning. If a parent provides more toeholds on the ladders of learning, children are more likely to succeed as they push upward in their growth toward achievements.

Preparations ahead of time boost the effectiveness of parent efforts to prime new learning, to scaffold opportunities for learning. Provide lots of discarded paper and crayons for children to draw. Keep assorted "beautiful junk" in a special place; empty egg cartons, pine cones collected on a walk, bubble paper from packaging, old greeting cards, and paper towel rolls plus some paste, blunt scissors, and Magic Markers are good ingredients for rainy day art activities.

Every parent needs a large repertoire of [discipline] techniques to use at different ages and stages of a child's growing up. Not all techniques work all the time with all youngsters!

Take children on small outdoor walks and to parks often. Give them opportunities to learn to swing, climb, balance, and coordinate their bodies with ease and grace. Also, teach them the names of weeds and flowers (dandelions and daisies are great!) growing by the roadside. Encourage children to notice and feel with their fingers the contrasting roughness and smoothness of the bark of different trees, such as a maple and a beech. Delight in the way clouds and sunshine light the land, the way cool air rustles and sways a flower stem, the way the earth smells fresh after a rain.

Express joy! Your own joy in the glories of the natural world sparks in your young child a deep pleasure, awareness, and appreciation for the world's beauty.

Creativity Turns Living Experiences into Learning Opportunities

Caregivers with limited financial resources need to scout their living space to use every opportunity to turn a household chore or routine into a *learning experience*. Store-bought toys may be too expensive; but adult cre-

ativity transforms every homey experience into a learning adventure (Honig, 1982b; Honig & Brophy, 1996). *Laundry time* can be used to teach colors, shapes, comparative sizes (of socks and of washcloths and towels), and the names for different materials and garments. Kids will love to feel important as they measure out laundry detergent up to the one-cup line and pour it into a wash tub or machine.

Cooking and baking times are a wonderful opportunity to increase hand dexterity skills in rolling, kneading, shaping, and measuring. And the tastes afterward are an extra reward for the helping youngster.

Grocery shopping is a superb perceptual and language learning experience for young children. Meat, dairy and fruit/vegetable departments give children opportunities to form conceptual categories. Why are peppers and celery and broccoli all in bins near one another? Where would hamburger be found? What items will need refrigeration? Which cartons or cans are heavier than others?

Encourage numerical estimations. As children grow and learn about numbers and letters, many take pride in being able to find a nutritious cereal box by the special letter on the box. They like to help stuff a plastic bag with string beans for supper. Many children by early school age can do estimates; they add up a dollar for this item (rounded off) and three dollars for that item, and so forth, and then come up with a fairly close estimate of how much the groceries will add up to. How proud your child feels. And how much practice in addition such estimates give her!

Teach children about money. People work to earn money. When money is in short supply, a child learns early that food and rent come first. Money, whether in pounds or dollars, for extras such as toys or snacks must be carefully budgeted.

Learning categories and learning gradations (such as little, big, bigger, biggest) are important cognitive tasks of the early years. The real world of shopping, cooking, clean-up times, and yard work provides rich opportunities for learning about number, shape, color, weight, bulk, categories of object, and other cognitive concepts. **Reframe** ordinary household experiences. Transform them into potential lesson times.

POSITIVE DISCIPLINE IDEAS: A GIFT FOR EVERY CAREGIVER AND PARENT

All parents, not just parents with limited resources, need help in acquiring discipline techniques beyond the dreary "hit" and "scold" and "go to your room" many folks learned in their families of origin. Every parent needs a large repertoire of techniques to use at different ages and stages of a child's growing up. Not all techniques work all the time with all youngsters!

> Most of the time, a young child is just acting like a child, not thinking in logical sequences, acting in-the-present time rather than planning ahead.

Parents who were raised by being belted or whipped in turn sometimes show powerful urges to use physical punishment. They hated the type of discipline they received but often believe it was justified. They need support to learn more appropriate child management skills. Sometimes young children's boisterous or overly intrusive games spark a feeling of rage in an adult. Grim and hostile parents are reflecting the anger they felt from adults far back in their own childhoods, when family members, furious with some of their behaviors, punished them harshly and branded them as "bad!"

Research has shown that **severe physical punishment (SPP)** was the major discipline method of parents whose youngsters ended up convicted of juvenile crimes. And, the worst crimes (as judged by independent professionals) were committed by the youths who had received the most SPP! (Welsh, 1976).

Let us cull from clinicians and researchers useful ideas about positive discipline that parents CAN use in order to raise responsible and cooperative children without instilling fear and deep anger against parental power (Briggs, 1975; Crary, 1990; Gordon, 1975; Honig, 1985b, 1996; Lickona, 1983). For example, the **redirection technique** helps a parent avoid willful battles with a toddler intent on messing up his big brother's model airplane. The parent invests a different, appropriate activity, such as wooden train tracks or a puzzle, or a jack-in-the-box, with interest so that the toddler turns toward the new and safer game.

Below are some further ideas to help adults re-think what discipline is about and how to use effective teaching techniques and avoid a punishment perspective.

Positive Attributions

Build up self esteem by generous use of **positive attributions** (Honig, 1996). Tell children what you admire about their behaviors and interactions.

Anger Management Techniques

Anger management techniques (such as counting to ten, or using words instead of fists) help children achieve self-control (Eastman & Rozen, 1984).

Teach Sharing

During a play group time, if two toddlers are struggling for a toy, supply an additional toy so each can play with a truck or have a supply of blocks. Talk about taking turns as a reasonable way to share a toy. Tell each child you will help with the taking turns by reminding each child in turn when the toy has been played with for an agreed upon number of minutes. Use a back rub and caress to soothe that child who has snatched a toy from another and as well the aggrieved child who is crying. Thus, you teach both the children that gentleness and kindness are necessary and important for each child.

Time Out as "Teach In"

Use time-out sparingly, and as a *"teach-in"* technique so that children can re-evaluate their inappropriate interactions and choose other ways to get their needs met (Honig, 1996).

Reframe a Problem in Terms of a Developmental Perspective

Adults can take a giant step toward devising new coping skills when they look at certain behaviors in terms of the stage a child is at or the curiosity a child has, or the need the child has to keep moving and exploring. Then certain behaviors, sometimes regarded as "bad" begin to seem just developmentally ordinary, such as a toddler's joy in jumping off a couch (find him someplace else that is appropriate and safe to jump off) or an infant's squeezing a banana through her fingers while watching in wonder.

How can a caregiver steer a child into more appropriate ways to experience vigorous body motions or to experience textures and squish clay?

Be Mindful of the Importance of Practising New Skills

Remember that children have to learn the initial steps for every new learning (and then practice that new skill). This helps an adult be tolerant even of toileting accidents or clumsy spills while a toddler pours juice. Perhaps a two-year-old cannot sit still but needs to run about a lot. He may not have the words for "poop" and "pee" yet. He may get intensely absorbed in his play and forget totally any signals coming from bladder or bowel. Punishing a two-year-old for a toileting accident when that particular child may not be ready to give up diapers for another year shows a lack of awareness of developmental norms for sphincter control. Toilet learning takes several years for some children to master. Male children have higher rates of enuresis. Little boys need particular understanding from parents who want compliance with their toilet training efforts (Honig, 1993).

Develop Realistic Expectations

More realistic expectations of young children's development supports a better understanding of how and when to discipline, and best of all, how to **prevent** discipline problems from arising. Expecting a newly cruising-about baby not to touch breakables or garbage in a bag left on a floor is more than the young one is capable of managing (Honig & Wittmer, 1990). Baby proofing a room full of interesting breakable art objects is a wise idea when curiosity is in full bloom. A toddler has little understanding of the difference between a shiny toy OK to play with and a shiny porcelain vase. Quite possibly, parental yelling if a toddler touches a treasured and fragile knick-knack on a coffee table will surely endow that particular item with increasing fascination and interest as a potential play toy.

Remind yourself that no baby, no school child, no parent, no spouse can ever be "perfect".

> After hearing me at a morning public lecture talk about what children need from their folks, a beautiful young teen mom with a nine-month-old child came to me with tears in her eyes. "Dr. Honig, you seem to know so much about little children. Teach me how to make my baby perfect so I won't have to hit her so much?"

Avoid Hostile Blame

Another danger sign among adults is when they assume that a child is doing unwanted or disapproved actions "on purpose" to displease or act mean to the adult. Babies soak their diapers. Preschoolers love to get all muddy and splash in puddles. They do not "mean" to cause more laundry work for a parent. Beware the dangers of **Projecting Evil** (a Freudian defense mechanism) onto young children. Parental rage is too often fueled in abuse cases by the adult's feeling that a small child deliberately set out to "hurt" or "defy" the adult. If we expect that young children have the same thinking skills as adults we will be very mad at some of their actions and "blame" them—for being children! Most of the time, a young child is just acting like a child, not thinking in logical sequences, acting in-the-present time rather than planning ahead. This focused-on-own-needs small person is sometimes messy, sometimes in short supply of inner controls, sometimes needing to dawdle or say "No". A year-old baby cannot comply perfectly with "No-no". A young preschooler finds it very hard to sit still comfortably for hours without a toy or books or playmates in a dentist's waiting room or at a religious ceremony.

Professionals must help parents gain more **realistic expectations** and understandings of young children's growth needs. Projecting evil onto children is a danger that regrettably leads to violence and inappropriate punishments rather than behavior guidance to help a youngster gain more mature behaviors.

IMPORTANCE OF THE NEW BRAIN RESEARCH

Apply Insights From the New Brain Research Findings

New brain research reveals that toddlers by 24 months have twice as many brain synapses as adults. Somewhere during the early school years, and by 10 years of age, nature starts to prune away brain connections that have not been wired well by frequent teaching and learning experiences. The motto for rich neural connections is "Use it or lose it!"

It is interesting that in England, compared with the United States, far fewer children are labelled "ADHD" (Attention Deficit and Hyperactivity Disorder) and British teachers are more likely to use behavior modification techniques rather than advocate the use of drugs.

Many families do not realize how early they CAN teach their little ones many kinds of lessons. By three weeks, if a baby has been talked to regularly, and a caregiver has waited with loving calmness for baby to respond with cooing throaty vowels, a baby can keep on cooing back in response to the caregivers' slow delighted talk with the baby held in "en face" position about one foot from the adult's face. The latest brain research reveals that **Parentese** (talk with babies using long drawn out vowels, short phrases, and a high pitched voice) is great for wiring in many rich neuron connections in the brain. This news means that to become good "teachers of the brain", caregivers need to have rich conversations with kids, read picture books frequently, sing songs, and offer their children experiences and adventures such as trips to the zoo, the public library, the supermarket, and local museums.

Figure Out Who Owns A Problem

Decide who owns a particular discipline problem. A teenager who dawdles in the mornings so long that she misses the school bus owns her problem. If a baby tears plant leaves from a favorite plant left on a low ledge, the parent owns the problem. If a parent expects a child with learning disabilities to do as well in school as an older brother who got high grades, the parent owns the problem. A parent's strong disapproval rather than support may contribute to possible school failure, and low child self esteem.

Some problems, of course, are owned by both parent and child. Have family meetings where each person can say what is bothering him about a rule, or an interaction, or a discipline in the family. When such meetings let each person have a say honestly about the week's positives and negatives, then such problems can be identified and hashed out with good will and a desire for reasonable compromise (Gordon, 1975).

Offer Choices

Toddlers who are contrary will often settle more easily into cooperation if offered a choice: "Do you want apple juice or orange juice? Do you want to sleep with your head at this end of the crib or the other end?" (when a tot has trouble setting into nap time). "You go choose two story books that you want me to read to you tonight". Offering choices often heads off a potential problem of crankiness or non-cooperation.

Think Through Household and Classroom Rules

How clear are your rules? Some children are scared that they will do something "wrong" inevitably because of the long lists of strict rules their folks insist on. Have few and clear house rules and be sure there are good reasons for the rules. Drinking milk is not a "must". A child can get calcium and Vitamin A from yellow cheese and from yoghurt. But not hurting a sibling IS a must in a family. *Make sure young children really understand your rules.* Ask a child who is not following a rule of the family to repeat to you what the household rule was. If the child is confused, he may not be aware of his "misbehavior."

Children have to learn about equity as well as fairness. Equity means taking into account special needs at special times for each person.

Adults get weary but need dogged persistence in explaining rules and the reasons for them over and over, especially for toddlers just learning to share, or children just learning how to balance homework responsibilities with their desire to rush out to play after school. "Don't need to wash my hands for supper 'cause they are clean" may mean that the preschooler needs to learn more about germs and the importance of keeping safe from sickness.

Do Not Ignore When Children Harm Others

Ignoring misbehavior only works for minor infractions. For example, if two children are verbally fussing or arguing, they may well be able to settle by themselves who gets to pull the wagon with blocks first. Aggression that is ignored will often escalate; it will not go away. If a child hits or kicks another, and the adult ignores this, the undesirable actions will not decrease but continue. Children then assume that the adult thinks hurting another child is allowed. Be firm about not allowing children to hurt others; but express that firmness without modeling physical hurt yourself. Talk so your child will listen; and be sure to listen so your child will open up to you (Faber & Mazlish, 1980).

Respect Each Child As A Person

Every person, big or little has a viewpoint and feelings of his or her own. A child is not personal property like furniture! Don't make comparisons between kids that make one child feel unloved, unpretty, or untalented compared with another. Screaming at or cursing a child, telling him he is rotten—these behaviors reflect parental anger and anguish, but in no way show that the adult remembers that this little child is a person and deserves to be treated with courtesy even when being disciplined.

Teach To Each Child's Temperament S3tyle

Respect also means that the adult needs to tune into a child's personality style and cluster of temperature traits. Children differ in their threshold of tolerance for distress. They differ in whether they approach or avoid the NEW—whether babysitters or foods or an unknown visiting relative.

Children may be impulsive or quietly reflective. Some are very active, always on the go. Others are quieter. Perceptive parents do not lump all children together. They notice the small differences in mood, in shyness or worrying, in adaptability or rigidity among their children and they are generous in tailoring their demands for more mature behaviors to the temperaments and abilities of each UNIQUE child. It is interesting that in England, compared with the United States, far fewer children are labelled "ADHD" (Attention Deficit and Hyperactivity Disorder) and British teachers are more likely to use behavior modification techniques rather than advocate the use of drugs.

Is a child shy and slow to warm up to new events, people and experiences? Is a child triggery and intense in responding to frustrations? Is a child's mood mostly upbeat and does the child bounce back fairly quickly from upsets? *Tuning into temperament helps you head off potential tantrums* and gives you better clues to guide your child into more peaceable ways of interacting with others (Honig, 1997).

Break Up Tasks Into Manageable Parts

Nobody likes being dictated to. When we give a vague order such as "Go clean up your messy room" a child may have no clear idea how and where to begin. But he sure feels that he cannot succeed and he may grumble and show morose resentment of his folks. Suggest smaller parts of this big task so that the child realizes what has to be done specifically. If you break the task down into manageable bits (put clothes in the hamper; stack books on the shelves; put away toy trucks and cars into the toybox) then a child feels more hopeful about being able to carry out small portions of a task that seemed initially so huge and vague.

Find Out How A Child Reasons When He Or She Misbehaves

When children seem unreasonable in their requests, try to require reasons. Sometimes young children give amusing reasons, such as "I should get four cookies because I am four." "I should go first because I am bigger." As children grow, let them know that you expect them to **think** about their actions and to think through reasons for how they are choosing to act.

Children's acting out gives a strong message that they have "empty" insides and deep needs for adult acceptance and caring.

Adults have to help young children actively learn how to reason and to think causally and sequentially. By asking children for reasons without putting them down, we encourage them to think more clearly: "Can you think of a **different** idea to get Bobby to let you hold his pet puppy?" "Can you think why Grandpa asked you to hold his hand before crossing this wide avenue?" "Can I get dinner ready and read to you at the same time? I can find

time to read to you **after** I have all the food cooking on the stove?" Children learn "polar opposites", such as "before" and "after" "same" and "different" more easily when they are actively utilized in real life discipline situations.

Offer Appropriate Incentives

If your school-age child wants you to take him to the park to play with some friends later in the day, think out loud together (Camp & Bash, 1985). He can finish his homework first and read his little brother a picture book story while you get dinner ready early so that you can then take the time off to go to the park with the children. "After you clean up your room we can play a game of checkers." "If you can take turns with Tanisha playing with the new dump truck or if you can figure out a way to play together, then you can have more play dates with her." This technique is sometimes called *"Grandma's Rule"*. That is, a low preferred activity, such as cleaning up, is followed by a highly preferred activity, such as a privilege or a treat. This timing pattern is more likely to result in an increase in the low-preferred activity. Unfortunately, many parents switch the timing. "Honey, be sure to do your homework after you come back from playing soccer!" is far less likely to result in completed homework!

Teach Ideas of Fairness

Introduce the language of fairness into your talks with children in their play with peers or siblings: "Each child needs to get a turn. Every child in the game needs to play by the same rules. Games will end up in fighting and they will not be fun if children do not follow the rules." Still, fairness may not always work. If one child has disabilities or is ill, then that child may need special attention and care. Children have to learn about **equity as well as fairness. Equity means taking into account special needs at special times for each person.**

Fantasy and Truth are Fuzzy Ideas For Preschoolers

Children have such strong longings and they often believe sincerely and strongly in the reality of fantasy characters, such as Ninja Turtles or He-Man. They sometimes have trouble distinguishing reality from their own wishes. A six-year old reported enthusiastically that she was a terrific swimmer, when she could barely take a few strokes in the water. In Menotti's Christmas opera about the three Wise Men, "Amahl and the night visitors", the boy Amahl tells his mother excitedly that he has seen a star with a tail as long as the sky. Parents may need to ask their children: "Is that a true-true story or a true-false one?" Do not be quick to brand a child as a "liar" when she makes up a fanciful tale or declares her imaginary playmate is sitting on the couch just where visiting Uncle Jim is about to seat himself. Remember how vivid children's imaginations are. Many young children are scared of "monsters" under the bed or in the closet. Many still blend fantasy and reality in ways adults find difficult to imagine!

Some make-believe tall tales of children represent deep longings. If your child pretends to others that she has a fabulously rich uncle who has promised her a pony, you may want to spend more real time doing loving activities together to help your youngster feel more at peace with the real world.

Be A Good Gatekeeper with TV

Be careful and judicious in the use of television. Some programs are prosocial. They give messages about how to handle impulsiveness or mean or mad feelings. Other television programs aimed at youngsters are incubators for teaching violent means of solving social problems. The cartoons are colorful. The animation is awesome. But the messages are pernicious. Sending kids to the television as a babysitter constantly is like using a narcotic to keep a child still. Enjoy activities, even peeling green peas or baking bread, or stripping the bed—together! Caring adults are good gatekeepers for choosing nourishing foods instead of junk food for children. Adults also need to be good gatekeepers for choosing programs that support self-reflectivity, positive solutions to social problems, and mistrust of easy or violent solutions. For example, in the United States there have recently been all too many violent solutions to ostracism and feelings of social rejection in schools with children shooting other children. Television programs with the Aardvark Arthur, the Teletubbies characters, Mr. Roger's Neighborhood neighbors, and the dragons in Dragon Tales all promote positive messages in solving social problems or personal issues. Be sure you are a good gatekeeper for television. Don't nag. Do arrange viewing situations, whether programs or videos or for positive learning.

Try To Figure Out What Is Worrying or Angering A Child

Anger, jealousy, resentment, and fear lead to acting out and misbehavior. Understanding your child's negative emotions may help you figure out how to approach and help your child.

Be careful about deciding what "causes" angry actions or misbehavior. Some families think a child should know right from wrong long before a child's thinking skills are well developed. Some children who were drug addicted in the womb show unmotivated and sudden aggressive actions, such as coming up behind an adult and biting the leg hard. Some children struggle with subtle thinking or perceptual deficits, a legacy from alcohol or drug addiction before they were born.

Blaming the Other Parent is Not a Useful Discipline Technique

Some folks blame the other parent. They say "The child gets his bad temper from his father. It's in his genes." Blaming the other parent for a child's troubling behaviors is guaranteed not to bring peace and good feelings in a family.

Use Victim-Centered Discipline Talk

Help children understand how others feel if they are attacked or hurt. Describe in vivid short sentences how a punch, a nasty word, a bite, a sneering remark hurts another's body and feelings. Galvanize your child to feel how it would be if the hurt had been done to him or her. Be firm in not accepting hurting as a means for your child to solve social conflicts. We do not shame children. They are not bad because they have a toileting accident sometimes or clumsily spill juice when they are toddlers. But if a child hurts another deliberately during the preschool years, we need to summon Eriksonian guilt. A child who understands how she would feel if someone hurt her or how he would feel if someone was mean to him is ready for you to lay your discipline talk on thick! Combine loving kindness with victim-centered discipline talk so that gradually the child comes to understand how kind ways help ease social difficulties far more than hurting ways. With your help, children learn inner self-control.

Use Empathic Listening

"Reflective Listening", sometimes called "Active listening" to the child's emotional message of aggravation, is a powerful tool that communicates an important message to your child: "My parent cares about me. My feelings are important to my folks. My parents want to help me figure out how to resolve my troubles rather than preaching at me or just getting angry." Simple "door-openers" help children open up and pour out their troubles. Try: "Looks like you had a rough day today, honey" (Gordon, 1975).

As you listen to a child's aggravations and woes with a peer or a parent or a teacher, try to reflect back to the child as best you can the genuine feelings you catch when he acts troubled or upset. Ridicule, put-downs, impatience—these are the swords that drive deep into children's hearts to make them feel that adults do not truly care about their feelings. Listen to your child's miseries. Listen and try to express your empathy with the child's upset feelings even when you do not agree with the scenario or think she or he is being childish.

Suppose Ricky is sad because his favorite friend now prefers a neighbor child as playmate and Ricky feels he has no one to play with. This problem seems as serious to a preschooler as adult problems seem to a parent. A teenage girl's worries about her weight or her popularity seem overblown to a parent, but desperately important to that girl. Don't suffer with her. Empathize and try to listen in a caring and supportive way.

Show Genuine Interest in Each Child

Be available and truly interested in talking with children in your care. Give them your full attention. Children hunger so deeply for personal attention. If adults are too involved in their own lives and needs, children express this emptiness in a variety of ways. They may turn away from parents and run with gangs of peers. They will sometimes steal coins out of parents' pockets. Sometimes they fight terribly with siblings or classmates. Children's acting out gives a strong message that they have "empty" insides and deep needs for adult acceptance and caring. Children have deep **emotional hunger for focused adult attention and emotional acceptance. Unconditional acceptance of each person heals the soul.** Can you think of a person in your own life who gave you that precious gift? Hopefully, a parent, a teacher, a spouse, a childcare provider, a religious leader in your faith community. And this gift makes a profound difference in healing past hurts.

Help Children Consider the **Consequences** *of Their Actions*

Many a youngster has never thought through exactly what will happen IF he hits Johnny or tears up his big brother's homework. It is really important for parents to probe and ask a lot: "What do think will happen next if you do that?" If Johnny fights with Billy over a toy, you may send Billy home and then Johnny will have nobody to play with the rest of the rainy weekend afternoon. Kids need encouragement to THINK, out loud, about what might happen IF they act in a certain way. When children are challenged to think of the consequences they often themselves decide that their action or idea is not helpful for themselves (Shure, 1994).

Challenge Children To Think Up Alternatives to Fighting

Help children get used to making a plan before a social problem arises. Encourage children to think up other ways of handling their social conflicts besides "not playing" with another child, or "hitting him". The more that teachers daily encouraged children to think up *alternative solutions* to their peer problems, the more likely they have been found to solve their social problems more appropri-

ately after three months of such classroom work (Shure & Spivack, 1978).

Find Community Resources, Books, and Programs That Support Families

To cope with the complex stresses and forces in society today, families need a lot of skills, a lot of insights, a lot of supports. Job loss, divorce, a child born with disabilities, death and illness, all impact on the family. Teachers and social service personnel can reach out to offer supports and services to increase peaceable family functioning and enhance children's lives.

Encourage Excellence, Not Perfection

Expect children to try hard. They know they can never be perfect and may deliberately fail or act clumsy if they feel very anxious that adults expect perfection. Praise good trying. Appreciate hard work and good efforts even when a child's grades are not as high as you would wish or even when she is clumsy when she gets to bat in a ball game.

Find Each Child's Gifts: Play as a Wonderful Discovery Channel for Learning a Child's Skills!

Sometimes a parent wants a child to be a terrific ball player because that was the parent's secret desire as a child. Or parents are so anxious about a child doing well in science and math that they do not realize that this child is talented in art but not as gifted for science. Learn the gifts of each child. The child who draws and doodles a lot in class may not be showing disrespect to the teacher. He may be showing a budding gift for cartooning or drawing. Children whose parents ignore their gifts and push other agendas on them (such as getting into a prestigious college 12 years later!) may start to lie and even to cheat on tests in school.

Some children do need help to develop their learning skills. Perhaps a child's family has moved and changed classrooms often. That child may not be able to keep up with school work. Be aware of when a child needs tutoring in school. Other children have more stable schooling situations, but they may have dyslexia or difficulties with reading or math. For example, some school age children reverse letters. They have troubles with figure-ground relationships (of black print on a white page) and do not see words clearly against the background of the page. Other children have perceptual-motor difficulties that make using a pencil to write clearly a very arduous task. Search for professional help when you see a clear need.

But also learn to appreciate the gifts your children do have. Some young children carry a tune flawlessly (Honig, 1995). Some kids can run with fleet feet. Some can recognize the model of every car that passes on the road.

Some kids can tell you the baseball batting statistics of every player on their favorite team. Some kids can soothe a playmate's upset by kind words. Be a not-so-secret admirer of your child and discover each gift with joy and gladness. If you watch your children at play with peers, you may catch their ingenuity at solving a social problem, such as trying to enter a peer group already playing house or pretending to be explorers on Mars.

Promote Children's Play

Provide rich play experiences by arranging for play dates and for quality preschool experiences. And then become a tuned-in NOTICER of the world of play. Read Vivien Paley's books, such as "The boy who would be a helicoptert" or "You can't say you can't play" to get more insights into the power of the world of play to socialize children just as the family is powerful in socializing children. Never permit bullying! Never permit catty clique behaviors. Talk about kindness with others and practice it yourself.

Don't Denigrate The Child's Other Parent

More and more marriages end in divorce, and second marriages tend to end even more frequently in divorce. In separations and divorce, parental bitterness and resentment belong to the adult, but so often heavy negative emotions spill over onto the children. Parental anger should not be sent as an arrow through the soul of a child where there has been a separation or divorce. Professionals need to help parents work through rage and grief so that these sorrowful poisons do not afflict children unduly. Already, young children in divorce often feel that it was their fault. Parents who feel betrayed or abandoned sometimes try to influence a child to turn against and hate the other parent. When possible, children need to feel that they are still loved by the other parent and they have total permission to love each parent. Enrolling children embroiled in divorce/custody issues in the "Banana Splits" programs social workers run in many schools is a good idea. Try to provide books and other materials to answer children's questions (Rofes, 1982). When mothers raise children alone, they may not realize that fathers are very precious to children (Biller & Meredith, 1975). Fathers are the preferred playmates of babies, and loss of affection from a divorced and absent father can cause long-lasting distress for children. Try to promote a climate of surety about each parent's caring for the children even when the parents cannot manage to live with each other.

Use Bibliotherapy

When children feel scared of the dark or worried about starting in a new school, stories have a wonderful power to heal. With stories, you find a way to reassure children so they feel more secure. Children identify with the loyal elephant in Dr. Seuss' "Horton hears a who". They do not always have to act out their resentments or disappointments. They can also identify with kind characters in stories.

In addition, children love mischievous characters, such as Pippo the monkey. They grin at the "Cat in the Hat". Everything gets fixed up just fine at the end of that Dr. Seuss story. Yet the Cat in the Hat surely acted naughty for a while!

Children sometimes misbehave when they want more attention. They act out with misbehavior in order to get attention, even when that attention is negative, such as yelling and spanking! A neighborhood library has good books about children's troubles. If you are going through a troubled time in your family, search for books such as "The boy who could make his mother stop yelling", for example.

Some children misbehave because they desperately want to feel powerful or exact revenge (for example, because they felt unwanted and unimportant when the new baby was born). Many problems hurt a child's soul, such as loss of a grandparent, or living with an alcoholic parent who humiliates the child so that he is afraid ever to invite a friend over to the home. Some children feel abandoned when a parent remarries and the stepparent obviously does not want the child around and never offers any affection to the child. The local library has many books you can read to help your child identify with a story child who has lived through such a problem and has managed to cope despite sorrow and worries.

Read stories that resonate for a child over and over. One youngster loved me to read daily for weeks Dr. Seuss' "The king's stilts". This is a story of a courageous little boy who digs up the king's buried stilts and returns them to the monarch (who loves to play on them at the end of a work day) and thus returns the king's joy and ability to govern well. That message, that a child could be scared of a mean and menacing adult (the king's prime minister in the story) and still finally become brave enough to do the right thing, seemed to resonate so deeply for this child. Another child, much younger, loved me to read "The enormous turnip" over and over. Somehow, naming all the family members as helpers in getting that huge turnip out of the ground was so satisfying. And he loved to point out that even Petya, the tiny beetle really helped too.

Toddlers love the Sam books too. Sam and Lisa quarrel over a toy car. Each one wants it. Each one smacks the other. Mama comes with another car so that each has a car to play with and they play together. These books resonate for toddlers who are learning, struggling, with the idea of sharing and taking turns. Choose your books to help children wrestle with such issues at every level. Choose books with cadences and poetry so that preschoolers can learn the refrains as in the book "Something from nothing". Preschoolers enthusiastically join in saying "Grandpa can fix it!". This is the positive refrain of the little boy Jacob every time his mama wants him to throw out something old and torn.

Create Your Own Stories to Reassure Worried Children

If a child has terrors or fears, for example, about starting kindergarten, make up stories about a little child (who very much resembles your child) who had a similar problem and how a healing, reassuring, good ending happened in that situation (Brett, 1986).

When parents are separating and getting a divorce, children often feel torn in pieces. They are afraid that something they did caused the breakup. They worry that if one parents has left, they may also be abandoned by the other parent. Make up stories that have endings clearly showing how each parent loves the child and showing the child where she will be living and how she will be kept safe and secure.

Help Siblings Get Along More Peacefully

Jealousy, the green-eyed monster, is often alive and well in families. Tattling and reporting important news are different. Make a distinction to your children between 1) tattling to hurt a sibling to get even or as one way to show jealousy, and 2) the importance of telling information to parents if there is a really important trouble where an adult **must** get involved. Praise each time that the siblings try to talk courteously and not trade sneering put downs. Talk with your children about the far future when they are all grown up and will have each other as the only close family persons. Share a good book about jealous siblings and how they dealt with the green eyed monster. Try to find time alone for meeting the special needs of each child. Take one grocery shopping while a friend or relative watches the other children. Bring one down to the laundry room to work together while the others are busy doing homework.

Use relaxation and vivid imagination techniques to help children relax, especially where there is sibling jealousy and too much rush and tension in the children's lives. Deep breathing exercises and conjuring peaceful scenes sometimes help bring down child tensions (Hendricks & Wills, 1975).

Assign Required and Admired Chores

Be sure that chores are not assigned just to get daily jobs done the parents don't want to do! Chores should depend on the age and ability of each child. Children should not feel that they are their parents' "slaves" but family helpers pitching in to make the household work easier. Give children a feeling that when they do their chores they are important, contributing members of the family so they feel proud to be useful and helpful. "I am a big helper. I

clear the table after dinner. My papa needs me to hold the nails and hand him a nail as he repairs the ripped porch screens." Swan and Stavros' work among poor inner-city families showed that children with required chores, whose parents praised their participation and gave them genuine admiration and appreciation felt very secure in the bosom of the family and performed with high achievement in the kindergarten and first grade classroom. "Me a big helper" is a proud and splendid boast from an older toddler!

Be a Good Matchmaker

Make the tasks you expect from each child be ones that the child can do. Encourage efforts and support early attempts to master new tasks in accordance with each child's ability (Honig, 1982b).

In a research study in New Orleans, Swan and Stavros (1973) found that low-income parents who required helpfulness (not coerced, but required) had children who were successful as kindergarten learners and in their social relationships with peers. They noted that fathers were mostly present in these low-income families with self-motivated learners. Parents had neat clean living environments, read daily to their young children, ate meals and talked together at dinner time, and found their children genuinely interesting persons.

Express Personal Pleasure With Each Child

Tell a child that you love him, that you love her. Hug that child frequently. Caress a child with warm (rather than cold or disapproving) voice tones. Shine your eyes at a child so that the sunshine of your smile and the pleasure in your tone of voice warm the deepest corners of your child's self.

Talk About Peer Pressure With Children

Peer pressure is very powerful in coercing some youngsters to misbehave. Sometimes peer pressure to have special sneakers or clothes or possessions will lead to children's stealing another's prized clothing item to gain peer admiration. Peer pressure can lead a teenager to drink immoderately, try drugs, or engage in unsafe sex. Families must talk frankly about peer pressure and how their child feels about it. A youngster can accept and more likely live by family values and family circumstances. IF the child feels a strong sense of rootedness and reassurance within the family rather than from the peer group.

Avoid the Use of Shame

Shame is an acid that corrodes the soul. Shame is often twinned with rage that fuels serious misbehavior. Do not shame your children or they may well feel that they need to get revenge on you and on the world. Perhaps a child acts defiant just to show that you cannot really make him eat a food he detests, you cannot make him fall asleep at a too-early bedtime for him. To get even, he will lie awake angry for hours. Power and revenge games are dangerous. They destroy a child's feelings of security and trust in responsible adults.

Encourage Competence

Even very young children need to feel they "can do it"—put a peg into a pegboard, roll a ball, pick up a wiggly spaghetti strand to feed themselves, throw a used Kleenex in the wastebasket, or other simple skills. Let them try, even if they are not expert, to accomplish tasks they are capable of doing, such as putting on a coat, or setting a table or pouring out dog food into the bowl on the floor. Children who give up easily or feel that they can never do their homework, never learn to ride a bide, for example, are **discouraged** children. Try patiently to support their small accomplishments. Figure out ways to decrease their discouraged feelings.

> Felicia asked for a wastebasket right by the table where she struggled nightly with homework math problems. She did not want all the papers with wrong answers and scribbles to pile up in front of her, almost accusing her of being "stupid". But with the handy wastebasket nearby, she was willing to struggle anew with a fresh sheet to try her math homework.

Provide Positive Attributions

Give praise for **specific** actions. Cheerfully tossing off "You're terrific!" or "That's wonderful!" makes a child feel uncomfortable. She knows how much she still has to learn, and how many times she goofs up. Notice specific times when praise can really boost self-esteem and brighten a child's day. For example, an adult could say: "You are a really good friend to Robbie. Did you notice how happy he was when you shared your markers with him. You know how to make another child feel comfortable and welcome here!"

Work Alongside A Young Child

By expecting too much, too fast, we sometimes force children to act incompetent to get out from under the disapproval they feel will be inevitable if they aren't superior (Dinkmeyer & McKay, 1982). When a job seems overwhelming to a young child, make sure you work alongside. "Clean up your room" may send a child into a temper tantrum or into trying to avoid the job entirely. But if you tackle the task cheerfully **together**, the child will enjoy your company and feel pride as he works to-

gether with you. When you break a task into smaller manageable bits, you **scaffold** the task for a youngster: "Which do you want to pick up first—the toys on the floor that go into your toy box or the clothes that go into the wash hamper?"

PROFESSIONALS AS PARTNERS WITH PARENTS

Professionals who work together with parents are not only teachers with a lot of information to share. They sometimes act as therapists. Sometimes they become caring friends of the family. Sometimes, as in Fraiberg's kitchen therapy model of home visitation, they become caring surrogate parents. They re-parent new parents whose ghosts of anguish and violence from the past are strongly impacting on the children in the present. Teachers especially need to "partner" with parents to form a strong team to support a child's early learning.

Sometimes, with very young mothers, professionals need to assist them in the process of **reflectivity**. The more that a new mother can reflect on her family of origin and how much during childhood she resented or was scared of harsh discipline, and decide that she does not want those feelings for her baby, the more affectionate and close will be her relationship with the new baby (Brophy & Honig, 1999).

In addition to support and knowledge, what other functions can personnel carry out to enhance positive family functioning?

Help Parents Find Ways To Give Themselves A Lift

Parents who feel happier with their own lives discipline more effectively and can share their happiness with children. Something as simple and inexpensive as a long bubble bath may relax an adult. Cleanup as a team after dinner with an adult partner helps any parent feel appreciated.

In a family with limited material resources, encourage parents to enlist imagination rather than material objects in order to bring special highlights into the family's day and into life. When rainy days in a row have resulted in short tempers, a family can plan to serve supper as a picnic on the living room floor. The children help make sandwiches. They spread the tuna salad and peanut butter on bread slices and wrap each sandwich. The family places all the picnic fixings in a basket and pretends they are walking to the picnic grounds—an old green sheet spread on the floor. Pretend games can break into the crankiness or hassles of daily living where severe financial constraints do not permit entertainments that "cost money".

Making collages out of bits of plastic egg cartons and other collected throw-aways can brighten an afternoon and provide art decorations to display on a refrigerator door so that children feel how proud you are of their talents.

Help Families to Network

Professionals need to introduce parents to others sometimes so they can form a support group when families feel isolated and alone. They could meet together at one another's home to talk about child issues with professional help or they can choose parenting materials to discuss. Help families feel comfortable in the world of the free public library or in a "Please Touch" museum. Introduce families to a drop-in store front center that welcomes families with respite child care, opportunities to swap children's used clothing and shopping coupons, as well as providing parenting classes and guitar lessons.

Find Respite Care For Overwhelmed Parents

Arrange for respite care when a parent is overwhelmed with caring for a disabled or emotionally disturbed child. Safe and secure respite care that a parent can count on and trust is one of the greatest gifts to give an exhausted parent. In a neighborhood, maybe parents can give each other coupons for helping out with childcare for each other. Such barter systems can provide needed respite without any money changing hands.

Assist Parents Trying to Join the Work Force

Help in finding job training and help in acquiring a high school diploma are other precious supports that families need as the bottom line in order to qualify for work positions to support their children. A resource room in a school or clinic can set out easy-to-read materials that focus on job training and on agencies that can help families in their search to become self sufficient.

Galvanize Specialist Help

When parents are behaving in seriously dysfunctional ways with children you need to act quickly and pinpoint the agencies and service to mobilize. Stresses can unnerve and make life difficult for parents. The five kinds of abuse that do occur in some families are: physical abuse, sexual abuse, physical neglect, emotional hostility, and emotional unavailability. Sometimes counseling and insight from child development experts and therapists can help. In urgent cases, when legal systems are threatening to remove a child from a home, then more strenuous professional help, such as Homebuilders provides (Kinney, Haapala & Booth, 1991), may be required. Homebuilders is an emergency service whereby a caseworker spends a great many hours for about six weeks in the home teaching the family members Gordon's (1975) Active Listening and I-statement techniques so that they can manage their

severe difficulties and get along more positively. Specialists in anger management can be enlisted to "tame the dragon of anger" in children and parents (Eastman & Rozen, 1994).

CONCLUSIONS

Enhancing parent involvement and training a highly skilled childcare provider workforce must become priority goals for nations if we are to improve children's lives and learning careers. As we support parents, particularly parents whose lives include undue stress from limited resources and chaotic and inappropriate role models from the past, we will be ensuring a brighter future not only for the families and children served but for our entire society. And as we support teachers in schools and care providers in nurseries and preschools with money, prestige, training, and our deep appreciation, we will also be ensuring that our children grow up to be happy, responsible, achieving citizens.

References

Baumrind, D. (1977). Some thoughts about childrearing. In S. Cohen and T. Comiskey (Eds.), *Child development: Contemporary perspectives* (pp. 248–258). Itasca, IL: F. E. Peacock.

Bettelheim, B. (1987). *A good enough parent: A book on childrearing.* New York: Random House.

Biller, H. and Meredith, D. (1975). *Father power: The art of effective fathering and how it can bring joy and freedom to the whole family.* New York: McKay.

Brett, D. (1986). *Annie stories.* Australia: Penguin.

Briggs, D. C. (1975). *Your child's self esteem.* New York: Doubleday.

Brophy-Herb, H. E. and Honig, A. S. (1999). Reflectivity: Key ingredient in positive adolescent parenting. *The Journal of Primary Prevention,* **19** (3), 241–250.

Camp, B. N. and Bash, M. A. (1985). *Think aloud. Increasing social and cognitive skills—a problem solving program for children.* Champaign, IL: Research Press.

Crary, E. (1990). *Pick up your socks and other skills growing children need: A practical guide to raising responsible children.* Seattle, WA: Parenting Press.

Dinkmeyer, D. and McKay, G. D. (1982). *The parent's handbook: STEP. Systematic training for effective parenting.* Circle Pines, MN: American Guidance Service.

Eastman, M. and Rozen, S. C. (1994). *Taming the dragon in your child: Solutions for breaking the cycle of family anger.* New York: John Wiley.

Erikson, E. (1970). *Childhood and society.* New York: Norton.

Faber, A. and Mazlish, E. (1980). *How to talk so kids will listen and listen so kids will talk.* New York: Rawson Wade.

Fraiberg, S. (Ed.) (1980). *Clinical studies in infant mental health: The first year of life.* New York: Basic Books.

Goleman, D. (1995). *Emotional intelligence.* New York: Basic Books.

Gordon, S. (1983). *Parenting: A guide for young people.* New York: Oxford.

Gordon, T. (1975). *Parent effectiveness training.* New York:

Hart, B. and Risley, T. R. (1995). *Meaningful differences in the everyday experiences of young American children.* Baltimore, MD: Paul H. Brookes.

Henricks, G. and Wills, R. (1975). *The centering book: Awareness activities for children, parents, and teachers.* Engelwood Cliffs, NJ: Prentice Hall.

Honig, A. S. (1979). *Parent involvement in early childhood education.* Washington, DC.: National Association for the Education of Young Children.

Honig, A. S. (1982a). The gifts of families: Caring, courage, and competence. In N. Stinnett, J. Defrain, K. King, H. Hingren, G. Fowe, S. Van Zandt, and R. Williams (Eds.), *Family strengths 4: Positive support systems* (pp. 331–349). Lincoln, NE: University of Nebraska Press.

Honig, A. S. (1982b). *Playtime learning games for young children.* Syracuse, NY: Syracuse University Press.

Honig, A. S. (1985a). The art of talking to a baby. *Working Mother,* **8** (3), 72–78.

Honig, A. S. (1985b). Research in review; Compliance, control and discipline. *Young Children,* Part 1, **40** (2), 50–58; Part 2, **40** (3), 47–52.

Honig, A. S. (1993, Fall). Toilet learning. *Day Care and Early Education.*

Honig, A. S. (1995). Singing with infants and toddlers. *Young Children,* **50** (5), 72–78.

Honig, A. S. (1996). *Behavior guidance for infants and toddlers.* Little Rock, AR: Southern Early Childhood Association.

Honig, A. S. (1997). Infant temperament and personality: What do we need to know? *Montessori Life,* **9** (3), 18–21.

Honig, A. S. and Brophy, H. E. (1996). *Talking with your baby: Family as the first school.* Syracuse, NY: Syracuse University Press.

Honig, A. S. and Morin, C. (2000). When should programs for teen parents and babies begin? *Journal of Primary Prevention,* **21** (1).

Honig, A. S. and Wittmer, D. S. (1990). Infants, toddlers and socialization. In J. R. Lally (Ed.,), *A caregiver's guide to social emotional growth and socialization* (pp. 62–80). Sacramento, CA: California State Department of Education.

Kinney, J. Haapala, D. and Booth, C. (1991). *Keeping families together: The Homebuilders model.* Hawthorne, NY: Aldine De Gruyter.

Lickona, T. (1983). *Raising good children: From birth through the teenage years.* New York: Bantam Books.

Rofes, E. (Ed.) (1982). *The kids' book of divorce.* New York: Vintage.

Shure, M. B. (1994). *Raising a thinking child: Help your young child to resolve everyday conflicts and get along with others.* New York: Henry Holt.

Shure, M. and Spivack, G. (1978). *Problem-solving techniques in child-rearing.* San Francisco, CA: Jossey Bass.

Swan, R. W. and Stavros, H. (1973A). Child-rearing practices associated with the development of cognitive skills of children in a low socio-economic area. *Early Child Development and Care,* **2**, 23–38.

Welsh, R. (1976). Violence, permissiveness and the overpunished child. *Journal of Pediatric Psychology,* **1**, 68–71.

Winnicott, D. W. (1987). *Babies and their mothers.* Reading, MA: Addison-Wesley.

---

*Keynote address presented at the Child and Family Development Conference, Charlotte, North Carolina, March, 2000.

From *Early Child Development and Care,* 2000, Vol. 163, pp. 79-106. © 2000 by Carfax Publishing Ltd. Reprinted by permission of Taylor & Francis Journals.

When Safety Is the Name of the Game

**Every year, millions of young athletes end up in the hospital.
What parents and kids can do to prevent sports injuries.**

By David Noonan

Fish gotta swim, birds gotta fly, kids gotta play. And that's what they do. Each year, an estimated 30 million young Americans, high-school age and under, participate in organized sports like football, basketball and soccer. Millions more race around every day on bikes, scooters, skates and skateboards and climb, jump and swing on playground equipment. The benefits of all that physical activity far outweigh the risks, especially these days, when obesity and inactivity plague the videogame generation.

Still, sports and recreation-related injuries are an ever-present threat to young athletes and a constant concern to their parents. With good reason. According to a recent study by the Centers for Disease Control, more kids receive medical attention for sports injuries each year than for injuries in automobile accidents. During the 12 months ending June 2001, nearly 2 million kids 14 and under were treated in emergency rooms for sports and recreation injuries. (Strains and sprains are the most common, followed by fractures.) The rate of sports injury among kids 5 to 14 is nearly three times the rate for people 25 to 44.

Those numbers add up to a major public-health issue, and the CDC, the American Academy of Pediatrics, the American Academy of Orthopaedic Surgeons and others are promoting a variety of guidelines and strategies to reduce them. "We want kids to get up off the couch, we're big cheerleaders for that," says Dr. Julie Gilchrist, a sports-injury expert at the CDC's Center for Injury Prevention and Control. "But be realistic in how you're doing it.

Make conscious choices about injury prevention. Don't just take it for granted."

Most kids get their first lumps riding their bikes and cavorting on the playground. The CDC estimates that more than 330,000 children from 5 to 14 are injured while bicycling each year. An additional 219,000 in that age group are hurt on monkey bars and other climbing equipment, swings and slides. Wearing a helmet that fits properly is the surest way to avoid serious injury on a bike. (Helmets are also the key to safer skateboarding, which accounts for about 50,000 injuries among people under 20 each year, including many head injuries.) At the playground, where 60 percent of injuries are due to falls, a soft surface to land on is a top priority. Wood chips, shredded tires and sand are good; packed-down soil is bad.

Organized sports, including football, are generally less risky for the 10-and-under crowd because the kids usually aren't big enough or fast enough to make collisions a serious problem. But that all changes when the hormones kick in. "At puberty, children gain muscle mass, speed and weight," says pediatric orthopedic surgeon J. Andy Sullivan, co-editor of the book "Care of the Young Athlete." "And the combination of those things allows them to run together hard enough to hurt each other."

There is no reliable way to compare the relative risks of various sports because the CDC doesn't track the level of participation. It knows how many people are injured playing basketball, for example (an estimated 977,000 each year, all ages), but it doesn't know how many people are playing the game, or for how long or how many days a week. "Basketball is one of the most common sports in all ages and areas of the U.S.," says Gilchrist, "and so just because it has the highest number of injuries doesn't mean that it's riskier."

Whatever the sport, injury prevention begins with the athletes and their parents. And the first thing they need to focus on, experts say, is conditioning. Being out of shape, a real problem for lots of kids, increases risk. Those who play only one sport have to be careful not to wait for their season to arrive before they begin working out; going from naps in the hammock to two-a-day football practices pretty much guarantees trouble. Appropriate gear in good condition is a must. And, simple as it sounds, knowing and learning basic skills also helps young athletes avoid injury. Baseball players should know how to slide correctly, football players how to tackle, soccer players how to head the ball.

Besides making sure their kids are fit and understand the fundamentals, parents can make any sport safer by attending games and practices, watching the coaches and encouraging them to emphasize injury prevention. (Which is hardly inconsistent with winning, since superior skill and safety go hand in hand.) Parents can also promote safety by urging officials to call stringent games. When a ref won't tolerate flagrant fouls, players usually get the message and rein themselves in (or they get ejected). The cleaner the game, the safer.

But there are no officials at practice, and that, in fact, is where most injuries happen because teams practice a lot more than they play actual games. "The safety of the athletes is really in the hands of the coaches at practice because usually you don't have trainers there," says Robert Ferraro, executive director of the National High School Coaches Association. Ferraro and Gilchrist both say trainers play a critical role in injury prevention because they focus on safety. "Coaches have other things on their minds, and to make them think about these things in addition to their other work is burdensome," says Gilchrist, who urges parents to press their local school officials to hire athletic trainers, if they don't already have them.

It's impossible to prevent all injuries, of course. Head injuries, which account for about 8 percent of the sports injuries treated in emergency rooms, are a special concern. Returning to play too soon after a concussion can be dangerous. A player who receives a second concussion before he recovers from the first can suffer long-lasting brain damage and even death. A child's brain may be more susceptible to this "second-impact syndrome" because it fits more tightly inside the skull than an adult's brain. Fortunately, such cases are rare.

Sprains and Strains

Threats change as kids move from the playground to organized sports.

Nonfatal sports injuries treated in emergency rooms, by activity, in thousands (2000–01):

Boys

Ages 5–9		Ages 10–14	
Bicycle riding	85.8	Football	145.0
Playground	67.9	Bicycle riding	124.0
Football	25.3	Basketball	118.0
Scooters	21.3	Baseball	47.5
Baseball	20.1	Skateboarding	39.2
Basketball	17.9	Soccer	29.0
Trampoline	14.7	Scooter	25.8
Swimming	12.3	Playground	21.0

Girls

Ages 5–9		Ages 10–14	
Playground	58.2	Basketball	53.1
Bicycle riding	53.0	Bicycle riding	38.9
Scooters	15.3	Soccer	28.1
Trampoline	14.1	Gymnastics	23.2
Swimming	9.7	Softball	19.9
Gymnastics	7.8	Scooters	16.1
Exercise	7.7	Playground	16.0
Skating	7.2	Trampoline	13.6

SOURCE: MORBIDITY AND MORTALITY WEEKLY REPORT

"Make conscious choices about injury prevention. Don't take it for granted."

—DR. JULIE GILCHRIST, CDC researcher

Even when a kid has a common injury, the decision about when to let him play again is critical. "It depends on the diagnosis and common sense, which a lot of people don't have," says Sullivan. "Number one, you want to know if the injury is healed. Number two, have they been rehabilitated?" In Sullivan's view, a young athlete is not rehabilitated until he or she has regained the full range of motion, strength and flexibility of the affected joint. If the injury is to the left ankle, for example, it has to be equal in all ways to the uninjured right ankle. In addition, the kid has to regain the same level of fitness and conditioning he was at before he got hurt. Bottom line for parents, coaches and kids: a little common sense and a lot of vigilance can prevent unnecessary pain.

The Blank Slate

The long-accepted theory that parents can mold their children like clay has distorted choices faced by adults trying to balance their lives, multiplied the anguish of those whose children haven't turned out as hoped, and mangled the science of human behavior

By Steven Pinker

IF YOU READ THE PUNDITS IN NEWSPAPERS AND MAGAZINES, you may have come across some remarkable claims about the malleability of the human psyche. Here are a few from my collection of clippings:

- Little boys quarrel and fight because they are encouraged to do so.
- Children enjoy sweets because their parents use them as rewards for eating vegetables.
- Teenagers get the idea to compete in looks and fashion from spelling bees and academic prizes.
- Men think the goal of sex is an orgasm because of the way they were socialized.

If you find these assertions dubious, your skepticism is certainly justified. In all cultures, little boys quarrel, children like sweets, teens compete for status, and men pursue orgasms, without the slightest need of encouragement or socialization. In each case, the writers made their preposterous claims without a shred of evidence—without even a nod to the possibility that they were saying something common sense might call into question.

Intellectual life today is beset with a great divide. On one side is a militant denial of human nature, a conviction that the mind of a child is a blank slate that is subsequently inscribed by parents and society. For much of the past century, psychology has tried to explain all thought, feeling, and behavior with a few simple mechanisms of learning by association. Social scientists have tried to explain all customs and social arrangements as a product of the surrounding culture. A long list of concepts that would seem natural to the human way of thinking—emotions, kinship, the sexes—are said to have been "invented" or "socially constructed."

At the same time, there is a growing realization that human nature won't go away. Anyone who has had more than one child, or been in a heterosexual relationship, or noticed that children learn language but house pets don't, has recognized that people are born with certain talents and temperaments. An acknowledgment that we humans are a species with a timeless and universal psychology pervades the writings of great political thinkers, and without it we cannot explain the recurring themes of literature, religion, and myth. Moreover, the modern sciences of mind, brain, genes, and evolution are showing that there is something to the commonsense idea of human nature. Although no scientist denies that learning and culture are crucial to every aspect of human life, these processes don't happen by magic. There must be complex innate mental faculties that enable human beings to create and learn culture.

Sometimes the contradictory attitudes toward human nature divide people into competing camps. The blank slate camp tends to have greater appeal among those in the social sciences and humanities than it does among biological scientists. And until recently, it was more popular on the political left than it was on the right.

But sometimes both attitudes coexist uneasily inside the mind of a single person. Many academics, for example, publicly deny the existence of intelligence. But privately, academics are *obsessed* with intelligence, discussing it endlessly in admissions, in hiring, and especially in their gossip about one another. And despite their protestations that it is a reactionary concept, they quickly invoke it to oppose executing a murderer with an IQ of 64 or to support laws requiring the removal of lead paint because it may lower a child's IQ by five points. Similarly, those who argue that gender differences are a reversible social construction do not treat them that way in their advice to their daughters, in their dealings with the opposite sex, or in their unguarded gossip, humor, and reflections on their lives.

No good can come from this hypocrisy. The dogma that human nature does not exist, in the face of growing evidence from science and common sense that it does, has led to contempt among many scholars in the humanities for the concepts of evidence and truth. Worse, the doctrine of the blank slate often distorts science itself by making an extreme position—that culture alone determines behavior—seem moderate, and by making the moderate position—that behavior comes from an interaction of biology and culture—seem extreme.

Although how parents treat their children can make a lot of difference in how happy they are, placing a stimulating mobile over a child's crib and playing Mozart CDs will not shape a child's intelligence.

For example, many policies on parenting come from research that finds a correlation between the behavior of parents and of their children. Loving parents have confident children, authoritative parents (neither too permissive nor too punitive) have well-behaved children, parents who talk to their children have children with better language skills, and so on. Thus everyone concludes that parents should be loving, authoritative, and talkative, and if children don't turn out well, it must be the parents' fault.

Those conclusions depend on the belief that children are blank slates. It ignores the fact that parents provide their children with genes, not just an environment. The correlations may be telling us only that the same genes that make adults loving, authoritative, and talkative make their children self-confident, well-behaved, and articulate. Until the studies are redone with adopted children (who get only their environment from their parents), the data are compatible with the possibility that genes make all the difference, that parenting makes all the difference, or anything in between. Yet the extreme position—that parents are everything—is the only one researchers entertain.

The denial of human nature has not just corrupted the world of intellectuals but has harmed ordinary people. The theory that parents can mold their children like clay has inflicted child-rearing regimes on parents that are unnatural and sometimes cruel. It has distorted the choices faced by mothers as they try to balance their lives, and it has multiplied the anguish of parents whose children haven't turned out as hoped. The belief that

human tastes are reversible cultural preferences has led social planners to write off people's enjoyment of ornament, natural light, and human scale and forced millions of people to live in drab cement boxes. And the conviction that humanity could be reshaped by massive social engineering projects has led to some of the greatest atrocities in history.

THE PHRASE "BLANK SLATE" IS A LOOSE TRANSLATION OF THE medieval Latin term tabula rasa—scraped tablet. It is often attributed to the 17th-century English philosopher John Locke, who wrote that the mind is "white paper void of all characters." But it became the official doctrine among thinking people only in the first half of the 20th century, as part of a reaction to the widespread belief in the intellectual or moral inferiority of women, Jews, nonwhite races, and non-Western cultures.

Part of the reaction was a moral repulsion from discrimination, lynchings, forced sterilizations, segregation, and the Holocaust. And part of it came from empirical observations. Waves of immigrants from southern and eastern Europe filled the cities of America and climbed the social ladder. African Americans took advantage of "Negro colleges" and migrated northward, beginning the Harlem Renaissance. The graduates of women's colleges launched the first wave of feminism. To say that women and minority groups were inferior contradicted what people could see with their own eyes.

Academics were swept along by the changing attitudes, but they also helped direct the tide. The prevailing theories of mind were refashioned to make racism and sexism as untenable as possible. The blank slate became sacred scripture. According to the doctrine, any differences we see among races, ethnic groups, sexes, and individuals come not from differences in their innate constitution but from differences in their experiences. Change the experiences—by reforming parenting, education, the media, and social rewards—and you can change the person. Also, if there is no such thing as human nature, society will not be saddled with such nasty traits as aggression, selfishness, and prejudice. In a reformed environment, people can be prevented from learning these habits.

In psychology, behaviorists like John B. Watson and B. F. Skinner simply banned notions of talent and temperament, together with all the other contents of the mind, such as beliefs, desires, and feelings. This set the stage for Watson's famous boast: "Give me a dozen healthy infants, well-formed, and my own specified world to bring them up in, and I'll guarantee to take any one at random and train him to become any type of specialist I might select—doctor, lawyer, artist, merchant-chief, and yes, even beggar-man and thief, regardless of his talents, penchants, tendencies, abilities, vocations, and race of his ancestors."

Watson also wrote an influential child-rearing manual recommending that parents give their children minimum attention and love. If you comfort a crying baby, he wrote, you will reward the baby for crying and thereby increase the frequency of crying behavior.

In anthropology, Franz Boas wrote that differences among human races and ethnic groups come not from their physical constitution but from their *culture*. Though Boas himself did not claim that people were blank slates—he only argued that all ethnic groups are endowed with the same mental abilities—his students, who came to dominate American social science, went further. They insisted not just that *differences* among ethnic groups must be explained in terms of culture (which is reasonable), but that *every aspect* of human existence must be explained in terms of culture (which is not). "Heredity cannot be allowed to have acted any part in history," wrote Alfred Kroeber. "With the exception of the instinctoid reactions in infants to sudden withdrawals of support and to sudden loud noises, the human being is entirely instinctless," wrote Ashley Montagu.

IN THE SECOND HALF OF THE 20TH CENTURY, THE IDEALS OF the social scientists of the first half enjoyed a well-deserved victory. Eugenics, social Darwinism, overt expressions of racism and sexism, and official discrimination against women and minorities were on the wane, or had been eliminated, from the political and intellectual mainstream in Western democracies.

At the same time, the doctrine of the blank slate, which had been blurred with ideals of equality and progress, began to show cracks. As new disciplines such as cognitive science, neuroscience, evolutionary psychology, and behavioral genetics flourished, it became clearer that thinking is a biological process, that the brain is not exempt from the laws of evolution, that the sexes differ above the neck as well as below it, and that people are not psychological clones. Here are some examples of the discoveries.

Hundreds of traits, from romantic love to humorous insults, can be found in every society ever documented.

Natural selection tends to homogenize a species into a standard design by concentrating the effective genes and winnowing out the ineffective ones. This suggests that the human mind evolved with a universal complex design. Beginning in the 1950s, linguist Noam Chomsky of the Massachusetts Institute of Technology argued that a language should be analyzed not in terms of the list of sentences people utter but in terms of the mental computations that enable them to handle an unlimited number of new sentences in the language. These computations have been found to conform to a universal grammar. And if this universal grammar is embodied in the circuitry that guides babies when they listen to speech, it could explain how children learn language so easily.

Similarly, some anthropologists have returned to an ethnographic record that used to trumpet differences among cultures and have found an astonishingly detailed set of aptitudes and tastes that all cultures have in common. This shared way of thinking, feeling, and living makes all of humanity look like a single tribe, which the anthropologist Donald Brown of the University of California at Santa Barbara has called the universal people. Hundreds of traits, from romantic love to humorous insults, from poetry to food taboos, from exchange of goods to

mourning the dead, can be found in every society ever documented.

One example of a stubborn universal is the tangle of emotions surrounding the act of love. In all societies, sex is at least somewhat "dirty." It is conducted in private, pondered obsessively, regulated by custom and taboo, the subject of gossip and teasing, and a trigger for jealous rage. Yet sex is the most concentrated source of physical pleasure granted by the nervous system. Why is it so fraught with conflict? For a brief period in the 1960s and 1970s, people dreamed of an erotopia in which men and women could engage in sex without hang-ups and inhibitions. "If you can't be with the one you love, love the one you're with," sang Stephen Stills. "If you love somebody, set them free," sang Sting.

But Sting also sang, "Every move you make, I'll be watching you." Even in a time when, seemingly, anything goes, most people do not partake in sex as casually as they partake in food or conversation. The reasons are as deep as anything in biology. One of the hazards of sex is a baby, and a baby is not just any seven-pound object but, from an evolutionary point of view, our reason for being. Every time a woman has sex with a man, she is taking a chance at sentencing herself to years of motherhood, and she is forgoing the opportunity to use her finite reproductive output with some other man. The man, for his part, may be either implicitly committing his sweat and toil to the incipient child or deceiving his partner about such intentions.

On rational grounds, the volatility of sex is a puzzle, because in an era with reliable contraception, these archaic entanglements should have no claim on our feelings. We should be loving the one we're with, and sex should inspire no more gossip, music, fiction, raunchy humor, or strong emotions than eating or talking does. The fact that people are tormented by the Darwinian economics of babies they are no longer having is testimony to the long reach of human nature.

ALTHOUGH THE MINDS OF NORMAL HUMAN BEINGS WORK IN pretty much the same way, they are not, of course, identical. Natural selection reduces genetic variability but never eliminates it. As a result, nearly every one of us is genetically unique. And these differences in genes make a difference in mind and behavior, at least quantitatively. The most dramatic demonstrations come from studies of the rare people who *are* genetically identical, identical twins.

Identical twins think and feel in such similar ways that they sometimes suspect they are linked by telepathy. They are similar in verbal and mathematical intelligence, in their degree of life satisfaction, and in personality traits such as introversion, agreeableness, neuroticism, conscientiousness, and openness to experience. They have similar attitudes toward controversial issues such as the death penalty, religion, and modern music. They resemble each other not just in paper-and-pencil tests but in consequential behavior such as gambling, divorcing, committing crimes, getting into accidents, and watching television. And they boast dozens of shared idiosyncrasies such as giggling incessantly, giving interminable answers to simple questions, dipping buttered toast in coffee, and, in the case of Abigail van Buren and the late Ann Landers, writing indistinguishable syndicated advice columns. The crags and valleys of their electro-encephalograms (brain waves) are as alike as those of a single person recorded on two occasions, and the wrinkles of their brains and the distribution of gray matter across cortical areas are similar as well.

Identical twins (who share all their genes) are far more similar than fraternal twins (who share just half their genes). This is as true when the twins are separated at birth and raised apart as when they are raised in the same home by the same parents. Moreover, biological siblings, who also share half their genes, are far more similar than adoptive siblings, who share no more genes than strangers. Indeed, adoptive siblings are barely similar at all. These conclusions come from massive studies employing the best instruments known to psychology. Alternative explanations that try to push the effects of the genes to zero have by now been tested and rejected.

People sometimes fear that if the genes affect the mind at all they must determine it in every detail. That is wrong, for two reasons. The first is that most effects of genes are probabilistic. If one identical twin has a trait, there is often no more than an even chance that the other twin will have it, despite having a complete genome in common (and in the case of twins raised together, most of their environment in common as well).

The second reason is that the genes' effects can vary with the environment. Although Woody Allen's fame may depend on genes that enhance a sense of humor, he once pointed out that "we live in a society that puts a big value on jokes. If I had been an Apache Indian, those guys didn't need comedians, so I'd be out of work."

Studies of the brain also show that the mind is not a blank slate. The brain, of course, has a pervasive ability to change the strengths of its connections as the result of learning and experience—if it didn't, we would all be permanent amnesiacs. But that does not mean that the structure of the brain is mostly a product of experience. The study of the brains of twins has shown that much of the variation in the amount of gray matter in the prefrontal lobes is genetically caused. And these variations are not just random differences in anatomy like fingerprints; they correlate significantly with differences in intelligence.

People born with variations in the typical brain plan can vary in the way their minds work. A study of Einstein's brain showed that he had large, unusually shaped inferior parietal lobules, which participate in spatial reasoning and intuitions about numbers. Gay men are likely to have a relatively small nucleus in the anterior hypothalamus, a nucleus known to have a role in sex differences. Convicted murderers and other violent, antisocial people are likely to have a relatively small and inactive prefrontal cortex, the part of the brain that governs decision making and inhibits impulses. These gross features of the brain are almost certainly not sculpted by information coming in from the senses. That, in turn, implies that differences in intelligence, scientific genius, sexual orientation, and impulsive violence are not entirely learned.

THE DOCTRINE OF THE BLANK SLATE HAD BEEN THOUGHT TO undergird the ideals of equal rights and social improvement, so it is no surprise that the discoveries undermining it have often

been met with fear and loathing. Scientists challenging the doctrine have been libeled, picketed, shouted down, and subjected to searing invective.

This is not the first time in history that people have tried to ground moral principles in dubious factual assumptions. People used to ground moral values in the doctrine that Earth lay at the center of the universe, and that God created mankind in his own image in a day. In both cases, informed people eventually reconciled their moral values with the facts, not just because they had to give a nod to reality, but also because the supposed connections between the facts and morals—such as the belief that the arrangement of rock and gas in space has something to do with right and wrong—were spurious to begin with.

We are now living, I think, through a similar transition. The blank slate has been widely embraced as a rationale for morality, but it is under assault from science. Yet just as the supposed foundations of morality shifted in the centuries following Galileo and Darwin, our own moral sensibilities will come to terms with the scientific findings, not just because facts are facts but because the moral credentials of the blank slate are just as spurious. Once you think through the issues, the two greatest fears of an innate human endowment can be defused.

One is the fear of inequality. Blank is blank, so if we are all blank slates, the reasoning goes, we must all be equal. But if the slate of a newborn is not blank, different babies could have different things inscribed on their slates. Individuals, sexes, classes, and races might differ innately in their talents and inclinations. The fear is that if people do turn out to be different, it would open the door to discrimination, oppression, or eugenics.

But none of this follows. For one thing, in many cases the empirical basis of the fear may be misplaced. A universal human nature does not imply that *differences* among groups are innate. Confucius could have been right when he wrote, "Men's natures are alike; it is their habits that carry them far apart."

Regardless of IQ or physical strength, all human beings can be assumed to have certain traits in common.

More important, the case against bigotry is not a factual claim that people are biologically indistinguishable. It is a moral stance that condemns judging an *individual* according to the average traits of certain *groups* to which the individual belongs. Enlightened societies strive to ignore race, sex, and ethnicity in hiring, admissions, and criminal justice because the alternative is morally repugnant. Discriminating against people on the basis of race, sex, or ethnicity would be unfair, penalizing them for traits over which they have no control. It would perpetuate the injustices of the past and could rend society into hostile factions. None of these reasons depends on whether groups of people are or are not genetically indistinguishable.

Far from being conducive to discrimination, a conception of human nature is the reason we oppose it. Regardless of IQ or physical strength or any other trait that might vary among people, all human beings can be assumed to have certain traits in common. No one likes being enslaved. No one likes being humiliated. No one likes being treated unfairly. The revulsion we feel toward discrimination and slavery comes from a conviction that however much people vary on some traits, they do not vary on these.

A second fear of human nature comes from a reluctance to give up the age-old dream of the perfectibility of man. If we are forever saddled with fatal flaws and deadly sins, according to this fear, social reform would be a waste of time. Why try to make the world a better place if people are rotten to the core and will just foul it up no matter what you do?

Parents often discover that their children are immune to their rewards, punishments, and nagging. Over the long run, a child's personality and intellect are largely determined by genes, peer groups, and chance.

But this, too, does not follow. If the mind is a complex system with many faculties, an antisocial desire is just one component among others. Some faculties may endow us with greed or lust or malice, but others may endow us with sympathy, foresight, self-respect, a desire for respect from others, and an ability to learn from experience and history. Social progress can come from pitting some of these faculties against others.

For example, suppose we are endowed with a conscience that treats certain other beings as targets of sympathy and inhibits us from harming or exploiting them. The philosopher Peter Singer of Princeton University has shown that moral improvement has proceeded for millennia because people have expanded the mental dotted line that embraces the entities considered worthy of sympathy. The circle has been poked outward from the family and village to the clan, the tribe, the nation, the race, and most recently to all of humanity. This sweeping change in sensibilities did not require a blank slate. It could have arisen from a moral gadget with a single knob or slider that adjusts the size of the circle embracing the entities whose interests we treat as comparable to our own.

SOME PEOPLE WORRY THAT THESE ARGUMENTS ARE TOO FANCY for the dangerous world we live in. Since data in the social sciences are never perfect, shouldn't we err on the side of caution and stick with the null hypothesis that people are blank slates? Some people think that even if we were certain that people differed genetically, or harbored ignoble tendencies, we might still want to promulgate the fiction that they didn't.

This argument is based on the fallacy that the blank slate has nothing but good moral implications and a theory that admits a human nature has nothing but bad ones. In fact, the dangers go both ways. Take the most horrifying example of all, the abuse of biology by the Nazis, with its pseudoscientific nonsense about superior and inferior races. Historians agree that bitter memories of the Holocaust were the main reason that human nature became taboo in intellectual life after the Second World War.

But historians have also documented that Nazism was not the only ideologically inspired holocaust of the 20th century. Many atrocities were committed by Marxist regimes in the name of egalitarianism, targeting people whose success was taken as evidence of their avarice. The kulaks ("bourgeois peasants") were exterminated by Lenin and Stalin in the Soviet Union. Teachers, former landlords, and "rich peasants" were humiliated, tortured, and murdered during China's Cultural Revolution. City dwellers and literate professionals were worked to death or executed during the reign of the Khmer Rouge in Cambodia.

And here is a remarkable fact: Although both Nazi and Marxist ideologies led to industrial-scale killing, *their biological and psychological theories were opposites*. Marxists had no use for the concept of race, were averse to the notion of genetic inheritance, and were hostile to the very idea of a human nature rooted in biology. Marx did not explicitly embrace the blank slate, but he was adamant that human nature has no enduring properties: "All history is nothing but a continuous transformation of human nature," he wrote. Many of his followers did embrace it. "It is on a blank page that the most beautiful poems are written," said Mao. "Only the newborn baby is spotless," ran a Khmer Rouge slogan. This philosophy led to persecution of the successful and of those who produced more crops on their private family plots than on communal farms. And it made these regimes not just dictatorships but totalitarian dictatorships, which tried to control every aspect of life, from art and education to child rearing and sex. After all, if the mind is structureless at birth and shaped by its experience, a society that wants the right kind of minds must control the experience.

None of this is meant to impugn the blank slate as an evil doctrine, any more than a belief in human nature is an evil doctrine. Both are separated by many steps from the evil acts committed under their banners, and they must be evaluated on factual grounds. But the fact that tyranny and genocide can come from an anti-innatist belief system as readily as from an innatist one does upend the common misconception that biological approaches to behavior are uniquely sinister. And the reminder that human nature is the source of our interests and needs as well as our flaws encourages us to examine claims about the mind objectively, without putting a moral thumb on either side of the scale.

From the book The Blank Slate *by Steven Pinker. Copyright © Steven Pinker, 2002. Printed by arrangement with Viking Penguin, a member of Penguin Putman Inc. Published in September 2002.*

Parents or Pop Culture?

Children's Heroes and Role Models

What kind of heroes a culture promotes reveals a great deal about that culture's values and desires.

Kristin J. Anderson and Donna Cavallaro

One of the most important features of childhood and adolescence is the development of an identity. As children shape their behavior and values, they may look to heroes and role models for guidance. They may identify the role models they wish to emulate based on possession of certain skills or attributes. While the child may not want to be exactly like the person, he or she may see *possibilities* in that person. For instance, while Supreme Court Justice Ruth Bader Ginsberg may not necessarily directly influence girls and young women to become lawyers, her presence on the Supreme Court may alter beliefs about who is capable of being a lawyer or judge (Gibson & Cordova, 1999).

Parents and other family members are important role models for children, particularly early on. Other influences may be institutional, such as schools, or cultural, such as the mass media. What kind of heroes a culture promotes reveals a great deal about the culture's values and desires. Educators not only can model important behaviors themselves, but also can teach about values, events, and people that a culture holds dear.

Television, movies, computer games, and other forms of media expose children to an endless variety of cultural messages. Which ones do children heed the most? Whom do children want to be like? Do their role models vary according to children's ethnicity and gender? Finally, what role can educators play in teaching children about role models they may never have considered?

This article examines the impact of the mass media on children's choices of heroes and role models. The authors address the questions posed above in light of results from a survey and focus groups conducted with children ages 8 to 13.

THE MENU OF POP CULTURE CHOICES

Television and Film for Children

Male characters—cartoon or otherwise—continue to be more prevalent in children's television and film than female characters. Gender-stereotyped behaviors continue to be the norm. For instance, male characters are more commonly portrayed as independent, assertive, athletic, important, attractive, technical, and responsible than female characters. They show more ingenuity, anger, leadership, bravery, and aggression, and they brag, interrupt, make threats, and even laugh more than female characters do. In fact, since male characters appear so much more frequently than female characters, they do more of almost *everything* than female characters. Also, while the behavior of female characters is somewhat less stereotypical than it was 20 years ago, in some ways male characters behave *more* stereotypically than 20 years ago (for instance, males are now in more leadership roles, are more bossy, and are more intelligent) (Thompson & Zerbinos, 1995). These gender-stereotyped images, and the inflexibility of male characters' roles, make for a restricted range of role models.

Parents, educators, and policymakers are also concerned about the aggressive and violent content in children's programs. Gerbner (1993) studied the violent content of children's programs and observed that "despite all the mayhem, only 3.2% of Saturday morning characters suffer any injury"; thus, children do not learn about the likely consequences of aggressive action. In children's shows, bad characters are punished 59 percent of the time. Even more telling, good characters who engage in violence are punished only 18 percent of the time. The characters that might be the most appealing to kids—the heroes and protagonists—rarely feel remorse, nor are they reprimanded or impeded when they engage in violence (National Television Violence Study, 1998). The authors found that 77 percent of the children surveyed watch television every day. Thus, many children may be learning to use violence as a problem-solving tool.

Characters in animated films also tend to follow stereotypes. While some positive changes in the portrayal of ethnic minority and female characters can be noted, both groups often remain narrowly defined in children's animated films. In his discussion of Disney films, Henry Giroux (1997) notes how the villains in the film *Aladdin* are racially stereotyped. The main character, Aladdin, the hero of the film, is drawn with very light skin, European features, and no accent. Yet the villains in the story appear as Middle Eastern caricatures: they have beards, large noses, sinister eyes, heavy accents, and swords. *Pocahontas*, who in real life was a young Native American girl, was portrayed by Disney as a brown-skinned, Barbie-like supermodel with an hourglass figure (Giroux, 1997). Consequently, animated characters, even those based on historical record, are either stereotyped or stripped of any meaningful sign of ethnicity. Fortunately, educators have the power to counter such unrealistic images with more accurate representations of historical characters.

Real-Life Television Characters

While some progress can be seen in the representation of ethnic minorities on television, the late 1990s actually brought a decrease in the number of people of color on prime time programming. In 1998, only 19 percent of Screen Actors Guild roles went to people of color. Roles for African American, Latinos, and Native Americans decreased from 1997 to 1998 (Screen Actors Guild [SAG], 1999). Women make up fewer than 40 percent of the characters in prime time. Female characters tend to be younger than male characters, conveying the message to viewers that women's youthfulness is more highly valued than other qualities. In terms of work roles, however, female characters' occupations are now less stereotyped, while male characters' occupations continue to be stereotyped (Signorielli & Bacue, 1999). This research suggests that girls' potential role models are somewhat less gender-stereotyped than before, while boy's potential role models are as narrowly defined as ever.

From Comic Book to Playground

Superheroes are the larger-than-life symbols of American values and "maleness." Perhaps the medium in which superheroes are most classically represented is comic books, which date back to the 1930s. The role of the hero is central to the traditional comic book. While female superheroes can be found in comics today (e.g., Marvel Girl, Phoenix, Shadow Cat, Psylocke), they represent only a small proportion—about 24 percent of Marvel Universe superhero trading cards (Young, 1993). Moreover, women and people of color do not fare well in superhero comics. To the extent that female characters exist, they often appear as victims and nuisances. People of color are marginalized as well. African American and Native American characters are more likely to be portrayed as villains, victims, or simply incompetent than as powerful and intelligent (Pecora, 1992).

One indirect way to gauge the impact of role models on children is to examine the nature of superhero play. Superhero play involving imitation of media characters with superhuman powers is more prevalent among boys than girls (Bell & Crosbie, 1996). This might be a function of the mostly male presence of superhero characters in comics and on television, or it may be due to girls receiving more sanctions from parents and teachers against playing aggressively. Children's imitations of superheroes in play concerns many classroom teachers, because it usually involves chasing, wrestling, kicking, and mock battles. Some researchers argue that superhero play may serve an important developmental function by offering children a sense of power in a world dominated by adults, thus giving children a means of coping with their frustrations. Superhero play also may allow children to grapple with ideas of good and evil and encourage them to work through their own anxieties about safety. Such play also may help children safely express anger and aggression (Boyd, 1997).

Other researchers and educators express concern that superhero play may legitimize aggression, endanger participants, and encourage stereotypical male dominance (Bell & Crosbie, 1996). One researcher observed children's superhero play in a school setting and found that boys created more superhero stories than girls did, and that girls often were excluded from such play. When girls were included they were given stereotypical parts, such as helpers or victims waiting to be saved. Even powerful female X-Men characters were made powerless in the boys' adaptations (Dyson, 1994). Thus, without teacher intervention or an abundance of female superheroes, superhero play may only serve to reinforce gender stereotypes.

One way to gauge popular culture's influence on superhero play is to compare the kind of play children engaged in before and after the arrival of television. In one retrospective study (French & Pena, 1991), adults between the ages of 17 and 83 provided information about their favorite childhood play themes, their heroes, and the qualities of those heroes. While certain methodological pitfalls common to retrospective studies were unavoidable, the findings are nevertheless intriguing. People who grew up before television reported engaging in less fantasy hero play and playing more realistically than kids who grew up with television. While media was the main source of heroes for kids who grew up with television, the previous generations found their heroes not only from the media, but also from direct experience, friends/siblings, and parents' occupations (French & Pena, 1991).

Recent Media Forms: Music Television and Video Games

Video games and music television videos are relatively recent forms of media. In a recent poll, girls and boys from various ethnic backgrounds reported that television and music were their favorite forms of media (Children Now, 1999). What messages about race/ethnicity and gender emerge from music videos—the seemingly perfect merger of children's favorite two media? Seidman (1999) found that the majority of characters were white (63 percent) and a majority were male (63 percent). When people of color, especially women of color, appeared in a video, their characters were much less likely to hold white collar jobs. In fact, their occupations were more gender-stereotyped than in real life. Gender role behavior overall was stereotypical. Thus, music television is yet another domain that perpetuates racial and gender stereotypes.

In the survey described below, the authors found that nearly half (48 percent) of the children surveyed played video and computer games every day or almost every day. Boys, however, were much more likely than girls to play these games. Of those who play computer/video games every day or almost every day, 76 percent are boys and only 24 percent are girls. Consequently, girls and boys might be differentially influenced by the images represented in video and computer games.

What *are* the images presented in video and computer games? Dietz's (1998) content analysis of popular video and computer games found that 79 percent of the games included aggression or violence. Only 15 percent of the games showed women as heroes or action characters. Indeed, girls and women generally were *not* portrayed—30 percent of the videos did not include girls or women at all. When female characters were included, 21 percent of the time they were the damsel in distress. Other female characters were portrayed as evil or as obstacles. This research points to at least two implications of these games. First, girls may not be interested in playing these video and computer games, because the implicit message is that girls are not welcome as players, and that girls and

women can only hope to be saved, destroyed, or pushed aside (see also Signorielli, 2001). Second, these images of girls and women found in video and computer games may influence boys' perceptions of gender.

In the past few years, a growing number of computer and video games geared toward girls have been made available by companies such as Purple Moon and Girl Games. These games have adventurous content without the violence typical of games geared toward boys. Two of the best-selling computer games for girls, however, have been *Cosmopolitan Virtual Makeover* and *Barbie Fashion Designer*. While these games may encourage creativity, ultimately their focus is on beauty. One columnist addresses the dilemma of creating games that will appeal to girls while fostering creativity and ingenuity:

> A girl given a doll is being told, "Girls play with dolls just like mommies take care of babies." A boy given a computer game is being told, "Boys play with computers just like daddies use them for work." A girl given *Barbie Fashion Designer* is being told, "Girls play with computers just like girls play with dolls." A lucky few might get the message that, as some girls exchange dolls for real babies, others might progress from *Barbie Fashion Designer* to real-life fashion designer, or engineering systems designer, or software designer. But there's a good chance that many will not. (Ivinski, 1997, p. 28)

As more and more educators begin using the Internet, CD-ROMS, and videos as teaching tools (Risko, 1999), they will be faced with the challenge of finding materials that fairly represent a wide range of characters, people, and behavior. Paradoxically, the use of "new" technology, such as CD-ROMs and computer games, implies that a student is going to enjoy a progressive, cutting-edge experience. However, educators must be vigilant about the content, as they should be with any textbook or film. The cutting-edge format of these new technologies does not guarantee nonstereotyped material.

A SURVEY OF CHILDREN'S ROLE MODELS AND HEROES

Whom do children actually choose as role models, and why? The authors surveyed children about their heroes and role models, both people they know and famous people or imaginary characters. Survey questions also addressed children's interaction with television, film, computer/video games, books, and comic books. The children talked about their answers in small groups. One hundred and seventy-nine children, ages 8 to 13, were surveyed from five day camp sites in central and southern California. The ethnic breakdown of the survey sample was as follows: 24 African Americans, 31 Asian

Americans, 74 Latinos, 1 Middle Eastern American, 2 Native Americans, 45 whites, and 2 "other." Ninety-five girls and 84 boys participated. The samples of ethnic and gender categories were then weighted so that each of these demographic groups, when analyzed, reflects their actual contribution to the total population of children in the United States.

Do Children Admire People They Know or Famous People?

The survey began with the following: "We would like to know whom you look up to and admire. These might be people you know, or they might be famous people or characters. You may want to be like them or you might just think they are cool." More respondents described a person they knew (65 percent) rather than a person they did not know, such as a person or character in the media (35 percent). When asked in focus groups why they picked people they knew instead of famous people, one 10-year-old white girl said, "I didn't put down people I don't know because when nobody's paying attention, they do something bad." Another student said, "Some [media figures] are just not nice. Some famous people act good on TV but they're really horrible." Thus, some children employed a level of skepticism when judging the worthiness of a role model.

Figure 1 represents the percentages of role models the children knew versus media heroes they identified. Similar to the overall sample, 70 percent of the African American and 64 percent of the White children chose people they knew as heroes. In contrast, only 35 percent of the Asian American kids and 49 percent of the Latino kids named people they knew. This latter finding seems paradoxical; Asian American and Latino children would seem more likely to choose people they know as role models because their ethnic groups are represented less frequently in mass media than are African Americans and whites. Perhaps Asian American and Latino children have internalized a message that they should not look up to fellow Asian Americans or Latinos as role models, or it may be a byproduct of assimilation. Obviously, further work in this area is needed.

On average, responses from girls and boys differed. While both girls and boys named people they knew as their heroes, 67 percent of the girls did so as compared with only 58 percent of the boys. Since boys and men are seen more frequently as sports stars, actors, and musicians, girls may have a smaller pool of potential role models from which to choose. Another factor might be that the girls in this study reported watching less television than the boys did, and so they may have known fewer characters. Sixty-seven percent of the girls reported watching television one hour a day or more, while 87 percent of the boys reported watching television this amount.

Do Children Choose Role Models Who Are Similar to Themselves?

One feature of role modeling is that children tend to choose role models whom they find relevant and with whom they can compare themselves (Lockwood & Kunda, 2000). Children who do not "see themselves" in the media may have fewer opportunities to select realistic role models. Two ways to assess similarity is to consider the ethnicity and gender of children's chosen role models. Do children tend to select heroes who are of their same ethnic background? Because data was not available on the ethnic background of the reported role models whom the children knew personally, the authors examined only the heroes from the media, whose backgrounds were known, to explore this question (see Figure 2). African American and white children were more likely to have media heroes of their same ethnicity (67 percent for each). In contrast, Asian American and Latino children chose more white media heroes than other categories (40 percent and 56 percent, respectively). Only 35 percent of the Asian Americans respondents, and 28 percent of the Latino respondents, chose media heroes of their own ethnicity.

How can we explain the fact that African American and white children are more likely to have media heroes of their same ethnicity, compared to Asian American and Latino children? There is no shortage of white characters for white children to identify with in television and film, and African Americans now make up about 14 percent of television and theatrical characters (SAG, 2000). While African American characters are represented less frequently than white characters, their representation on television, film, and music television is much higher than for Asian American and Latino characters (e.g., Asians represent 2.2 percent, and Latinos represent 4.4 percent, of television and film characters) (SAG, 2000). Also, fewer famous athletes are Asian American or Latino, compared to African American or white.

Also of interest was whether children choose role models of the same, or other, gender. Overall, children in this study more often chose a same-gender person as someone they look up to and admire. This pattern is consistent across all four ethnic groups, and stronger for boys than girls. Only 6 percent of the boys chose a girl or woman, while 24 percent of the girls named a boy or man. Asian American boys actually picked male heroes exclusively. Asian American girls chose the fewest female role models (55 percent) compared to the other girls (see Figure 3). These findings associated with Asian American children present a particular challenge for educators. Asian Americans, and particularly Asian American women, are seldom presented as heroes in textbooks. This is all the more reason for schools to provide a broader and more diverse range of potential role models.

Figure 1

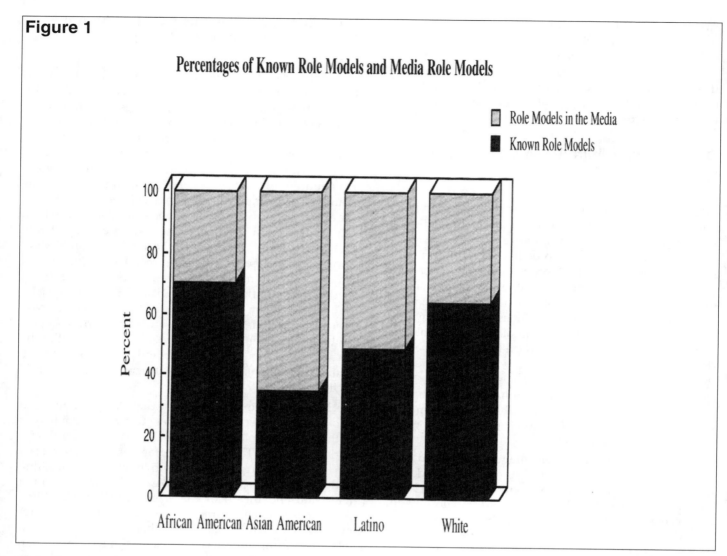

Percentages of Known Role Models and Media Role Models

Role Models in the Media
Known Role Models

At the same time, it has been reported that boys will tend to imitate those who are powerful (Gibson & Cordova, 1999). Thus, while boys tend to emulate same-gender models more than girls do, boys may emulate a woman if she is high in social power. Therefore, boys may be especially likely to have boys and men as role models because they are more likely to be portrayed in positions of power. It also has been noted that college-age women select men *and* women role models with the same frequency, whereas college-age men still tend to avoid women role models. The fact that young women choose both genders as role models might be a result of the relative scarcity of women in powerful positions to serve as role models (Gibson & Cordova, 1999).

Who Are Children's Role Models and Heroes?

Overall, children most frequently (34 percent) named their parents as role models and heroes. The next highest category (20 percent) was entertainers; in descending or-

der, the other categories were friends (14 percent), professional athletes (11 percent), and acquaintances (8 percent). Authors and historical figures were each chosen by only 1 percent of the children.

Patterns were somewhat different when ethnicity was taken into account. African American and white children chose a parent more frequently (30 percent and 33 percent, respectively). In contrast, Asian Americans and Latinos chose entertainers (musicians, actors, and television personalities) most frequently (39 percent for Asian Americans and 47 percent for Latinos), with parents coming in second place. When gender was taken into account, both girls and boys most frequently mentioned a parent (girls 29 percent, boys 34 percent), while entertainers came in second place. Figure 4 illustrates these patterns.

When taking both ethnicity and gender into account, the researchers found that Asian American and Latina girls most frequently picked entertainers (50 percent of the Asian American girls and 41 percent of the Latinas), while African American and white girls chose parents (33 percent and 29 percent, respectively). Asian American boys most frequently named a professional athlete (36

Figure 2

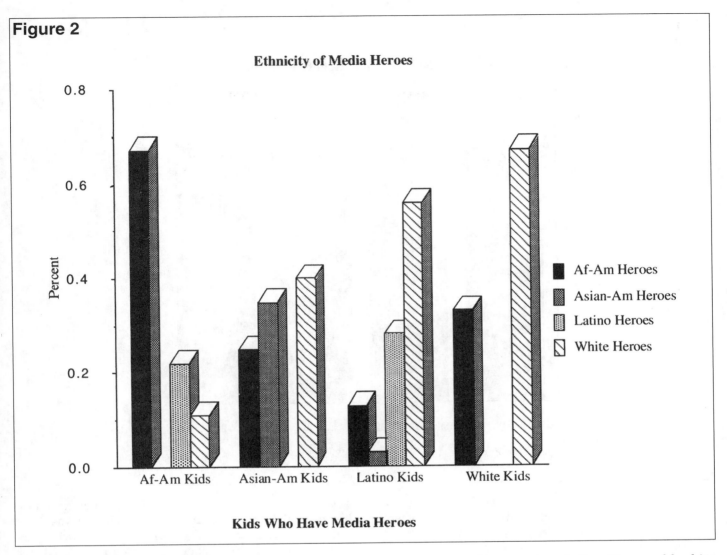

Ethnicity of Media Heroes

Kids Who Have Media Heroes

percent), African American boys most frequently picked a parent (30 percent), Latino boys most frequently chose entertainers (54 percent), and white boys picked parents (38 percent).

What Qualities About Their Role Models and Heroes Do Children Admire?

When asked why they admired their heroes and role models, the children most commonly replied that the person was nice, helpful, and understanding (38 percent). Parents were appreciated for their generosity, their understanding, and for "being there." For instance, an 11-year-old African American girl who named her mother as her hero told us, "I like that she helps people when they're in a time of need." Parents were also praised for the lessons they teach their kids. A 9-year-old Asian American boy told us, "I like my dad because he is always nice and he teaches me."

The second most admired feature of kids' role models was skill (27 percent). The skills of athletes and entertain-

ers were most often mentioned. One 12-year-old white boy said he admires Kobe Bryant because "he's a good basketball player and because he makes a good amount of money." A 10-year-old Asian American girl chose Tara Lipinski because "she has a lot of courage and is a great skater." A 9-year-old Latino boy picked Captain America and said, "What I like about Captain America is his cool shield and how he fights the evil red skull." The third most frequently mentioned characteristic was a sense of humor (9 percent), which was most often attributed to entertainers. For instance, a 10-year-old Latino boy picked Will Smith "because he's funny. He makes jokes and he dances funny."

These findings held true for children in all four ethnic groups and across the genders, with two exceptions: boys were more likely than girls to name athletes for their skill, and entertainers for their humor. Given the media attention to the U.S. women's soccer team victory in the World Cup in 1999, and the success of the WNBA (the women's professional basketball league), the researchers expected girls to name women professional athletes as their heroes. However, only four girls in the study did so. Despite recent

Figure 3

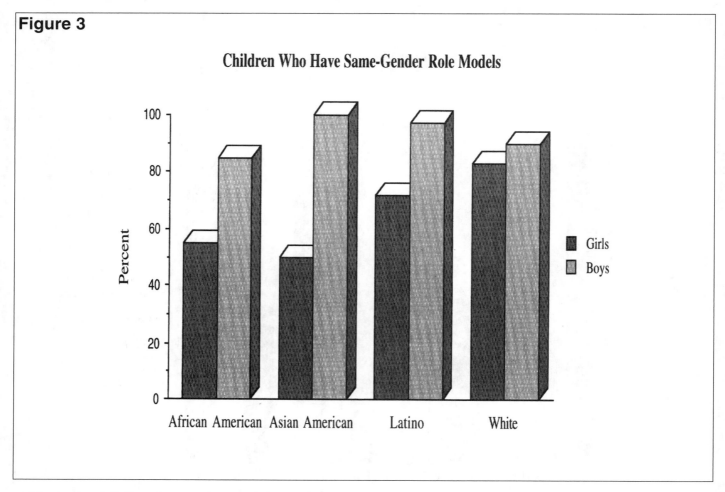

When children's heroes were media characters, African American and white children were more likely to name media heroes of their same ethnicity. In contrast, Asian American and Latino children tended to name media heroes who were not of their same ethnicity.

Summary and Implications

Whether the children in this study had heroes they knew in real life, or whether they chose famous people or fictional characters, depended, to some extent, on the respondents' ethnicity and gender. Overall, however, the most frequently named role model for kids was a parent. This is good news for parents, who must wonder, given the omnipresence of the media, whether they have any impact at all on their children. Popular culture was a significant source of heroes for children as well. Entertainers were the second most frequently named role models for the children, and the number increases significantly if you add professional athletes to that category. The attributes that children valued depended on whom they chose. For instance, children who named parents named them because they are helpful and understanding. Media characters were chosen because of their skills. When children's heroes were media characters, African American and white children were more likely to name media heroes of their same ethnicity. In contrast, Asian American and Latino children tended to name media heroes who were not of their same ethnicity. Children kept to their own gender when choosing a hero; boys were especially reluctant to choose girls and women as their heroes.

The frequency with which boys in this study named athletes as their role models is noteworthy. Only four girls in the study did the same. The implications of this gender difference are important, because many studies find that girls' participation in sports is associated with a number of positive attributes, such as high self-esteem and self-efficacy (Richman & Shaffer, 2000). Therefore, school and community support of girls' athletic programs and recognition of professional women athletes would go

strides in the visibility of women's sports, the media continue to construct men's sports as the norm and women's sports as marginal (e.g., references to men's athletics as "sports" and women's athletics as "women's sports").

Figure 4

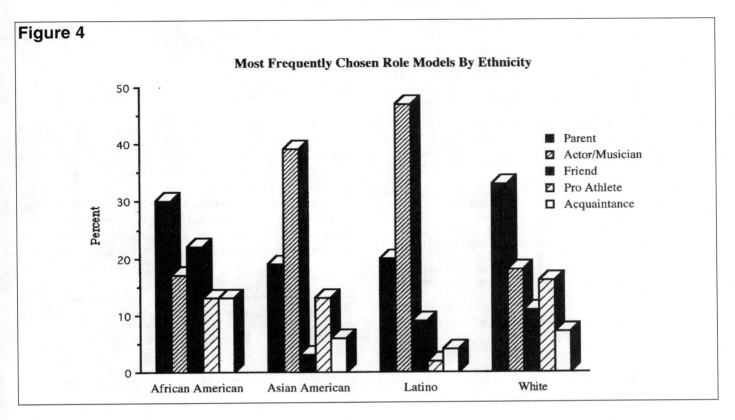

Most Frequently Chosen Role Models By Ethnicity

a long way to encourage girls' participation in sports, as well as boys' appreciation of women athletes as potential role models.

The mass media are hindered by a narrow view of gender, and by limited, stereotyped representations of ethnic minorities. Parents and educators must take pains to expose children to a wider variety of potential role models than popular culture does. Historical figures and authors constituted a tiny minority of heroes named by the children surveyed. Educators can play a significant role by exposing students to a wide range of such historical heroes, including people from various professions, people of color, and women of all races.

Finally, educators could capitalize on children's need for guidance to expose them to a greater variety of role models. Doing so affirms for the children that their race and gender are worthy of representation. A variety of potential heroes and role models allows children to appreciate themselves and the diversity in others.

References

Bell, R., & Crosbie, C. (1996, November 13). Superhero play of 3-5-year-old children. Available: http://labyrinth.net.au/~cccav/sept97/superhero.html.

Boyd, B. J. (1997). Teacher response to superhero play: To ban or not to ban. *Childhood Education, 74*, 23–28.

Children Now. (1999, September). *Boys to men: Messages about masculinity.* Oakland, CA: Author.

Dietz, T. L. (1998). An examination of violence and gender role portrayals in video games: Implications for gender socialization. *Sex Roles, 38*, 425–433.

Dyson, A. H. (1994). The ninjas, the X-men, and the ladies: Playing with power and identity in an urban primary school. *Teachers College Record, 96*, 219–239.

French, J., & Pena, S. (1991). Children's hero play of the 20th century: Changes resulting from television's influence. *Child Study Journal, 21*, 79–94.

Gerbner, G. (1993). *Women and minorities on television: A study in casting and fate.* A report to the Screen Actors Guild and the American Federation of Radio and Television Artists, Philadelphia: The Annenberg School of Communication, University of Pennsylvania.

Gibson, D. E., & Cordova, D. I. (1999). Women's and men's role models: The importance of exemplars. In A. J. Murrell, F. J. Crosby, & R. J. Ely (Eds.), *Mentoring dilemmas: Developmental relationships within multicultural organizations* (pp. 121–141). Mahwah, NJ: Lawrence Erlbaum Associates.

Giroux, H. A. (1997). Are Disney movies good for your kids? In S. R. Steinberg & J. L. Kincheloe (Eds.), *Kinderculture: The corporate construction of childhood* (pp. 53–67). Boulder, CO: Westview Press.

Ivinski, P. (1997). Game girls: Girl market in computer games and educational software. *Print, 51*, 24–29.

Lockwood, P., & Kunda, Z. (2000). Outstanding role models: Do they inspire or demoralize us? In A. Tesser, R. B. Felson, et al. (Eds.), *Psychological perspectives on self and identity* (pp. 147–171). Washington, DC: American Psychological Association.

National Television Violence Study. Vol. 3. (1998). Thousand Oaks, CA: Sage.

Pecora, N. (1992). Superman/superboys/supermen: The comic book hero as socializing agent. In S. Craig (Ed.), *Men, masculinity, and the media* (pp. 61–77). Newbury Park, CA: Sage.

Richman, E. L., & Shaffer, D. R. (2000). "If you let me play sports": How might sport participation influence the self-esteem of adolescent females? *Psychology of Women Quarterly, 24*, 189–199.

Risko, V. J. (1999). The power and possibilities of video technology and intermediality. In L. Semali & A. Watts Pailliotet (Eds.), *Intermediality: The teachers' handbook of critical media literacy* (pp. 129–140). Boulder, CO: Westview Press.

Screen Actors Guild. (1999, May 3). *New Screen Actors Guild employment figures reveal a decline in roles for Latinos, African American and Native American Indian performers.* Press Release. Available: www.sag.org

Screen Actors Guild. (2000, December 20). *Screen Actors Guild employment statistics reveal percentage increases in available roles for African Americans and Latinos, but total number of roles to minorities decrease in 1999.* Press Release. Available: www.sag.org.

Seidman, S. A. (1999). Revisiting sex-role stereotyping in MTV videos. *International Journal of Instructional Media, 26,* 11.

Signorielli, N. (2001). Television's gender role images and contribution to stereotyping: Past, present, future. In D. G. Singer & J. L. Singer (Eds.), *Handbook of children and the media* (pp. 341–358). Thousand Oaks, CA: Sage.

Signorielli, N., & Bacue, A. (1999). Recognition and respect: A content analysis of prime-time television characters across three decades. *Sex Roles, 40,* 527–544.

Thompson, T. L., & Zerbinos, E. (1995). Gender roles in animated cartoons: Has the picture changed in 20 years? *Sex Roles, 32,* 651–673.

Young, T. J. (1993). Women as comic book superheroes: The "weaker sex" in the Marvel universe. *Psychology: A Journal of Human Behavior, 30,* 49–50.

Authors' Notes:

This project was conducted in conjunction with Mediascope, a not-for-profit media education organization. The terms "hero" and "role model" tend to be used interchangeably in the literature. When a distinction between the terms is made, role models are defined as known persons (e.g., parents, teachers) and heroes are defined as figures who may be less attainable, or larger than life. Both kinds of persons and figures are of interest here; therefore, the terms are used interchangeably, and we specify whether known people or famous figures are being discussed.

Kristin J. Anderson is Assistant Professor, Psychology and Women's Studies, Antioch College, Yellow Springs, Ohio. Donna Cavallaro is graduate student, counseling psychology, Santa Clara University, Santa Clara, California.

From *Childhood Education,* Spring 2002, pp. 161–168. Reprinted by permission of the authors and the Association for Childhood Education International. © 2002 by the Association for Childhood Education International.

BROWN V. BOARD

A Dream Deferred

Fifty years ago, a landmark ruling seemed to break Jim Crow's back and usher in an era of hope for integrated education. But the reality has fallen short of the promise. The fight for decent schooling for black kids goes on.

By Ellis Cose

SOMETIMES HISTORY serves as a magnifying mirror—making momentous what actually was not. But *Brown v. Board of Education of Topeka, Kansas,* is the real thing: a Supreme Court decision that fundamentally and forever changed America. It jump-started the modern civil-rights movement and excised a cancer eating a hole in the heart of the Constitution.

So why is the celebration of its 50th anniversary so bittersweet? Why, as we raise our glasses, are there tears in our eyes? The answer is simple: *Brown,* for all its glory, is something of a bust.

Clearly *Brown* altered forever the political and social landscape of an insufficiently conscience-stricken nation. "*Brown* led to the sit-ins, the freedom marches… the Civil Rights Act of 1964… If you look at *Brown* as… the icebreaker that broke up… that frozen sea, then you will see it was an unequivocal success," declared Jack Greenberg, former head of the NAACP Legal Defense & Educational Fund Inc. and one of the lawyers who litigated *Brown.* Still, measured purely by its effects on the poor schoolchildren of color at its center, *Brown* is a disappointment—in many respects a failure. So this commemoration is muted by the realization that *Brown* was not nearly enough.

While most white and Hispanic Americans (59 percent for each group) think their community schools are doing a good or excellent job, only 45 percent of blacks feel that way, according to an exclusive NEWSWEEK Poll. That is up considerably

from the 31 percent who thought their schools were performing well in 1998, but it means a lot of people are still unhappy with the deck of skills being dealt to black kids.

Increasingly, black and Latino kids are likely to find themselves in classrooms with few, if any, nonminority faces. The shift is due in part to Supreme Court decisions that undermined *Brown.*

Only 38 percent of blacks think those schools have the resources necessary to provide a quality education, according to the poll. And African-Americans are not alone in feeling that funding should increase. A majority of the members of all ethnic groups support the notion that schools attended by impoverished minority children ought to have equivalent resources to those attended by affluent whites. Indeed, most Americans go even further. They say schools should be funded at "whatever level it takes to raise minority-student achievement to an acceptable national standard." Sixty-one percent of whites, 81 percent of Hispanics and a whopping 93 percent of blacks agree with that statement—which is to say they agree

> Most white and Hispanic Americans (59% for each group) think their local schools do a good or excellent job. Only 45% of blacks feel that way.

with the proposition of funding schools at a level never seriously countenanced by the political establishment: a total transformation of public education in the United States.

So now, 50 years after the court case that changed America, another battle is upon us—and only at this moment becoming clear. It began at the intersection of conflicting good intentions, where the demands of politicians and policymakers for high educational standards collided with the demands of educators and children's advocates for resources. Throw in a host of initiatives spawned, at least in part, by frustration at low student achievement—vouchers, charter schools, privatization, curbs on social promotion, high-stakes testing (all issues now swirling around the presidential campaign)—and you have the making of an educational upheaval that may rival *Brown* in its ramifications. It may in some ways be the second phase of *Brown*: a continuation by other means of the battle for access to a decent education by those whom fortune left behind.

On May 17, 1954, the day the walls of segregation fell, the Supreme Court actually handed down two decisions, involving five separate cases—in South Carolina, Virginia, Delaware, Kansas and Washington, D.C.—all of which came collectively to be known as *Brown*. Instead of abolishing segregation straightaway, the justices sought advice on how—and when—desegregation was to come about. So *Brown* spawned what came to be known as *Brown* II—a decision in May 1955 that provided neither a timetable nor a plan. Instead it ordered the South to proceed with "all deliberate speed," which the South took as an invitation to stall. But something more was wrong.

THE DECISION RESTED ON AN ASSUMPTION that simply wasn't true: that once formal, state-mandated segregation ended, "equal educational opportunities" would be the result. A half century later, school segregation is far from dead and the goal of educational equality is as elusive as ever. Since the early 1990s, despite the continued growth of integration in other sectors of society, black and Latino children are increasingly likely to find themselves in classes with few, if any, nonminority faces.

The shift is due, at least in part, to Supreme Court decisions that essentially undermined *Brown*. In 1974 the court ruled that schools in white suburbs were not obliged to admit black kids from the inner city. And in 1992 the court decided that local school boards, even if not in full compliance with desegregation orders, should be released from court supervision as quickly as possible. "Racial balance is not to be achieved for its own sake," proclaimed the court.

For most black parents, of course, *Brown* was never about integration "for its own sake"—though blacks strongly support integration. Instead, it was about recognition of the fact that unless their children went to school with the children of the whites

who controlled the purse strings, their children were likely to be shortchanged.

Most blacks are no longer convinced their kids necessarily do better in integrated settings. Some 57 percent of black parents say the schools' racial mixture makes no difference, significantly more than the 41 percent who said that in 1988. But they also know resource allocation is not colorblind. Hence, 59 percent of blacks, 52 percent of Hispanics and 49 percent of whites agree that it will be impossible to provide equal educational opportunities for all "as long as children of different races in this country basically go to different schools."

Today, by virtually any measure of academic achievement, blacks, Puerto Ricans and Mexican-Americans are, on average, far behind their white and Asian-American peers. A range of factors, from bad prenatal care to intellectually destructive neighborhood or home environments, have been implicated to explain the disparity. Certainly one reason for the difference is that blacks (and Puerto Ricans and Mexican-Americans) do not, for the most part, go to the same schools, or even the same types of schools, as do the majority of non-Hispanic whites. They are more likely to go to schools such as those found in parts of rural South Carolina—schools that, were it not for the American flags proudly flying over the roofs, might have been plucked out of some impoverished country that sees education as a luxury it can barely afford.

Take a tour of Jasper County and you will find a middle school with a drainpipe in the corridor, which occasionally spills sewage into the hallway. You'll find labs where the equipment doesn't work, so children have to simulate, rather than perform, experiments. In nearby Clarendon County resources are also lacking. Were Thurgood Marshall to find himself in Clarendon County today, "he would think [*Brown*] had been reversed," state Sen. John Marshall told a visitor. So Clarendon County is again in court, refighting the battle for access to a decent education that Clarendon's children, and all the children of *Brown*, presumably won a long time ago.

In 1951, kids walked out to protest school conditions in Farmville, Va. Despite *Brown*, relief did not come. The schools were shuttered for five years. Today the dream of integration is thriving there.

The saga of Clarendon County began in 1947 with a simple request for a bus. The county's white schoolchildren already had 30 schoolbuses at their disposal. Though black children outnumbered whites by a margin of nearly three to one, they had not a single bus. So a local pastor, J. A. DeLaine, went on a cru-

Blacks (83%) and Hispanics (91%) are more likely than whites (73%) to feel it's important to use standardized tests to raise academic standards

sade. His request for transportation led angry whites to burn down his church and his home, to shoot at him and to literally run him out of town under cover of night. It also spawned a lawsuit known as *Briggs v. Elliot*, which challenged the doctrine of "separate but equal" and was later bundled into *Brown*.

Instead of integrating its school systems, as *Brown* had decreed, South Carolina maneuvered to keep segregation alive. It structured school districts in such a way that blacks were largely lumped together, and having clustered them together, the state "systematically neglected to adequately fund those districts," says Steve Morrison, a partner in the law firm that is currently suing the state for additional resources for Clarendon and more than 30 other counties.

It is a sign of how much, in some respects, attitudes have changed that the state's largest law firm—Nelson Mullins Riley & Scarborough—is on the side of the plaintiffs. During a conversation in the offices of the law firm that bears his name, Richard Riley, former governor of South Carolina and former U.S. secretary of Education, remarked, "If *Brown* had been 100 percent successful, we wouldn't have this situation." In opening arguments Carl Epps, another Nelson Mullins attorney, compared the suit to Brown itself, calling it the kind of case that comes along only "every generation or two."

Certainly, when aggregated with a multitude of similar cases, the Clarendon case—known as *Abbeville County School District, et al. v. The State of South Carolina, et al.*—represents a major shift in tactics among those fighting for the educational rights of poor people. Once upon a time the emphasis was on "equity": on trying to ensure that the most economically deprived students were provided with resources equal to those lavished on the children of the rich. Now the cases are about whether states are providing sufficient resources to poor schools to allow the students who attend them to effectively compete in society. They are called "adequacy" cases, and they aspire to force states to produce graduates capable of functioning competently as citizens and as educated human beings.

The shift in strategy stems, in part, from the Supreme Court's making equity cases more difficult to win but leaving the door open to adequacy claims. In a seminal moment for this new movement, the Kentucky Supreme Court decided in 1989 that students in Kentucky had a right to a much better education than they were receiving. In response, the legislature totally overhauled the state's educational system.

Elsewhere, legislative reforms—so far—have been less dramatic as politicians have fought efforts to mandate spending increases. But in several states, including New York, judges are looking on adequacy suits with favor. Indeed, last week a group of high-profile businessmen called on New York politicians to heed the call for more and smarter education funding. The notion that schools ought to invest more in those whose need is greatest goes against American tradition, but it seems an idea

whose time is coming. Conversely, the notion that integration ought to be an explicit goal driving policy seems to be an idea whose time (at least among most whites) has passed. While close to two thirds of blacks and Hispanics feel that "more should be done" to integrate schools, only one third of whites agree. And only 18 percent of whites think whites receive a better education if they are in a racially mixed environment.

THIS IS NOT TO SAY THAT THE PUSH FOR integration has been a total failure. Indeed, in Farmville, Va., a small town little more than an hour's drive southwest of Richmond, the state capital, the dream of school integration is thriving. In the early 1950s, black high-school students in Farmville were relegated to a tiny structure. Students who could not be accommodated in the main building were relegated to flimsy shacks covered with tar paper, each heated with a single wood-burning stove. As former student leader John Stokes recalls, "The buildings were so bad that the people sitting near the windows or the door had to wear an overcoat, and the person sitting near the stove burned up." In 1951 the students walked out and took their complaints to the NAACP. That led to a case called *Davis v. County School Board of Prince Edward County,* which was eventually made part of *Brown*.

After the Supreme Court declared the era of separate but equal over, Virginia's legislature prohibited expenditure of funds on integrated schools. And when delay was no longer an option, Prince Edward County closed its public schools altogether. From the fall of 1959 through much of 1964 the schools were shuttered. Those whites whose parents had a little money could go to Prince Edward Academy, the newly established "private" school. But most blacks, who were barred from the (state subsidized) segregation academies, saw their educational hopes wither.

On May 25, 1964, the Supreme Court finally brought Prince Edward County's resistance to an end. "The time for mere 'deliberate speed' has run out," wrote Justice Hugo Black. But it was only this year that the Virginia State Legislature (prodded by Viola Baskerville, a black delegate, and Ken Woodley, editor of The Farmville Herald) passed a bill to provide some belated scholarship assistance to those who had missed school so long ago.

For Farmville's current generation of high-school students, integration has become a way of life. The racial composition (60 percent black, 39 percent white, in a high school of nearly 3,000) is a source of delight: "I talk about being proud that we are diverse," says school superintendent Margaret Blackmon. And nearly three fourths of those who graduate from Prince Edward County High go to college.

One reason Prince Edward County was able to integrate successfully no doubt has to do with size. Once desegregation was

66% of blacks and 67% of Hispanics favor vouchers, as do 54% of whites. But they're unlikely to get vouchers to send kids to any school they want

forced on it, tiny Farmville didn't really have the option of carving out separate black and white districts. And once the region's racial madness ended and the segregation academy fell on hard times, the public school seemed a less objectionable alternative. There was, in other words, no real room for whites to flee and, as time wore on, increasingly less reason to do so. In much of the rest of America, there are plenty of places to run. Nonetheless, to visit a place like Farmville, with full knowledge of its wretched history, is to experience a certain wistfulness—to wonder about what might have been.

If integration is not the answer (at least not now), what is? If the heat generated around the issue is any indication, there are two popular answers: testing and choice, considered either separately or in combination.

In one state after another, politicians have seized on tests as the solution. Without question, testing is popular with the public. And though it may come as a surprise to some, testing is particularly popular with the black and Latino public. Blacks (83 percent) and Hispanics (91 percent) are much more likely than whites (73 percent) to believe that it is important or very important to use "standardized tests to raise academic standards and student achievement." Some 74 percent of blacks and 64 percent of Hispanics think "most" or "some" minority students would show academic improvement if required to pass standardized tests before being promoted from one grade to another.

My guess is that the numbers measure support more for the idea of testing than for the reality of what testing has become. The idea—that ability can be recognized and developed, that deficiencies can be diagnosed and remedied—is impossible to argue with. It is far from clear at this juncture that that is what is happening.

When it comes to children of color, we ask the wrong question. We ask, 'Why are you such a problem?' when we should ask, 'What have we not given you that we routinely give to upper-middle-class white kids?'

In a report assessing the first-year results of the No Child Left Behind Act in 11 urban districts, researchers from the Civil Rights Project at Harvard concluded: "In each of the districts we studied, fewer than 16% of eligible students requested and received supplemental educational services. In most of these districts it was less than 5% of the eligible students, and in some it was less than 1%."

The use of choice as a tool of educational reform has also been controversial, particularly when it comes to the issue of vouchers. On one side are those who claim that poor kids in ghettos and barrios have the right (and ought to receive public money) to leave crummy schools and seek a quality education

elsewhere. On the other side are those who say that vouchers will not appreciably increase the options of children attending wretched schools but will instead deprive public schools of resources they can ill afford to lose.

In the last several years, voucher programs have sprouted in a number of states. Florida's program—actually three different programs—is the most ambitious. In December 2003 an audit of those programs by the state's chief financial officer led to several probes for criminal irregularities. In a blistering editorial in February, The Palm Beach Post, which had written several critical investigative pieces on the programs, concluded that "as the state is running it, the entire voucher program is a fraud." Even the Florida Catholic Conference, a presumptive beneficiary of the programs, appealed for reforms. At the very least the conference wanted schools to be accredited, to have some kind of track record and to give standardized tests so parents would know how the schools were performing relative to others.

Certainly there is evidence that voucher programs can help some students. And most people view vouchers in a positive light. Some 66 percent of blacks and 67 percent of Hispanics favor vouchers, as do 54 percent of whites. But most people understand quite clearly that in the real world they are not likely to get a voucher that will allow them to send a child to any school of their dreams. So it is not inconsistent that a majority of Americans favor increasing funding for public education over providing parents with vouchers. Nor it is surprising that blacks, even more than whites, strongly support funding for public schools.

The voucher debate is bound to rage for years to come. With the backing of the Bush administration, Washington, D.C., is launching an ambitious new voucher experiment. Indeed, George W. Bush is running for re-election as the education president, as the leader who championed No Child Left Behind and who is making schools accountable with testing regimes and more demanding curricula. Not to be outdone, John Kerry has come up with his own education proposals, which include programs to keep young people, particularly people of color, in school and more funding for NCLB and special education.

The national dialogue on education that is emerging from the rhetoric of warring politicians—and from all these suits, all this testing and all these experiments with choice—must ultimately get beyond what happens in the school to what is happening in the larger society, and in the larger environment in which children exist.

In too many ways, when it comes to children of color, we continue to ask the wrong questions. We poke and probe and test those kids as we wrinkle our brows and ask, with requisite concern, "Why are you such a problem? What special programs do you need?" when we should be asking, "What have we not given to you that we routinely give to upper-middle-class white kids? What do they have that you don't?"

The answer is simple. They have a society that grants them the presumption of competence and the expectation of success; they have an environment that nurtures aspiration, peers who provide support and guardians who provide direction. If we are serious about realizing the promise of *Brown*, about decently educating those who begin with the least, we will have to ponder deeply how to deliver those things where they are desperately needed.

In the end, it may be that the true and lasting legacy of *Brown* has little to do with desegregation as such. It may instead be that *Brown* put us on a path that will, ideally, let us see children of color—and therefore our entire country—in a wholly new and beautiful light.

UNIT 5

Development During Adolescence and Young Adulthood

Unit Selections

Key Points to Consider

- Are advanced placement (AP) courses and tests good for high school students?

- Why are more adolescents choosing to postpone sex? What does this mean for education, career preparation, and marriage?

- Why are college students so stressed-out? What can be done to reduce campus pressures?

- If she works, and he doesn't, will the marriage last?

- What are DINS? How is this new American cultural phenomenon affecting marriage and childrearing?

- Can brain power be boosted with drugs? If so, should it be?

 **Links: www.dushkin.com/online/**
These sites are annotated in the World Wide Web pages.

ADOL: Adolescent Directory On-Line
http://education.indiana.edu/cas/adol/adol.html

Adolescence: Change and Continuity
http://www.personal.psu.edu/nxd10/adolesce.htm

AMA—Adolescent Health On-Line
http://www.ama-assn.org/ama/pub/category/1947.html

American Academy of Child and Adolescent Psychiatry
http://www.aacap.org/

Ask NOAH About: Mental Health
http://www.noah-health.org/english/illness/mentalhealth/mental.html

The term "adolescence" was coined in 1904 by G. Stanley Hall, one of the world's first psychologists. He saw adolescence as a discrete stage of life bridging the gap between sexual maturity (puberty) and socioemotional and cognitive maturity. At the beginning of the twentieth century, it was typical for young men to begin working in middle childhood (there were no child labor laws), and for young women to become wives and mothers as soon as they were fertile and/or spoken for. At the turn of the twenty-first century, the beginning of adolescence is marked by the desire to be independent of parental control. The end of adolescence, which once coincided with the age of legal maturity (usually 16 or 18, depending on local laws), has now been extended upwards. Although legal maturity is now 18 (voting, enlisting in the armed services, owning property, marrying without permission), the social norm is to consider persons in their late teens as adolescents, not adults. The years between 18 and 21 are often problematic for youth tethered between adult and not-adult status. They can be married, with children, living in homes of their own, running their own businesses, yet not be able to

drive their cars in certain places or at certain times. They can go to college and participate in social activities, but they cannot legally drink. Often the twenty-first birthday is viewed as a rite of passage into adulthood in the United States because it signals the legal right to buy and drink alcoholic beverages. "Maturity" is usually reserved for those who have achieved full economic as well as socioemotional independence as adults.

Erik Erikson, the personality theorist, marked the passage from adolescence to young adulthood by a change in the nuclear conflicts of two life stages: identity versus role confusion and intimacy versus isolation. Adolescents struggle to answer the question, "Who am I?" Young adults struggle to find a place within the existing social order where they can feel intimacy rather than isolation. In the 1960s, Erikson wrote that females resolve both their conflicts of identity and intimacy by living vicariously through their husbands, an unacceptable idea today.

As adolescence has been extended, so too has young adulthood. One hundred years ago, life expectancy did not extend too far beyond menopause for women and retirement for men.

Young adulthood began when adolescents finished puberty. Parents of teenagers were middle-aged, between 35 and 55. Later marriages and delayed childbearing have redefined the line between young adulthood and middle age. Many people today consider themselves young adults well into their 40s.

Jean Piaget, the cognitive theorist, marked the end of the development of mental processes with the end of adolescence. Once full physical maturity, including brain maturity, was achieved, one reached the acme of his or her abilities to assimilate, accommodate, organize, and adapt to sensations, perceptions, associations, and discriminations. Piaget did not feel cognitive processing of information ceased with adulthood. He believed, however, that cognitive judgments would not reach a stage higher than the abstract, hypothetical, logical reasoning of formal operations. Today many cognitive theorists believe post-formal operations are possible. The dialectics and the relativistic processes described in this book's preface are descriptive of some ideas about post-formal thinking.

The article "The 100 Best High Schools in America" has a misleading title. Rather than simply naming best schools, this literary composition describes what makes a high school an excellent environment for learning. Stretching young minds should be the fundamental purpose of education, according to Jay Mathews. He believes the surge of schools now offering courses which qualify a student for advanced placement in college has been instrumental in revitalizing the 100 Best Schools. After taking advanced placement (AP) courses, students take AP tests. Many colleges now consider these AP test scores as important as, or more important than, scholastic achievement tests (SATs). The AP test score is the frosting on the cake of success. The AP course curricula challenge students to do more than they believe they can do. They also learn how to use resources and time wisely, and to view learning as a lifelong challenge.

"Choosing Virginity" is also a misleading title. The author does not claim that American adolescents are all chaste, or even that large numbers of them are taking vows to save sex for marriage. Some are making such promises in religious services. Others are embracing the concepts of self-respect, self-identity, and self-esteem. One area which they can control and which can contribute to their sense of empowerment is their sexuality. Many adolescents who decide to postpone sex until they feel emotionally ready for it are concentrating instead on their education and career choices. This article, plus the preceding "100 Best Schools" article, gives a very positive view of contemporary adolescents and of our youth entering the twenty-first millennium.

The last selection in the Adolescence portion of this unit addresses some of the pressures and stressors that are weighing down our college students. Jane Brody, in "Hello to College Joys," gives an anti-thetical description of what happens to young people attending institutions of higher learning. Campus counseling centers are reporting an alarming increase in the numbers of students with serious psychological problems. She presents some fresh approaches to alleviating emotional distress. These include self-help practices and low cost mental health services.

The first article about young adulthood addresses the current economic recession and the increasing numbers of couples who rely on the wife to be the primary wage earner. Traditional female careers (e.g., health care and education) have not been downsized to the same degree as traditional male jobs. It is also more common for a wife to have more years of education than her husband. While most women still prefer to marry a financially secure man, our culture is gradually finding it acceptable for the wife to be the major wage earner, and the husband to be the household engineer and the childcare provider.

Despite its title, "We're Not in the Mood," this article actually has useful advice about making marriages work in the new millennium. Stress can have ripple effects not only in the bedroom but also on mental and physical health maintenance. Kathleen Deveny offers suggestions for revitalizing sex and health.

The last article of this unit reviews some of the ways in which neuroscientific discoveries may boost our brain power in the years to come. "The Battle for Your Brain" discusses the pros and cons of doing so. Bioethicists weigh in with their opinions about changing the human brain in order to improve mood, memory, intelligence, and perhaps more.

The 100 Best High Schools in America

The surge in the number of students taking AP tests is changing life inside America's classrooms—and altering the rules of the college-admissions game. A look at a new set of winners for 2003.

BY JAY MATHEWS

In THE 1970s, MIKE RILEY WAS A YOUNG CHICAGO TEACHER trying to save failing inner-city students. He found they blossomed if he simply sat them down each day after class and made sure they did their homework. "They went from F's to honor roll, and I realized that… they weren't dumb kids, just kids we hadn't connected to," he says. Riley learned that even the most apathetic students responded to a challenge—as long as they had the right support.

Today he is the superintendent of schools in Bellevue, Wash., a hilly and ethnically diverse Seattle suburb on the leading edge of a movement to take this lesson to the next level. Riley wants to make the hardest classes in U.S. high schools today—the college-level Advanced Placement (AP) or International Baccalaureate (IB) courses—mandatory for nearly all graduates. If he succeeds, he will help accelerate a transformation of American secondary education that has sparked intense debate among educators.

This month more than a million students in 14,000 high schools took 1,750,000 AP exams, a 10 percent increase over last year and twice the number of these college-level tests taken in 1996. That means that 245 more schools are eligible for the 2003 Challenge Index, which ranks 739 public schools according to the ratio of AP or IB tests taken by all students divided by the number of graduat-ing seniors. Schools that select more than half their students by exams or other academic criteria are not eligible, because they have few, if any, of the average students who need a boost from AP or IB. Some of these magnet schools achieve extraordinary results, partly because they get the best students. In the last index, in 2000, only 494 schools were included. (AP's younger, European-based counterpart, IB, is also on the rise, with 77,285 tests given in American schools this month.) The index uses AP and IB as a measure because schools that push these tests are most likely to stretch young minds—which should be the fundamental purpose of education.

AN ELITE REBELLION: Some private schools contend they can create a better curriculum and a few have dropped AP—although students can still take the tests

Some experts think AP is growing so fast and spreading so far it could eventually supplant the SAT and the ACT as America's most influential test. At Harvard—the dream school for many high-performing seniors—the dean of ad-

The Cream of THE CROP

Public schools are ranked according to a ratio devised by Jay Matthews: the number of Advanced Placement or International Baccalaureate tests taken by all students at a school in 2002 divided by the number of graduating seniors. For a list of every school scoring more than 1,000, see Newsweek.com.

	SCHOOL	RATIO
1	International Academy*–Bloomfield Hills, Mich.	6.323
2	Stanton College Prep*–Jacksonville, Fla.	5.639
3	Paxon*–Jacksonville, Fla.	4.668
4	Alabama School of Fine Arts–Birmingham, Ala.	4.567
5	Jericho–N.Y.	4.519
6	George Mason*–Falls Church, Va.	4.365
7	Myers Park*–Charlotte, N.C.	4.086
8	Science Academy of South Texas–Mercedes, Texas	4.024
9	H-B Woodlawn–Arlington, Va.	3.961
10	Los Angeles Center for Enriched Studies–Calif.	3.893
11	Manhasset–N.Y.	3.840
12	Wyoming–Cincinnati	3.782
13	Bellevue–Wash.	3.755
14	Highland Park–Dallas	3.693
15	Edgemont–Scarsdale, N.Y.	3.673
16	International–Bellevue, Wash.	3.643
17	Great Neck South–Great Neck, N.Y.	3.640
18	Newport–Bellevue, Wash.	3.625
19	Cold Spring Harbor–N.Y.	3.573
20	Mills University Studies–Little Rock, Ark.	3.564
21	Lincoln Park Academy*–Ft. Pierce, Fla.	3.521
22	W.T. Woodson*–Fairfax, Va.	3.448
23	Yorktown–Arlington, Va.	3.422
24	St. Petersburg*–Fla.	3.403
25	Brighton–Rochester, N.Y.	3.357
26	Great Neck North–Great Neck, N.Y.	3.298
27	Greeley–Chappaqua, N.Y.	3.240
28	Washington-Lee*–Arlington, Va	3.192
29	Wheatley–Old Westbury, N.Y.	3.146
30	Langley–McLean, Va.	3.144
31	Indian Hill–Cincinnati	3.100
32	Ft. Myers*–Fla.	3.075
33	Pittsford Mendon–Pittsford, N.Y.	3.053

34	Vandermeulen–Port Jefferson, N.Y.	3.040
35	Weston–Mass.	3.009
36	Westlake–Austin, Texas	3.004
37	Richard Montgomery*–Rockville, Md.	2.969
38	University Laboratory–Urbana, Ill.	2.932
39	Miami Palmetto-Miami, Fla.	2.914
40	Pittsford Sutherland–Pittsford, N.Y.	2.881
41	Lyndon B. Johnson–Austin, Texas	2.879
42	Enloe*–Raleigh, n.C.	2.879
43	Rye–N.Y.	2.878
44	Eastside*–Gainsville, Fla.	2.868
45	Walter Johnson–Bethesda, Md.	2.878
46	Westfield–Chantilly, Va.	2.848
47	La Jolla–Calif.	2.802
48	Providence–Charlotte, N.C.	2.800
49	Banneker–Washington, D.C.	2.796
50	Gunn–Palo Alto, Calif.	2.791
51	Hewlett–N.Y.	2.780
52	East Chapel Hill–Chapel Hill, N.C.	2.774
53	University–Irvine, Calif.	2,772
54	Atlantic Commuinty*–Delray Beach, Fla.	2.745
55	Robinson*–Fairfax, Va.	2.736
56	Wilson Magnet*–Rochester, N.Y.	2.735
57	Westwood*–Austin, Texas	2.709
58	Bernards–Bernardsville, N.J.	2.707
59	Miller Place–N.Y.	2.700
60	Syosset–N.Y.	2.699
61	Wootton–Rockville, Md.	2.699
62	South Side*–Rockville Centre, N.Y.	2.690
63	Millburn–N.J.	2.673
64	Kennedy–Bellmore, N.Y.	2.668
65	Harding Univ.*–Charlotte, N.C.	2.665
66	Steveson–Lincolnshire, Ill.	2.658
67	Foshay Learning Center–Los Angeles	2.651
68	Chagrin Falls–Ohio	2.625
69	Chantilly–Va.	2.620
70	East Hampton–N.Y.	2.598
71	North Shore–Glen Head, N.Y.	2.592
72	Buchholz–Gainsville, Fla.	2.573
73	Scarsdale–N.Y.	2.565
74	Churchill–Potomac, Md.	2.557
75	Torrey Pines–San Diego	2.541

continued on following page

The Cream of the Crop continued

76	Edina–Minn.	2.528
77	Roslyn–Roslyn Heights, N.Y.	2.505
78	Duxbury–Mass.	2.502
79	Mamaroneck–N.Y.	2.500
80	Bellaire*–Texas	2.493
81	Stonewall Jackson*–Manassas, Va.	2.489
82	Monta Vista–Cupertino, Calif.	2.470
83	Whitman–Bethesda, Md.	2.450
84	Ardsley–N.Y.	2.448
85	Lynbrook–San Jose, Calif.	2.442
86	Fairfax–Va.	2.436
87	Spurce Creek*–Port Orange, Fla.	2.435
88	Palos Verdes Peninsula–Rolling Hills Estates, Calif.	2.435
89	East Mecklenburg*–Charlotte, N.C.	2.434
90	Irondequoit–Rochester, N.Y.	2.432
91	Bronxville–N.Y.	2.429
92	Calhoun–Merrick, N.Y.	2.419
93	Troy*–Fullerton, Calif.	2.407
94	Sunny Hills*–Fullerton, Calif.	2.384
95	Oak Park–Calif.	2.382
96	Lewiston-Porter–Youngstown, N.Y.	2.367
97	North Hollywood–Los Angeles	2.349
98	Garden City–N.Y.	2.346
99	Sumner Academy*–Kansas City, Kans.	2.340
100	Croton-Harmon–Croton-on-Hudson, N.Y.	2.338

*GAVE IB TESTS. AP AND IB PARTICIPATION RATES ARE INDICATORS OF A SCHOOL'S EFFORTS TO GET STUDENTS TO EXCEL AND PREPARE FOR COLLEGE. SCHOOLS THAT CHOSE MORE THAN HLAF OF THEIR STUDENTS BY ENTRANCE EXAMINATIONS OR OTHER ACADEMIC QUALIFICATIONS WERE NOT CONSIDERED BECAUSE THEY HAVE VERY FEW OF THE AVERAGE STUDENTS THAT AP AND IB ARE USED TO HELP AND INSPIRE.

missions says AP is already a better predictor of college grades than the SAT. One reason could be that students get only one shot at the AP, unlike the SATs, which many retake several times in order to boost their scores. More important, AP tests a whole year of learning, while the SAT assesses a specific set of skills that many educators think have little relation to academic potential in college. College-admissions officers at many schools say that AP and IB have acquired the status of backstage passes at a rock concert. Selective universities begin to ask questions if they see that applicants have not taken the tests available at their high schools. Even freshmen and sophomores are crowding into AP courses once open only to juniors and seniors. At Miller Place High School on New York's Long Island, guidance director Joseph W. Connolly says 40

percent of this year's 10th graders took AP European history—an unheard-of proportion a decade ago.

Both AP and IB students answer lengthy free-response questions that are graded by actual human beings (AP also has multiple-choice questions). If their scores are high enough, students can earn college credit. They also get a taste of the higher-level exams they'll face on campus. Jordan Wish, a senior at Richard Montgomery High School in Rockville, Md., took two AP and four IB tests this month—25 hours of tests with not much time for sleep each night. "Right now I am not feeling so good," Wish said as he crammed in some last-minute studying for the difficult AP physics test. But he thinks the extra effort will be good preparation for Princeton, where he'll be a freshman this fall.

LEADING THE WAY: At the Science Academy of South Texas, many students from disadvantaged backgrounds learn to defy the odds

Proponents say AP and IB have exposed many average suburban teenagers to a level of instruction once reserved only for honor students and, even more significantly, have energized inner-city schools. From 1998 to 2002, AP participation by underrepresented minority students increased 77 percent and participation by low-income students increased 101 percent, while overall participation rose only 48 percent. But some administrators and university educators warn that pushing the programs too far and too quickly could dilute their benefits. A recent report by the National Research Council says AP and IB courses should delve more deeply into fewer topics. A few colleges have become more demanding as well. Last year Harvard announced that it would give advanced standing only to students who had the top AP grade, a 5, the equivalent of a college A, on four required AP tests. There are complaints that many of the new AP—students are failing the tests. And some high-school principals say that it is better for their more-ambitious students to take courses at local colleges rather than enroll in AP or IB. "There are many of us who would celebrate the exit of AP from high-school life," says Marilyn Colyar, assistant principal at San Marino High School in California. "I certainly believe in a rigorous curriculum for all students," she says, "but "a class can be challenging and relevant, AP or not."

THE CONTROVERSY OVER AP HAS BECOME PARTICULARLY intense in the private schools and affluent public schools that were the first to adopt the program in 1956, when it was little more than a way to keep high-performing seniors from getting bored. Andrew Meyers, head of the history department at the Ethical Culture Fieldston School in New York City, says he was not sympathetic three years ago when a student complained about being forced to stay on the AP superhighway without stopping to explore some intriguing side roads. But then, Meyers says, he realized that whenever a student in his AP American-history course asked a thoughtful question not quite on the topic, he often heard himself saying, "That's interesting… but we have to move on to the next era." Fieldston, Dalton, Exeter and a few other private schools have declared themselves AP-free zones. Instead of the AP history course he used to teach each spring, Meyers is offering one of his favorite electives, "Inventing Gotham," during which each student devises a historical tour of New York City. Similar electives are being offered at other schools shedding the AP label, although many of their students still take AP tests in order to impress colleges.

Many advocates of college-level courses say the prep schools are guilty of an elitist reaction to programs that are helping more and more average and below-average schools, as if AP and IB were last year's high fashions that had to be thrown out because similar clothes were being sold at Kmart. At the average high school, "the —kids would not get into elite colleges if they did not have AP courses," says Nicholas Lemann, author of "The Big Test," a history of the SAT, "but Fieldston knows that for socioeconomic reasons, their kids do not need AP to persuade those colleges to take them." Lemann and others fear that the rarefied complaints of privileged schools could slow the spread of AP and IB to poor districts where students need the challenge.

Some teachers have accused the College Board, which sponsors the AP, of promoting the program in order to collect the $80 test fees from all those students eager for an advantage in the college-admissions race. (IB is even more expensive, but schools usually pay the test fees.) Educators also bicker over the growing use of AP as a measure of school quality. NEWSWEEK's list of top high schools has been compared to U.S. News & World Report's annual "America's Best Colleges" list by educators who say such rankings distort the strengths of individual schools. The National Research Council report complained that the NEWSWEEK list had "taken on a life of its own," with high schools publishing their ratings and schools not making the list posting "disclaimers on their Web sites indicating why they are not there."

DESPITE THIS CRITICISM, THE MAJORITY OF EDUCATORS SAY they continue to support the growth of AP and IB. A recent straw-poll survey by the American School Board Journal found that 80 percent of readers wanted more of their students to take the college-level courses. And initial opposition often disappears if schools provide extra help for students who need it. Pat Hyland, principal of Mountain View (Calif.) High School, says she heard many worries when she opened her AP courses to all, but they soon

faded away. "We have added tutorial sessions and a variety of other measures to bolster the kids," she says.

Many communities have found that adding AP really turns a school around. Seven years ago, when Tim Berkey became principal of Perry High School in a rural area east of Cleveland, there were no AP or IB classes at all. He told teachers about the marked change in student attitude and achievement he had seen at his previous school, Adlai Stevenson in suburban Chicago, when the AP program was opened to everyone willing to work that hard. Five years ago Perry High started with 87 AP tests; this month it administered 214. "We believed in kids, held high expectations, provided them with the resources, tools and challenging opportunities, and then simply got out of their way," Berkey says.

Lemann, who thinks the SAT hinders educational improvement, says AP and IB have had the opposite effect—much to the surprise of many educators who are generally opposed to the spread of standardized tests. "It has become a wonderful and effective way to produce a massive upgrading of the high-school curriculum," Lemann says. "These were unintended consequences, but good unintended consequences."

The commitment to giving more high schoolers a useful dose of college exam-week trauma has turned an old elementary-school building in Bloomfield Hills, Mich., into an IB hothouse—and the top school on the 2003 NEWSWEEK list. Five hundred teenagers, picked by lottery from 13 local districts, have enrolled in the International Academy, while their neighborhood friends shy away from the workload. "I had no idea what I was getting myself into," says Bhavana Bhaya, a senior who took 30 hours of IB exams this month at the public school near Detroit, "but I am glad I am here." The effort paid off, says senior James Kurecka. He was afraid his 1270 SAT score and 27 ACT score would not have been enough to get into the University of Michigan's prestigious College of Engineering; he believes the IB label did the trick.

TAKING THE CHALLENGE: Admissions deans say that AP is a better predictor of college success than the SAT and that they look for students who've pushed themselves

Even students whose grades and test scores in high school were mediocre are more likely to graduate from college if they have had some challenging high-school — courses such as AP and IB, according to a 1999 study by U.S. Education Department researcher Clifford Adelman. That finding was particularly true for minorities. The Science Academy of South Texas, a public school that draws students from three rural counties in the Rio Grande Valley, has sent several migrant workers' children to high-tech colleges by exposing them to difficult AP assignments. Norma Flores, a senior, says she often started school late in the fall because her migrant-laborer family needed her in the cornfields. "I had to work twice as hard to catch up," she says. But next fall, fortified by college-level courses, she will study aerospace engineering at the University of Texas-Pan American campus in Edinburg.

Riley, the superintendent in Bellevue, says the criticism of AP and IB demonstrates how ubiquitous these programs have become, and how many previously ignored students are being helped. "Elitists will always try to find higher ground when it becomes apparent that others can scale their hill," he says. "While AP's standards, tests and curriculum have not changed, there are those who once thought the program was the gold standard but now see it as tarnished. What's the only, and I underscore only, thing that has changed? More kids are included." And like his students in Chicago nearly 30 years ago, he's betting that they will all thrive.

ALTERNATIVE SCHOOLS

Daring to Be Different

Reformers around the country have found new ways to motivate teens and they're inspiring others to break the mold

BY JAY MATHEWS

Tests aren't the only way to judge a high school. In the past decade, educators around the country have created dozens of intriguing models for reform. They include virtual high schools where all classes are online and "theme" schools based on environmental issues or the health-care profession. These schools tend to have "a strong identity shared by families and faculty alike," says Thomas Toch, writer-in-residence at the National Center on Education and the Economy and author of "High Schools on a Human Scale," published this month by Beacon Press. Some examples:

Urban Academy Laboratory High School, New York City: This public school of 120 students has made debate a teaching tool in every classroom. "What's your evidence?" could be the school motto; one of the most popular courses is officially titled "Are You Looking for an Argument?"

Despite drawing a typically urban mix of students, with many minorities and children of low-income parents, the school has a 3 percent dropout rate, while 95 percent of graduates go to college.

Christo Rey Jesuit High School, Chicago: Ninety-three percent of the 440 students at this Roman Catholic school come from low-income families, so Cristo Rey has found a novel way of financing private education that is now spreading to other cities. Per-student costs are $8,450, but the tuition is only $2,200. The rest of the money comes from students' own labor. Each of them puts in an eight-hour day, five days a month, in one of an assortment of banks, law firms and other private firms on Chicago's Loop, which pay $25,000 a year for each clerical job staffed by four rotating students. The work ethic pays off in other ways as well; 85 percent of graduates head for college.

Schools for Educational Evolution & Development (SEED) Public Charter School, Washington, D.C.: Drive past a small park in a low-income neighborhood of southeast Washington, and suddenly you find a brand-new prep school, resembling an old-line New England boarding school. The 230 students from mostly minority families live at the school all week in gleaming new dorms with computer connections, study halls and round-the-clock teachers. Two young management consultants came up with the idea, and it has created an atmosphere where distracted public-school children can finally focus on their studies.

Girard Academic Music Program, Philadelphia: This fifth-through-12th-grade school of 520 students in south Philadelphia draws mostly children from low-income families. Everyone studies music theory and "all of them can read and write their own music," says counselor Mae Pasquariello. Music lessons in every instrument (except piano) are free. There is also a strong emphasis on English, math, science and social science.

Marcus Garvey School, Los Angeles: A private school with 285 students, Marcus Garvey has a strong Afrocentric curriculum and scores that are often two years or more above grade level. It is in the Crenshaw district of South-Central Los Angeles, and some parents use the school to get their children up to the academic level of magnet programs in the public system.

Minnesota New Country School (MNCS), Henderson, Minn.: One of the first charter schools in the country, MNCS, located in a rural area 60 miles southwest of Minneapolis, proves that innovation isn't confined to cities. The school is run by a team of teachers (there's no principal) and students' work is project-based, says teacher Dean Lind, whose official title is "advisor." Students are required to make a 30-minute presentation in order to graduate. Topics for one recent senior class included "Building a Garden Pond," "History of Nursing" and "Theoretical Physics."

Choosing Virginity

A New Attitude: Fewer teenagers are having sex. As parents and politicians debate the merits of abstinence programs, here's what the kids have to say.

BY LORRAINE ALI AND JULIE SCELFO

THERE'S A SEXUAL REVOLUTION GOING ON IN AMERICA, AND believe it or not, it has nothing to do with Christina Aguilera's bare-it-all video "Dirrty." The uprising is taking place in the real world, not on "The Real World." Visit any American high school and you'll likely find a growing number of students who watch scabrous TV shows like "Shipmates," listen to Eminem—and have decided to remain chaste until marriage. Rejecting the get-down-make-love ethos of their parents' generation, this wave of young adults represents a new counterculture, one clearly at odds with the mainstream media and their routine use of sex to boost ratings and peddle product.

According to a recent study from the Centers for Disease Control, the number of high-school students who say they've never had sexual intercourse rose by almost 10 percent between 1991 and 2001. Parents, public-health officials and sexually beleaguered teens themselves may be relieved by this "let's not" trend. But the new abstinence movement, largely fostered by cultural conservatives and evangelical Christians, has also become hotly controversial.

As the Bush administration plans to increase federal funding for abstinence programs by nearly a third, to $135 million, the Advocates for Youth and other proponents of a more comprehensive approach to sex ed argue that teaching abstinence isn't enough. Teens also need to know how to protect themselves if they do have sex, these groups say, and they need to understand the emotional intensity inherent in sexual relationships.

The debate concerns public policy, but the real issue is personal choice. At the center of it all are the young people themselves, whose voices are often drowned out by the political cacophony. Some of them opened up and talked candidly to NEWSWEEK about their reasons for abstaining from sex until marriage. It's clear that religion plays a critical role in this extraordinarily private decision. But there are other factors as well: caring parents, a sense of their own unreadiness, the desire to gain some semblance of control over their own destinies. Here are their stories.

The Wellesley Girl

ALICE KUNCE SAYS SHE'S A FEMINIST, BUT NOT THE "ARMY-boot-wearing, shaved-head, I-hate-all-men kind." The curly-haired 18-year-old Wellesley College sophomore—she skipped a grade in elementary school—looks and talks like what she is: one of the many bright, outspoken students at the liberal Massachusetts women's college. She's also a virgin. "One of the empowering things about the feminist movement," she says, "is that we're able to assert ourselves, to say no to sex and not feel pressured about it. And I think guys are kind of getting it. Like, 'Oh, *not* everyone's doing it'."

But judging by MTV's "Undressed," UPN's "Buffy the Vampire Slayer" and just about every other TV program or movie targeted at teens, everyone *is* doing it. Alice grew up with these images, but as a small-town girl in Jefferson City, Mo., most teen shows felt alien and alienating. "You're either a prudish person who can't handle talking about sex or you're out every Saturday night getting some," she says. "But if you're not sexually active and you're willing to discuss the subject, you can't be called a prude. How do they market to that?" The friend from back home she's been dating since August asked not to be identified in this story, but Alice doesn't mind talking candidly about what they do—or don't do. "Which is acceptable? Oral, vaginal or anal sex?" she asks. "For me, they're all sex. In high school, you could have oral sex and still call yourself a virgin.

148

Now I'm like, 'Well, what makes one less intimate than the other?'"

Alice, a regular churchgoer who also teaches Sunday school, says religion is not the reason she's chosen abstinence. She fears STDs and pregnancy, of course, but above all, she says, she's not mature enough emotionally to handle the deep intimacy sex can bring. Though most people in her college, or even back in her Bible-belt high school, haven't made the same choice, Alice says she has never felt ostracized. If anything, she feels a need to speak up for those being coerced by aggressive abstinence groups. "Religious pressure was and is a lot greater than peer pressure," says Alice, who has never taken part in an abstinence program. "I don't think there are as many teens saying 'Oh come on, everybody's having sex' as there are church leaders saying 'No, it's bad, don't do it. It'll ruin your life.' The choices many religious groups leave you with are either no sex at all or uneducated sex. What happened to educating young people about how they can protect themselves?"

The Dream Team

Karl Nicoletti wasted no time when it came to having "the talk" with his son, Chris. It happened five years ago, when Chris was in sixth grade. Nicoletti was driving him home from school and the subject of girls came up. "I know many parents who are wishy-washy when talking to their kids about sex. I just said, 'No, you're not going to have sex. Keep your pecker in your pants until you graduate from high school'."

"If you're abstinent, it's like you're the one set aside from society because you're not 'doing it'."

AMANDA WING, 17,
who plans to stay a virgin until marriage

Today, the 16-year-old from Longmont, Colo., vows he'll remain abstinent until marriage. So does his girlfriend, 17-year-old Amanda Wing, whose parents set similarly strict rules for her and her two older brothers. "It's amazing, but they did listen," says her mother, Lynn Wing. Amanda has been dating Chris for only two months, but they've known each other for eight years. On a Tuesday-night dinner date at Portabello's (just across from the Twin Peaks Mall), Amanda asks, "You gonna get the chicken parmesan again?" Chris nods. "Yep. You know me well." They seem like a long-married couple—except that they listen to the Dave Matthews Band, have a 10:30 weeknight curfew and never go beyond kissing and hugging. (The guidelines set by Chris's dad: no touching anywhere that a soccer uniform covers.)

"Society is so run by sex," says Chris, who looks like Madison Avenue's conception of an All-American boy in his Abercrombie sweat shirt and faded baggy jeans. "Just look at everything—TV, movies. The culture today makes it seem OK to have sex whenever, however or with whoever you want. I just disagree with that." Amanda, who looks tomboy comfy in baggy brown cords, a white T shirt and chunky-soled shoes, feels the same way. "Sex should be a special thing that doesn't need to be public," she says. "But if you're abstinent, it's like *you're* the one set aside from society because you're not 'doing it'."

The peer pressure in this town of 71,000 people in the shadow of the Rocky Mountains is substantially less than in cosmopolitan Denver, 45 minutes away. ("It figures you had to come all the way out here to find a virgin," one local said.) Chris joined a Christian abstinence group called Teen Advisors this year. "We watched their slide show in eighth grade and it just has pictures of all these STDs," he says. "It's one of the grossest things you've ever seen. I didn't want to touch a girl, like, forever." He now goes out once a month and talks to middle schoolers about abstinence. Amanda saw the same presentation. "It's horrible," she says. "If that doesn't scare kids out of sex, nothing will." Could these gruesome images put them off sex for life? Chris and Amanda say no. They're sure that whoever they marry will be disease-free.

To most abstaining teens, marriage is the golden light at the end of the perilous tunnel of dating—despite what their parents' experience may have been. Though Amanda's mother and father have had a long and stable union, Karl Nicoletti separated from Chris's mother when Chris was in fifth grade. His fiancée moved in with Chris and Karl two years ago; Chris's mother now has a year-and-a-half-old son out of wedlock. Chris and Amanda talk about marriage in the abstract, but they want to go to college first, and they're looking at schools on opposite sides of the country. "I think we could stay together," Chris says. Amanda agrees. "Like we have complete trust in each other," she says. "It's just not hard for us." Whether the bond between them is strong enough to withstand a long-distance relationship is yet to be seen. For now, Chris and Amanda mostly look ahead to their next weekly ritual: the Tuesday pancake lunch.

The Survivor

Remaining a virgin until marriage is neither an easy nor a common choice in Latoya Huggins's part of Paterson, N.J. At least three of her friends became single mothers while they were still in high school, one by an older man who now wants nothing to do with the child. "It's hard for her to finish school," Latoya says, "because she has to take the baby to get shots and stuff."

Latoya lives in a chaotic world: so far this year, more than a dozen people have been murdered in her neighborhood. It's a life that makes her sexuality seem like one of the few things she can actually control. "I don't even want a boyfriend until after college," says Latoya, who's studying to be a beautician at a technical high school. "Basically I want a lot out of life. My career choices are going to need a lot of time and effort."

Latoya, 18, could pass for a street-smart 28. She started thinking seriously about abstinence five years ago, when a national outreach program called Free Teens began teaching classes at her church. The classes reinforced what she already knew from growing up in Paterson—that discipline is the key to getting through your teen years alive. Earlier this year she dated a 21-year-old appliance salesman from her neighborhood, until Latoya heard that he was hoping she'd have sex with him. "We decided that we should just be friends," she explains, "before he cheated on me or we split up in a worse way."

So most days Latoya comes home from school alone. While she waits for her parents to return from work, she watches the Disney Channel or chills in her basement bedroom, which she's decorated with construction-paper cutouts of the names of her favorite pop stars, such as Nelly and Aaliyah. She feels safe there, she says, because "too many bad things are happening" outside. But bad things happen inside, too: last year she opened the door to a neighbor who forced his way inside and attempted to rape her. "He started trying to take my clothes off. I was screaming and yelling to the top of my lungs and nobody heard." Luckily, the phone rang. Latoya told the intruder it was her father, and that if she didn't answer he would come home right away. The man fled. Latoya tries not to think about what happened, although she feels "like dying" when she sees her attacker on the street. (Her parents decided not to press charges so she wouldn't have to testify in court.) Her goal is to graduate and get a job; she wants to stay focused and independent. "Boys make you feel like you're special and you're the only one they care about," she says. "A lot of girls feel like they need that. But my mother loves me and my father loves me, so there's no gap to fill."

The Beauty Queen

EVEN THOUGH SHE LIVES 700 MILES FROM THE NEAREST ocean, Daniela Aranda was recently voted Miss Hawaiian Tropic El Paso, Texas, and her parents couldn't be prouder. They've displayed a picture of their bikini-clad daughter smack-dab in the middle of the living room. "People always say to me 'You don't look like a virgin'," says Daniela, 20, who wears super-sparkly eye shadow, heavy lip liner and a low-cut black shirt. "But what does a virgin look like? Someone who wears white and likes to look at flowers?"

Daniela models at Harley-Davidson fashion shows, is a cheerleader for a local soccer team called the Patriots and hangs out with friends who work at Hooters. She's also an evangelical Christian who made a vow at 13 to remain a virgin, and she's kept that promise. "It can be done," she says. "I'm living proof." Daniela has never joined an abstinence program; her decision came from strong family values and deep spiritual convictions.

Daniela's arid East El Paso neighborhood, just a mile or so from the Mexican border, was built atop desert dunes, and the sand seems to be reclaiming its own by swallowing up back patios and sidewalks. The city, predominantly Hispanic, is home to the Fort Bliss Army base, breathtaking mesa views—and some of the highest teen-pregnancy rates in the nation. "There's a lot of girls that just want to get pregnant so they can get married and get out of here," Daniela says.

But she seems content to stay in El Paso. She studies business at El Paso Community College, dates a UTEP football player named Mike and works as a sales associate at the A'gaci Too clothing store in the Cielo Vista Mall. She also tones at the gym and reads—especially books by the Christian author Joshua Harris. In "Boy Meets Girl," she's marked such passages as "Lust is never satisfied" with a pink highlighter. She's also saved an article on A. C. Green, the former NBA player who's become a spokesman for abstinence. "My boyfriend's coach gave it to him because the other guys sometimes say, 'Are you gay? What's wrong with you?' It's proof that if a famous man like Green can do it, so can he."

"I feel that part of me hasn't been triggered yet," she says. "Sex is one of those things you can't miss until you have it."

LENÉE YOUNG, 19,
who has never had a boyfriend

Daniela has been dating Mike for more than a year. He's had sex before, but has agreed to remain abstinent with her. "He's what you call a born-again virgin," she says. "Or a secondary abstinent, or something like that. We just don't put ourselves in compromising situations. If we're together late at night, it's with my whole family."

Daniela knows about temptation: every time she walks out onstage in a bathing suit, men take notice. But she doesn't see a contradiction in her double life as virgin and beauty queen; rather, it's a personal challenge. "I did Hawaiian Tropic because I wanted to see if I could get into a bikini in front of all these people," she says. "I wasn't thinking, 'Oh, I'm going to win.' But I did, and I got a free trip to Houston's state finals. I met the owner of Hawaiian Tropic. It's like, wow, this is as good as it gets."

The Ring Bearer

LENEE YOUNG IS TRYING TO WRITE A PAPER FOR HER SPANISH class at Atlanta's Spelman College, but as usual she and her roommates can't help getting onto the subject of guys. "I love Ludacris," Lenée gushes. "I love everything about him. Morris Chestnut, too. He has a really pretty smile. Just gorgeous." But Lenée, 19, has never had a boyfriend, and has never even been kissed. "A lot of the guys in high school had already had sex," she says. "I knew that would come up, so I'd end all my relationships at the very beginning." Lenée decided back then to remain a virgin until marriage, and even now she feels little temptation to do what many of her peers are doing behind closed dormitory doors. "I feel that part of me hasn't been triggered yet," she says. "Sex is one of those things you can't miss until you have it."

Last summer she went with a friend from her hometown of Pittsburgh to a Silver Ring Thing. These popular free events meld music videos, pyrotechnics and live teen comedy sketches with dire warnings about STDs. Attendees can buy a silver ring—and a Bible—for $12. Then, at the conclusion of the program, as techno music blares, they recite a pledge of abstinence

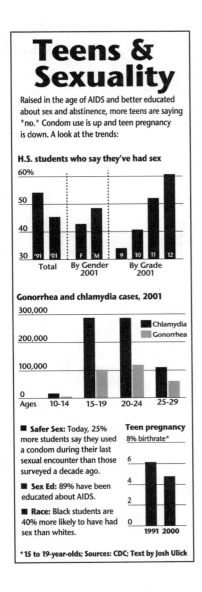

Teens & Sexuality

Raised in the age of AIDS and better educated about sex and abstinence, more teens are saying "no." Condom use is up and teen pregnancy is down. A look at the trends:

H.S. students who say they've had sex

Gonorrhea and chlamydia cases, 2001

- **Safer Sex:** Today, 25% more students say they used a condom during their last sexual encounter than those surveyed a decade ago.
- **Sex Ed:** 89% have been educated about AIDS.
- **Race:** Black students are 40% more likely to have had sex than whites.

Teen pregnancy
8% birthrate*

*15 to 19-year-olds; Sources: CDC; Text by Josh Ulick

Young was the only woman who said no, and everybody in the room was stunned. "Are you serious? We gotta find you a boyfriend!" But Lenée wasn't embarrassed. "I don't feel like I've missed out," she says. "I just feel like my time will come." Until then, she sports that shiny silver ring.

The Renewed Virgin

LUCIAN SCHULTE HAD ALWAYS PLANNED TO WAIT UNTIL HE was married to have sex, but that was before a warm night a couple of years ago when the green-eyed, lanky six-footer found himself with an unexpected opportunity. "She was all for it," says Lucian, now 18. "It was like, 'Hey, let's give this a try'." The big event was over in a hurry and lacked any sense of intimacy. "In movies, if people have sex, it's always romantic," he says. "Physically, it did feel good, but emotionally, it felt really awkward. It was not what I expected it to be."

While the fictional teens of "American Pie" would have been clumsily overjoyed, Lucian, raised Roman Catholic, was plagued by guilt. "I was worried that I'd given myself to someone and our relationship was now a lot more serious than it was before," he says. "It was like, 'Now, what is she going to expect from me?'" Lucian worried, too, about disease and pregnancy. He promised himself never again.

Lucian, now an engineering major at the University of Alberta in Canada, is a "renewed virgin." His parents are strong proponents of chastity, and he attended school-sponsored abstinence classes. But the messages didn't hit home until he'd actually had sex. "It's a pretty special thing, and it's also pretty serious," he says. "Abstinence has to do with 'Hey, are you going to respect this person?'" He has dated since his high-school affair, and is now hoping a particular cute coed from Edmonton will go out with him. "But I'll try to restrict myself to kissing," he says. "Not because I think everything else is bad. But the more you participate with someone, the harder it's going to be to stop."

It's not easy to practice such restraint, especially when those around him do not. Lucian lives in a single room, decorated with ski-lift tickets and a "Scooby-Doo" poster, in an all-male dorm, but he says most students "get hitched up, sleep around and never see each other again." Meanwhile he does his best to push his own sexual urges from his mind. "I try to forget about it, but I have to say it sucks. Homework is a good thing to do, and going out for a run usually works." He also goes to Sunday mass. Lucian figures he can hold out until he's married, which he hopes will be by the time he's 30. "I'm looking forward to an intimate experience with my wife, who I'll truly love and want to spend the rest of my life with," says Lucian. "It's kind of corny, but it's for real."

and don their rings. "My friend, who's also a virgin, said I needed to go so I could get a ring," Lenée says. "It was fun, like the music and everything. And afterwards they had a dance and a bonfire."

The idea of abstinence was not new to Lenée. In high school she participated in a program sponsored by the University of Pittsburgh Medical Center called Postponing Sexual Involvement. Her mother had discussed it with her—once—the week before she left for college. Two of her closest friends are also virgins; the trio jokingly call themselves The Good Girls Club. But student life can sometimes be a shock to her sensibilities. "Another friend of mine and this guy were talking about how they didn't use a condom. He said, 'I like it raw.' I was like, 'Oh, my goodness'."

And then there was the recent party that began with truth-or-dare questions. The first one: have you ever kissed a boy?

With SARAH DOWNEY and VANESSA JUAREZ

Hello to College Joys: Keep Stress Off Campus

By JANE E. BRODY

Adults are often quick to tell college students: "Enjoy yourselves. This is the best time of your lives." But for an increasing number of students, the college experience is marred by chronic anxiety, stress and distress.

College counselors report a sharp increase in the need and demand for mental health services, and that can sometimes result in long waiting lists, making the troubled students' problems even worse.

In recent years more than 80 percent of campuses have noted significant increases in serious psychological problems, including severe stress, depression, anxiety and panic attacks, according to an annual survey of counseling centers by Dr. Robert P. Gallagher of the University of Pittsburgh.

Causes of Stress Abound

Some of this emotional distress can be attributed to financial worries in these economically uncertain times. Looking at the dismal employment situation, many students with college loans fret about how they will be able to repay them.

Furthermore, family support systems are not what they used to be for students whose parents are separated, divorced or remarried. Even within colleges, there may now be less support from peers, with the increase in nontraditional students who live on their own off campus rather than in dormitories.

But also, a host of new drugs have enabled more students with mental illnesses to attend college.

These challenges can land on top of traditional causes of student distress like broken romantic relationships, bad grades, insufficient sleep, difficulty making friends, failing to join fraternities or sororities, homesickness or simply feeling overwhelmed by the amount of work that has to be done.

The burden is especially heavy for student athletes who constantly have to juggle the demands of schoolwork and teamwork and for students who have to work to help pay for their schooling.

It does not take much to send a vulnerable 18-year-old into an emotional descent. I recall feeling as if I were in an academic sinkhole and close to suffering an emotional meltdown at the start of my sophomore year.

Although I had good grades in hard courses as a freshman biochemistry major, I began to doubt my interest in the field and questioned whether I had even chosen the right college. I became anxious, depressed and paranoid, thinking that no one liked me and that everyone was speaking ill of me.

But before I abandoned my major and college, I consulted a psychologist at the campus health center, who helped to turn my academic goals and my outlook on college life in a more positive direction.

After tests and talk revealed no underlying mental illness, the therapist suggested that I find an activity that I might enjoy and that would help me feel more a part of college life. So I joined my college's monthly magazine, began writing and editing science-related articles and eventually realized that my passion lay in writing about science rather than doing it. The rest is history.

Strategies Gone Awry

Far too many students turn to tobacco and alcohol to assuage their emotional crises and, in the process, make them worse. Recent studies have shown, for example, that smoking cigarettes causes rather than alleviates stress.

The stress that smokers typically experience when not smoking is induced by nicotine withdrawal, prompting them to believe that they cannot cope with life without cigarettes. But if they had not become hooked on nicotine to begin with or if they broke their addictions by quitting cigarettes (and nicotine replacements), most would eliminate the need to smoke to relieve stress.

Smoking by college students soared in the 1990's, and by 1999 one-third of students were reportedly current smokers, many of them having started after entering college. But more and more colleges are making it very hard to be a smoker on campus. Many forbid smoking in all campus buildings. Some campuses have become entirely smoke free and instead offer smoking-cessation programs for students and faculty members.

Drinking alcohol—especially binge drinking—has long been a troublesome college pastime, even when most students are younger than the legal drinking age. Many students drink alcohol simply to be part of the crowd. Others drink to help them relax and forget their problems.

But what most students—in fact, most people—do not realize is that alcohol is a depressant that only temporarily masks ill feelings but in the end makes matters worse. And binge drinking is plain dangerous. A few students each year die directly from alcohol intoxication. Many more die indirectly by doing something stupid while drunk.

Meanwhile, some colleges are working hard to help students resist the temptation to drink and are providing alternative activities to those where alcohol is most likely to flow. Rather than being stigmatized for refusing alcohol, students who participate in such activities are increasingly seen as campus leaders.

Another all-too-common but ill-conceived mechanism for coping can lead to an eating disorder. The problem may start with stress-induced compulsive eating, leading to weight gain or a fear of it. Desperate attempts to control unwanted pounds may lead to risky diets or even bulimia, the binge-and-purge syndrome that is said to afflict up to 15 percent of young women on some campuses.

Fresh Approaches

Young people with emotional problems often think that they are the only ones so afflicted and that no one understands them. But few if any such problems are unique, and talking about them to a good listener, professional or otherwise, can often make matters seem less serious and more manageable.

It can also lead to creative solutions for even seemingly impossible problems.

A student overwhelmed by a difficult course load may find that dropping an especially troublesome course and taking it or an alternative in summer school or the next semester is far more workable.

Those plagued with monetary worries can consult financial aid offices and explore options like scholarships, part-time or summer jobs or government loans that do not have to be paid back until after graduation.

Instead of using food, drugs, alcohol or tobacco in a counterproductive attempt to relieve stress, students might consider any of a number of wholesome relaxation techniques including meditation, yoga and physical exercise.

Sometimes a short walk or bike ride can help gain a healthier perspective and renewed vigor for dealing with challenging tasks. No matter how busy a student is academically, everyone needs a break and some fun from time to time to restore emotional reserves.

Finally, when emotional distress seems beyond self-help solutions, troubled students should not hesitate to seek professional counseling on campus or off.

Often the campus medical clinic can provide free or low-cost mental health services.

Using such help no longer provokes a stigma. Rather, it is a smart move that can be lifesaving. Plus, you never know where it might lead. It led me, for example, to a very rewarding career.

She Works, He Doesn't

She's got an advanced degree, A HIGH-PAYING JOB and a boss who loves her. He just got a pink slip. Or maybe her career has more EARNING POTENTIAL. Or maybe he's THE NURTURING ONE. The number of American families in which the SOLE WAGE EARNER is the woman is small, but many economists think it's growing.

BY PEG TYRE AND DANIEL MCGINN

SINCE THE BEGINNING OF TIME, ANTHROPOLOGISTS BELIEVE, women have been programmed to seek a mate who can provide for a family—whether that means dragging the mastodon back to the cave or making the payments on the Volvo. So when Laurie Earp walked down the aisle, she joined hands with a man most brides would consider a good catch: a lawyer. "By marrying a lawyer," she says, "I thought he'd be able to bring in money." Freed from the need to earn a big paycheck, Laurie imagined herself in a part-time job, one that allowed her to spend long afternoons with their children.

54%
of Americans know a couple where the woman is clearly the major wage earner and the man's career is secondary, according to the NEWSWEEK Poll.

For a time the Earps realized that vision. Jonathan earned a six-figure salary as a lawyer at Napster, while Laurie worked leisurely hours as a fund-raising consultant. But last May Jonathan was laid off; he still can't find work. So, reluctantly, Laurie has become the breadwinner. On a recent evening their son, Dylan, 5, skipped through their home in Oakland, Calif., praising how well his stay-at-home dad cares for him. But Dylan is the only one pleased with the turnabout. "This is not the life I wanted," says Laurie, who's heading off to an after-dinner meeting with clients. Meanwhile, Jonathan spends his days doing housework and preparing badly cooked dinners. "I hate it all," he says.

Men who identify with their jobs are HIT HARDEST. Younger couples—the ones who GREW UP LISTENING to 'Free to Be... You and Me'—tend to take the turnabout more IN STRIDE.

Like several million American families, the Earps are experiencing the quiet, often painful transformation that takes place when Dad comes home with a severance package. The unemployment rate hit 6 percent last month, and while that's low by historical standards, some economists say it underestimates the difficulties facing laid-off workers—especially white-collar men who've been victimized by corporate downsizings. Despite Alan Greenspan's predictions of rosier times on the horizon, some experts talk of a growing problem of "underemployment" that goes beyond the nation's 8.8 million jobless. Their numbers include people forced to accept part-time work, all those newfound "consultants" who are playing computer solitaire but producing little income, and "discouraged workers" who've given up job hunting altogether.

The good news, at least for the 1.7 million unemployed men who are married, is that their wives are better equipped than any generation in history to pick up the financial slack. Women are currently earning more college degrees and M.B.A.s than men. In 1983, women made up 34 percent of high-paying "executive, administrative and managerial" occupations; in 2001 they were nearly half of that category. They've also weathered the recession better than men, because traditionally female industries like health care and education have suffered less than male-dominated businesses like manufacturing. Although the average woman's wage still trails a man's (78 cents to the dollar), enough women are breaking into better-paying professions that in 30.7 percent of married households with a working wife, the wife's earnings exceeded the husband's in 2001. Many of these women were born and bred for the office; they wouldn't want it any other way.

Laurie and Jonathan Earp: Oakland, Calif.

SHE

While her husband was at Napster, Laurie worked part time and hung out with her kids. Now she's ratcheted up her hours. "It's a lot of stress," she says.

HE

He's the main caregiver, runs the house and is also trying to start a small business making notecards for kids' lunch-boxes. He misses his old life: "I make bad dinners," he says.

Within these homes, some of the husbands have voluntarily dialed back their careers (or quit work entirely) to care for kids and live off their wives' income. Some experts use a new phrase to describe high-income female providers: Alpha Earners. For some families, this shift works wonderfully; for others (especially those forced into it by layoffs), it creates tensions. Regardless, it's a trend we'd better get used to. Like runners passing the baton in a track event, many 21st-century couples will take turns being the primary breadwinner and the domestic god or goddess as their careers ebb and flow. Says marriage historian Stephanie Coontz: "These couples are doing, in a more extreme form, what most couples will have to do in the course of their working lives."

Most experts believe the number of families converting to the "Mr. Mom" lifestyle remains quite small. According to the Bureau of Labor Statistics, just 5.6 percent of married couples feature a wife who works and a husband who doesn't. But that information is misleading: most of those nonworking husbands are retired, disabled or full-time students, not househusbands who care for the kids. On the other hand, many of the men who have put their careers on the back burner to watch the kids still have part-time or entrepreneurial gigs of some sort, so they

---

Sandra and Tom Núñez: Dallas, Texas

SHE

A software engineer for IBM, Sandra's still feeding their infant daughter, Ava, in the wee hours. She's glad Tom quit his job. "I'd rather have him here," she says.

HE

Was a vet's assistant, but the money wasn't worth the time away. Their son, Andrew, now 3, was ill, and Tom didn't want the boy in day care. "He's not going to suffer," he says.

---

don't show up in that number. So to better understand the Alpha Earner phenomenon, some researchers focus instead on those households where the wife outearns the husband. They're crunching the data to eliminate men who are retirees or students, and to seek families where the wife's career appears dominant (by finding, say, households where the wife earns 60 percent or more of the family income). Until the 1990s these numbers were tiny. But University of Maryland demographer Suzanne Bianchi recently began analyzing new 2001 data. Her initial results suggest that 11 percent of marriages feature an Alpha Earner wife. There's probably one in your neighborhood: in the NEWSWEEK Poll, 54 percent of Americans said they "personally know a couple where the woman is clearly the major wage earner and the man's career is secondary."

The shift is showing up more frequently in pop culture, too. "Friends" fans spent much of this season watching Monica support her unemployed husband, Chandler. (To recycle an old Thursday-night catch-phrase: "Not that there's anything wrong with that.") Eddie Murphy hits theaters this week in "Daddy Day Care," in which he plays a laid-off dad whose wife becomes the primary breadwinner. In the bookstores, Alpha Earners are at the heart of Allison Pearson's novel "I Don't Know How She Does It" and "The Bitch in the House," a collection of feminist essays. "There are few things that make a man less attractive to women than financial instability," writes one contributor. "We can deal with men in therapy, we can deal with men crying, but I don't think gender equality will ever reach the point where we can deal with men broke."

Fathers who voluntarily choose the househusband role are challenging that sensibility. Last month three Chicago men gathered for breakfast at a suburban strip mall. Each has a wife with a lucrative job—two in finance, one in market research—and each man had achieved enough workplace success that he felt able to ease off the throttle. Ron Susser, 43, was chief financial officer for a consulting firm; today he practices the 4 O'Clock Shuffle, his name for his frantic afternoon cleaning binge. "When my wife comes home, she expects the pantry to be stocked, the

Richer or Poorer, Sickness and Health

Women have always worked, of course. But as economic conditions and social expectations have evolved over the millenniums, so have gender roles in marriage. Here's a brief look at some of the ways couples have shared the load.

Hunter-Gatherers

15,000 years ago: Prehistoric women forage for plants while their cavemen husbands hunt. In many climates, it is the gathering that keeps them alive.

Adam and Eve

Literature's first couple adheres to conventional sex roles: God creates Eve, the first woman, as the "help meet" for a lonely Adam.

The Middle Ages

Fifth century to 1300: Although women often work, they are prevented by law from controlling their own money.

The Renaissance

1300–1600: What's love got to do with it? This 15th-century wedding portrait by Jan van Eyck is a visual marriage contract. Matrimony is used to build capital, amass land and consolidate power.

The Age of Austen

Marriage is the sole option for upper- and middle-class women. In 1916, Jane Austen writes: "Single women have a dreadful propensity for being poor, which is one argument in favour of matrimony."

The Victorians

In the 19th century, middle- and upper-class women aspire to a life of purity, submissiveness, piety and domesticity.

Turn of the Century

With both men and women working and earning money, it becomes possible to choose a mate based on attraction and compatibility.

'The Man in the Gray Flannel Suit'

This 1956 film, starring Gregory Peck (left), reflects the dissatisfaction of a husband and commuter who is the sole breadwinner.

The Birth-Control Pill

1960s: For the first time, reliable birth control becomes available to all American women, kicking off the sexual revolution. It also allows women to time their pregnancies in order to pursue career and family as they wish.

Gloria Steinem

In the early 1970s, the feminist movement ignites a generation of women who demand equal pay for equal work. Says Steinem: "We have become the husbands we wanted to marry."Thirty years later women's wages still lag behind men's.

'Kramer vs. Kramer'

This 1979 movie explores a generation's uneasiness with traditional gender roles in marriage. The movie wins five Academy Awards.

Margaret and Denis Thatcher

In office from 1979 to 1990, the first female British P.M. is one of the most powerful politicians of her time. She lives at 10 Downing Street with her househusband, Denis.

Monica and Chandler

Recently Chandler quit work to be with his chef wife, Monica. But getting a new job isn't a high priority.

Bill and Hillary

She's a senator now, but back in 2000 Bill made news when he announced he would support his wife's political career after he left the White House.

Jennifer Sey and Winslow Warren, San Francisco, Calif.

SHE

Earns more than 100,000 a year at Levi Strauss. She planned to take time off to help raise the kids, but her salary was too good. She just had a second baby.

HE

Was laid off from a failed dot-com two years ago and has been raising their son Virgil, now 2 1/2, ever since. He loves looking after Virgil, "but it can be a little lonely."

house to be in order and dinner cooked—I consider that my job," Susser says. David Burns, 49, was a computer consultant; today he's a Brownie leader. Scott Keeve, 52, oversaw 150 employees for a food distributor. When the nanny told his two kids she'd quit if they didn't behave, Keeve took the job himself. Like so many women before them, these guys are learning to adapt to a job without paychecks, business lunches or "attaboys." You get the sense that if the Lifetime cable channel installed cameras in their homes, there's a ready-made reality show to be found in their bouts of ambivalence.

For Bill Laut, a former real-estate appraiser, those moments come frequently. While his wife, Sheila, racks up frequent-flier miles as a business-development executive, Bill hauls their 6-year-old triplets to the grocery store, where strangers gawk. "Your poor wife," they say, to which Laut has a standard reply: "I look around very dramatically and then ask them, 'Do you see her here?'" When his kids were younger, he'd be watching football with friends, and talk would inevitably turn to work. "I changed 27 diapers today," Bill would interject, only to be heckled: "Get a job!" "At parties I feel like an outcast," Bill says. "I tell people what I do and some of them are thinking, 'What a freeloader.' Everyone pats you on the back, but I wonder, are they patronizing me or being sincere?"

But on good days, many househusband-by-choice families are so jubilant about their lifestyle they sound like the "after" example in an ad for antidepressants. Dan and Lynn Murray were both Chicago lawyers when Lynn became pregnant with *their* triplets. Assessing their lives, they decided Lynn was happier in the office. "I'm sort of a type-A personality who likes to control my environment, and there's more of that at work than at home," she says. Today Dan cares for their five children; Lynn hopes he never returns to work. Brian and Maria Sullivan of Highland Park, Ill., saw their income drop 40 percent when Brian quit his sales job to care for their two kids, now 5 and 3 (Maria's a VP with a big computer company). Brian had resisted quitting, but now he sees the upside. "How many dads get to potty-train their kids?" he says. When they're teenagers, Brian would like to spend some afternoons on the golf course. "That's fine as long as he's chaperoning every field trip and is there at every sports practice," Maria says.

25%
of respondents to the NEWSWEEK Poll think it is generally 'not acceptable' for a wife to be the major wage earner

Many such couples have simply decided that no matter how much lip service companies pay to "family friendly" policies, it's simply not possible to integrate two fast-track careers and kids without huge sacrifices. So they do a cold-eyed calculation, measuring the size and upside potential of each parent's paycheck, and opting to keep whoever's is larger. For the highest-achieving women, the trend is striking. Last fall Fortune reported that more than one third of its "50 Most Powerful Women in Business" have a stay-at-home man (it dubbed them "trophy husbands"). But this trend reaches women far below the executive-vice-president rank. Patty Lewis, 42, is a video producer and meeting planner in east Dallas; her husband, Spencer Prokop, 45, is an actor. When son Chase arrived, her income was steadier, so Prokop stayed home. Dad feels isolated, and he's given up on lugging Chase along to occasional auditions. "This notion that I would have this time to work on myself—well, that goes right out the window," says Prokop, who misses the lux-

ury of uninterrupted bathroom time. After Lewis's 12-hour work-days, she's often too beat for spousal conversation. Sometimes Prokop thinks he's nagging his wife the same way his stay-at-home mom nagged his father. While they've no regrets that Chase enjoyed a full-time dad for 3 1/2 years, Prokop is ready for a change. Their son started day care two weeks ago.

The wives of these househusbands have one universal regret: they spend too little time with their children. Of course, two-career couples with kids in day care express similar sentiments. Still, becoming the family's only revenue stream can add a dose of anxiety, even to a job you love. "I feel an intense pressure being the sole wage earner," says Sally Williams, 28, a Philadelphia lawyer with a 4-year-old daughter and a stay-at-home husband. "The house, the car—everything is riding on my shoulders." Some Alpha Earners say colleagues assume that their husbands are deadbeats who can't hold jobs. They also complain about the other extreme: how the novelty of Dad's dialing back can lead people to lavish him with too much praise. Says Beth Burkstrand-Reid, a lawyer in Washington, D.C.: "I'm doing a good job of supporting the family, [but] no one is giving *me* a pat on the back."

Feminists see the emerging era—when it's no longer the default choice that the kids will be watched by Mom, the nanny or a day-care center—as a necessary evolution. "The first half [of the feminist vision] was to liberate women from domestic servitude," says Suzanne Levine, a founding editor of Ms. Magazine and author of "Father Courage: What Happens When Men Put Family First." "The second half was to integrate the men back into the family." But while many dads now help with 3 a.m. feedings, it hasn't led to wholesale acceptance of wives as breadwinners. In the NEWSWEEK Poll, 41 percent of Americans agreed that "it is much better for everyone involved if the man is the achiever outside the home and the woman takes care of the home and family." One in four said it was "generally not acceptable" for a woman to be the major wage earner in a marriage.

34%
of men say that if their wife earned more money, they'd consider quitting their job or reducing their hours

While those attitudes may fester, the data suggest women's economic power will only grow. And as you plot out those trend lines a few decades, it's easy to imagine more-dramatic implications. For example, conventional wisdom is that once a man earns a certain income, whether his wife works becomes optional. Does that

Hoping for the Best, Ready for the Worst

Thanks to recession and divorce, today's college kids are determined to break the rules about sex roles

BY BARBARA KANTROWITZ

A few years ago, when the University of Connecticut women's basketball team first captured the NCAA title, a popular bumper sticker declared the Storrs campus a place where the men are men and the women are champions. And with the Lady Huskies still stars, UConn students aren't afraid to break stereotypes. So last week senior Christopher Kyne, 22, was confident about heading to South Carolina after graduation because his girlfriend has a good job at the Medical University of South Carolina. "We're going on her money," he says. He hopes to enter grad school and become a teacher, partly because it's a family-friendly career. In the future, he says, "I'd be 100 percent satisfied if my wife made enough money so I could be a stay-at-home dad."

50%
of women say that when it came time to choose a mate, they considered his earning potential 'not at all important'

Openness to flexible roles in marriage and family distinguishes this generation of college students from their parents, say researchers who've studied their progress. The battle over whether mothers should work is moot now; families need the money. Young women are more ready to pick up the slack and the men feel less of a stigma if they stay home. Everyone is desperate to avoid his parents' mistakes. In the early 1980s, these kids' baby-boomer mothers swarmed into the work force without any of the supports common today—maternity leave, part-time career paths, flexible schedules. The children saw marriages crumble under the strain. They also watched the economy ricochet. In the current downturn, many of their forty-something fathers are out of work with little chance of getting rehired. In this context, rigid roles seem quaint,

says Kathleen Gerson, a sociologist at New York University who is writing a book called "The Children of the Gender Revolution." "If the economic opportunities are there for the woman, fine. As long as they are there for *somebody*."

They're hopeful but pragmatic, and understand that the real world can crush ideals. Many of these young women hope for a close family life, but with nearly half of all marriages eventually ending in divorce, they're prepared to be breadwinners. "That's a big thing for our age group," says Lucy Swetland, a 21-year-old junior who watched friends' mothers struggle. Even though her parents are married, she's learned that "you can't depend on someone else to carry you through." Women still want to have it all—although maybe not all at the same time. Jennifer Carosella, a 21-year-old senior, is going to law school so she can earn six-figure income. But at some point, she also wants to be home with her children—as her own mother was.

How comfortably the men adapt depends largely on the examples their fathers set, says University of Chicago sociologist Barbara Schneider, coauthor of "The Ambitious Generation." UConn junior Alfred Guante, 21, whose parents are divorced, was the main male figure in his household for much of his childhood—and being responsible for his family is important to him: "I think it's a man's role to get a job." But unlike many men in earlier generations, he would have no objections to his wife's working as well. Drama student Jeremy Andrews was inspired by his father, an engineer who trained as a nurse. It was a backup when his company left town so he could avoid dislocating his family. His father found another engineering job, but rarely missed his four sons' games, while his mother, a nurse, worked long hours. That gives Andrews the confidence to try acting—even if it doesn't bring in a steady paycheck.

Rather than bemoan a legacy of social upheaval, his generation seems determined to embrace possibilities. "You're not stuck in what you do," says UConn sophomore Caitlin Fitzpatrick. "People have four or five careers. There are so many opportunities." Maybe this time, the balancing act will work.

mean work will become equally optional for men whose wives bring home big paychecks? For many families, it appears so: in the NEWSWEEK Poll, 34 percent of men said that in their relationship, if the wife landed a big pay raise, the husband would consider not working or reducing his hours.

Steve and Kim Taylor: Ft. Thomas, Ky.

SHE

For 10 years Kim has been the steady earner, rising from the mailroom to a management position at Cincinnati Bell. She's supportive of her husband: "I have more than I hoped for."

HE

Steve left a steady factory job for a sales gig, but his career in sales never took off. For the past two years his professional life has been a series of dashed hopes and disappointments. After looking in vain for a new career, he recently took a job as a local courier and is caring for their son, Ben.

Here's a related twist: we know many women consider a man's earning potential when choosing spouses. (Why do you think they're hiding the bachelors' occupations on "Mr. Personality"?) But as women's earnings rise, are more men paying attention to women's earning potential when they choose a mate? Yes, says University of Wisconsin economist Maria Cancian, who believes high-earning women are starting to be seen by men as a "good catch." As for high-powered women, Cancian wonders if their view may be changing, too. "Are we now in a situation where very career-oriented women might look for husbands that are less career oriented" and better equipped to nurture the kids full time?

Those questions will take years to answer. In the short term, there are aspects of this role reversal that are less cheery. By all accounts, the shift to wife as breadwinner is far more difficult when it's forced on couples because of Hubby's layoff. Predicting which families will suffer most is largely intuitive. Men who identify closely with their jobs or believe in traditional gender roles are hit hardest. Younger couples—the ones who grew up listing to "Free to Be… You and Me" while their moms were at work—tend to take the turnabout more in stride (sidebar).

But there are also wrinkles that aren't obvious. Working-class families may suffer less psychic whiplash because lesser-skilled workers have always been more susceptible to layoffs. As layoffs have crept up into white-collar ranks, they've taken more families by surprise. "When transitions are unexpected, then people are more likely to think it's somehow your fault, and that compounds the problems," says University of California, Berkeley, marriage researcher Philip Cowan.

Sherie Zebrowski was so unprepared for her husband Sean's layoff that she thought he was kidding when he came home with the news. The $80,000-plus-commissions he'd earned as an Austin, Texas, software salesman had allowed Sherie to care for their two children, train for triathlons and teach Sunday school. After his layoff two years ago, Sean spent months unsuccessfully looking for a similar job. For a while, the couple just hung on. "I tried not to fault him—he was good at what he did," Sherie says. "But after a while, you can't help but question: Is he looking in the right places? Could he be doing more?" To pay the bills, Sherie began turning her hobby—decorative painting—into a business. Soon she was working 10-hour days—and doing most of the housework while Sean surfed the Web. When their parish priest asked how they were doing, Sherie burst into tears. She told the priest: "I understand how the stress of being unemployed can break up a marriage."

So the Zebrowskis sat down for what they recall as The Talk. "I said, 'Either get a job at a checkout counter or you have to help me," Sherie says. So Sean created a marketing plan for her painting business. He began estimating jobs and boosting prices. They began hiring subcontractors. They're surviving, but it's far from ideal. "I'm still looking for a job," Sean says. "When I get it, Sherie can go back to sleeping in. This is not what I want to do, but I like to eat. I will get back to selling software. It's just a matter of when."

One element of the Zebrowskis' experience is near universal: among these couples, who does the housework becomes a battlefield. Some men claim wives develop bionic eyesight once the husband is home all day. "I don't tend to see dirt, but she can spot a single molecule," says Brian Reid, a former reporter who now cares for daughter Clio while his wife practices law. Sociologists speculate that some men actually do *less* housework when they stop working. Why? Being out of work already threatens their manhood, and taking on "feminine" tasks like cleaning the toilet might only make them feel worse.

Bill and Sheila Laut: Hudson, Ohio

SHE

Six weeks after the triplets were born, Sheila went back to her corporate job and Bill quit working. Now she makes more than their two previous incomes combined.

HE

Bill does the child care, cooking, cleaning and laundry. He says: "I don't get a paycheck, but I make that paycheck happen. Sheila couldn't excel if I didn't do what I do."

For families of laid-off househusbands, there's a more obvious source of marital tension: money. During the Internet boom, Gregg Wetterman prospered by organizing networking parties for Dallas techies. His wife, Jennie, remembers those days fondly. "The summer of 2001, I was at the pool every day," Jennie says. "I went scuba diving, sky diving—I must have read 30 books that summer." But when the tech bubble burst, Gregg bounced through a series of unstable jobs. As his career outlook became bleaker, an old boss of Jennie's called and asked if she wanted a management job at Old Navy. Says Gregg: "When she got the opportunity, I said, 'You don't have to,' but inside I was saying, 'Please, please, please… '"

32%
of those polled are worried about their family's major wage earner losing his or her job, compared with 44% in 1991

While Jennie works 50 hours a week, Gregg carts their kids to school and works on documentary films (he hasn't sold anything yet). Their two cars have a combined 286,000 miles; they've ditched their cell phones to cut expenses. At the kitchen table, the tension is palpable. Gregg argues it's smarter for him to keep pursuing non-paying opportunities related to his aspirations—filmmaking and technology marketing—than to take an unpleasant job just to pay the bills. When the economy picks up, he figures he'll find something that pays well in his field. But he realizes the family can't wait forever. "I'm not pulling my weight financially," he says. Jennie is sometimes resentful. "I would just like for everybody to do their part," she says. "I don't want to be in this situation two years down the road. I'll have to put my foot down." Gregg says it may not come to that. "There's no telling," he says "Jennie could get a better job."

For many couples, switching in and out of roles may become a routine part of life. Counselors say that 21st-century careers will involve more jumps between industries and more time out of work for retraining or as a result of downsizing. Ted and Jenny Cater, 40 and 43, already have that routine down pat. In 1999 Ted, a salesman, relocated to San Francisco with his company. When his employer went bankrupt, Jenny, who works in marketing, immediately received a call about a $100,000-a-year job in Atlanta. So they moved her career to the front burner; Ted stayed home with daughter Megan. Then two months ago Jenny was laid off. They're expecting a baby next month, but by July they'll both be job hunting. "Whoever wins the best position wins a ticket back to coffee breaks and time to check e-mail," Jenny says. "Not that we don't want to say at home with the kids, but we are both geared for working."

Some younger couples are talking about these issues long before kids or joblessness enters their lives. Jennifer McCaskill is a 33-year-old Washington, D.C., lawyer; Ryan Schock, 28, is an accountant. As they look ahead to their September wedding, they're already talking about who might care for their future children. "Quite honestly, I don't want to stay at home," McCaskill says. "I won't make partner if I'm not working full time—and my earnings potential is higher." Schock's response: he'd love to be a full-time father. "He has a lot more patience than I do," McCaskill says. "I think he would be a better parent for our kids." With his master's degree and experience, Schock doesn't think a few years off would kill his career. "She would lose more than I would," Schock says. As more Alpha Earners roam the earth, that kind of outlook may be worth a premium. Forget doctors or lawyers. For a certain kind of woman, a laid-back guy like Ryan Schock may become the ultimate good catch.

With KAREN SPRINGEN, PAT WINGERT, ELLISE PIERCE, NADINE JOSEPH, VANESSA JUAREZ, DANIEL I. DORFMAN, JULIE SCELFO, TARA WEINGARTEN and HILARY SHENFELD

WE'RE NOT IN THE MOOD

For married couples with kids and busy jobs, sex just isn't what it used to be. How stress causes strife in the bedroom—and beyond.

BY KATHLEEN DEVENY

FOR MADDIE WEINREICH, SEX HAD ALWAYS BEEN A JOY. IT helped her recharge her batteries and reconnect with her husband, Roger. But teaching yoga, raising two kids and starting up a business—not to mention cooking, cleaning and renovating the house—left her exhausted. She often went to bed before her husband, and was asleep by the time he joined her. Their once steamy love life slowly cooled. When Roger wanted to have sex, she would say she was too beat. He tried to be romantic; to set the mood he'd light a candle in their bedroom. "I would see it and say, 'Oh, God, not that candle'," Maddie recalls. "It was just the feeling that I had to give something I didn't have."

Lately, it seems, we're just not in the mood. We're overworked, anxious about the economy—and we have to drive our kids to way too many T-Ball games. Or maybe it's all those libido-dimming antidepressants we're taking. We resent spouses who never pick up the groceries or their dirty socks. And if we actually find we have 20 minutes at the end of the day—after bath time and story time and juice-box time and e-mail time—who wouldn't rather zone out to Leno than have sex? Sure, passion ebbs and flows in even the healthiest of relationships, but judging from the conversation of the young moms at the next table at Starbucks, it sounds like we're in the midst of a long dry spell.

It's difficult to say exactly how many of the 113 million married Americans are too exhausted or too grumpy to get it on, but some psychologists estimate that 15 to 20 percent of couples have sex no more than 10 times a year, which is how the experts define sexless marriage. And even couples who don't meet that definition still feel like they're not having sex as often as they used to. Despite the stereotype that women are more likely to dodge sex, it's often the men who decline. The number of sexless marriages is "a grossly underreported statistic," says therapist Michele Weiner Davis, author of "The Sex-Starved Marriage."

IF SO, THE PROBLEM MUST BE HUGE, GIVEN HOW MUCH WE already hear about it. Books like "The Sex-Starved Marriage," "Rekindling Desire: A Step-by-Step Program to Help Low-Sex and No-Sex Marriages" and "Resurrecting Sex" have become talk-show fodder. Dr. Phil has weighed in on the crisis; his Web site proclaims "the epidemic is undeniable." Avlimil, an herbal concoction that promises to help women put sex back into sexless marriage, had sales of 200,000 packages in January, its first month on the market. The company says it's swamped with as many as 3,000 calls a day from women who are desperately seeking desire. Not that the problem is confined to New Agers: former U.S. Labor secretary Robert Reich jokes about the pressure couples are under in speeches he gives on overworked Americans. Have you heard of DINS? he asks his audience. It stands for dual income, no sex.

Sex and the Century: A History

Over the past 100 years, our understanding of sexual behavior has changed dramatically—and it's still evolving. From Sigmund to Sarah Jessica and Lucy to Lorena, here are some of the highlights:

1905 Sigmund Freud's 'Three Essays on Sexuality' misinform generations about the nature of the female orgasm.

1934 Henry Miller's 'Tropic of Cancer,' a semifictional memoir, debuts in Paris. But the expatiriate's libidinous adventures get banned in the United States.

1952 Lucille Ball is the first pregnant woman to play a mother-to-be in a sitcom—but she isn't allowed to say the word 'pregnancy' on TV.

1953 Alred Kinsey publishes 'Sexual Behavior in the Human Female,' the first major U.S. survey on women's sexual habits. He finds that Americans' attitudes don't match their behavior—50 percent have had premarital sex.

December 1953 Marilyn Monroe takes it all off in the first issue of Playboy. Hugh Hefner's open love letter to bachelorhood.

1960 The Food and Drug Administration OKs the birth-control pill, fueling the sexual revolution.

1962 Helen Gurley Brown publishes her best-selling book 'Sex and the Single Girl.'

1965 In *Griswold v. Connecticut*, the Supreme Court rules that the government cannot regulate a married couple's use of birth control.

1966 William Masters and Virginia Johnson's 'Human Sexual Response' finds that half of all U.S. Marriages are plagued by some kind of sexual inadequacy.

1970 Female college students nationwide adopt 'Our Bodies, Ourselves' as their bible on health and sexuality.

1973 In *Roe v. Wade*, the Supreme Court decides that a woman's right to privacy encompasses her decision to terminate a pregnancy.

1981 State Supreme Court cases in Massachusetts and New Jersey rule that husbands can be prosecuted for raping their wives—overturning the centuries-old marital-rape exception.

1984 Researchers isolate the virus responsible for causing AIDS.

1987 In 'Fatal Attraction,' Michael Douglas and Glenn Close share a one-night stand that turns mighty ugly. Mmm, rabbit.

1993 Lorena Bobbit cuts off her husband's penis with a kitchen knife. Men nationwide cross their legs a little tighter.

June 2003 HBO's 'Sex and the City,' which candidly chronicles the love lives of four professional, single women in New York City, kicks off its final season.

—MELISSA BREWSTER

LOOKING FOR LOVE: New Yorkers Rosemary Breslin and her husband, Tony Dunne, joke that they've shelved sex till 2004.

Marriage counselors can't tell you how much sex you should be having, but most agree that you should be having *some*. Sex is only a small part of a good union, but happy marriages usually include it. Frequency of sex may be a measure of a marriage's long-term health; if it suddenly starts to decline, it can be a leading indicator of deeper problems, just like "those delicate green frogs that let us know when we're destroying the environment," says psychologist John Gottman, who runs the Family Research Lab (dubbed the Love Lab) at the University of Washington. Marriage pros say intimacy is often the glue that holds a couple together over time. If either member of a couple is miserable with the amount of sex in a marriage, it can cause devastating problems—and, in some cases, divorce. It can affect moods and spill over into all aspects of life—relationships with other family members, even performance in the office.

Best-selling novels and prime-time sit-coms only reinforce the idea that we're not having sex. In the opening pages of Allison Pearson's portrait of a frazzled working mom, "I Don't Know How She Does It," the novel's heroine, Kate Reddy, carefully brushes each of her molars 20 times. She's not fighting cavities. She's stalling in the hopes that her husband will fall asleep and won't try to have sex with her. (That way, she can skip a shower the next morning.) And what would Ray Romano joke about on his hit series "Everybody Loves Raymond" if he didn't have to wheedle sex out of his TV wife? Romano, who has four kids, including 10-year-old twins, says his comedy is inspired by real life. "After kids, everything changes," he told NEWSWEEK. "We're having sex about every three months. If I have sex, I know my quarterly estimated taxes must be due. And if it's oral sex, I know it's time to renew my driver's license."

"It wasn't that I didn't love him. It had nothing to do with him. What it boiled down to was being exhausted."

—TARA PATERSON

Yet some couples seem to accept that sexless marriage is as much a part of modern life as traffic and e-mail. It's a given for Ann, a 39-year-old lawyer with two kids who lives in Brooklyn. When she and her husband were first married, they had sex almost every day. Now their 5-year-old daughter comes into their bedroom every night. Pretty soon, the dog starts whining to get on the bed, too. "At 3 or 4 a.m., I kick my husband out for snoring and he ends up sleeping in my daughter's princess twin bed with the Tinkerbell night light blinking in his face," she says. "So how are we supposed to have sex?"

The statistical evidence would seem to show everything is fine. Married couples say they have sex 68.5 times a year, or slightly more than once a week, according to a 2002 study by the highly respected National Opinion Research Center at the University of Chicago, and the NORC numbers haven't changed much over the past 10 years. At least according to what people tell researchers, DINS are most likely an urban myth: working women appear to have sex just as often as their stay-at-home counterparts. And for what it's worth, married people have 6.9 more sexual encounters a year than people who have never been married. After all, you can't underestimate the value of having an (occasionally) willing partner conveniently located in bed next to you.

But any efforts to quantify our love lives must be taken with a shaker of salt. The problem, not surprisingly, is that people aren't very candid about how often they have sex. Who wants to sound like a loser when he's trying to make a contribution to social science? When pressed, nearly everyone defaults to a respectable "once or twice a week," a benchmark that probably seeped into our collective consciousness with the 1953 Kinsey Report, a study that's considered flawed because of its unrepresentative, volunteer sample.

"As a result, we have no idea what's 'normal'," says Pepper Schwartz, a sociologist and author of "Everything You Know About Love and Sex Is Wrong." Her best guess: three times a week during the first year of marriage, much less over time. When people believe they have permission to complain, she says, they often admit to having sex less than once a month: "And these are couples who like each other!"

In fact, the problem may be just as much perception as reality. Because we have the 100-times-a-year myth in our minds, and because there are so many movies and TV shows out there with characters who frequently have better-than-you-get sex, it's easy to think that everybody else is having more fun. Forget the four hotties on HBO's "Sex and the City." Even Ruth Fisher, the frumpy, middle-aged widow on the network's "Six Feet Under," gets lucky week after week. Armed with birth-control pills and dog-eared copies of "The Sensuous Woman," boomers were the front line of the sexual revolution. They practically invented guilt-free, premarital sex, and they know what they're missing better than any previous generation in history. "Boomers are the first generation to imagine that they can have exciting monogamous sex through old age," says Marty Klein, a marriage and sex therapist in Palo Alto, Calif. "The collision between that expectation and reality is pretty upsetting for most people."

And sexlessness has a long and rich tradition. In Aristophanes' bawdy play "Lysistrata," written in 411 B.C., Spartan and Athenian women agree to withhold sex from their husbands until the two warring city-states make peace. Virginia Woolf's Mrs. Dalloway was in a sexless marriage; it's likely Dorothea Brooke and Edward Casaubon, characters in George Eliot's "Middlemarch," were, too. And what about the "frigid" housewives of the 1950s?

Marriage experts say there's no single reason we're suddenly so unhappy with our sex lives. Many of us are depressed; last year Americans filled more than 200 million prescriptions for antidepressants. The sexual landscape may have been transformed in the last 40 years by birth control, legalized abortion and a better understanding of women's sexuality. But women have changed, too. Since they surged into the workplace in the 1970s, their economic power has grown steadily. Women now make up 47 percent of the work force; they're awarded 57 percent of all bachelor's degrees. About 30 percent of working women now earn more than their husbands.

Like never before, women have the financial clout to leave their husbands if they choose. In his new book, "Mismatch: The Growing Gulf Between Women and Men," sociologist Andrew Hacker says women are less and less inclined to stay married when they're not emotionally satisfied. Wives say they were the driving force in 56.2 percent of divorces, according to Hacker, while men say they were the ones who wanted out only 23.3 percent of the time. When women have those kinds of choices, marital "duties" become options and the debate over how much, or how little, sex to have is fundamentally altered.

MEANWHILE, FAMILIES HAVE CHANGED. THE YEAR AFTER the first child is born has always been a hazardous time for marriages—more divorces happen during those sleepless months than at any other time in a marriage, except for the very first year. But some researchers say parents are now obsessed with their children in a way that can be unhealthy. Kids used to go to dance class or take piano lessons once a week; now parents organize an array of activities—French classes, cello lessons and three different sports—that would make an air-traffic controller dizzy. And do you remember being a child at a restaurant with your parents and having every adult at the table focus on your happiness? No? That's probably because you weren't taken along.

Working parents who wish they could spend more time with their kids often compensate by dragging their brood everywhere with them. That means couples are sacrificing sleep and companionship. Parents of infants sometimes stop thinking of themselves as sexual beings altogether. Gottman recalls treating a couple with a 4-month-old; the wife was nursing. One morning the husband reached over and caressed his wife's breast. The woman sat bolt upright in bed and said, "Those are for *Jonathan*." "They laugh about it now," Gottman says. "But you can understand why a guy might withdraw in that kind of situation."

"We say, 'Meet me in the bedroom at noon.' We put on music and light candles and take some time to enjoy each other."

REGENA THOMASHAUER

There's another theme winding through popular culture and private conversations. Because let's face it: no one is *really* too tired to have sex. Arguing over whether you should have sex can easily take longer than the act itself. For many couples, consciously or not, sex has become a weapon. A lot of women out there are mad. Working mothers, stay-at-home moms, even women without kids. They're mad that their husband couldn't find the babysitter's home number if his life depended on it. Mad that he would never think to pick up diapers or milk on his way home. Mad that he doesn't have to sing all the verses of "The Wheels on the Bus" while trying to blow-dry his hair. Those of us who were weaned on "Fear of Flying" or "Our Bodies, Ourselves" understand that we're responsible for our own orgasms. But then couldn't somebody else take responsibility for the laundry once in a while?

Researchers say women have some legitimate gripes. Most two-income couples without children divide up the household chores pretty evenly. After the kids come, however, men may be happy to play with Junior, but they actually do *less* around the house. Men's contributions to household chores increased dramatically in the '70s and '80s, but haven't changed much since then, according to Andrew Cherlin, a sociologist at Johns Hopkins. And it isn't just that Dad isn't doing the dishes. Researchers say many new fathers—55 percent—actually start spending *more time* at work after a child is born. Experts can only

speculate on why: fathers may suddenly take their role as breadwinner more seriously. Others may feel slighted by how much attention their wives lavish on the new baby.

But men are mad, too. "The big loser between job, kids and the dogs is me," says Alex, a 35-year-old financial executive from Manhattan. "I need more sex, but that's not the whole story. I want more time alone with my wife and I want more attention." They may not be perfect, but most husbands today do far more around the house than their fathers would have ever dreamed of doing. They're also more involved than ever in their children's lives. And they want points for it, points they're not getting.

Experts say very few women openly withhold sex. More often, lingering resentments slowly drive a wedge between partners. After two kids and 10 years of marriage, Bill, an actor in his 50s, loves his wife, Laurie (not their real names), though he'd like to have sex more often than the once or twice a month they average now. Laurie, a graphic designer in her 40s, agreed to hire a babysitter and make a standing Saturday-night date. But when Saturday rolled around, she was too tired to go out. They missed the next week's appointment, too. She's tired, she says, but resentful, too. "I get angry because he doesn't help around the house enough or with the kids. He sees the groceries sitting on the counter. Why doesn't he take them out of the bag and put them away? How can I get sexy when I'm ticked off all the time?"

Advice on how to stay connected, however, varies widely. Traditionally, marriage counselors have focused on bridging emotional gaps between husbands and wives, with the idea that better sex flows out of better communication. More important than a fancy meal at a restaurant (where you can still have a rip-roaring fight, of course) is to just make time to sit down and talk. The Weinreichs managed to rekindle romance after their sons, now 18 and 21, got a little older. All it really took, Maddie says, was being more committed to intimacy.

But a new breed of marriage therapists take a more action-oriented approach. Regena Thomashauer, a relationship counselor and author of "Mama Gena's Owner's and Operator's Guide to Men," agrees that scheduling time together is essential. Use the time to have sex, she urges. Michele and Marcelo Sandoval, 40 and 42, respectively, sought help from Thomashauer when they were expecting their first child; now they make two "dates" a week. "We call them dates," says Marcelo, "but we know it means sex, and we make it a priority."

Author Weiner Davis has a similar strategy: just do it. Don't wait until you're in the mood. And view thoughtful gestures, such as letting your spouse sleep in, as foreplay. Chris Paterson, 31, and his wife, Tara, 29, say Weiner Davis has helped them. Early in their marriage, they had sex nearly every night. But after she gave birth to their first child, Tara lost interest. Their nightly sessions became infrequent events. In addition to raising the kids, now 6 and 2, both Tara and Chris run their own businesses—she has a Web site called justformom.com and he's a general contractor. Tara says she's just exhausted. Chris also shoulders part of the blame. "I haven't always been the most romantic, getting-her-in-the-mood kind of individual," he says. Since talking to Weiner Davis and reading her book, Chris and Tara say they now have sex almost once a week, when they "try really hard."

"When you have young children and you're working, your husband goes from the top of the food chain to the bottom."

MADDIE WEINREICH

Most therapists do agree on one thing. You can't force a sexy situation. There's nothing wrong with dressing up like a cowgirl or answering the front door in "black mesh stockings, and an apron—that's all," a la Marabel Morgan's 1973 classic, "Total Woman." But if it feels silly, it won't work. Rosemary Breslin, 45, a writer and filmmaker in New York, says she still has a great relationship with her husband, Tony Dunne. "But one of the things I ask him is, 'Are we going to have sex in 2003 or are we shelving it to 2004?' I asked him what he would do if I put on a black negligee, and he said he would laugh." Maybe she should persuade him to help out a little more around the house. After all, we know there's nothing sexier these days than a man who takes out the trash without being asked.

With HOLLY PETERSON, PAT WINGERT, KAREN SPRINGEN, JULIE SCELFO, MELISSA BREWSTER, TARA WEINGARTEN and JOAN RAYMOND

The *Battle* for Your Brain

Science is developing ways to boost intelligence, expand memory, and more. But will you be allowed to change your own mind?

By *Ronald Bailey*

"We're on the verge of profound changes in our ability to manipulate the brain," says Paul Root Wolpe, a bioethicist at the University of Pennsylvania. He isn't kidding. The dawning age of neuroscience promises not just new treatments for Alzheimer's and other brain diseases but enhancements to improve memory, boost intellectual acumen, and fine-tune our emotional responses. "The next two decades will be the golden age of neuroscience," declares Jonathan Moreno, a bioethicist at the University of Virginia. "We're on the threshold of the kind of rapid growth of information in neuroscience that was true of genetics 15 years ago."

One man's golden age is another man's dystopia. One of the more vociferous critics of such research is Francis Fukuyama, who warns in his book *Our Posthuman Future* that "we are already in the midst of this revolution" and *"we should use the power of the state to regulate it"* (emphasis his). In May a cover story in the usually pro-technology *Economist* worried that "neuroscientists may soon be able to screen people's brains to assess their mental health, to distribute that information, possibly accidentally, to employers or insurers, and to 'fix' faulty personality traits with drugs or implants on demand."

There are good reasons to consider the ethics of tinkering directly with the organ from which all ethical reflection arises. Most of those reasons boil down to the need to respect the rights of the people who would use the new technologies. Some of the field's moral issues are common to all biomedical research: how to design clinical trials ethically, how to ensure subjects' privacy, and so on. Others are peculiar to neurology. It's not clear, for example, whether people suffering from neurodegenerative disease can give informed consent to be experimented on.

Last May the Dana Foundation sponsored an entire conference at Stanford on "neuroethics." Conferees deliberated over issues like the moral questions raised by new brain scanning techniques, which some believe will lead to the creation of truly effective lie detectors. Participants noted that scanners might also be able to pinpoint brain abnormalities in those accused of breaking the law, thus changing our perceptions of guilt and innocence. Most nightmarishly, some worried that governments could one day use brain implants to monitor and perhaps even control citizens' behavior.

But most of the debate over neuroethics has not centered around patients' or citizens' autonomy, perhaps because so many of the field's critics themselves hope to restrict that autonomy in various ways. The issue that most vexes *them* is the possibility that neuroscience might enhance previously "normal" human brains.

The tidiest summation of their complaint comes from the conservative columnist William Satire. "Just as we have anti-depressants today to elevate mood;" he wrote after the Dana conference, "tomorrow we can expect a kind of Botox for the brain to smooth out wrinkled temperaments, to turn shy people into extroverts, or to bestow a sense of humor on a born grouch. But what price will human nature pay for these nonhuman artifices?"

Truly effective neuropharmaceuticals that improve moods and sharpen mental focus are already widely available and taken by millions. While there is some controversy about the effectiveness of Prozac, Paxil, and Zoloft, nearly 30 million Americans have taken them, with mostly positive results. In his famous 1993 book *Listening to Prozac*, the psychiatrist Peter Kramer describes patients taking the drug as feeling "better than well." One

Prozac user, called Tess, told him that when she isn't taking the medication, "I am not myself."

One Pill Makes You Smarter...

That's exactly what worries Fukuyama, who thinks Prozac looks a lot like *Brave New World*'s soma. The pharmaceutical industry, he declares, is producing drugs that "provide self-esteem in the bottle by elevating serotonin in the brain." If you need a drug to be your "self," these critics ask, do you really have a self at all?

Another popular neuropharmaceutical is Ritalin, a drug widely prescribed to remedy attention deficit hyperactivity disorder (ADHD), which is characterized by agitated behavior and an inability to focus on tasks. Around 1.5 million schoolchildren take Ritalin, which recent research suggests boosts the activity of the neurotransmitter dopamine in the brain. Like all psychoactive drugs, it is not without controversy. Perennial psychiatric critic Peter Breggin argues that millions of children are being "drugged into more compliant or submissive state[s]" to satisfy the needs of harried parents and school officials. For Fukuyama, Ritalin is prescribed to control rambunctious children because "parents and teachers...do not want to spend the time and energy necessary to discipline, divert, entertain, or train difficult children the old-fashioned way."

Unlike the more radical Breggin, Fukuyama acknowledges that drugs such as Prozac and Ritalin have helped millions when other treatments have failed. Still, he worries about their larger social consequences. "There is a disconcerting symmetry between Prozac and Ritalin," he writes. "The former is prescribed heavily for depressed women lacking in self-esteem; it gives them more the alpha-male feeling that comes with high serotonin levels. Ritalin, on the other hand, is prescribed largely for young boys who do not want to sit still in class because nature never designed them to behave that way. Together, the two sexes are gently nudged toward that androgynous median personality, self-satisfied and socially compliant, that is the current politically correct outcome in American society."

> What really worries critics is that Prozac and Ritalin may be the pharmacological equivalent of bearskins and stone axes compared to the new drugs that are coming.

Although there are legitimate questions here, they're related not to the chemicals themselves but to who makes the decision to use them. Even if Prozac and Ritalin can help millions of people, that doesn't mean schools should be able to force them on any student who is unruly or bored. But by the same token, even if you accept the most radical critique of the drug—that ADHD is not a real disorder to begin with—that doesn't mean Americans who exhibit the symptoms that add up to an ADHD diagnosis should not be allowed to alter their mental state chemically, if that's an outcome they want and a path to it they're willing to take.

Consider Nick Megibow, a senior majoring in philosophy at Gettysburg College. "Ritalin made my life a lot better, he reports. "Before I started taking Ritalin as a high school freshman, I was doing really badly in my classes. I had really bad grades, Cs and Ds mostly. By sophomore year, I started taking Ritalin, and it really worked amazingly. My grades improved dramatically to mostly As and Bs. It allows me to focus and get things done rather than take three times the amount of time that it should take to finish something." If people like Megibow don't share Fukuyama's concerns about the wider social consequences of their medication, it's because they're more interested, quite reasonably, in feeling better and living a successful life.

What really worries critics like Satire and Fukuyama is that Prozac and Ritalin may be the neuropharmacological equivalent of bearskins and stone axes compared to the new drugs that are coming. Probably the most critical mental function to be enhanced is memory. And this, it turns out, is where the most promising work is being done. At Princeton, biologist Joe Tsien's laboratory famously created smart mice by genetically modifying them to produce more NMDA brain receptors, which are critical for the formation and maintenance of memories. Tsien's mice were much faster learners than their unmodified counterparts. "By enhancing learning, that is, memory acquisition, animals seem to be able to solve problems faster," notes Tsien. He believes his work has identified an important target that will lead other researchers to develop drugs that enhance memory.

A number of companies are already hard at work developing memory drugs. Cortex Pharmaceuticals has developed a class of compounds called AMPA receptor modulators, which enhance the glutamate-based transmission between brain cells. Preliminary results indicate that the compounds do enhance memory and cognition in human beings. Memory Pharmaceuticals, co-founded by Nobel laureate Eric Kandel, is developing a calcium channel receptor modulator that increases the sensitivity of neurons and allows them to transmit information more speedily and a nicotine receptor modulator that plays a role in synaptic plasticity. Both modulators apparently improve memory. Another company, Targacept, is working on the nicotinic receptors as well.

All these companies hope to cure the memory deficits that some 30 million baby boomers will suffer as they age. If these compounds can fix deficient memories, it is likely that they can enhance normal memories as well. Tsien points out that a century ago the encroaching senility of Alzheimer's disease might have been considered part of the "normal" progression of aging. "So it depends on how you define normal," he says. "Today we know that most people have less good memories after age 40 and I don't believe that's a normal process."

Eight Objections

And so we face the prospect of pills to improve our mood, our memory, our intelligence, and perhaps more. Why would anyone object to that?

Eight objections to such enhancements recur in neuro-ethicists' arguments. None of them is really convincing.

• *Neurological enhancements permanently change the brain.* Erik Parens of the Hastings Center, a bioethics think tank, argues that it's better to enhance a child's performance by changing his environment than by changing his brain—that it's better to, say, reduce his class size than to give him Ritalin. But this is a false dichotomy. Reducing class size is aimed at changing the child's biology too, albeit indirectly. Activities like teaching are supposed to induce biological changes in a child's brain, through a process called *learning*.

Fukuyama falls into this same error when he suggests that even if there is some biological basis for their condition, people with ADHD "clearly...can do things that would affect their final degree of attentiveness or hyperactivity. Training, character, determination, and environment more generally would all play important roles." So can Ritalin, and much more expeditiously, too. "What is the difference between Ritalin and the Kaplan SAT review?" asks the Dartmouth neuroscientist Michael Gazzaniga. "It's six of one and a half dozen of the other. If both can boost SAT scores by, say, 120 points, I think it's immaterial which way it's done."

• *Neurological enhancements are anti-egalitarian.* A perennial objection to new medical technologies is the one Patens calls "unfairness in the distribution of resources." In other words, the rich and their children will get access to brain enhancements first, and will thus acquire more competitive advantages over the poor.

This objection rests on the same false dichotomy as the first. As the University of Virginia's Moreno puts it, "We don't stop people from giving their kids tennis lessons," If anything, the new enhancements might *increase* social equality. Moreno notes that neuropharmaceuticals are likely to be more equitably distributed than genetic enhancements, because "after all, a pill is easier to deliver than DNA."

• *Neurological enhancements are self-defeating.* Not content to argue that the distribution of brain enhancements won't be egalitarian enough, some critics turn around and argue that it will be too egalitarian. Parens has summarized this objection succinctly: "If everyone achieved the same relative advantage with a given enhancement, then ultimately no one's position would change; the 'enhancement' would have failed if its purpose was to increase competitive advantage."

This is a flagrant example of the zero-sum approach that afflicts so much bioethical thought. Let's assume, for the sake of argument, that everyone in society will take a beneficial brain-enhancing drug. Their relative positions may not change, but the overall productivity and wealth of society would increase considerably, making everyone better off. Surely that is a social good.

• *Neurological enhancements are difficult to refuse.* Why exactly would everyone in the country take the same drug? Because, the argument goes, competitive pressures in our go-go society will be so strong that a person will be forced to take a memory-enhancing drug just to keep up with everyone else. Even if the law protects freedom of choice, social pressures will draw us in.

For one thing, this misunderstands the nature of the technology. It's not simply a matter of popping a pill and suddenly zooming ahead. "I know a lot of smart people who don't amount to a row of beans," says Gazzaniga. "They're just happy underachieving, living life below their potential. So a pill that pumps up your intellectual processing power won't necessarily give you the drive and ambition to use it."

Beyond that, it's not as though we don't all face competitive pressures anyway—to get into and graduate from good universities, to constantly upgrade skills, to buy better computers and more productive software, whatever. Some people choose to enhance themselves by getting a Ph.D. in English; others are happy to stop their formal education after high school. It's not clear why a pill should be more irresistible than higher education, or why one should raise special ethical concerns while the other does not.

• *Neurological enhancements undermine good character.* For some critics, the comparison to higher education suggests a different problem. We should strive for what we get, they suggest; taking a pill to enhance cognitive functioning is just too easy. As Fukuyama puts it: "The normal, and morally acceptable, way of overcoming low self-esteem was to struggle with oneself and with others, to work hard, to endure painful sacrifices, and finally to rise and be seen as having done so."

"By denying access to brain-enhancing drugs, people like Fukuyama are advocating an exaggerated stoicism," counters Moreno. "I don't see the benefit or advantage of that kind of tough love." Especially since there will still be many different ways to achieve things and many difficult challenges in life. Brain-enhancing drugs might ease some of our labors, but as Moreno notes, "there are still lots of hills to climb, and they are pretty steep." Cars, computers, and washing machines have tremendously enhanced our ability to deal with formerly formidable tasks. That doesn't mean life's struggles have disappeared—just that we can now tackle the next ones.

• *Neurological enhancements undermine personal responsibility.* Carol Freedman, a philosopher at Williams College, argues that what is at stake "is a conception of ourselves as responsible agents, not machines." Fukuyama extends the point, claiming that "ordinary people" are eager to "medicalize as much of their behavior as possible and thereby reduce their responsibility for their own actions." As an example, he suggests that people who claim to suffer from ADHD "want to absolve themselves of personal responsibility."

But we are not debating people who might use an ADHD diagnosis as an excuse to behave irresponsibly. We are speaking of people who use Ritalin to change their behavior. Wouldn't it be more irresponsible of them to not take corrective action?

• *Neurological enhancements enforce dubious norms.* There are those who assert that corrective action might be irresponsible after all, depending on just what it is that you're trying to correct. People might take neuropharmaceuticals, some warn, to conform to a harmful social conception of normality. Many bioethicists—Georgetown University's Margaret Little, for example—argue that we can already see this process in action among women who resort to expensive and painful cosmetic surgery to conform to a social ideal of feminine beauty. Never mind for the moment that beauty norms for both men and women have never been so diverse. Providing and choosing to avail oneself of that surgery makes one complicit in norms that are morally wrong, the critics argue. After all, people should be judged not by their physical appearances but by the content of their characters.

That may be so, but why should someone suffer from society's slights if she can overcome them with a nip here and a tuck there? The norms may indeed be suspect, but the suffering is experienced by real people whose lives are consequently diminished. Little acknowledges this point, but argues that those who benefit from using a technology to conform have a moral obligation to fight against the suspect norm. Does this mean people should be given access to technologies they regard as beneficial only if they agree to sign on to a bioethical fatwa?

Of course, we should admire people who challenge norms they disagree with and live as they wish, but why should others be denied relief just because some bioethical commissars decree that society's misdirected values must change? Change may come, but real people should not be sacrificed to some restrictive bioethical utopia in the meantime. Similarly, we should no doubt value depressed people or people with bad memories just as highly as we do happy geniuses, but until that glad day comes people should be allowed to take advantage of technologies that improve their lives in the society in which they actually live.

Furthermore, it's far from clear that everyone will use these enhancements in the same ways. There are people who alter their bodies via cosmetic surgery to bring them closer to the norm, and there are people who alter their bodies via piercings and tattoos to make them more individually expressive. It doesn't take much imagination to think of unusual or unexpected ways that Americans might use mind-enhancing technologies. Indeed, the war on drugs is being waged, in part, against a small but significant minority of people who prefer to alter their consciousness in socially disapproved ways.

• *Neurological enhancements make us inauthentic.* Parents and others worry that the users of brain-altering chemicals are less authentically themselves when they're on the drug. Some of them would reply that the exact opposite is the case. In *Listening to Prozac*, Kramer chronicles some dramatic transformations in the personalities and attitudes of his patients once they're on the drug. The aforementioned Tess tells him it was "as if I had been in a drugged state all those years and now I'm clearheaded."

> Cars, computers, and washing machines have tremendously enhanced our ability to deal with formerly formidable tasks. That doesn't mean life's struggles have disappeared—just that we can now tackle the next ones.

Again, the question takes a different shape when one considers the false dichotomy between biological and "nonbiological" enhancements. Consider a person who undergoes a religious conversion and emerges from the experience with a more upbeat and attractive personality. Is he no longer his "real" self? Must every religious convert be deprogrammed?

Even if there were such a thing as a "real" personality, why should you stick with it if you don't like it? If you're socially withdrawn and a pill can give you a more vivacious and outgoing manner, why not go with it? After all, you're choosing to take responsibility for being the "new" person the drug helps you to be.

Authenticity and Responsibility

"Is it a drug-induced personality or has the drug cleared away barriers to the real personality?" asks the University of Pennsylvania's Wolpe. Surely the person who is choosing to use the drug is in a better position to answer that question than some bioethical busybody.

This argument over authenticity lies at the heart of the neuroethicists' objections. If there is a single line that divides the supporters of neurological freedom from those who would restrict the new treatments, it is the debate over whether a natural state of human being exists and, if so, how appropriate it is to modify it. Wolpe makes the point that in one sense cognitive enhancement resembles its opposite, Alzheimer's disease. A person with Alzheimer's loses her personality. Similarly, an enhanced individual's personality may become unrecognizable to those who knew her before.

Not that this is unusual. Many people experience a version of this process when they go away from their homes to college or the military. They return as changed people with new capacities, likes, dislikes, and social styles, and they often find that their families and friends no longer relate to them in the old ways. Their brains have been changed by those experiences, and they are not the same people they were before they went away. Change makes most people uncomfortable, probably never more so than when it happens to a loved one. Much of the neuro-Luddites' case rests on a belief in an unvarying, static personality, something that simply doesn't exist.

It isn't just personality that changes over time. Consciousness itself is far less static than we've previously assumed, a fact that raises contentious questions of free will and determinism. Neuroscientists are finding more and more of the underlying automatic processes operating in the brain, allowing us to take a sometimes disturbing look under our own hoods. "We're finding out that by the time we're conscious of doing something, the brain's already done it," explains Gazzaniga. Consciousness, rather than being the director of our activities, seems instead to be a way for the brain to explain to itself why it did something.

Haunting the whole debate over neuroscientific research and neuroenhancements is the fear that neuroscience will undercut notions of responsibility and free will. Very preliminary research has suggested that many violent criminals do have altered brains. At the Stanford conference, *Science* editor Donald Kennedy suggested that once we know more about brains, our legal system will have to make adjustments in how we punish those who break the law. A murderer or rapist might one day plead innocence on the grounds that "my amygdala made me do it." There is precedent for this: The legal system already mitigates criminal punishment when an offender can convince a jury he's so mentally ill that he cannot distinguish right from wrong.

> Like any technology, neurological enhancements can be abused. But critics have not made a strong case for why individuals should not be allowed to take advantage of breakthroughs.

Of course, there are other ways such discoveries might pan out in the legal system, with results less damaging to social order but still troubling for notions of personal autonomy. One possibility is that an offender's punishment might be reduced if he agrees to take a pill that corrects the brain defect he blames for his crime. We already hold people responsible when their drug use causes harm to others—most notably, with laws against drunk driving. Perhaps in the future we will hold people responsible if

they fail to take drugs that would help prevent them from behaving in harmful ways. After all, which is more damaging to personal autonomy, a life confined to a jail cell or roaming free while taking a medication?

The philosopher Patricia Churchland examines these conundrums in her forthcoming book, *Brainwise: Studies in Neurophilosophy.* "Much of human social life depends on the expectation that agents have control over their actions and are responsible for their choices," she writes. "In daily life it is commonly assumed that it is sensible to punish and reward behavior so long as the person was in control and chose knowingly and intentionally." And that's the way it should remain, even as we learn more about how our brains work and how they sometimes break down.

Churchland points out that neuroscientific research by scientists like the University of Iowa's Antonio Damasio strongly shows that emotions are an essential component of viable practical reasoning about what a person should do. In other words, neuroscience is bolstering philosopher David Hume's insight that "reason is and ought only to be the slave of the passions." Patients whose affects are depressed or lacking due to brain injury are incapable of judging or evaluating between courses of action. Emotion is what prompts and guides our choices.

Churchland further argues that moral agents come to be morally and practically wise not through pure cognition but by developing moral beliefs and habits through life experiences. Our moral reflexes are honed through watching and hearing about which actions are rewarded and which are punished; we learn to be moral the same way we learn language. Consequently, Churchland concludes "the default presumption that agents are responsible for their actions is empirically necessary to an agent's learning, both emotionally and cognitively, how to evaluate the consequences of certain events and the price of taking risks."

It's always risky to try to derive an "ought" from an "is," but neuroscience seems to be implying that liberty—i.e., letting people make choices and then suffer or enjoy the consequences—is essential for inculcating virtue and maintaining social cooperation. Far from undermining personal responsibility, neuroscience may end up strengthening it.

For Neurological Liberty

Fukuyama wants to "draw red lines" to distinguish between therapy and enhancement, "directing research toward the former while putting restrictions on the latter." He adds that "the original purpose of medicine is, after all, to heal the sick, not turn healthy people into gods" He imagines a federal agency that would oversee neurological research, prohibiting anything that aims at enhancing our capacities beyond some notion of the human norm.

"For us to flourish as human beings, we have to live according to our nature, satisfying the deepest longings that we as natural beings have," Fukuyama told the Christian review *Books & Culture* last summer. "For example, our nature gives us tremendous cognitive capabilities, capability for reason, capability to learn, to teach ourselves things, to change our opinions, and so forth. What follows from that? A way of life that permits such growth is better than a life in which this capacity is shriveled and stunted in various ways." This is absolutely correct. The trouble is that Fukuyama has a shriveled, stunted vision of human nature, leading him and others to stand athwart neuroscientific advances that will make it possible for more people to take fuller advantage of their reasoning and learning capabilities.

Like any technology, neurological enhancements can be abused, especially if they're doled out—or imposed— by an unchecked authority. But Fukuyama and other critics have not made a strong case for why *individuals*, in consultation with their doctors, should not be allowed to take advantage of new neuroscientific breakthroughs to enhance the functioning of their brains. And it is those in-

dividuals that the critics will have to convince if they seriously expect to restrict this research.

It's difficult to believe that they'll manage that. In the 1960s many states outlawed the birth control pill, on the grounds that it would be too disruptive to society. Yet Americans, eager to take control of their reproductive lives, managed to roll back those laws, and no one believes that the pill could be re-outlawed today.

Moreno thinks the same will be true of the neurological advances to come. "My hunch," he says, "is that in the United States, medications that enhance our performance are not going to be prohibited." When you consider the sometimes despairing tone that Fukuyama and others like him adopt, it's hard not to conclude that on that much, at least, they agree.

Ronald Bailey is **reason's** *science correspondent and the editor of Global Warming and Other Eco-Myths: How the Environmental Movement Uses False Science to Scare Us to Death (Prima Publishing).*

UNIT 6

Development During Middle and Late Adulthood

Unit Selections

Key Points to Consider

- Does laughter serve biological functions? If so, what are the uses of laughter that are regulated by our primitive instincts?

- What are the three deadly threats alcohol abuse poses?

- Do stressors contribute to America's epidemic of back pain?

- What hard truths should workers know to keep their jobs in America?

- What is "the changing face" of America's elderly population?

- Why do some people live over 100 years in good health? What are their secrets?

- What new insights have come from the study of the Mankato nuns?

- What are the ethics of terminal care? Who should prepare advance care directives? When?

 **Links: www.dushkin.com/online/**
These sites are annotated in the World Wide Web pages.

Alzheimer's Disease Research Center
http://alzheimer.wustl.edu/adrc2//

American Psychological Association's Division 20, Adult Development and Aging
http://www.aging.ufl.edu/apadiv20/apadiv20.htm

Grief Net
http://rivendell.org

Lifestyle Factors Affecting Late Adulthood
http://www.school-for-champions.com/health/lifestyle_elderly.htm

National Aging Information Center (NAIC)
http://www.aoa.dhhs.gov/naic/

Joseph Campbell, a twentieth-century sage, said that the privilege of a lifetime is being who you are. This ego-confidence often arrives during middle and late adulthood, even as physical-confidence declines. There is a gradual slowing of the rate of mitosis of cells of all the organ systems with age. This gradual slowing of mitosis translates into a slowed rate of repair of cells of all organs. By the 40s, signs of aging can be seen in skin, skeleton, vision, hearing, smell, taste, balance, coordination, heart, blood vessels, lungs, liver, kidneys, digestive tract, immune response, endocrine functioning, and ability to reproduce. To some extent, moderate use of any body part (as opposed to disuse or misuse) helps it retain its strength, stamina, and repairability. However, by middle and late adulthood persons become increasingly aware of the aging effects of their organ systems on their total physical fitness. A loss of height occurs as spinal disks and connective tissues diminish and settle. Demineralization, especially loss of calcium, causes weakening of bones. Muscles atrophy, and the slowing of cardiovascular and respiratory responses creates a loss of stamina for exercise. All of this may seem cruel, but it occurs very gradually and need not adversely affect a person's enjoyment of life.

Healthful aging, at least in part, seems to be genetically preprogrammed. The females of many species, including humans, outlive the males. The sex hormones of females may protect them from some early aging effects. Males, in particular, experience earlier declines in their cardiovascular system. Diet and exercise can ward off many of the deleterious effects of aging. A reduction in saturated fat (low density lipid) intake coupled with regular aerobic exercise contributes to less bone demineralization, less plaque in the arteries, stronger muscles (including heart and lung muscles), and a general increase in stamina and vitality. An adequate intake of complex carbohydrates, fibrous foods, fresh fruits, fresh vegetables, unsaturated fats (high density lipids), and water also enhances good health.

Cognitive abilities do not appreciably decline with age in healthy adults. Research suggests that the speed with which the brain carries out problems involving abstract (fluid) reasoning may slow but not cease. Complex problems may simply require more time to solve with age. On the other hand, research suggests that the memory banks of older people may have more crystallized (accumulated and stored) knowledge and more insight. Creativity also frequently spurts after age 50. One's ken (range of knowledge) and practical skills (common sense) grow with age and experience. Older human beings also become experts at the cognitive tasks they frequently do. Many cultures celebrate these abilities as the "wisdom of age."

The first article about middle adulthood speaks to the urge to laugh. New brain research reported in "Emotions and the Brain: Laughter" suggests that laughing is a form of instinctive social bonding. We do not make a conscious decision to laugh. We are often unaware that we are laughing. And laughter is contagious. It makes us healthier by enhancing our immune responsivity and reducing our stress hormones. The "wisdom of age" may allow us to be more frivolous, and to take more pleasure in happy friendships within our families and communities. Children laugh freely. Somehow many adults learn to suppress laughter and to be more serious. Perhaps some wisdom and maturity is evidenced by not trying to suppress this important biological response.

The second article about middle adulthood speaks to "Alcohol's Deadly Triple Threat." Karen Springen and Barbara Kantrowitz discuss gender-differences in alcohol abuse. Men drink openly and seek help if they become addicted. Women more often hide their drinking. They risk their children's health, as well as their own with their alcohol abuse.

The third article discusses the explosion of back ailments in North America. They are the number two reason for visits to physicians, after respiratory infections. Claudia Kalb reports that 80% of Americans will experience the agony of back pain in their lives. Stress is often an etiological factor. Holistic treatment, including psychotherapy, massage therapy, acupuncture, and chiropractic manipulation are less expensive, and much less risky, than surgery.

The fourth adulthood selection outlines "12 Things You Must Know to Survive and Thrive in America." Ellis Cose's article is described as a roster of hard truths for a new age. They may be hard, but they are also valuable truths that everyone needs to know to succeed.

Erik Erikson suggested that the most important psychological conflict of late adulthood is achieving a sense of ego integrity. This is fostered by self-respect, self-esteem, love of others, and a sense that one's life has order and meaning. The articles in the subsection on late adulthood reflect Erikson's concern with experiencing ego integrity rather than despair.

"Aging's Changing Face" by Willow Lawson describes older Americans with a sense of ego integrity. They are upbeat about their age and look forward to getting up every morning. They have good sex lives, many friends, and do interesting things (e.g., education, athletic challenges). Their optimism contributes to their continuing good health.

In "Secrets of the Centenarians," Maya Pines portrays the lives of several people who are over the age of 100 but who appear to be in their 70s or early 80s. Researchers have identified genetic markers on the fourth pair of chromosomes which may contribute to longevity and good health. It may be possible in the future to manipulate the single-nucleotide polymorphisms (SNPs) to allow everyone to live as long as the centenarians being studied.

The next article discusses the longitudinal study of Mankato nuns that has helped unlock many of the secrets of Alzheimer's disease. The Human Genome Project revealed where some genetic precursors are located. The nuns have now shed light on environmental triggers, and on lifestyles that protect the brain from mental deterioration. Cardiovascular disease and lack of folic acid are triggers. Cognitive exercises and positive emotions seem to help ward off mental deterioration.

The last article describes end-of-life care. The author, Helen Sorenson, discusses the conflicting opinions which create turmoil for patients, family, friends, and health care professionals when death is imminent. "Navigating Practical Dilemmas in Terminal Care" gives useful information on how to reduce such conflicts. Family conferences should occur well ahead of the end-of-life to discuss the terms of advance care directives. Asking questions and communicating openly can prevent misunderstandings.

Emotions and the Brain:
Laughter

IF EVOLUTION COMES DOWN TO SURVIVAL OF THE FITTEST, THEN WHY DO WE JOKE AROUND SO MUCH? NEW BRAIN RESEARCH SUGGESTS THAT THE URGE TO LAUGH IS THE LUBRICANT THAT MAKES HUMANS HIGHER SOCIAL BEINGS

BY STEVEN JOHNSON

ROBERT PROVINE WANTS ME TO SEE HIS TICKLE Me Elmo doll. Wants me to hold it, as a matter of fact. It's not an unusual request for Provine. A professor of psychology and neuroscience at the University of Maryland, he has been engaged for a decade in a wide-ranging intellectual pursuit that has taken him from the panting play of young chimpanzees to the history of American sitcoms—all in search of a scientific understanding of that most unscientific of human customs: laughter.

The Elmo doll happens to incorporate two of his primary obsessions: tickling and contagious laughter. "You ever fiddled with one of these?" Provine says, as he pulls the doll out of a small canvas tote bag. He holds it up, and after a second or two, the doll begins to shriek with laughter. There's something undeniably comic in the scene: a burly, bearded man in his mid-fifties cradling a red Muppet. Provine hands Elmo to me to demonstrate the doll's vibration effect. "It brings up two interesting things," he explains, as I hold Elmo in my arms. "You have a bestselling toy that's a glorified laugh box. And when it shakes, you're getting feedback as if you're tickling."

Provine's relationship to laughter reminds me of the dramatic technique that Bertolt Brecht called the distanciation effect. Radical theater, in Brecht's vision, was supposed to distance us from our too-familiar social structures, make us see those structures with fresh eyes. In his study of laughter, Provine has been up to something comparably enlightening, helping us to recognize the strangeness of one of our most familiar emotional states. Think about that Tickle Me Elmo doll: We take it for granted that tickling causes laughter and that one person's laughter will easily "infect" other people within earshot. Even a child knows these things. (Tickling and contagious laughter are two of the distinguishing characteristics of childhood.) But when you think about them

from a distance, they are strange conventions. We can understand readily enough why natural selection would have implanted the fight-or-flight response in us or endowed us with sex drives. But the tendency to laugh when others laugh in our presence or to laugh when someone strokes our belly with a feather—what's the evolutionary advantage of that? And yet a quick glance at the Nielsen ratings or the personal ads will tell you that laughter is one of the most satisfying and sought-after states available to us.

Funnily enough, the closer Provine got to understanding why we laugh, the farther he got from humor. To appreciate the roots of laughter, you have to stop thinking about jokes.

THERE IS A LONG, SEMI-ILLUSTRIOUS HISTORY OF SCHOLARLY investigation into the nature of humor, from Freud's *Jokes and Their Relation to the Unconscious*, which may well be the least funny book about humor ever written, to a British research group that announced last year that they had determined the World's Funniest Joke. Despite the fact that the researchers said they had sampled a massive international audience in making this discovery, the winning joke revolved around New Jersey residents:

A couple of New Jersey hunters are out in the woods when one of them falls to the ground. He doesn't seem to be breathing; his eyes are rolled back in his head. The other guy whips out his cell phone and calls the emergency services. He gasps to the operator: "My friend is dead! What can I do?"

The operator says: "Take it easy. I can help. First, let's make sure he's dead." There is silence, then a shot is heard. The guy's voice comes back on the line. He says, "OK, now what?"

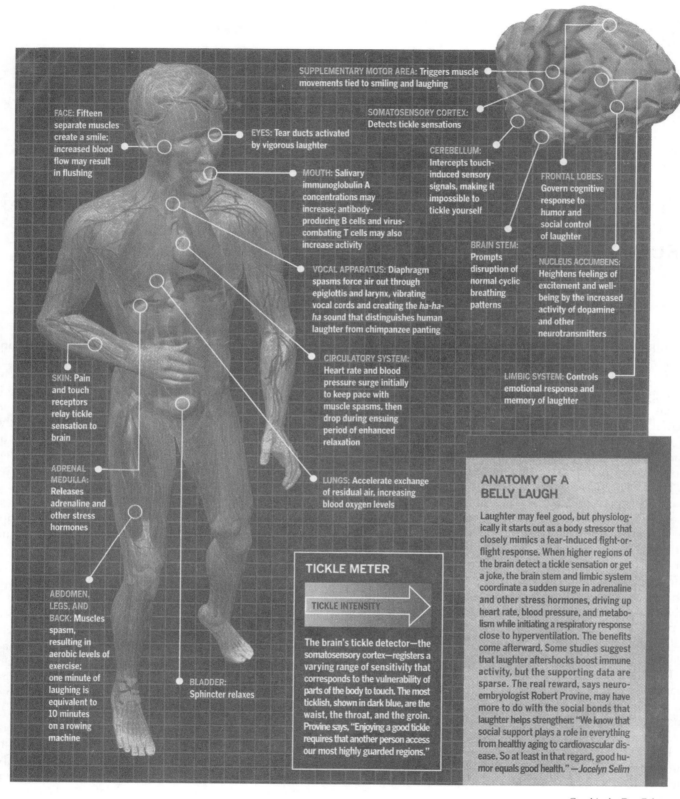

SUPPLEMENTARY MOTOR AREA: Triggers muscle movements tied to smiling and laughing

SOMATOSENSORY CORTEX: Detects tickle sensations

CEREBELLUM: Intercepts touch-induced sensory signals, making it impossible to tickle yourself

FRONTAL LOBES: Govern cognitive response to humor and social control of laughter

BRAIN STEM: Prompts disruption of normal cyclic breathing patterns

NUCLEUS ACCUMBENS: Heightens feelings of excitement and well-being by the increased activity of dopamine and other neurotransmitters

LIMBIC SYSTEM: Controls emotional response and memory of laughter

FACE: Fifteen separate muscles create a smile; increased blood flow may result in flushing

EYES: Tear ducts activated by vigorous laughter

MOUTH: Salivary immunoglobulin A concentrations may increase; antibody-producing B cells and virus-combating T cells may also increase activity

VOCAL APPARATUS: Diaphragm spasms force air out through epiglottis and larynx, vibrating vocal cords and creating the *ha-ha-ha* sound that distinguishes human laughter from chimpanzee panting

CIRCULATORY SYSTEM: Heart rate and blood pressure surge initially to keep pace with muscle spasms, then drop during ensuing period of enhanced relaxation

SKIN: Pain and touch receptors relay tickle sensation to brain

ADRENAL MEDULLA: Releases adrenaline and other stress hormones

ABDOMEN, LEGS, AND BACK: Muscles spasm, resulting in aerobic levels of exercise; one minute of laughing is equivalent to 10 minutes on a rowing machine

BLADDER: Sphincter relaxes

LUNGS: Accelerate exchange of residual air, increasing blood oxygen levels

TICKLE METER

TICKLE INTENSITY

The brain's tickle detector—the somatosensory cortex—registers a varying range of sensitivity that corresponds to the vulnerability of parts of the body to touch. The most ticklish, shown in dark blue, are the waist, the throat, and the groin. Provine says, "Enjoying a good tickle requires that another person access our most highly guarded regions."

ANATOMY OF A BELLY LAUGH

Laughter may feel good, but physiologically it starts out as a body stressor that closely mimics a fear-induced fight-or-flight response. When higher regions of the brain detect a tickle sensation or get a joke, the brain stem and limbic system coordinate a sudden surge in adrenaline and other stress hormones, driving up heart rate, blood pressure, and metabolism while initiating a respiratory response close to hyperventilation. The benefits come afterward. Some studies suggest that laughter aftershocks boost immune activity, but the supporting data are sparse. The real reward, says neuro-embryologist Robert Provine, may have more to do with the social bonds that laughter helps strengthen: "We know that social support plays a role in everything from healthy aging to cardiovascular disease. So at least in that regard, good humor equals good health." —*Jocelyn Selim*

Graphics by Don Foley

This joke illustrates that most assessments of humor's underlying structure gravitate to the notion of controlled incongruity: You're expecting *x*, and you get *y*. For the joke to work, it has to be readable on both levels. In the hunting joke there are two plausible ways to interpret the 911 operator's instructions—either the hunter checks his friend's pulse or he shoots him. The context sets you up to expect that he'll check his friend's pulse, so the—admittedly dark—humor arrives when he takes the more unlikely path. That incongruity has limits, of course: If the hunter chooses to do something utterly nonsensical—untie his shoelaces or climb a tree—the joke wouldn't be funny.

A number of studies in recent years have looked at brain activity while subjects were chuckling over a good joke—an attempt to locate a neurological funny bone. There is evidence that the frontal lobes are implicated in "getting" the joke while the brain regions associated with motor control execute the physical response of laughter. One 1999 study analyzed patients with damage to the right frontal lobes, an integrative region of the brain where emotional, logical, and perceptual data converge. The brain-damaged patients had far more difficulty than control subjects in choosing the proper punch line to a series of jokes, usually opting for absurdist, slapstick-style endings rather than traditional ones. Humor can often come in coarse, lowest-common-denominator packages, but actually getting the joke draws upon our higher brain functions.

When Provine set out to study laughter, he imagined that he would approach the problem along the lines of these humor studies: Investigating laughter meant having people listen to jokes and other witticisms and watching what happened. He began by simply observing casual conversations, counting the number of times that people laughed while listening to someone speaking. But very quickly he realized that there was a fundamental flaw in his assumptions about how laughter worked. "I started recording all these conversations," Provine says, "and the numbers I was getting—I didn't believe them when I saw them. The speakers were laughing more than the listeners. Every time that would happen, I would think, 'OK, I have to go back and start over again because that can't be right.'"

Speakers, it turned out, were 46 percent more likely to laugh than listeners—and what they were laughing at, more often than not, wasn't remotely funny. Provine and his team of undergrad students recorded the ostensible "punch lines" that triggered laughter in ordinary conversation. They found that only around 15 percent of the sentences that triggered laughter were traditionally humorous. In his book, *Laughter: A Scientific Investigation*, Provine lists some of the laugh-producing quotes:

I'll see you guys later./Put those cigarettes away./I hope we all do well./It was nice meeting you too./We can handle this./I see your point./I should do that, but I'm too lazy./I try to lead a normal life./I think I'm done./I told you so!

The few studies of laughter to date had assumed that laughing and humor were inextricably linked, but Provine's early research suggested that the connection was only an occasional one. "There's a dark side to laughter that we are too quick to overlook," he says. "The kids at Columbine were laughing as they walked through the school shooting their peers."

As his research progressed, Provine began to suspect that laughter was in fact about something else—not hu-

mor or gags or incongruity but our social interactions. He found support for this assumption in a study that had already been conducted, analyzing people's laughing patterns in social and solitary contexts. "You're 30 times more likely to laugh when you're with other people than you are when you're alone—if you don't count simulated social environments like laugh tracks on television," Provine says. "In fact, when you're alone, you're more likely to talk out loud to yourself than you are to laugh out loud. Much more." Think how rarely you'll laugh out loud at a funny passage in a book but how quick you'll be to make a friendly laugh when greeting an old acquaintance. Laughing is not an instinctive physical response to humor, the way a flinch responds to pain or a shiver to cold. It's a form of instinctive social bonding that humor is crafted to exploit.

PROVINE'S LAB AT THE BALTIMORE COUNTY CAMPUS OF THE University of Maryland looks like the back room at a stereo repair store—long tables cluttered with old equipment, tubes and wires everywhere. The walls are decorated with brightly colored pictures of tangled neurons, most of which were painted by Provine. (Add some Day-Glo typography and they might pass for signs promoting a Dead show at the Fillmore.) Provine's old mentor, the neuroembryologist Viktor Hamburger, glowers down from a picture hung above a battered Silicon Graphics workstation. His expression suggests a sense of concerned bafflement: "I trained you as a scientist, and here you are playing with dolls!"

The more technical parts of Provine's work—exploring the neuromuscular control of laughter and its relationship to the human and chimp respiratory systems—draw on his training at Washington University in St. Louis under Hamburger and Nobel laureate Rita Levi-Montalcini. But the most immediate way to grasp his insights into the evolution of laughter is to watch video footage of his informal fieldwork, which consists of Provine and a cameraman prowling Baltimore's inner harbor, asking people to laugh for the camera. The overall effect is like a color story for the local news, but as Provine and I watch the tapes together in his lab, I find myself looking at the laughters with fresh eyes. Again and again, a pattern repeats on the screen. Provine asks someone to laugh, and they demur, look puzzled for a second, and say something like, "I can't just laugh." Then they turn to their friends or family, and the laughter rolls out of them as though it were as natural as breathing. The pattern stays the same even as the subjects change: a group of high school students on a field trip, a married couple, a pair of college freshmen.

At one point Provine—dressed in a plaid shirt and khakis, looking something like the comedian Robert Klein—stops two waste-disposal workers driving a golf cart loaded up with trash bags. When they fail to guffaw on cue, Provine asks them why they can't muster one up.

"Because you're not funny," one of them says. They turn to each other and share a hearty laugh.

"See, you two just made each other laugh," Provine says.

"Yeah, well, we're coworkers," one of them replies.

The insistent focus on laughter patterns has a strange effect on me as Provine runs through the footage. By the time we get to the cluster of high school kids, I've stopped hearing their spoken words at all, just the rhythmic peals of laughter breaking out every 10 seconds or so. Sonically, the laughter dominates the speech; you can barely hear the dialogue underneath the hysterics. If you were an alien encountering humans for the first time, you'd have to assume that the laughing served as the primary communication method, with the spoken words interspersed as afterthoughts. After one particularly loud outbreak, Provine turns to me and says, "Now, do you think they're all individually making a conscious decision to laugh?" He shakes his head dismissively. "Of course not. In fact, we're often not aware that we're even laughing in the first place. We've vastly overrated our conscious control of laughter."

The limits of our voluntary control of laughter are most clearly exposed in studies of stroke victims who suffer from a disturbing condition known as central facial paralysis, which prevents them from voluntarily moving either the left side or the right side of their faces, depending on the location of the neurological damage. When these individuals are asked to smile or laugh on command, they produce lopsided grins: One side of the mouth curls up, the other remains frozen. But when they're told a joke or they're tickled, traditional smiles and laughs animate their entire faces. There is evidence that the physical mechanism of laughter itself is generated in the brain stem, the most ancient region of the nervous system, which is also responsible for fundamental functions like breathing. Sufferers of amyotrophic lateral sclerosis—Lou Gehrig's disease—which targets the brain stem, often experience spontaneous bursts of uncontrollable laughter, without feeling mirth. (They often undergo a comparable experience with crying as well.) Sometimes called the reptilian brain because its basic structure dates back to our reptile ancestors, the brain stem is largely devoted to our most primal instincts, far removed from our complex, higher-brain skills in understanding humor. And yet somehow, in this primitive region of the brain, we find the urge to laugh.

We're accustomed to thinking of common-but-unconscious instincts as being essential adaptations, like the startle reflex or the suckling of newborns. Why would we have an unconscious propensity for something as frivolous as laughter? As I watch them on the screen, Provine's teenagers remind me of an old Carl Sagan riff, which begins with his describing "a species of primate" that likes to gather in packs of 50 or 60 individuals, cram together in a darkened cave, and hyperventilate in unison, to the point of almost passing out. The behavior is described in such a way as to make it sound exotic and somewhat foolish, like salmon swimming furiously upstream to their deaths or butterflies traveling thousands of miles to rendezvous once a year. The joke, of course, is that the primate is *Homo sapiens*, and the group hyperventilation is our fondness for laughing together at comedy clubs or theaters, or with the virtual crowds of television laugh tracks.

I'm thinking about the Sagan quote when another burst of laughter arrives through the TV speakers, and without realizing what I'm doing, I find myself laughing along with the kids on the screen, I can't help it—their laughter is contagious.

WE MAY BE THE ONLY SPECIES ON THE PLANET THAT LAUGHS together in such large groups, but we are not alone in our appetite for laughter. Not surprisingly, our near relatives, the chimpanzees, are also avid laughers, although differences in their vocal apparatus cause the laugher to sound somewhat more like panting. "The chimpanzee's laughter is rapid and breathy, whereas ours is punctuated with glottal stops," says legendary chimp researcher Roger Fouts. "Also, the chimpanzee laughter occurs on the inhale and exhale, while ours is primarily done on our exhales. But other than these small differences, chimpanzee laughter seems to me to be just like ours in most respects."

Chimps don't do stand-up routines, of course, but they do share a laugh-related obsession with humans, one that Provine believes is central to the roots of laughter itself: Chimps love tickling. Back in his lab, Provine shows me video footage of a pair of young chimps named Josh and Lizzie playing with a human caretaker. It's a full-on ticklefest, with the chimps panting away hysterically when their bellies are scratched. "That's chimpanzee laughter you're hearing," Provine says. It's close enough to human laughter that I find myself chuckling along.

Parents will testify that ticklefests are often the first elaborate play routine they engage in with their children and one of the most reliable laugh inducers. According to Fouts, who helped teach sign language to Washoe, perhaps the world's most famous chimpanzee, the practice is just as common, and perhaps more long lived, among the chimps. "Tickling… seems to be very important to chimpanzees because it continues throughout their lives," he says. "Even Washoe at the age of 37 still enjoys tickling and being tickled by her adult family members." Among young chimpanzees that have been taught sign language, tickling is a frequent topic of conversation.

Like laughter, tickling is almost by definition a social activity. Like the incongruity theory of humor, tickling relies on a certain element of surprise, which is why it's impossible to tickle yourself. Predictable touch doesn't elicit the laughter and squirming of tickling—it's unpredictable touch that does the trick. A number of tickle-related studies have convincingly shown that tickling exploits the sensorimotor system's awareness of the difference between self and other: If the system orders your hand to move toward your belly, it doesn't register surprise when the nerve endings on your belly report being stroked. But if the touch is being generated by another sensorimotor system, the belly stroking will come as a surprise. The pleasant laughter of tickle is the way the brain responds to that touch. In both human and chimpanzee societies, that touch usually first appears in parent-child interactions and has an essential role in creating those initial bonds. "The reason [tickling and laughter] are so important," Roger Fouts says, "is because they play a role in maintaining the affinitive bonds of friendship within the family and community."

A few years ago, Jared Diamond wrote a short book with the provocative title *Why Is Sex Fun?* These recent studies suggest an evolutionary answer to the question of why tickling is fun: It encourages us to play well with others. Young children are so receptive to the rough-and-tumble play of tickle that even pretend tickling will often send them into peals of laughter. (Fouts reports that the threat of tickle has a similar effect on his chimps.) In his book, Provine suggests that "feigned tickle" can be thought of as the Original Joke, the first deliberate behavior designed to exploit the tickling-laughter circuit. Our comedy clubs and our sitcoms are culturally enhanced versions of those original playful childhood exchanges. Along with the suckling and smiling instincts, the laughter of tickle evolved as a way of cementing the bond between parents and children, laying the foundation for a behavior that then carried over into the social lives of adults. While we once laughed at the surprise touch of a parent or sibling, we now laugh at the surprise twist of a punch line.

Bowling Green State University professor Jaak Panksepp suggests that there is a dedicated "play" circuitry in the brain, equivalent to the more extensively studied fear and love circuits. Panksepp has studied the role of rough-and-tumble play in cementing social connections between juvenile rats. The play instinct is not easily suppressed. Rats that have been denied the opportunity to engage in this kind of play—which has a distinct choreography, as well as a chirping vocalization that may be the rat equivalent of laughter—will nonetheless immediately engage in play behavior given the chance. Panksepp compares it to a bird's instinct for flying. "Probably the most powerful positive emotion of all—once your tummy is full and you don't have bodily needs—is vigorous social engagement among the young," Panksepp says. "The largest amount of human laughter seems to occur in the midst of early childhood—rough-and-tumble play, chasing, all the stuff they love."

Playing is what young mammals do, and in humans and chimpanzees, laughter is the way the brain expresses the pleasure of that play. "Since laughter seems to be ritualized panting, basically what you do in laughing is replicate the sound of rough-and-tumble play," Provine says. "And you know, that's where I think it came from. Tickle is an important part of our primate heritage.

Touching and being touched is an important part of what it means to be a mammal."

THERE IS MUCH THAT WE DON'T KNOW YET ABOUT THE NEU-rological underpinnings of laughter. We do not yet know precisely why laughing feels so good; one recent study detected evidence that stimulating the nucleus accumbens, one of the brain's pleasure centers, triggered laughter. Panksepp has performed studies that indicate opiate antagonists significantly reduce the urge to play in rats, which implies that the brain's endorphin system may be involved in the pleasure of laughter. Some anecdotal and clinical evidence suggest that laughing makes you healthier by suppressing stress hormones and elevating immune system antibodies. If you think of laughter as a form of behavior that is basically synonymous with the detection of humor, the laughing-makes-you-healthier premise seems bizarre. Why would natural selection make our immune system respond to jokes? Provine's approach helps solve the mystery. Our bodies aren't responding to wisecracks and punch lines; they're responding to social connection.

In this respect, laughter reminds us that our emotional lives are as much outward bound as they are inner directed. We tend to think of emotions as private affairs, feelings that wash over our subjective worlds. But emotions are also social acts, laughter perhaps most of all. It's no accident that we have so many delicately choreographed gestures and facial expressions—many of which appear to be innate to our species—to convey our emotions. Our emotional systems are designed to share our feelings and not just represent them internally—an insight that Darwin first grasped more than a century ago in his book *The Expression of the Emotions in Man and Animals.* "The movements of expression in the face and body, whatever their origin may have been, are in themselves of much importance for our welfare. They serve as the first means of communication between mother and infant; she smiles approval, and thus encourages her child on the right path.… The free expression by outward signs of an emotion intensifies it."

And even if we don't yet understand the neurological basis of the pleasure that laughing brings us, it makes sense that we should seek out the connectedness of infectious laughter. We are social animals, after all. And if that laughter often involves some pretty childish behavior, so be it. "I mean, this is why we're not like lizards," Provine says, holding the Tickle Me Elmo doll on his lap. "Lizards don't play, and they're not social the way we are. When you start to see play, you're starting to see mammals. So when we get together and have a good time and laugh, we're going back to our roots. It's ironic in a way: Some of the things that give us the most pleasure in life are really the most ancient."

Alcohol's Deadly Triple Threat

Women get addicted faster, seek help less often and are more likely to die from the bottle

By Karen Springen and Barbara Kantrowitz

Pat Staples's childhood gave birth to the demons that nearly killed her. Her father was a volatile alcoholic. "I was physically, verbally and emotionally abused," she says. "Nose broken, head into the walls." In kindergarten she started dreaming about running away; she finally escaped in 1959, at the age of 20, when she married young to get out of the alcoholic house. But she couldn't flee her past. Over the years she gradually became an addict herself first with pills and then with alcohol. Still, her life seemed good on the surface. The marriage endured, defying the odds, and she and her husband had two healthy daughters. "Our house was on the home tour," she says. "Our kids were perfect."

The reality was far more bleak. She felt constantly under stress, anxious and terrified. "I was taking pills and drinking to keep it up," she says. Her husband started marking the bottles in the bar area, but she would just add water so he couldn't tell how much she had drunk. He checked the trash, too, and when she could no longer hide the empty bottles under newspapers, she started stashing them on the hill behind their house. Finally, one day in 1985, Staples went into the kitchen to get more ice for her vodka and saw her younger daughter, Tracy, then a high-school senior, making soup. The sweet smile on Tracy's face triggered something in Staples. "I looked at her, and I walked over, and I put my arms around her, and I said, 'Tracy, I need help'." Tracy replied, "I'm so proud of you." A few weeks later, when Staples entered the Betty Ford Center in Rancho Mirage, Calif., she was hemorrhaging rectally. "The alcohol had stripped the veins in my stomach," says Staples, now 64. "I would be dead today if I hadn't gotten sober."

Staples's grim assessment echoes new research about the devastating effects of alcohol on women. "Women get ad- dicted faster with less alcohol, and then suffer the conse- quences more profoundly than men do," says Susan Foster, director of policy research and analysis at the National Cen- ter on Addiction and Substance Abuse at Columbia Univer- sity. A single drink for a woman has the impact of two drinks for a man. One reason: women's bodies contain proportion- ately less water than men's, and a given amount of alcohol produces a higher concentration in the bloodstream. For women, anything more than one drink a day (five ounces of wine or a 12-ounce bottle of beer) is considered risky. The limit for men is two. Women who start drinking young and become heavy drinkers as they get older are more vulnerable to a range of major health problems, from infertility to os- teoporosis to cancer. At the same level of consumption, con- trolling for body size, women seem more likely than men to develop alcohol-related liver disease.

But new evidence about the dangers of alcohol hasn't stopped women from drinking. Researchers say that about 60 percent of American women consume alcohol on a reg- ular basis and about 5 percent average two or more drinks a day. Many female alcoholics keep their drinking secret for years. "Our culture is still more critical of women who are intoxicated than of men who are intoxicated," says psy- chologist Nancy Waite-O'Brien of the Betty Ford Center. Women who drink heavily are denigrated as sluts, while a man may be praised for his hollow leg. That bias means many women drink in secret and don't seek help until ma- jor health problems make denial impossible.

Most experts say the best way to spare women from al- coholism is to get them when they're young. People who drink before they're 15 are four times as likely to be alco- hol-dependent or have alcohol problems when they're adults. Drinking can also damage the still-developing teenage brain, according to the American Medical Association. Unfortunately, that message isn't getting out. Even though drinking under the age of 21 is illegal in all 50 states, 41 percent of ninth graders reported drinking in the past month, according to National Institutes of Health literature. Other studies have shown that more teen girls are getting drunk, and they're trying to keep up with the boys, drink for drink. "It puts them at risk of sexual assault, of physical violence," says Foster.

Many teen girls see drinking as cool, a way to be social. Elizabeth Anderson, now 26, started drinking with her friends when she was a 15-year-old high-school student in suburban Boulder, Colo. A year later she had her first blackout. Still, she did well in school, graduating in the top 10 percent of her class. She continued drinking at the University of Colorado, where she graduated with degrees in French and advertising. At 22 she crashed her car after drinking. At 23 she got a DUI. She doesn't remember much of the next year—there were more blackouts, and eventually she was fired. At 24 she was deep in debt and finally called her father for help. He got her into rehab, and she says she's been sober ever since. She avoids drinking parties and begs off when friends go to bars. Instead, she cherishes the friends she has made through a 12-step program—people who can understand what she's been through. "More than anything, what keeps me sober is looking at my life today," she says.

As women get older, their drinking threatens their children's health as well. During pregnancy especially, doctors say, women should abstain completely. "We haven't established that there's any safe level of drinking during pregnancy or lactation," says Foster. Fetal alcohol syndrome is the leading preventable cause of mental retardation in the United States. And it's not the only risk children face when pregnant women drink. Fetal alcohol spectrum disorders, which affect as many as 40,000 infants a year, can include a range of physical, mental, behavioral and learning problems.

Some studies indicate that women in unhappy or stressful relationships are the most likely to turn to alcohol for comfort. Women who have never been married or who are divorced are more likely to drink heavily than married women. And women who were sexually abused as children are more than three times as likely to suffer from alcohol problems, according to Sharon Wilsnack of the University of North Dakota School of Medicine and Health Sciences, who has conducted a 20-year study of women and alcohol. Depression is a common trigger for drinking in women. What women should watch for, doctors say, is a pattern of using alcohol to be less stressed or angry. "Alcohol is pretty good in the early stages at dealing with bad feelings," says Wilsnack. But ultimately drinking becomes as big a problem as depression and can even exacerbate negative feelings.

Wilsnack and her colleagues found that women are less likely to drink as they age—which is a good thing, because older women who drink heavily are at much higher risk for diseases of aging. Heavy alcohol use irreversibly weakens bones, and while there's some evidence that one drink a day may decrease the risk of heart disease, there's also research suggesting that the same amount of alcohol can increase the risk of breast cancer. A woman with a family history of heart disease but no family history of alcoholism or breast cancer could have a drink a day, but a woman with a family history of those diseases might want to abstain.

If you drink at all, drink sensibly—aim for no more than one drink a day. Don't drink alone. And don't drink to medicate your moods. If you think you have a problem, seek help. "It's not a moral issue," says Staples. "It's a disease. It needs to be treated by professionals who understand the disease. If a person wants it, there is help and there is hope." That's a message you can't get in a bottle.

THE GREAT BACK PAIN DEBATE

Is massage better for you than surgery? As millions of people seek relief from this ancient ailment, doctors are trying simpler, less invasive ways to end the agony.

BY CLAUDIA KALB

STOP RUBBING YOUR SORE BACK for a minute and take a quick tour of Mother Nature's engineering masterpiece: the human spine. Pretend you are Alice, so tiny you can climb among the muscles, nerves, bones and ligaments that make up the very core of your body. Crawl down the 24 vertebrae that encase and protect the spinal cord, from the cervical spine to the thoracic area to the lumbar region, that pesky lower back. Note the 23 rubbery white discs: the cartilage inner tubes that cushion the vertebrae. Observe the dozens of spinal nerves threading out from the cord between the bones. Poke the bands of muscle that wrap and support the bony column. Now focus on the tugs and thuds of daily life. The quick bend when you pick up your sobbing 2-year-old, the pounding of your feet as you run to catch the bus, the steady pull of your untoned belly, the dull pressure as you sit bleary-eyed in front of your computer, the sudden twist of your golf swing. Feel, too, the constant emotional stress we all live with: worries about aging parents, the kids' grades, a tax audit. Finally, imagine

(or recall) that knife-in-the-back moment when something suddenly goes wrong with all that gorgeous spinal anatomy: *Owwwwwww!*

Like an expensive but temperamental sports car, the human spine is beautifully designed and maddeningly unreliable. If you're a living, breathing human being, you have probably suffered the agony of back pain. Eighty percent of Americans will battle the condition at some point in their lives, making it the No. 2 reason for doctor visits (after coughs and other respiratory infections). Already, back-pain sufferers cost this country more than $100 billion annually in medical bills, disability and lost productivity at work. And as long as we continue to lead overweight, sedentary and stressful lives, that number is unlikely to go anywhere but up.

As it does, legions of new back-pain sufferers, many desperate and even disabled, will seek relief. When they do, they'll quickly discover just how complicated their problem really is, with its mystifying mix of physical symptoms and psychological underpinnings. The reality is that

BEYOND THE KNIFE

HOW THEY WORK
Treatments like massage, chiropractic manipulation and acupuncture relax, stretch and stimulate the back.

PROS
Cheaper and less risky than surgery. No recovery time, plenty of hands-on TLC.

CONS
Dearth of good research to prove efficacy.

the torment will usually go away on its own—impossible as that may seem when you're writhing on the kitchen floor. But pain is pain, and Americans, especially baby boomers, want a quick fix. The result: spinal-fusion surgery, the most costly (about $34,000 a pop) and invasive form of therapy, has spiked dramatically—77 percent in the United States between 1996 and 2001. But many of these procedures simply don't work. Doctors, worried that far too many patients seem far too willing to go under the knife, are now actively looking for simple, more effective ways to treat one of the most vexing problems in medicine. "We've come to the point where we have to think out of the box," says Dr. David Eisenberg, head of Harvard Medical School's Osher Institute, where he is studying non-surgical alternatives like massage and acupuncture. "The time is now."

KEEP MOVING SITTING FOR LONG STRETCHES IS BAD FOR YOUR DISCS, WHICH RELY ON MOVEMENT TO KEEP THEM HYDRATED AND HEALTHY.

Back pain can originate anywhere in the elaborate spinal architecture. Degenerated discs, which may lead to herniation and compressed nerves, are a common problem. Then there are those wrenching spasms provoked by muscle, tendon and ligament injuries, which can drop grown men to the floor. What's most mysterious about back problems is the disconnect between anatomical defects and pain. Unlike blood pressure and cholesterol, which can be easily measured with arm cuffs and blood tests, lower-back pain has no objective way—the volume of tears? the intensity of a grimace?—to be gauged. In many cases, the precise cause of pain remains unknown. Imaging tests have found that two people with herniated discs can lead radically different lives: one spends his days popping painkillers, the other waltzes through life like Fred Astaire. In one well-known study, researchers sent 98 healthy people through an MRI machine: two thirds had abnormal discs even though none complained of pain. In other research, experts compared a group of patients who reported back pain with a control group who didn't. Close to two thirds of the pain patients had cracks in their discs, so-called high-intensity zones, or HIZs. But so did 24 percent of the noncomplainers. "The real issue," says Dr. Eugene Carragee, the study's lead author and director of Stanford's Orthopaedic Spine Center, "is, why do some people have a mild backache and some have really crippling pain?"

The answer, Carragee and others believe, has as much to do with the mind as it does with the body. In the HIZ study, the best predictor of pain was not how bad the defect looked but the patient's psychological distress. Depression and anxiety have long been linked to pain; a recent Canadian study found that people who suffer from severe depression are four times more likely to develop intense or disabling neck or low-back pain. At the Integrative Care Center of New York's Hospital for Special Surgery, physiatrist Gregory Lutz says he routinely sees men who have two things in common: rip-roaring sciatica and an upcoming wedding date. The problem in their back, possibly a degenerated or herniated disc, probably already existed, says Lutz, but was intensified by the ole premarriage jitters.

LIKE A TEMPERAMENTAL SPORTS CAR, THE HUMAN SPINE IS BEAUTIFUL DESIGNED BUT MADDENINGLY UNRELIABLE

In 2001, 250,000 spinal-fusion procedures were performed, most of them to treat disc problems. When they're young and healthy, discs are plump with water, which keeps them hydrated and buoyant—the perfect consistency to work as shock absorbers for the vertebrae. But over time, the daily stress of walking, sitting, twisting and just plain aging dries them out "like grapes that turn into raisins," says Dr. Nick DiNubile, an orthopedic surgeon at the University of Pennsylvania.

As discs deteriorate, their tough outer shell weakens. One swing on the tennis court or even just lifting a briefcase can burst the interior gel through the casing, like jelly squishing out of a doughnut. The result is the famous herniated disc. Some go unnoticed, but when a disc bulges against one of the two long sciatic nerves, which run from the spinal cord down the leg, the pain can be excruciating. Teri Klein, 45, de-

scribes it as going through childbirth "for all three of my kids at once."

Photographer Nancy Newberry vividly remembers the "kunk, kunk, kunk" she heard seven years ago when she slipped on some stairs at the Bronco Bowl arena in Dallas. After two years of persistent pain, she was floored by a searing jolt as she bent over during a photo shoot. She tried painkillers, hot and cold ultrasound therapy, cortisone injections, electrical muscle stimulation and a year of physical therapy. Nothing much helped. Frustrated, cranky and crazy from pain, Newberry reluctantly gave in to surgery. Doctors removed a cracked disc, then fused her vertebrae together with a bone graft. Five years later, the pain is duller but it lingers, and Newberry still keeps a stash of painkillers in her medicine cabinet. "I'll never be the same as I was," she says.

Fusion surgery was originally designed to treat serious instability or deformity of the spine. Over the past 10 to 15 years, the patient pool has gradually expanded to include more run-of-the-mill disc problems. The increase in all spinal surgery has been prompted in part by technical advances promising better outcomes. Perhaps the most tantalizing new development is the artificial cobalt-chrome disc. Dr. Jeffrey Goldstein, a spine surgeon at NYU-Hospital for Joint Diseases, has inserted dozens of the implants into patients as part of a U.S. clinical trial. He believes the discs, like knee replacements, will give patients more mobility than traditional fusion. And they'll get out of bed a lot sooner, too. The key, he says, is "to be very specific and very careful about patient selection. Not everyone with bad discs should have an operation."

Perhaps too many already do, says Dr. Richard Deyo, a professor of medicine and health services at the University of Washington. In a paper published in The New England Journal of Medicine in February, Deyo and two colleagues issued a major challenge to the field. They charged that there are insufficient data to justify treating disc degeneration with spinal fusion. They also pointed to confounding issues like the variation in surgery rates and complications such as nerve injuries or infection. And then there's the quirky relationship between a surgeon's handicraft and how a patient actually feels: sometimes a first-rate fusion does little for pain, while a less impressive piece of work does wonders. Deyo's view: back pain "is part of living and being a human being."

NO BED REST A DAY OR TWO IS OK AFTER AN INJURY, BUT TOO MUCH LYING AROUND WILL WEAKEN KEY MUSCLES THAT SUPPORT THE BACK.

For more and more Americans, complementary and alternative therapies are the way to go. Chiropractic treatment, the most popular nonsurgical back therapy, is booming, with 60,000 chiropractors practicing worldwide today, a 50 percent increase since 1990. Some happy clients visit their chiropractors more than their barbers. While experts generally agree that the treatment, which involves spinal manipulation and stretching, is safe for the lower back, there's not a lot of data on how effective it is in the long term. "At this point, we don't really know," says Dr. Dan Cherkin of the Center for Health Studies in Seattle, who is

---

STAYING HEALTHY

HOW IT WORKS
Regular exercise, weight control and care when lifting and bending could prevent the torment of back pain from ever happening.

PROS
Strong muscles and less disc stress. A sense of well-being to accompany that happy back.

CONS
None at all.

---

now conducting the first large trial of the practice. Of course, in the grip of pain, patients don't necessarily care about data—they just want relief, and a lot of them get it from the "adjustments" chiropractors make to their backs. Massage has seen an increasing number of addicted patients, too, and research shows it can help knead out persistent pain; one study even found that patients took fewer medications during treatment. Steven Smith, a physical therapist at the Schuldt Performance Center in Deerfield, Ill., uses massage on back-pain sufferers to loosen up tight muscles and increase blood flow. It's not exactly a spa-like experience—Smith uses an electrical vibrator to distract patients from the pain of his fingers pushing into their muscles. "You've got to get in there deep to break those spasms," he says. Acupuncture is also popular, though, again, there's a dearth of evidence about its effectiveness. But even conventional doctors say if it makes you feel better, go for it. Dr. Jeffrey Ngeow, an anesthesiologist by training, pushes the tiny needles into patients at New York's Integrative Care Center. He says acupuncture, which seems to stimulate the release of feel-good endorphins, won't provide instant relief, but it will have a cumulative effect. Patients describe a lingering euphoria—a nice state to be in whether you've got a lumbar problem or not.

It was a flood of interest in alternative medicine that prompted the Hospital for Special Surgery to open

---

its complementary-medicine center four years ago. Now about 13,000 patients a year, many with bad backs, see its rehab specialists, massage therapists and chiropractors, as well as taking yoga and tai chi classes and working with personal trainers to help strengthen muscles-any noninvasive approach they can find to relieve the pain. Craig Jordan, 41, is a typical patient. He used to run six miles a day and thought he was man enough to pick up a leather club chair on his own; the gesture herniated two discs. Like so many others in the beleaguered-back population, Jordan tried every wacky thing out there. "Faith healing, hanging from the ceiling, clicking my heels together and wishing I was home—you name it, I've done it." Jordan now gets acupuncture twice a week and shots of anesthesia three times a year to numb the pain. Last week, feeling especially stressed by tax deadlines, he decided to start biofeedback, a technique that trains the mind to believe it can overcome pain. "You never get rid of the pain," says Jordan, though he says his treatments provide some relief. "You learn to live with it."

HOLD THE FRIES EXTRA WEIGHT STRAINS YOUR BACK MUSCLES AND SPINE. LOSE THE CIGARETTES, TOO. SMOKING IS BAD FOR YOUR DISCS.

If a patient's attitude can help process the pain, can more creative thinking among the experts improve the odds of beating it? Harvard's Eisenberg is spearheading a pilot program to find out. Over 18 weeks, a diverse group of 25 specialists who rarely see each other in clinic corridors—orthopedists, neurologists, chiropractors, massage therapists, acupuncturists and others—met to educate one another on how they diagnose and treat back pain. The goal: to see if there is a more efficient, multidisciplinary way to attack the problem—and to make it cost-effective, too. Next month at Boston's Brigham and Women's Hospital, the first pa-

HOW IT WORKS

Simply acknowledging repressed rage can help relieve the tension that causes back pain.

PROS

A mind-body approach requires no risky surgery, and patients say it gives quick relief.

CONS

Sarno provides scant scientific evidence. Critics say his approach is little more than a placebo.

tients will meet with one doctor and one complementary-medicine provider, who will then consult with the rest of the team to devise a treatment plan. "From a caring-physician point of view, I really want to know what we can do to treat people better," says Dr. Stephen Lipson, a team member and Harvard spine surgeon.

To the south, in New York City, a lone crusader thinks he has another answer. Dr. John Sarno, an attending physician at NYU Medical Center's Rusk Institute of Rehabilitation Medicine, believes that almost all back pain is rooted in bottled-up emotions. For 30 years, even as high-tech imaging and fancy surgical interventions have made their way into the discs and vertebrae of millions of American backs, Sarno has thrown every ounce of his energy into the inner workings of the mind.

In weekly lectures to his patients, Sarno uses a slide show and a pointer to explain how repressed rage—over your parents' divorce, sexual abuse, trouble at work—can stress the body, leading to mild oxygen deprivation, which he says will eventually manifest itself as muscle spasm, nerve dysfunction, numbness and pain. Recovery begins with recognizing the connection between mind and body. Every new patient is required to attend Sarno's two-hour presentation, and by then most will have read his 183-page book "Healing Back Pain" as well. Alessandro Giangola, 28, says his hourlong office visit with Sarno felt like psychotherapy. The doctor performed some simple tests: running a paper clip up and down Giangola's arm to test sensation, checking his reflexes. "Your health is fine," he told Giangola. Then he asked questions: How was your childhood? What causes the anger? Patients are assigned "homework," which starts with listing every source of repressed anger in their life. Then every day, in a quiet place, they must meditate for 15 minutes on one item on the list. Tapping into the fury helps alleviate the pain. "Pain is created by the brain to make sure the rage doesn't come out," Sarno tells his patients. "It protects you by giving you something physical to pay attention to instead."

DON'T FEAR PAIN IF YOU AVOID DOING THE THINGS YOU LOVE, IT WON'T HELP YOU GET BETTER AND YOU COULD BECOME DEPRESSED

Sarno has published no academic research on his theory and can offer little scientific proof that he's right. But his satisfied patients, who he says number in the thousands, swear by his methods and treat him like some kind of lumbar messiah. Giangola, a tennis instructor and guitar player, has had back pain for 10 years, and yes, he's tried everything, even a vegetarian diet (no real explanation for that one). Several months ago, a friend told him about Sarno's book; Giangola flew through it in two hours. Immediately the pain, which he now believes stems from his parents' divorce, began to lift. "I was floored," he says. Skeptics say that Sarno is offering a placebo, which could miss the true cause of the pain. Giangola says the man "is good for humanity."

After centuries of agony, humanity could certainly use some relief. But more important than the success of any given treatment is the good news that both back-pain sufferers and the medical establishment are embracing bold new ways to think about that most exquisite and frustrating work of art: the spine.

12 Things You Must Know to Survive And Thrive in America

Excerpt: Black men face a new America, one in which there are no limits to their dreams—at least for some. A roster of hard truths for the new age.

BY ELLIS COSE

THOSE OF US WITH FOREBEARS BRANDED by history hold in our hearts an awful truth: to be born black and male in America is to be put into shackles and then challenged to escape. But that is not our only truth, or even the one most relevant. For in this age of new possibilities, we are learning that the shackles forged in slavery are far from indestructible, that they will yield, even break, provided that we attack them shrewdly.

Today's America is not our grandfathers' or even our fathers' America. We are no longer forced to hide our ambition while masking our bitterness with a grin. We don't face, as did our forefathers, a society committed to relentlessly humiliating us, to forcing us to play the role of inferiors in every civilized sphere. This doesn't mean that we are on the verge of achieving the all-encompassing revolution, of reaching that lofty state of exalted consciousness that sweeps all inequities away. What it does mean is that we have a certain social and cultural leeway; that, in a way our forefathers could only dream about, we are free to define our place in the world.

That freedom is nowhere near absolute. But today's obstacles are not nearly as daunting as those faced by our ancestors. It's the difference between stepping into the ring with both hands lashed behind your back and stepping in with one hand swinging free.

Still, if the one hand is all you have, you must use it twice as well as your opponent uses his. And because you have so much less room for error, you must fight strategically, understanding when to retreat and when to go all out and how to deflect the blows that inevitably will come your way. You must under-stand, in short, how to compete in this new arena, where the rules are neither what they seem nor quite what they used to be. So what I have set out below is a list of things that may help us in our competition. Call them new world rules, or keys to sur-vival, or Cose's commandments; or, better yet, call them hard truths of this new age—an age of both unlimited potential and soul-crushing inequality.

1. **Play the race card carefully, and at your own peril**. As Johnnie Cochran cleverly demonstrated when he saved O. J. Simpson's hide, there is a time when playing the race card makes perfectly good sense. In November 2000, researchers at the University of Michigan published a study showing that white mock jurors were especially likely to find blacks guilty in seemingly racially neutral situations. But when an explicit ra-cial context was provided, when an assailant's offense was pro-voked by a perceived racial insult, whites were no longer so likely to see blacks as more guilty; they treated black and white defendants more or less equally. The lesson seems to be that there is some value in certain circumstances in reminding peo-ple about the reality of racism; for when they are reminded of racism (which is different from being accused of it), they make a greater attempt to be fair. Life, however, usually is not con-ducted under controlled experimental conditions. And as the Simpson trial demonstrated, Americans see racially charged in-cidents very differently. We (meaning blacks) have been so bat-tered by and sensitized to racism that we sometimes see it where

it doesn't exist. Whites have such an emotional investment in denying that they are racists that they often refuse to acknowledge racism when it is perfectly obvious to us. Other racial groups, depending on their experiences and sensitivities, also view racially tinged incidents through an ethnocentric lens. Given such psychologically complex phenomena as racial guilt and racial pain, you are not likely to find much empathy or understanding when you bring racial complaints to whites. The best you can generally hope for is an awkward silence accompanied by the suspicion that you are crying wolf. This is not to say that you should grin and bear bad treatment, but that you are generally better off finding a less charged terrain than that of racial grievance on which to fight the battle.

2. **Complain all you like about the raw deal you have gotten in life, but don't expect those complaints to get you anywhere**. America likes winners, not whiners. And one of the encouraging developments of this new, more enlightened age is that America even, at times, embraces winners who are black. There is a certain strong incentive to do so, since the very existence of black winners can be made into a rather fantastical argument that discrimination no longer hinders black advancement. Whiners, on the other hand, simply remind too many Americans of history they would prefer to forget, and of unpleasant current realities they would prefer not to face. Thankfully, we have moved past the time when whites collectively spent much time hating us; these days they mostly just don't care. Did that boss (teacher, classmate, administrator, stranger) call you stupid because of your color, or despite it? Were you assumed to be a ballplayer instead of a scholar simply because you're black? Was your rival promoted ahead of you because he's white? Was your intellect (ability, judgment) questioned in an instance where your white colleague's would not have been? You can drive yourself crazy trying to figure it out and also end up wasting a lot of energy that could be best directed elsewhere. An editor in Chicago, where I began my writing career, gave me a valuable piece of advice. "If you're going to be a writer," he said, "you'd better develop a thick skin." Much the same could be said about just being a black man in America. If you are going to survive with your sanity and emotional health intact, you're going to have to learn not to sweat much of the routine stuff that makes being a black man difficult. If you can engage life with a certain amount of humor, or at least with a sense of charity, you'll not only be happier but a lot less likely to need blood-pressure medication.

3. **Expect to do better than the world expects of you; expect to live in a bigger world than the one you see**. One of the most unfortunate realities of growing up as a black male in America is that we are constantly told to lower our sights; we are constantly nudged, unless we are very lucky and privileged, in the direction of mediocrity. Our dreams, we are told in effect, cannot be as large as other folks' dreams; our universe, we are led to believe, will be smaller than that of our nonblack peers. Franklin Raines, head of the Fannie Mae Corporation, speaks of

his early exposure to a life beyond inner-city Seattle as "a period of time when my world grew bigger," when his sophistication and exposure increased. What Raines really is describing is the natural progression of knowledge and the optimal progression of life. When Arthur Ashe wrote that his "potential is more than can be expressed within the bounds of my race or ethnic identity," he was speaking for all of us. When Maurice Ashley, America's first black grandmaster of chess, talks of a "rope of destiny pulling me along," he is talking of something we all should feel. For those of us who are accustomed to hearing, "You will never amount to much," dreams may be all that give us the strength to go on. And as we dream big dreams, we also must prepare ourselves to pursue them, instead of contenting ourselves with fantasies of a wonderful existence that will be forever beyond our reach.

4. **Don't expect support for your dreams from those who have not accomplished very much in their lives**. The natural reaction of many people (especially those who believe they share your background) is to feel threatened or intimidated or simply to be dismissive if you are trying to do things they have not done themselves. As a very young man and a "junior leader" in my neighborhood Boys Club, I was invited to a dinner at which multimillionaire W. Clement Stone spoke. After delivering a stirring talk detailing his personal journey of success, Stone handed out an inspirational book (whose title I can no longer recall), which I took with me to bed that evening. Don't share your dreams with failures, warned the book, which went on to explain that people who had not done much in their own lives would be incapable of seeing the potential in yours. While that is certainly not true in all cases, it is true much too often. The book's observation helped me to understand why some people I knew seemed more interested in telling me what I could never accomplish than in helping me achieve what I could. It also helped me understand why I owed it to myself to tune out the voices around me telling me to lower my sights.

5. **If someone is bringing out your most self-destructive tendencies, acknowledge that that person is not a friend.** No one should, willy-nilly, toss away friendship. People who will care for you, who will support and watch out for you, are a precious part of a full and blessed life. But people who claim to be friends are not always friends in fact—as Mike Gibson, an ex-prisoner who is now a Morehouse student, ultimately learned. His time behind bars taught Gibson to "surround myself with people who want to see me do good." On the streets he learned that when things got tough, the very buddies who had encouraged him to break the law were nowhere to be found: "When I was in the cell, I was there by myself… I always found myself alone." It's easy to be seduced by those who offer idiotic opinions disguised as guidance. It's even easier to find people who attach themselves to you for their own selfish reasons, or who will say they have your back when, in reality, they're only looking out for themselves. It's sometimes a bit harder to let them go,

which sometimes is what you must do in the interest of your own survival.

Too many of us are trying to cope alone, when we would be much better off if we would just reach out for help.

6. **Don't be too proud to ask for help, particularly from those who are wiser and older**. While working on a previous book, "Color-Blind," I interviewed mathematician Philip Uri Triesman, who has had astounding success teaching advanced mathematics to black students who previously had not done very well. Unlike Chinese-American students who typically studied in groups, blacks, he had discovered, tended to study alone. For blacks, the solitary study ritual seemed to be a matter of pride, reflecting their need to prove that they could get by without help, that they were not inferior to whites. By getting them, in effect, to emulate some of what the Chinese-Americans were doing, Triesman spurred the black students to unprecedented levels of accomplishment. Too often (and not only in math), we feel we have to face our problems alone. We are uncomfortable admitting our pain, our inexperience, our incompetence; and, as a result, we sometimes ignore resources we usefully could tap. Whether in schools, in the streets or in corporate suites, too many of us are trying to cope alone when we would be much better off if we reached out for help.

7. **Recognize that being true to yourself is not the same as being true to a stupid stereotype**. A few years ago when I visited Xavier University, a historically black college in New Orleans, I was moved by a student who proudly proclaimed the university to be a school full of nerds. At a time when many black men and boys are trying their best to act like mack-daddies and bad-ass muthas, Xavier (which sends more blacks to medical schools than any other university) is saying that it has another image in mind: blackness really has nothing to do with projecting a manufactured, crude street persona. Xavier celebrates accomplishment instead of denigrating it, and it makes no apologies for doing so. We desperately need to promote archetypes other than rappers, thugs and ballplayers of what it is possible and desirable for us to be—if for no other reason than that so few of us can find success on such limited terrain.

8. **Don't let the glitter blind you**. Almost invariably when I have spoken to people who had made their living selling drugs, they talk a lot like "Frank," who said, "I didn't want to be the only dude on the streets with busted-up shoes, old clothes." They talk of the money, the women, the cars, the gold chains—the glamour, the glitter of the dealer's life. Only later do most acknowledge that the money, for most dealers, is not all that good, and that even when it is, it generally doesn't last very long—partly because the lifestyle so often leads to either prison or an early grave. Maybe you don't care about that. Nonetheless, I urge you to realize that you have a better chance (provided you prepare for it) of getting a big job at a major corporation than of making big money for a long time on the streets—and the benefits and security are a hell of a lot better.

9. **Don't expect competence and hard work alone to get you the recognition or rewards you deserve**. For all our skepticism about the so-called system, it sometimes seems that people of color are the only ones alive who truly believe in the meritocracy. We work hard, pour all our energy into our jobs and then are stunned and shattered when our hard work is not rewarded. Why, we ask, is our ability not being recognized? Why is our hard work being overlooked? Why can't they see our talent? The answers are as varied as the possible circumstances, but the general rule is that any organization (government, private business, educational or other) is essentially a social body that rewards those fully engaged in the game. To the extent we try to hold ourselves above that process, we end up losing.

It is never too late to accomplish something in life. But lost ground can be very hard to make up.

10. **You must seize the time, for it is already later than you think**. When working on "The Rage of a Privileged Class," a book I published in 1994, I was touched by a confession from Basil Paterson, lawyer, high-ranking Democratic National Committee official and former deputy mayor of New York. "It's too late for me to get rich because I spent too much time preparing for what I've got... Most of us are 10 years behind what we should have been. We didn't get credentials until we were older than other folks," he said. Paterson was talking of a particular generation, one hobbled by a much more blatant, more virulent form of discrimination than exists for the most part today; but the essence of what he said is still true—at least for those without well-to-do parents or fancy educations. Daniel Rose, founder of the Harlem Educational Activities Fund, tells his young disciples: "Your chief competitor started yesterday. And you are already a day behind." While it is never too late to accomplish something in life, lost ground is hard to make up, and it only gets harder the longer one waits, as competition becomes even stiffer and opportunities dry up.

11. **Even if you have to fake it, show some faith in yourself**. Confidence, lightly worn, can be contagious, and you might even manage to fool yourself into letting go of your doubts. "A lot of our kids don't believe in themselves because they've been told by so many people that they ain't worth s—t.

I was labeled the bad kid, so I know how that feels," says Chicago youth worker J. W. Hughes. "Go to any high school with black males and tell them they are smart enough to go to any university in the world. Many of them will say, 'Not me.' I know that because [I was] one of them," says Zachary Donald, a member of the Omega Boys Club, a San Francisco-based nonprofit dedicated to rescuing young souls from the street. So much energy has been expended undermining our confidence, picking apart our faith in ourselves, that we sometimes forget faith does not depend on the beliefs of others or on demonstrating a list of accomplishments. "Faith is the substance of things hoped for, the evidence of things not seen," says the Bible (Hebrews 11:1). And there is so much that we have not yet seen, so much waiting to be revealed when it comes to our potential on this planet. But the first step is to believe that we can go where others say we can't.

12. **Don't force innocent others to bear the price of your pain**. Sister Simone Ponnet, executive director of Abraham House (a New York Roman Catholic organization that works with prisoners and their families), spoke feelingly of ex-convicts and prisoners who lamented growing up fatherless, or with abusive fathers, and then ended up treating their own children no better. Even some of us who haven't been locked down at times feel so much pain, so much anger that we feel justified in taking out our frustrations on everyone around us. Threatened in so many realms, unable to control the forces enveloping us, we sometimes try too hard to exert control in the few areas we think we can: sometimes over women, sometimes over children and sometimes over random souls unlucky enough to get in our way. Before giving in to the temptation to turn loved ones into targets, we should remind ourselves that those who love us are the best hope we have to regain whatever humanity we have lost; that they, in other words, are our salvation.

ALL THAT I HAVE SAID ABOVE FOCUSES on the personal, on what we, as individuals, can do to improve the quality of our lives. This is not to say that I believe the only problems we have in America are individual ones. Nothing could be farther from the truth. Huge and systemic problems remain that prevent America from being the best country that it can be. We continue, as a country, to leave our young people uneducated and, often, illiterate. We continue to stress incarceration where we should be stressing human reclamation. We continue to confound the dream of true equality by rejecting the investments in remediation and infrastructure needed to achieve it. We continue to permit society to label young black men as undesirable, as troublemakers, and we throw up our hands in exasperation when the self-fulfilling prophecy becomes fact. I could go on, but those are subjects for another day.

Here I am purposely less concerned with the systemic than with the personal, with some things you might want to consider as you figure out how to live your life. And, as such, I would like to end on a hopeful note, by restating what I sincerely believe to be true: there is more leeway than there has ever been in history for you to become whatever you would be; for you to accomplish whatever you dream; for you to escape the prisons of stereotypes and caricatures that our forefathers could not avoid.

We are entitled to our big dreams, just as we deserve an America that is as welcoming to us as it is to a white kid from Cuba, Croatia or Ireland. We deserve, in other words, the fairness we have always been promised, and the opportunity to compete free of the burdens we have always carried, burdens economic, emotional and historical, burdens that still stand in the way of our receiving our due and of America achieving a true meritocracy.

AGING'S CHANGING FACE:
Science is Reshaping the Way we Think about the Older Body, Memory and Sex Drive.

by Willow Lawson

In just three years, the first of 80 million baby boomers will turn 60, an age once associated with early bird dinner specials and slow driving in the fast lane.

But today, age 60 looks like Geraldo Rivera, Mick Jagger and Lauren Hutton, all of whom will enter their seventh decade this year.

More and more, how we grow old is a personal choice. Older folks are going back to school in their 50s, starting businesses in their 60s, training for triathlons in their 70s and, yes, having sex in their 80s.

This is a good thing, according to researchers who have found that negative stereotypes about aging can actually shorten your life. A Yale University study last year in the *Journal of Personality and Social Psychology* found that people who have a positive perception of aging tend to live seven and a half years longer than those who don't. The difference may be the result of a better response to stress or even just the will to live, according to the study.

WHAT BRAIN DRAIN?

Recent research has found that memory studies can intimidate elderly subjects into performing poorly. Older subjects score higher on memory tests if they aren't explicitly told that the study is about memory and aging, according to a study by researchers at North Carolina State University in Raleigh.

We are swayed by our own expectations. The new research, reported in the *Journal of Gerontology,* found that elderly subjects scored 20 to 30 percent worse on memory tests after reading a pessimistic newspaper account about aging and memory than those who read a cheerful article about growing older.

People who have an upbeat outlook on aging are also more likely to take control and responsibility for their health. Curbing lifestyle diseases caused by obesity, lack of exercise, smoking and chronic stress is perhaps the big-

Staying in Touch

"Honda has an intelligent robot for household help," says one participant at the Brain-Mind Roundtable. "The question is: Just how far do we want this to go?"

This isn't an undergraduate discussion about artificial intelligence, but part of a conversation on SeniorNet, an online community for the over-50 set.

For the aging, the Internet provides a healthy escape from emotional isolation. Some 40 percent of the elderly own computers, according to a SeniorNet survey. The number is steadily growing. "For those who can't get out much, the Net can be an enormously helpful way to improve their day," says Louis J. Marino Jr., M.D., head of geriatric psychiatry at Brown University's Butler Hospital.

Many seniors surf health Web sites for referrals and information about medical conditions. More are simply e-mailing their kids and grandchildren, and creating Web sites that help them stay in touch with family and friends, and keep their minds active.

—Mark Baard

gest hurdle in the aging game. Nearly 55 percent of Americans are overweight and some 22 percent are obese, according to the National Institutes of Health. The rates are even higher for Americans over age 50. These are startling numbers when one considers the impact this will have on future rates of heart disease, diabetes, high blood pressure and arthritis. Arthritis alone plagues half of all Americans over age 64.

"People of all ages are always looking for a magic bullet," says Fox Wetle, Ph.D., assistant dean of the Brown School of Medicine in Rhode Island. Wetle says that while there is no easy way out, exercise may be the "magic shotgun."

Troubling health trends—such as obesity—notwithstanding, new research shows a bright future for those of us entering midlife. Many symptoms long associated

Did You Know?

WILTING TASTE BUDS?
After menopause, sugar may not taste as sweet, say researchers at Ankara University in Turkey. Further research is needed to understand why some women experience this change, which may cause a preference for sweeter foods.

EXCESS VITAMINS
Older dietary supplement users may not need them. Half of Americans over 65 take a multivitamin or supplement. However, they are often lean, active individuals who don't smoke and don't need a dietary boost.

MIDLIFE CRISIS
In 2002, traffic deaths rose to their highest levels since 1990. One of the steepest increases in death was among motorcycle riders 50 and older. Rates of fatal crashes for this group rose by 24 percent.

RETIREMENT BLUES
A woman's occupation impacts how she adjusts to retirement, according to a study from Ohio State University. Women doctors, teachers and other professionals have a tougher time adjusting to the end of a career than those who are considered non-professionals, such as clerical workers.

WEAK IN THE KNEES
Arthritis is the fifth most expensive medical condition in the U.S., costing $16 billion last year. Obesity contributes to osteoarthritis, especially in the knees. As the obese adult population ages, doctors expect an explosion in the rate of the disease.

MIND THE STAIRS
Older women who use antidepressants or narcotics are at increased risk for bone fractures, according to a study from the VA Medical Center in Minneapolis. It is unclear if women on these medications are more likely to fall, or if a loss in bone density is part of the problem. Falls are the leading cause of accidental death for people over age 75.

NEVER TOO LATE
Older women who start exercising after the age of 65 may live longer, according to a study in the *Journal of the American Medical Association*. Newly active women had a 36 percent lower risk of heart disease and a 51 percent lower risk of cancer than those who didn't exercise.

Sources: British Dental Journal, NIH, National Highway Traffic Safety Administration, Journal of Women and Aging, Agency for Healthcare Research and Quality, Archives of Internal Medicine, National Safety Council.

---

with aging are actually signs of disease, according to recent studies.

Between the ages of 30 and 90, the brain loses about 10 percent of its volume. Forgetfulness isn't an automatic result, however. Scientists have recently found that loss of brain cells due to aging isn't as steep as once thought. In fact, they now believe memory problems aren't a natural part of growing older. Studies have shown that people with bad memories as older adults probably had the same deficiency when they were younger. But later in life, we may attribute it to aging.

Crossword puzzles, practicing the piano and playing chess exercise the brain, counteracting these natural changes. Exercise helps cognitive function too, studies show.

I WANT YOUR SEX

Older people are still amorous with surprising frequency, according to a study presented recently at the annual meeting of the American Urological Association.

More than 4,000 people between the ages of 40 and 80 were polled in the U.S., Canada, Australia and New Zealand. Around 30 percent of men aged 70 to 80 reported having sex five times in the past month, although only 8 percent of women reported doing so. Most women said the lack of sex was due to the absence of a partner. Indeed, the study found women were more likely to be widowed.

Still, sexual dysfunction was an issue for both sexes, with some 40 percent of men reporting problems such as erectile dysfunction.

Public Enemy No. 1

Heart disease has been the leading cause of death in the U.S. since 1900, a fact easily forgotten by Americans who are worried about myriad forms of cancer and infectious disease. One in three men and one in ten women will develop heart disease by age 60, according to the American Heart Association.

How people handle a diagnosis of heart disease largely influences how they recover from it, says Wayne Sotile, M.D., author of *Thriving With Heart Disease*.

Women are especially vulnerable to anger and anxiety when told they have heart disease. There is so much focus on breast cancer and other diseases that they often aren't aware of their risk.

Unfortunately, women usually have less support at home to help them fight the condition. "A male patient is more likely to have a daughter or other family member who says, 'I'll diet with you, or I'll quit smoking with you,'" Sotile says. "Women are more likely to worry about inconveniencing their family."

The key to life with heart disease is avoiding the anxiety and stress that often plague people who have it. Research has shown that depression, anger and relationship conflicts can affect the clotting of blood and the electrical activity of the heart.

"There's more immediate anxiety with this disease," according to Sotile. "No one with cancer says, 'If I make love, I might die' or 'If I take out the garbage, I might die.'"

The good news is that dietary changes and moderate exercise, especially for the most sedentary individuals, can make a big difference.

Says Sotile: "This really is a second-chance illness."

IT'S IMPORTANT TO HAVE SOCIAL SUPPORT FOR GENERAL HEALTH. WE ALL NEED SOMETHING TO GET US UP IN THE MORNING.

Exercise is an antidote for that too, perhaps even more so than pills, according to a two-year study from the Cologne University Medical Center in Germany.

Researchers studied men with circulatory problems and prescribed either an exercise program, the prescription drug Viagra or a placebo. The exercise group, which focused on working pelvis and leg muscles, reported 80 percent better erections, while Viagra resulted in a 74 percent increase in sexual arousal.

But it's not just sex that matters. Social support makes both men and women less vulnerable to health problems, according to a study at the University of California at Irvine. People ages 58 to 90 who described themselves as lonely were particularly at risk.

"It's really important to have confidantes and social support for general health," says Wetle. "We all need something to look forward to that will get us up in the morning."

Secrets of the Centenarians

*In certain families, small genetic variations bring good health and long life.
Can researchers apply this knowledge to benefit us all?*

By Maya Pines

IS THERE A FORMULA FOR LIVING TO the age of 100 or beyond? HHMI investigator Louis M. Kunkel believes there is, and he's working hard to define it.

Besides a healthy dose of good luck (Kunkel says it helps to not be killed in a war or a traffic accident), one key to longevity is a highly unusual combination of gene variants that protects against the customary diseases of old age. Several research teams are now in the process of uncovering these genes.

Kunkel, director of the Genomics Program at Children's Hospital in Boston, and his associates recently identified a genetic variant that is particularly prominent among sibling pairs in the New England Centenarian Study, perhaps the world's largest pool of centenarians. They are seeking additional genetic variants that might retard—or perhaps even prevent—many of the diseases that debilitate the old. "People with this rare combination of genes clearly age more slowly," Kunkel says. "When they reach 90, they don't look any older than 70."

Hundreds of centenarians around the world are now contributing their blood and medical histories to the search for these precious genes. They have become a key resource for researchers who hope that as these genes are revealed, their good effects may be reproduced in other people with the help of new drugs.

CLUSTERED IN FAMILIES

Kunkel was drawn to the hunt for longevity genes about six years ago, through a chance encounter with Thomas T. Perls, a Boston University Medical School geriatrician who had enrolled a large group of centenarians for his New England Centenarian Study. Kunkel's own research was focused on a deadly genetic disorder called Duchenne muscular dystrophy, which affects mostly boys. In 1986, he discovered a mutation that causes this muscle-wasting disease, and he is still working on a therapy for it (see Cures for Muscle Diseases?). But he could not resist the opportunity to also apply his knowledge of genetics to what he heard from Perls.

The two men were acquainted through Perls's wife, Leslie Smoot, who happened to be a postdoc in Kunkel's lab. When they met on a street in Cambridge, Massachusetts, in 1997 and started talking about their work, "Tom told me that many of the centenarians whose lineage he was examining were clustered in families," Kunkel recalls. "I realized that's just got to be genetics. We soon started a collaboration."

For his part, Perls remembers that at the beginning of his study he thought the centenarians had little in common except for their age. But he soon realized that many of them had an unusually large number of equally aged relatives. "We had a 108-year-old man who blew out his birthday candles next to his 102-year-old sister," Perls recalls. "They told us they had another sibling who was 103, and yet another who was only 99. Two other siblings—also centenarians—had passed away. Four siblings had died in childhood. So here was an incredible clustering, 5 or maybe 6 siblings out of 10! We've since found about 7 families like that." This implied that all these families carried especially protective genes. Shortly after the two scientists met, a new postdoc arrived in Kunkel's lab—Annibale A. Puca, a young Italian neurologist who wanted to work in genetics—and Kunkel suggested he take on this new project. "I warned him it was going to be a lot of work and high risk, but he said okay," Kunkel says, "and he spearheaded the whole program."

Puca and Perls rapidly expanded the group of centenarians, recruiting them through alumni associations, newspaper clippings, and state census lists. After taking samples of the centenarians' blood, the researchers extracted DNA from it and started looking for genetic markers—specific stretches of DNA that might occur more frequently among these extremely old men and women than among a group of younger people who were the study's controls. Most scientists believed that human longevity is far too complicated a trait to be influenced by only a few genes. There are so many independent mechanisms of aging that "the chance that only a few major genes control longevity in man is highly unlikely," wrote a self-styled "pessimist" on this issue, George M. Martin of the University of Washington in Seattle, in the journal *Mechanisms of Ageing and Development* in 2002. But Kunkel's

Who Are These Centenarians?

"Centenarians tend to be independent, assertive, funny, and gregarious," says Boston University Medical School geriatrician Thomas T. Perls, who at 43 has probably met more people over the age of 100 than anybody else. "They also seem to manage stress very well, which makes sense, since we know that not handling stress predisposes you to cardiovascular disease and high blood pressure."

During a fellowship in geriatrics at Harvard Medical School in the early 1990s, Perls took care of 40 patients at Boston's Hebrew Rehabilitation Center for the Aged. Two of his healthiest patients, who looked as if they were in their seventies, were actually over 100 years old. "They were in really terrific shape," he says. "It was so different from what I expected! This sparked my interest."

As a result, Perls founded the New England Centenarian Study in 1994, becoming one of only a few researchers studying the very old at that time. He started out by looking for people over 100 in eight towns around Boston, using census records, voter registration files, and the media. Later, he expanded the study by adding centenarians from all over the United States. Now it includes 1,600 centenarians and 500 of their children. About 20 percent of the centenarian women in his study had given birth after the age of 40, Perls found, compared to a national average of only 3 percent of mothers. "It showed that these women were aging very slowly," he says.

He also studied the centenarians' siblings and concluded that their chances of living to their early nineties were four times greater than average. More recently, Perls examined the centenarians' children. At the age of 70, he found, they had a 24 percent reduction in mortality compared to the general population, as well as about a 60 percent reduction in the risk of heart disease, hypertension, and diabetes.

More than 90 percent of the centenarians had been in good health and completely independent until their early to mid-90s, Perls says. "They lived the vast majority of their lives with good function," he emphasizes. "So it's not a matter of 'the older you get, the sicker you get' but rather 'the older you get, the healthier you've been.' This is a different way of thinking about aging."

By the time people reach the century mark, however, the healthy ones are in the minority. "We found that 25 percent of the centenarians were doing well, but the remaining 75 percent had mild to severe impairment," Perls reports. "In the end, they die of cardiovascular disease or something that's related to frailty, such as pneumonia."

This fits in well with the theories of Leonard Hayflick, of the University of California, San Francisco, who showed in 1961 that there are limits to the number of times a normal human cell can divide. Even under the most favorable conditions, he said, noncancerous human cells die after about 50 cell divisions (this is now called the "Hayflick limit"). Eliminating the leading causes of death in old age—cardiovascular diseases, stroke, and cancer—"will only result in an increase of about 15 years in human life expectancy," Hayflick declared in the November 9, 2000, issue of *Nature*. Although these 15 years would be a great gift, assuming that people remained healthy during that time, nothing could stop "the inevitable increase in errors and disorders in the cells of vital organs" that results from age, he pointed out. Even the cells' repair processes would become disordered, leading to extreme vulnerability and death.

Then would it be a good thing for more people to live to 100? "Absolutely," says Perls. "Centenarians are sentinels of the health of older people. Our goal is not to get a bunch of individuals to be 120 or 130, but to discover which genes are most protective and then use this information to get a majority of people living almost all their lives in good health, as centenarians generally do."

lab took a different view. "In lower organisms, such as nematodes, fruit flies, and yeast, there are only a few genes that need to be altered to give a longer life span," Kunkel says. "My feeling was that there were only a few genes, perhaps four to six, in humans that would do the same."

The team proceeded to examine genetic markers for the entire genomes of 308 people, selected because they belonged to 137 sibships (sets of siblings) in which at least one member was over 98 and the others were over 90. "From early on, we saw a blip of a peak on chromosome 4," says Kunkel. "Eventually, in 2001, we found a linkage between one region of this chromosome and longevity."

SEARCH FOR A SNP

It was "phenomenal" to get a real linkage from such a slight hint in the original data, Kunkel declares. But that didn't mean further research would be easy. This stretch of DNA was so large—12 million DNA base pairs long—that it seemed it could contain as many as 200 genes. Furthermore, the researchers knew that

within these genes they would have to look for variations in single bases of DNA—"single-nucleotide polymorphisms," or SNPs (pronounced "snips"). "SNPs really represent the difference between individuals," Kunkel explains. "Everybody's DNA is 99.9 percent identical—it's the SNPs that make us unique and allow certain people to live longer. Even though most of our DNA is alike, the 0.1 percent variation means that we have more than 10 million SNPs across the genome. And we're on the verge of being able to map them." For Kunkel, the critical question was "how would we find the one SNP in a single gene that might help a person to live much longer than average?"

The groundbreaking work of the Human Genome Project had not yet been completed at that time, and Kunkel realized that finding this particular SNP would be both expensive and time-consuming. It would also be quite different from zeroing in on a missing or severely garbled gene, as had been done for cystic fibrosis, muscular dystrophy, and other single-gene disorders. The widespread diseases of aging—heart disease, stroke, diabetes, cancer, and Alzheimer's disease—are much more complex and are triggered by subtle gene variations that produce only slightly altered proteins, Kunkel says. These

Cures for Muscle Diseases?

Ever since Louis M. Kunkel discovered the cause of Duchenne muscular dystrophy (DMD) in 1986, he has been laboring to find a cure for this muscle-wasting disease. DMD—the result of an error in a single gene—attacks 1 out of every 4,000 newborn boys, progressively crippling and then killing them at an early age.

Kunkel saw that patients with DMD lacked a protein, dystrophin, which this gene would have produced if it were functioning normally. So he knew he had to replace the protein somehow. He and others tried many methods—gene therapy to deliver a normal gene to the defective muscle cell, drugs to help restore the mission protein, and cell therapy to inject normal cells into muscle or blood—but despite some partial successes in animals, nothing really worked.

Kunkels lab worked mostly with *mdx* mice, a naturally mutant strain that lack dystrophin. When he and his colleagues attempted to cure these crippled mice with injections of muscle stem cells from normal mice, "some of the donor cells did go into the damaged muscles." he recalls, "but we never got more then 1 to 2 percent of the muscles repaired. Part of the problem was that when you inject cells into a mouses tail vein, which is the most accessible part of its circulation, the donor cells to through all the organs—the lungs, liver, heart, and so on—and out through the arterial system. Most of the cells get filtered and lost, and don't contribute to the therapy."

Today, however, Kunkel feels he is on the verge of success. The big breakthrough came last summer when a team of Italian scientists headed by Giulio Cossu of Milans Stem Cell Research Institute announced it had found a new route for the injection of stem cells into dystrophic mice directly into an artery. The cells seemed to lodge within the capillary system near the injection site. From there, about 30 percent of them migrated to the diseased muscles. Not only did the cells get there, he says, but at later time points, you could see a larger number of donor cells than at the earliest point, as if they were trying to divide.

"Can we improve on this?" asks Kunkel with a glint in his eye. "If we can get the stem cells into 50 percent of the dystrophic muscles, thats basically a cure."

They had trouble at first because "the mouse artery was 10 times smaller than our smallest injection needles—it was like trying to hit it with a hammer!" Kunkel says. Though a tail vein is even smaller than an artery, it can be hit much more easily because it is right under the surface of the skin and can be made to swell up by warming it. In the new system, the mouse had to be anesthetized and opened up to expose its artery, which was lifted out—a complex procedure.

"It wasnt until we started collaborating with some vascular surgeons who had been doing heart transplants in mice that we were able to get the stem cells into the mouse arteries efficiently," he says. In humans, of course, reaching an artery would not be a problem given that human arteries are so much larger.

Getting the stem cells into the muscles was just the first step. Unless these cells supplied enough dystrophin, the diseased muscles would not be repaired. So Kunkel also tried to find different stem cells that could do the job more effectively. In 1999 his lab and that of his colleague Richard Mulligan announced they could restore some of the missing dystrophin in mdx mice with the aid of a new kind of stem cells called "side population" (SP) cells, which seemed to work much better. These SP cells had to be taken from muscle tissue, however. Last year Kunkel's lab succeeded in deriving similar SP cells from adult skin, which is easier to obtain. Since they originate in adult tissue, both kinds of SP cells will be much less controversial then embryonic stem cells.

"Its my belief that you can do a lot of therapeutic intervention with adult-derived cells," says Kunkel. He notes that the new stem cells seem ready to differentiate into every type of muscle tissue, which implies that they have the potential to treat many forms of muscle disease.

The combination of new cell type and a new delivery system "may revolutionize how one does therapy for muscle diseases," Kunkel suggests. "When we get it perfected in mice, we'll go to humans." He thinks this might happen in a couple of years.

---

proteins may either work a little better or be less active than those in the normal population, and several of them may work in concert. Searching for a single SNP would require doing thousands of genetic analyses on each of his subjects (now numbering 653) and comparing the results with the control group. "We estimated it would cost at least $5 million," Kunkel said. "It finally cost $8 million and took one-and-a-half years."

Ultimately, all that painstaking work paid off. The paper announcing the discovery of a SNP that contributes to longevity was published in the November 25, 2003, issue of the *Proceedings of the National Academy of Sciences*.

NOW FOR THE OTHERS

The long-sought SNP turned out to lie within the gene for microsomal transfer protein, or MTP, which had been known since the mid-1980s to be involved in cholesterol metabolism.

"It's quite clear that to live to be 100, you've got to maintain your cholesterol at a healthy level," says Kunkel. "It makes perfect sense. We know that increased LDL (the 'bad' cholesterol) and lowered HDL (the 'good' cholesterol) raise your cardiovascular risk and that cardiovascular diseases account for a large percentage of human mortality. So variations in the genes involved in cholesterol packaging will influence your life span. It's as if these centenarians had been on Lipitor [a cholesterol-lowering drug] from birth!"

This discovery might lead to drugs that are tailored to intervene in the cholesterol pathway. Because the MTP gene was already in the public domain, however, it could not be patented, much to the disappointment of the former Centagenetix Corporation (founded by Puca, Perls, and Kunkel and now a part of Elixir Pharmaceuticals of Cambridge, Massachusetts), which had bankrolled most of the study.

In any event, this SNP "cannot be the whole story," Kunkel declares. "There must be other gene variations that enable people to avoid age-related diseases. Some of our original families did not show linkages to chromosome 4." Nor did a group of centenarians who were tested in France.

Determined to find some of the other SNPs that produce longevity, Kunkel says he's going back to his sample and will redo the whole study. "We now have 310 sibships," he says. "Our genetic markers are much denser. I believe we can get 10 times the power in our next screen than we had in the first."

Moreover, the work can be done much more rapidly and inexpensively than last time, he notes, given the giant strides that have been made recently in human genetics. Not only has the entire human genome been sequenced, but many of the errors in the original draft have been corrected. Equally important, all the known genes in the genome are now available on a single Affymetrix DNA chip, allowing researchers to promptly identify which genes are activated and which are damped down in any given situation. In addition, as many as 10,000 different human SNPs have been placed on a single chip.

Similar tools have already turned up new gene variants in yeast, worms, and flies. But Kunkel will use the chips to analyze the DNA of humans. Once his lab gets started on the new longevity project, he believes, it will not take very long to get some definitive answers. He hopes these will lead to drugs that could mimic the protective effects of the centenarians' genes.

GOLD STANDARD

In fact, these studies foreshadow a far-reaching attack on all complex diseases—not just those of the aged but others, such as autism and hypertension. None of these ills could be tackled efficiently in the past. "The centenarians are the ideal control group for such research," Kunkel says. "To reach 100, you must have good alleles [versions of the genes] at all points. So if one wants to find the genes that are connected with hypertension, for instance, one can look across the genome for genes that are highly active in the hypertensive population but down-regulated in centenarians. Ultimately, that's what the centenarians' genes will be used for."

He believes that in the future, "every person who comes to our genetic clinic—or goes through any type of care system—with what appears to be a complex disease should be analyzed in detail. I mean that we should gather all the information we can about each patient's symptoms, the family history of these symptoms, any environmental insults the patient suffered, any learning disability—anything that would allow us to categorize the patient and [the patient's] family into subtypes of the disease which could be more related to one another and thus more likely to involve the same gene." To make this happen, Kunkel has just appointed a director of phenotyping (the Greek roots of this word mean "classifying phenomena into specific types") who will collect, categorize, and catalogue such patient information.

"We will also analyze the patients' genes but only in the context of the category of symptoms they exhibit," he says. "The samples we collect—under appropriate protocols—will be available to the national groups of patients and researchers that are organizing to find the underlying genetic bases of specific diseases." Eventually, he hopes, many complex disorders such as heart disease, diabetes, and autism will be broken down into more specific categories, which in turn may lead to more precise treatments or ways of preventing the disorder. Kunkel expects this process to accelerate in the near future as more patients' genes are compared with those of the gold standard for humans—the centenarians.

THE NUN STUDY ALZHEIMER'S

How one scientist and 678 sisters are helping unlock the secrets of Alzheimer's

By MICHAEL D. LEMONICK and ALICE PARK MANKATO

IT'S THE DAY AFTER EASTER, AND THE first crocus shoots have ventured tentatively above the ground at the convent on Good Counsel Hill. This is Minnesota, however; the temperature is 23°F and the wind chill makes it feel far colder. Yet even though she's wearing only a skirt and sweater, Sister Ada, 91, wants to go outside. She wants to feed the pigs.

But the pigs she and the other nuns once cared for have been gone for 30 years. Sister Ada simply can't keep that straight. In recent years, her brain, like a time machine gone awry, has been wrenching her back and forth between the present and the past, depositing her without warning into the days when she taught primary schoolchildren in Minnesota or to the years when she was a college student in St. Paul. Or to the times when she and the sisters had to feed the pigs several times a day.

Like some 4 million Americans, Sister Ada (not her real name) is suffering from Alzheimer's disease; as the years go by, she'll gradually lose her memory, her personality and finally all cognitive function. But advanced age does not automatically lead to senility. Ada's fellow nun, Sister Rosella, 89, continues to be mentally sharp and totally alert, eagerly anticipating the celebration of her 70th anniversary as a sister without the slightest sign of dementia. In a very real sense, this pair of retired schoolteachers haven't finished their teaching careers. Along with hundreds of other nuns in their order, the School Sisters of Notre Dame, they have joined a long-term study of Alzheimer's disease that could teach the rest of us how to escape the worst ravages of this heartbreaking illness.

The groundbreaking research they are helping conduct probably won't lead directly to any new drugs, and it's unlikely to uncover a genetic or biochemical cause of Alzheimer's. Doctors know, however, that preventing disease can be a lot easier and cheaper than trying to cure it. It was by studying the differences between people who get sick and people who don't—the branch of medical science known as epidemiology—that doctors discovered the link between smoking and lung cancer, between cholesterol and heart disease, between salt and high blood pressure. Epidemiology also led to the understanding that cooked tomatoes may help protect against prostate cancer, and that fruits and vegetables tend to stave off cancers of all sorts.

Now it's Alzheimer's turn. Precious little is known about this terrible illness, which threatens to strike some 14 million Americans by 2050. Its precise cause is still largely mysterious, and effective treatments are still years away. But epidemiologists are beginning to get a handle on what kinds of people are most seriously ravaged by Alzheimer's—and, conversely, which people tend to escape relatively unscathed.

Much of this knowledge comes from a single, powerful piece of ongoing research: the aptly named Nun Study, of which Sisters Ada and Rosella are part.

Since 1986, University of Kentucky scientist David Snowdon has been studying 678 School Sisters—painstakingly researching their personal and medical histories, testing them for cognitive function and even dissecting their brains after death. Over the years, as he explains in Aging with Grace (Bantam; $24.95), a moving, intensely personal account of his research that arrives in bookstores this week, Snowdon and his colleagues have teased out a series of intriguing—and quite revealing—links between lifestyle and Alzheimer's.

Scientists know that genes can predispose people to Alzheimer's disease. But as described in nearly three dozen scientific papers, Snowdon's study has shown, among other things, that a history of stroke and head trauma can boost your chances of coming down with debilitating symptoms of Alzheimer's later in life; and that a college education and an active intellectual life, on the other hand, may actually protect you from the effects of the disease.

Perhaps the most surprising result of the Nun Study, though, is the discovery that the way we express ourselves in language, even at an early age, can foretell how long we'll live and how vulnerable we'll be to Alzheimer's decades down the line. Indeed, Snowdon's latest finding, scheduled to be announced this week, reinforces that notion. After analyzing short autobiographies of almost 200 nuns, written when they first took holy orders, he found that the sisters who had expressed the most positive emotions in their writing

M. Nicholas Kunkel

12

A Short Sketch of my Life

When I was first told that I saw the light of day on a Tuesday noon, there automatically ran through my mind the old nursery rhyme pretending to predict one's fate by making it depend on the day of the week on which one was born. It goes something like this

"Monday's child is fair of face,

Tuesday's child is full of grace"

Now, I don't want to feign that I had dreamed of being a nun from the age of reason but it at least was a good encouragement and something to strive for as an ideal. I remember little of my baby days and what I do I have had to take on hearsay. From all accounts I was perfectly normal with regard to mischief and, being the first of my fond parents' offspring, might have ... had God not blessed them ...

A Way with Words

Analyzing autobiographical sketches written by the sisters in their 20s, before they took their vows, Snowdon discovered that the number of ideas they packed into their sentences was a powerful predictor of who would develop Alzheimer's 60 years later

LOW IDEA DENSITY, HIGH RISK	HIGH IDEA DENSITY, LOW RISK
I was born in Eau Claire, Wis., on May 24, 1913, and was baptized in St. James Church. My father, Mr. L. M. Hallacher, was born in the city of Ross, County Cork, Ireland, and is now a sheet-metal worker in Eau Claire.	When I was first told that I saw the light of day on a Tuesday noon, there automatically ran through my mind the old nursery rhyme pretending to predict one's fate by making it depend on the day of the week on which one was born.

as girls ended up living longest, and that those on the road to Alzheimer's expressed fewer and fewer positive emotions as their mental functions declined.

These findings, like many of Snowdon's earlier conclusions, will undoubtedly spark a lively debate. As laboratory scientists and clinicians are quick to point out, cause and effect are notoriously difficult to tease out of population studies like this one, and exactly what the emotion-

Alzheimer's link means has yet to be established. But even hard-nosed lab scientists admit that the Nun Study has helped sharpen the focus of their research. The study has impressed the National Institutes of Health enough that it has provided $5 million in funding over the past decade and a half. "It is," says Dr. Richard Suzman, director of the National Institute on Aging, "a very innovative, pioneering study."

Snowdon wasn't out to change the world when he first began visiting the convent of the School Sisters of Notre Dame on Good Counsel Hill in Mankato, Minn. He wasn't even planning to study Alzheimer's disease. Snowdon was desperately trying to find a research project that would secure his position at the University of Minnesota. He was a young assistant professor of epidemiology at the time—a field he'd been introduced to as a young boy who raised chickens to earn money. "I learned a lot about what it takes to stay healthy from taking care of those chickens," he recalls. "That's what epidemiology is all about—the health of the whole flock."

Chicken studies wouldn't cut it with the Minnesota administration though, so Snowdon was interested when a graduate student, an ex-nun, told him about the aging sisters at her former order, living out their retirement in a convent just two hours away. He was already familiar with the advantages of studying religious groups, whose relatively uniform backgrounds mean fewer variations in lifestyle to confound the data. An order of nuns whose economic status, health care and living conditions were especially uniform would be an excellent starting place for an epidemiological study of the aging process. So he went out for a series of visits. Both Snowdon and the sisters had to overcome inhibitions—theirs at becoming research subjects, his from a Roman Catholic school background that made him uncomfortable asking personal questions of a nun. But they finally agreed that he would quiz them periodically to learn about what factors might be involved in promoting a healthy old age.

At first, the study didn't look as if it would reveal much. For one thing, Snowdon wasn't really sure what aspect of aging to focus on. For another, he had to count on the nuns to recall those aspects of their lives, including the years before entering the order, that had differed—and memory, even among the mentally competent, is notoriously unreliable. But then, after several months, he stumbled on two olive-green metal file cabinets—the personal records of all the young women who had taken their vows at the Mankato convent. "Everything changed when we discovered the archives," says Snowdon.

Because the records were relatively standardized, Snowdon could extend his study of aging far beyond the few years in late life that such studies traditionally cover. Most precious of all were the autobiographies written by each sister on her entry into the order. They were full of basic information about where the sisters were born, who their parents and siblings were, and why each one decided to join the order. With these documents, moreover, Snowdon now had an objective measure of the sisters' cognitive abilities while they were still young and in their prime. An epidemiologist could not have designed a better way to evaluate them across time. "For

many years," says the National Institute's Suzman, "we had an inadequate sense of how connected late-life health, function and cognition were to early life. But in the past decade, spurred by the Nun Study, there is a growing appreciation for that connectedness."

The first results, compiled after a year of research, confirmed earlier studies suggesting that people with the most education were most independent and competent later in life (most of the sisters were teachers; many had master's degrees). And breaking with academic tradition—but establishing one of his own—Snowdon first presented his conclusions, not through a journal or a conference but directly to the nuns. Recalls Sister Rita Schwalbe, then one of the convent's administrators: "He threw us a thank-you party, and we thought that was it."

Not even close. Snowdon's study attracted the attention of leading Alzheimer's researchers, who explained to him that the elderly women represented an ideal population for studying this mysterious disease. On average, 10% of people over 65 come down with Alzheimer's, a number that rises to 50% by age 85. Given the aging population of the convent, they knew that a significant proportion of the nuns would have the disease.

The most serious drawback to studying the sisters for Alzheimer's is that there's only one sure way to diagnose it: examine the patient's brain after he or she dies. If he were to proceed, Snowdon would need written permission to perform autopsies, not only on the Mankato nuns but also, to get a large enough sample, on members of the order at six other Notre Dame convents as well. "They really had to trust us," he says. "We could have turned out to be Dr. Frankensteins for all they knew."

So one day in 1990, a nervous Snowdon stood in front of the assembled sisters in Mankato, many of whom he'd got to know as friends, and made his pitch. "We sat in our chairs and held our breath," recalls Sister Rita Schwalbe, who by then had joined Snowdon's research team. "Then one of the sisters piped up, 'He can have my brain, what good is it going to do me when I'm six feet under?' And that broke the ice."

In all, more than 90% of the sisters living in the Mankato convent agreed to donate their brains. After visiting six other convents, Snowdon ended up with a 68% consent rate overall, one of the highest in any tissue-donation study. "I didn't really know what it was going to be about," says Sister Nicolette, an engaging 93-year-old

HOW SHARP IS YOUR MEMORY?

Snowdon uses a longer version of the following quiz to pick up signs of memory loss. You can use it to test your own memory. If you are concerned about the results, discuss them with your physician.

VERBAL FLUENCY

How many animals can you name in 60 seconds?

WORD-LIST MEMORY

1. Have a friend read the following 10 words aloud:

    Leg
    Cheese
    Tent
    Motor
    Flower
    Stamp
    Cup
    King
    Forest
    Menu

2. Try to commit them to memory.
3. Go over the list twice more, each time in a different order. How many can you recall on the third try?

DELAYED WORD RECALL TEST

Wait five minutes. Now how many words can you recall?

WORD RECOGNITION

1. Ask your friend to write 20 words on separate index cards—the 10 words from the list above mixed in with ten different words
2. Have your friend show you the cards one at a time
3. How many words can you pick out from the original list?

ADD UP YOUR SCORES. If the total is less than 29, you may have difficulty with short-term memory. Ask your doctor about doing a more thorough exam.

who is the only one of the 16 girls who took their vows in 1925 to both survive and remain mentally intact. "But I thought if science could learn something from this program, then I was glad to be a part of it."

In 1991, the first participant, a resident of Good Counsel Hill convent, died, and the Nun Study received its first brain.

Snowdon, who had accepted a position at the University of Kentucky's Sanders-Brown Center on Aging, was working with a team of neurologists and psychologists to devise a battery of tests for assessing the sisters' mental and physical abilities—tests that could later be correlated with the results of brain exams. He joined forces with James Mortimer, an eminent researcher on aging then at the Minneapolis Veterans Administration Medical Center, to study the nuns' youthful autobiographies in more detail, and their relationship led to an interesting discovery: autopsies by other scientists had shown that the physical destruction wrought by Alzheimer's didn't inevitably lead to mental deterioration. The reason, according to one leading theory, was that some folks might have an extra reserve of mental capacity that kept them functioning despite the loss of brain tissue.

So he and Mortimer, along with University of Kansas psychologist Susan Kemper, began analyzing the autobiographies for evidence of such extra capacity. Kemper, an expert on the effects of aging on language usage, had earlier shown that "idea density"—the number of discrete ideas per 10 written words—was a good marker of educational level, vocabulary and general knowledge. Grammatical complexity, meanwhile, was an indicator of how well memory was functioning.

Applying these measures to the sisters' autobiographies, Snowdon and Kemper found to their astonishment that the elderly sisters who showed signs of Alzheimer's had consistently authored essays low in both idea density and grammatical complexity a half-century or more earlier. One of the lowest-scoring samples begins: "My father, Mr. L.M. Hallacher, was born in the city of Ross, County Cork, Ireland, and is now a sheet-metal worker in Eau Claire." By contrast, one of the highest-scoring essays conveys the same type of information but in a dramatically different way: "My father is an all-around man of trades, but his principal occupation is carpentry, which trade he had already begun before his marriage with my mother."

Idea density turns out to be an astonishingly powerful predictor of Alzheimer's disease—at least among the School Sisters of Notre Dame. Snowdon found by reading nuns' early writings, he could predict, with 85% to 90% accuracy, which ones would show the brain damage typical of Alzheimer's disease about 60 years later. "When we first looked at the findings," says Snowdon, "we thought, 'Oh my God, it's in the bag by the time you're in your 20s.'"

But Alzheimer's is not that simple. One especially telling case: Sister Bernadette (not her real name), who had shown no outward signs of Alzheimer's and whose youthful autobiography was rich with ideas and grammatical complexity, turned out at death to be riddled with the plaques and tangles of Alzheimer's (see diagram). Says Snowdon: "Lesson No. 1 in my epidemiology training is that there are hardly any diseases where one factor alone, even in infectious disease, will always cause illness."

These results posed a chicken-and-egg problem: Did higher brain capacity protect the sisters from developing the symptoms of dementia, or were those with lackluster biographies already suffering very early signs of some brain abnormality that predisposed them to mental decline later? That question remains unanswered—but follow-up studies, to be published next month in the journal Psychology and Aging, suggest that exercising what brain capacity you have offers some protection. While all the sisters show age-related decline in mental function, those who had taught for most of their lives showed more moderate declines than those who had spent most of their lives in service-based tasks. And that, says Kemper, supports the commonsense idea that stimulating the brain with continuous intellectual activity keeps neurons healthy and alive. (Of course, notes Snowdon, these activities are not absolute protectors. For some, a genetic predisposition may override even a lifetime of learning and teaching.)

Another crucial finding from the Nun Study came in 1997, by which time Snowdon had accumulated some 100 brains for analysis. He and neurologist Dr. William Markesbery, director of the Alzheimer's Disease Research Center at the University of Kentucky, were intrigued by an idea advanced by other researchers that strokes and other brain trauma might contribute to the dementia of Alzheimer's disease. Selecting only the brains of sisters who had earned a bachelor's degree—to eliminate any differences attributable to education—they found that among nuns with physical evidence of Alzheimer's in the brain, those who had evidence of strokes as well almost inevitably showed outward symptoms of dementia. But only half the nuns without strokes were comparably afflicted. Says Suzman, of the National Institute on Aging: "This is one of the first studies to look at the cardiovascular component of Alzheimer's disease."

It's also one of the first to suggest a way to stave off Alzheimer's symptoms. "If your brain is already progressing toward Alzheimer's," says Snowdon, "strokes or head trauma (which can produce similar kinds of brain damage) can put you over the edge." His advice: wear a helmet while biking, motorcycling or playing contact sports; buckle your seat belt; and drive a car with air bags. Meanwhile, keep strokes at bay by keeping your cardiovascular system in shape: avoid tobacco, get regular exercise and eat a balanced, healthy diet.

WHERE ARE THEY NOW?

Nuns, ages 75 to 102, who volunteered to join the Nun Study in 1986	678
Nuns who have died	334
Brain autopsies that have been performed	more than 300
Nuns, ages 84 to 106, who survive	344
Nuns who are symptom free	about 100

Diet may play a role in Alzheimer's in other ways as well. In 1998 British researchers announced that Alzheimer's victims have low concentrations in their blood of the nutrient folate, also called folic acid. That's an intriguing result, especially in light of other studies showing that folic acid deficiency plays a role in some forms of mental retardation in children and in cognitive problems in adults. So Snowdon began looking at levels of folic acid, along with 18 other micronutrients (including beta carotene, magnesium, zinc and cholesterol) in blood samples of 30 sisters who had died since the study began.

Sure enough, he found that the sisters with high folate levels showed little evidence of Alzheimer's-type damage in their brain after death. This makes a certain amount of sense; folate tends to counteract the effects of homocysteine, an amino acid produced in the body that has been implicated in cardiovascular disease. Plenty of folate in the blood would thus mean less chance of stroke—and might even protect brain cells from damage by homocysteine in the brain.

Unfortunately, the other micronutrients haven't panned out so well. It makes sense that antioxidants like vitamin E and vitamin C, which soak up cell-damaging "free-radical" molecules in the body, would protect against cell destruction. Although vitamin E looked promising in an earlier study, neither substance had an obvious effect on the Notre Dame sisters. Nor, on the other side of the equation, did mercury or aluminum in the diet, both of which had been implicated in earlier studies as possible triggers for Alzheimer's.

But another hunch turned out to be far more productive. When Snowdon and Kemper first read the sisters' autobiographies in the early 1990s, they noted that the writings differed not just in the density of ideas they contained but also in their emotional content. "At the time," he says, "we saw that idea density was much more related to later cognitive ability. But we also knew that there was something interesting going on with emotions." Studies by other scientists had shown that anger and depression can play a role in heart disease, so the team decided to take another look.

This time they searched for words suggesting positive emotions (such as happiness, love, hope, gratitude and contentment), as well as negative ones (sadness, fear, confusion and shame). Snowdon found that the sisters expressing negative emotions did not live as long as the sisters conveying more positive ones. He has already begun another analysis, comparing the emotional content of the nuns' early autobiographies with the ones they penned in late life, as part of the Nun Study. As mental abilities decline, his preliminary review has found, the expression of positive emotions also drops. While he suspects the whittling away of positive feelings are a consequence of the neurological changes of Alzheimer's, it is still possible that emotional states may play a role in determining cognitive function. To find out, Snowdon will next compare the emotional content of the sisters' writings with their autopsied brains, to see if positive emotions work to keep nerve connections snapping and if negative emotions dampen and eventually extinguish them.

By now, 15 years after he first climbed Good Counsel Hill, Snowdon has identified half a dozen factors that may predict or contribute to Alzheimer's disease. He could sit each sister down right now and tell her what her chances are. But should he? As he has all along, Snowdon will put his dilemma to the sisters themselves: next month he will meet with the Notre Dame leadership to discuss whether to break the news to the high-risk nuns—and how to answer the inevitable questions about what they might do to prevent or slow down the disease.

"So far," he says, "I have a certain comfort level in making some recommendations because there are other good reasons for preventing strokes, for reading, for taking folic acid. If our findings showed something that had no other known benefit besides preventing Alzheimer's, then we would be on much thinner ice." Even so, it's not clear precisely how much folic acid to take, and Snowdon's team is divided on whether to boost the intake of vitamins C and E beyond the normal recommended doses (Markesbery says yes; Snowdon says not until we know more).

These questions will become more urgent as the population bulge of the baby boom generation reaches the Alzheimer's years—and new research is showing that those years may start earlier than anyone had thought. Just two months ago, scientists suggested that many cases of a condition known as mild cognitive impairment, in which patients in their 40s and 50s exhibit memory and recall problems, are very likely the first step on the way to Alzheimer's disease. If so, then it's important to start slowdown strategies as soon as possible. A cure for Alzheimer's is still the ultimate goal, but, says Snowdon, "until there is a magic bullet that can stop the plaques and tangles from growing, we're going to have to take a multipronged approach that will include things like avoiding head injuries and strokes and adding nutritional supplements like folate and antioxidants."

Meanwhile, the Nun Study will continue. Snowdon and his team are attempting to study the sisters' brains before they die, using MRI scans to track how the brain deteriorates with age and how such changes correlate with those in speech, memory and behavior. And to ensure that the sisters' generous gift to science will continue to educate others, Snowdon is trying to have the brain bank and archive records permanently endowed. That way, future generations will continue to benefit from lessons that women like Sisters Ada, Rosella and Nicolette are teaching all of us about how to age with grace and good health.

From *Time*, May 14, 2001, pp. 54-64. © 2001 by Time Inc. Reprinted by permission.

NAVIGATING PRACTICAL DILEMMAS in TERMINAL CARE

Helen Sorenson, MA, RRT, FAARC

Introduction

It has been stated that one-fourth of a person's life is spent growing up and three-fourths growing old. The aging process is universal, progressive, irreversible and eventually decremental.[1] Cellular death is one marker of aging. When cells are not replaced or replicated at a rate constant enough to maintain tissue or organ function, the eventual result is death of the organism.

Although not an unexpected endpoint for any human being, death unfortunately is often fraught with turmoil and dilemmas. Patients, family, friends, caregivers and health care professionals often get caught up in conflicting opinions regarding how terminal care should be approached. For the patient, the result often is suboptimal symptom management, an increased likelihood of being subjected to painful and often futile therapy and the unnecessary prolonging of death. For the family and friends of the patient, the psychosocial consequences can be devastating. Conflict at the bedside of a dying loved one can result in long-lasting and sometimes permanent rifts in family relationships.

There are some complicated issues surrounding terminal care, such as fear, lack of trust, lack of understanding, lack of communication, and stubbornness on the part of both the physician's and family members. There are moral, ethical, economic, cultural and religious issues that must be considered. Some of the dilemmas in terminal care come up more frequently than others. This paper will discuss some of the more commonly encountered ones. And possible interventions and/or alternate ways of coming to concordance regarding end-of-life care will be presented for consideration by the reader.

Fear/Death Anxiety

A degree of fear is the natural response of most individuals to the unknown. Despite many attempts at conceptualization and rationalization, preparing for death involves coming to terms with a condition unknown in past or present experience. Fear of death has been referred to in the literature as death anxiety. Research indicates that younger people have a higher level of death anxiety than older people.[2] The reasons are not difficult to understand. Younger adults in our society are often

shielded from death. Many young adults may not have had close contact with individuals dying from a terminal or chronic disease. When younger people confront death, it is most likely that of a grandparent, a parent, a sibling or a friend. Death is commonly from an acute cause. Grief is intense, with many unanswered questions and psychological ramifications.

Older adults have had more experience with death, from having lost a spouse, colleagues, a friend or relatives over the years. They undoubtedly will have experienced grief and worked through loss at some time in their life. Older adults may be more apt to express the fear of dying alone.

When facing a terminal diagnosis and impending death older adults are more likely to be concerned with "mending fences" and seeking forgiveness for perceived wrongdoing. There is a need on the part of many adults to put their affairs in order and resolve any outstanding financial matters. Some interesting research on death anxiety and religiosity conducted by Thorson & Powell,[3] revealed that persons higher in religiosity were lower in death anxiety.

How can the potential dilemma caused by fear be circumscribed? Possibly allowing patients to discuss the issue may ease death anxiety, but patients may be advised not to talk about funeral arrangements, since "they're not going to die." While well intended, the statement may not be helpful. Instead of preventing the patient from discussing "depressing thoughts," encouraging frank discussions about end-of-life issues may ease death anxiety. Asking the patient to verbalize his or her fears may lead to understanding the fears and alleviate the anxiety they cause.

It is important to guard against treating dying patients as though they are no longer human. For example, asking if a person would like to talk to a minister, priest or rabbi does not impinge the religious belief of the patient—it simply allows another avenue to reduce death anxiety.

Issues of Trust

Patients who have been under the care of a personal physician for an extended period of time generally exhibit a high level of trust in the diagnosis, even when the diagnosis is that of a terminal disease. Good end-of-life care requires a measure of continuity among caregivers. The patient who has had the same physician from the onset of a serious illness to the terminal stages of the disease has a substantial advantage.[4]

Planning, family support and social services, coordinated to meet the patient's needs, can be more easily arranged if there is an atmosphere of trust and confidence.

Health care today however, has become increasingly fragmented. A physician unknown to the family and/or patient may be assigned to a case. It is difficult for very sick patients to develop new relationships and establish trust with an on-going stream of care providers.[5] When circumstances are of an immediate and critical nature, issues of trust become paramount. Lack of trust in the physician and/or the health care system can erode into a lack of confidence in a diagnosis, which often results in a conflict between the patient, the family and the health care system.

Navigating this dilemma can be challenging. Recommending that the services of a hospitalist or a palliative care team be requested may be beneficial. Patients and families that are versed in the standard of care for the specific terminal disease may be in a better position to ask questions and make suggestions. Trust is associated with honesty. Conversely, trust can be eroded by what is perceived as the incompetence of or duplicity by health care providers.

An increased, concerted effort to communicate effectively all pertinent information to a patient and family and members of the health care team caring for the patient may not instantly instill confidence, but it may forestall any further erosion of trust. It is a good feeling to think that everyone on the team is pulling in the same direction.

Issues of Communication

Communication, or lack of adequate communication is problematic. A recent article published in *Critical Care Medicine* stated, "In intensive care settings, suboptimal communication can erode family trust and fuel so called 'futility disputes'."[6] Lack of communication does not imply wrongdoing on the part of the caregivers, nor does it imply lack of comprehension or skills in patients and families. The message is delivered, but not always in language that is readily understandable. While the message may be received, at times it is not comprehended due to the nature of the message or the emotional state of the recipient.

A few years ago, during a conversation about end-of-life care, a nurse shared with the author a situation she had encountered. The patient, an elderly female, had undergone a biopsy of a tumor. The physician, upon receiving the biopsy report, asked the nurse to accompany him to the patient's room to deliver the results. The patient was told "the results of the biopsy indicate that the tumor was not benign, so I am going to refer you to Dr. ***, an

oncologist, for further treatment." The physician asked for questions from the patient and, receiving none, left the room. The patient then got on the phone, called her family and stated: "Good news, I don't have cancer." The nurse left the room and called the physician, who expressed surprise that the patient had misunderstood the message. Reluctantly, he returned to the patient's room and in simple terms told her that she did indeed have cancer and that Dr. *** was a cancer specialist who would discuss treatment options with her and her family. Did the physician, on the first visit, tell the patient she had cancer—of course. Did the patient receive the message—unfortunately, no.

Although anecdotal, the case demonstrates a situation in which there was poor communication. Had the nurse not intervened, how long would it have been before the patient was adequately apprised of her condition?

Because quality communication with patients and families is imperative, the dilemma deserves attention. Many articles have been written, discussing optimal times, situations and environments best suited for end-of-life care discussions. Unfortunately, end-of-life does not always arrive on schedule or as planned.

Because of the severity of some illnesses, intensive care units may be the environment where the futility of further care becomes apparent. Intensive care units are busy places, sometimes crowded, and replete with a variety of alarms and mechanical noises on a continual basis. About 50 percent of patients who die in a hospital are cared for in an intensive care unit within three days of their death. Over thirty percent spend at least ten days of final hospitalization in an intensive care unit.[7] This is a particularly sobering reality for patients with chronic lung disease. Many COPD patients have had serious exacerbations, have been admitted to intensive care units, and many have been on mechanical ventilation. Fortunately, the medications, therapeutic interventions, and disease management skills of physicians and therapists often can turn the exacerbation around. Unfortunately, the airway pathology may not be reversible.

How and when and with whom should communication about the gravity of a situation be handled? Ideally, it should occur prior to any crisis; realistically, when it becomes obvious that a patient is unlikely to survive. Regardless of the answer, effective communication is vitally important.

Because few intensive care unit (ICU) patients (less than 5%) are able to communicate with the health care providers caring for them at the time that withholding/withdrawing life support decisions are made,[8] there is a real need to share information with and seek input from the family.

A recent article published as a supplement to *Critical Care Medicine* reviewed the importance of talking with families about end-of-life care. Although few studies provide hard evidence on how best to initiate end-of-life discussions in an ICU environment, Curtis, et al[9] provides a framework that could serve as a model for clinicians and families alike. The proposed components of the conference would include: preparation prior to the conference, holding the conference, and finishing the conference.[9]

Preparing in Advance of the ICU-Family Conference

It is important for the participating clinician to be informed about the disease process of the patient, including: diagnosis, prognosis, treatment options, and probably outcomes of various treatments. It is important also for the clinician to identify areas of uncertainty or inconsistencies concerning the diagnosis, prognosis, or potential treatments. Any disagreements between subspecialists involved in the care of the patient should be resolved before the family conference. Additionally, in preparing for the family conference, it is advantageous for the clinician to have some familiarity with the attitudes of the family and the patient toward illness, life-extending therapy, and death. When possible, the determination of who will attend the conference should be done advance of the conference. The location of the conference should also be pre-determined: a quiet private setting, with adequate comfortable seating is ideal. Asking all participants to turn off cell phones and pagers is appropriate and will prevent unwanted distraction. (If the patient is able to participate in the conference but is too ill to leave the ICU, then the conference should take place in the patient's room in the ICU.)

Holding the ICU Family-Conference About End-of-Life Care

Assuring that all participants are introduced and understand the reason for the conference will facilitate the process. It is also helpful to discuss conference goals and determine what the patient and his or her family understand about the prognosis. If the patient is unable to participate in the conference, it may be opportune to pose the question: "What would the patient want?" Explaining during the conference that withholding life-sustaining treatment is not withholding care is an important distinction. Another recommended approach to achieve concord in the conference is to tolerate silence. Giving the family time to absorb any information they have just received, and allowing them to formulate questions, will result in better and more goal-oriented discussions. When families are able to communicate the fears and emotions they may have, they are better able to cope with difficult decisions.

Finishing the Conference

After the patient and/or family have been provided with the facts and have achieved an understanding of the disease and the treatment issues, the clinician should make recommendations regarding treatment options. It is a disservice, for example, to give family members the impression that they are single-handedly making the deci-

sion to "pull the plug" on a loved on. Soliciting any follow-up questions, allowing adequate time, and making sure the family knows how to reach you, should end the conference on a positive note.

Understanding Choices

Another commonly encountered dilemma in terminal care is the number of choices involved, as well as the medical terminology that sometimes mystifies the choices. Advanced directives, living wills, health care proxies, durable powers of attorney for health care; what they are, what they mean, how much weight they carry, are they honored, and does everyone who needs them have them? Not long ago during a conversation with a chaplain at a hospital, the advice shared with me—to pass on to others—was to give family members the gift of knowledge. The final gift you give them may be the most important gift of all. Let them know your wishes.

When advanced directives became available in the late 1980's, it was presumed that the document would solve all the problems and that terminal care would adhere to the patient's wishes. The Study to Understand Prognoses and Preferences for Outcomes and Risks of Treatment (SUPPORT), initiated in 1988, however, showed severe shortcomings in end-of-life care.[10]

Advanced directives, as a legal document, have not necessarily lived up to expectations. A viable option is a Durable Power of Attorney for Health Care, in which a trusted individual is designated to make health care decisions when the patient cannot.

Another option is to have advanced planning sessions with family members. If the patient and his or her family can come to consensus about terminal care in advance, and the doctor is in agreement with any decisions, unnecessary suffering probably can be avoided. (When death becomes imminent and the patient's wishes are not followed, waste no time in seeking a meeting with the hospital ethics committee.)

Adaptive Techniques

There is no "recipe" that, if followed precisely, will allow for the successful navigation of all potential dilemmas. There is no way to prepare for each eventuality that accompanies terminal illness and death. Knowledge remains the safest shield against well-meaning advice-givers. Asking questions of caregivers is the best defense against misunderstanding and mismanagement of the patient.

The University of Iowa Research Center is working on an evidence-based protocol for advanced directives, which outlines in a step-by-step fashion assessment criteria that factor in the patient's age, primary language, and mental capacity for making health care treatment decisions. The protocol also provides a check-list format for health care providers, the documentation thereof is easily accessible and in a prominent position in the patient's chart. [11]

Another alternative health care benefit being proposed is called MediCaring, which emphasizes more home-based and supportive health care and discourages hospitalization and use of aggressive treatment.[12] While not specifically aimed at solving end-of-life care issues, there may be parts of MediCaring that mesh well with terminal care of the oldest old.

Whether in a home setting, a community hospital or an intensive care unit, terminal care can result in moral, ethical, economic, religious, cultural and/or personal/family conflict. Even when death is universally accepted as a normal part of the life cycle, there will be emotional dilemmas to navigate around. Additional education and research initiatives, however, may result in increased awareness that this currently is an unsolved problem, for the patient, the family, and the health care providers. Notwithstanding, however, the medical community should continue to persevere in trying to understand patients' and families' fears and needs, the need for quality communication with questions and answers in lay vocabulary. The clinician's task is to balance communication and understanding with medical delivery.

References

1. Thorson JA. Aging in a Changing Society, 2000. 2nd Ed. Taylor & Francis, Philadelphia, PA.

2. Thorson JA & Powell FC. Meaning of death and intrinsic religiosity. Journal of Clinical Psychology. 1990;46: 379-391.

3. Thorson JA & Powell FC. Elements of death anxiety and meanings of death. Journal of Clinical Psychology. 1998;44: 691-701.

4. Lynn J. Serving patients who may die soon and their families. JAMA. 2001;285(7): 925–932.

5. Pantilat SZ, Alpers A, Wachter RM. A new doctor in the house: ethical issues in hospitalist systems. JAMA. 1999;282: 171-174.

6. Fins JJ & Soloman MZ. Communication in the intensive care setting: The challenge of futility disputes. Critical Care Medicine: 2001;29(2) Supplement.

7. Quill TE & Brody H. Physician recommendations and patient autonomy: Finding a balance between physician power and patient choice. Ann Internal Med. 1996;25: 763-769.

8. Prendergast T.J. & Luce JM. Increasing incidence of withholding and withdrawal of life support from the critically ill. Am J Respir Crit Care Med. 1997;155: 15-20.

9. Curtis JR et al. The family conference as a focus to improve communication about end-of-life care in the intensive care unit: Opportunities for improvement. Critical Care Medicine. 2001;29(2) Supplement. PN26-N33.

10. Pioneer Programs in Palliative Care: Nine Case Studies (2000). The Robert Wood Johnson Foundation in cooperation with the Milbank Memorial Fund, New York, NY.

11. Evidence-based protocol: Advanced Directives. Iowa City, IA: University of Iowa Gerontological Nursing Interventions Research Center. 1999 .
Available; [http://www.guideline.gov/index.asp].

12. Lynn. J. et al. MediCaring: development and test marketing of a supportive care benefit for older people. Journal of the American Geriatric Society. 1999;47(9) 1058-1064.

Helen Sorenson, Assistant Professor, Department of Respiratory Care, University of Texas Health Science Center at San Antonio in San Antonio, Texas. Ms. Sorenson is also Managing Editor of "Emphysema/COPD: The Journal of Patient Centered Care."

Test Your Knowledge Form

We encourage you to photocopy and use this page as a tool to assess how the articles in *Annual Editions* expand on the information in your textbook. By reflecting on the articles you will gain enhanced text information. You can also access this useful form on a product's book support Web site at *http://www.dushkin.com/online/*.

NAME:

DATE:

TITLE AND NUMBER OF ARTICLE:

BRIEFLY STATE THE MAIN IDEA OF THIS ARTICLE:

LIST THREE IMPORTANT FACTS THAT THE AUTHOR USES TO SUPPORT THE MAIN IDEA:

WHAT INFORMATION OR IDEAS DISCUSSED IN THIS ARTICLE ARE ALSO DISCUSSED IN YOUR TEXTBOOK OR OTHER READINGS THAT YOU HAVE DONE? LIST THE TEXTBOOK CHAPTERS AND PAGE NUMBERS:

LIST ANY EXAMPLES OF BIAS OR FAULTY REASONING THAT YOU FOUND IN THE ARTICLE:

LIST ANY NEW TERMS/CONCEPTS THAT WERE DISCUSSED IN THE ARTICLE, AND WRITE A SHORT DEFINITION:

We Want Your Advice

ANNUAL EDITIONS revisions depend on two major opinion sources: one is our Advisory Board, listed in the front of this volume, which works with us in scanning the thousands of articles published in the public press each year; the other is you—the person actually using the book. Please help us and the users of the next edition by completing the prepaid article rating form on this page and returning it to us. Thank you for your help!

ANNUAL EDITIONS: Human Development 05/06

ARTICLE RATING FORM

Here is an opportunity for you to have direct input into the next revision of this volume.
We would like you to rate each of the articles listed below, using the following scale:

1. **Excellent: should definitely be retained**
2. **Above average: should probably be retained**
3. **Below average: should probably be deleted**
4. **Poor: should definitely be deleted**

Your ratings will play a vital part in the next revision.
Please mail this prepaid form to us as soon as possible.
Thanks for your help!

RATING	ARTICLE
	1. The Age of Genetic Technology Arrives
	2. Brave New Babies
	3. Inside the Womb
	4. The Mystery of Fetal Life: Secrets of the Womb
	5. The War Over Fetal Rights
	6. Four Things You Need to Know About Raising Baby
	7. Who's Raising Baby?
	8. Vaccines and Autism, Beyond the Fear Factors
	9. Four Perspectives on Child Care Quality
	10. Guilt Free TV
	11. Raising a Moral Child
	12. Implicit Learning
	13. The New Science of Dyslexia
	14. Metacognitive Development
	15. Trick Question
	16. The Future of Computer Technology in K–12 Education
	17. The New Gender Gap
	18. Girls, Boys and Autism
	19. "High Stakes Are for Tomatoes"
	20. Raising Happy Achieving Children in the New Millennium
	21. When Safety is the Name of the Game
	22. The Blank Slate
	23. Parents or Pop Culture? Children's Heroes and Role Models
	24. Brown v. Board: A Dream Deferred
	25. The 100 Best High Schools in America
	26. Choosing Virginity
	27. Hello to College Joys: Keep Stress Off Campus
	28. She Works, He Doesn't
	29. We're Not in the Mood
	30. The Battle for Your Brain
	31. Emotions and the Brain: Laughter
	32. Alcohol's Deadly Triple Threat
	33. The Great Back Pain Debate
	34. 12 Things You Must Know to Survive and Thrive in America
	35. Aging's Changing Face

RATING	ARTICLE
	36. Secrets of the Centenarians
	37. The Nun Study: Alzheimer's
	38. Navigating Practical Dilemmas in Terminal Care

(Continued on next page)

BUSINESS REPLY MAIL
FIRST CLASS MAIL PERMIT NO. 551 DUBUQUE IA

POSTAGE WILL BE PAID BY ADDRESEE

McGraw-Hill/Dushkin
2460 KERPER BLVD
DUBUQUE, IA 52001-9902

ABOUT YOU

Name _____   Date _____

Are you a teacher? ❐   A student? ❐
Your school's name _____

Department _____

Address _____   City _____   State _____ Zip _____

School telephone # _____

YOUR COMMENTS ARE IMPORTANT TO US!

Please fill in the following information:
For which course did you use this book?
_____

Did you use a text with this ANNUAL EDITION? ❐ yes ❐ no
What was the title of the text?
_____

What are your general reactions to the *Annual Editions* concept?
_____

Have you read any pertinent articles recently that you think should be included in the next edition? Explain.
_____

Are there any articles that you feel should be replaced in the next edition? Why?
_____

Are there any World Wide Web sites that you feel should be included in the next edition? Please annotate.
_____

May we contact you for editorial input? ❐ yes ❐ no
May we quote your comments? ❐ yes ❐ no